Vojtěch Kolman
Tomáš Murár (eds.)

Devouring One's Own Tail

Autopoiesis in Perspective

CHARLES UNIVERSITY
KAROLINUM PRESS 2022

KAROLINUM PRESS is a publishing department of Charles University
Ovocný trh 560/5, 116 36 Prague 1, Czech Republic
www.karolinum.cz

EUROPEAN UNION
European Structural and Investment Funds
Operational Programme Research,
Development and Education

MINISTRY OF EDUCATION,
YOUTH AND SPORTS

This work was supported by the European Regional Development Fund
project "Creativity and Adaptability as Conditions of the Success of Europe
in an Interrelated World" (reg. no.: CZ.02.1.01/0.0/0.0/16_019/0000734)
implemented at Charles University, Faculty of Arts. The project is carried
out under the ERDF Call "Excellent Research" and its output is aimed at
employees of research organizations and Ph.D. students.

Cover and layout by Jan Šerých
Set and printed in the Czech Republic by Karolinum Press
First English edition
A catalogue record for this book is available from the National Library
of the Czech Republic.

ISBN 978-80-246-5131-6
ISBN 978-80-246-5132-3 (pdf)

The original manuscript was reviewed by Prof. RNDr. Ladislav Kvasz, DSc., Dr.,
Doc. Mgr. Ondřej Beran, PhD.

List of Contents

Part 4: Society in an Autopoietic Perspective

"All That Is Straight Lies": Introduction

Vojtěch Kolman

'All that is straight lies,' murmured the dwarf contemptuously.
'All truth is crooked, time itself is a circle.'
Friedrich Nietzsche: *Thus Spoke Zarathustra*

1 The Circle or the Ruler?

Nietzsche's wordplay with "all that is straight lies" and "all truth is crooked" may be both part of his doctrine of the eternal recurrence of all things as well as his program of the revaluation of values – even somewhere in the spirit of Goethe's Hexenküche with its magic square innuendo "nine is one" and "ten is none" (Goethe 2004, 36). For us, though, the modest, conceptual reading is more relevant, with the central opposition between the straight line and the full circle, or what they traditionally represent: two basic paths our experience can take. The first path proceeds linearly, replacing the old truth with the new one, and so on, *ad infinitum*. The second path returns after several steps back to its beginning, only to start the same route anew. Both might resemble a living organism, perhaps the legendary snake uroboros, at first crawling away in a desperate quest to appease an ever-existing hunger and later being at relative rest while devouring its own tail. As such, they are either too mundane or too mysterious, too short or too long for our mind to capture, as Kant (1998, A529/B557) says in his analysis of the antinomies of pure reason.

In this volume, the second path is deliberately chosen, with a full awareness of its mysterious and paradoxical nature – as the very title *devouring its own tail* indicates. The ostensible reason for this is to provide a frame for the representative outputs of the broad *interdisciplinary* project KREAS, devoted to the *autopoietic* concept of experience, i.e. experience which is its own *product* and *goal*. [1] The very concept of autopoiesis, however, provides an additional and rather traditional reason for taking the "crooked" path rather than the "straight" one: if read linearly, as a mere means to some external goal, *experience* becomes reducible to this goal, and, as such, worthless as soon as it might be replaceable by anything leading to the same result. Wittgenstein phrased it as aptly with respect to the experience of music, his point, though, remaining quite general:

> It has sometimes been said that what music conveys to us are feelings of joyfulness, melancholy, triumph, etc. etc. and what repels us in this account is that it seems to say that music is an instrument for producing in us sequences of feelings. And from this one might gather that any other means of producing such feelings would do for us instead of music. – To such an account we are tempted to reply "Music conveys to us *itself*!" (Wittgenstein 1958, 178)

The less traditional and more challenging part of the "autopoietic" choice, as captured in the volume's title, is the focus on the *negative side* of it, namely that to "convey to us itself" it must "devour itself", as means to its own sustenance and growth. This is, obviously, the part which arouses not only interest but also some discomfort because something like that does not seem possible in the world governed by the *positive* sciences of which the *thermodynamical laws* are only an example.

The suggestion given in this volume is to follow the autopoietic world-view back to the concept of *creativity* that, by definition, brings into the world something which *was not* there – at least not in the merely positive sense of the word. This is done from a large variety of viewpoints, including those of philosophy, philology, aesthetics, and the specialized sciences such as linguistics, archeology, or the religious and media studies. What is common to all of them, and as such can be mentioned already here, at the very beginning, is the phenomenon of the shared language, being a particularly good example of such a *negativity* at work.

---

1   For further details, see *Creativity and Adaptability as Conditions for the Success of Europe in an Interrelated World* at https://kreas.ff.cuni.cz/en/. Accessed 14 August 2021.

2 The Metaphor of the Metaphor

To make this last point explicit, I will simply follow Nietzsche's (1979) seemingly radical, but not unfounded claim that by *naming* different things the same – e.g. very different individual animals by the general description of "snake" – one obviously *lies*, i.e. blurs the natural differences while ignoring the other, more transparent ones, e.g. that between the snake and the earthworm. What the autopoietic – i.e. *self*-creating – worldview adds to this experience is presenting it in a *cautiously positive way*, roughly along the lines of Hegel's "elaboration" on Nietzsche's idiosyncratic idea: by being the medium of generalization, both from the given situation as well as the subjectivity of the given speaker, language lies, but, in this lying, Hegel adds, it is *more truthful* since without it no experience proper would be even possible.[2]

This, of course, could be easily laughed off as a philosophical "mumbo jumbo", as Carnap or Russell in their project of the *logical analysis of language* would certainly do ("in saying that language is lying," they would ask, "are you lying or telling the truth?"). But before we do that too, just let us think, as a kind of exercise, of the phenomenon of *metaphor* that Nietzsche explicitly drives at. In saying, e.g. that my colleague is a weasel, I am obviously stating something that *is not true* in the usual sense of the word, and what is more, I am stating this while presupposing that those who I am addressing know that it is not true and they also know that I know that. Without this presupposition, the statement would not be a *metaphor*, but rather a *mistake* or a *suggestion* to extend the concept of a weasel by a new exemplar, i.e. a mere stipulation or an analytic sentence. Thus, in using the metaphor, I am lying for the benefit of a bigger truth, to reveal something new not only about the world around us – e.g. my colleague's insincerity or manipulative nature – but also about the standard use of our words, *despite and because* it is at variance with them.

In the light of this, Carnap's prospective objection is misplaced, or rather ignorant, failing to notice that Nietzsche's claim "language is

---

2   Hegel writes: "We also *express* the sensuous as a universal, but what we say is: *This*, i.e., the *universal this*, or we say: *it is*, i.e., *being as such*. We thereby of course do not *represent* to ourselves the universal. This or being as such, but we *express* the universal; or, in this sensuous-certainty we do not at all say what we *mean*. However, as we see, language is the more truthful. In language, we immediately refute what we *mean to say*, and since the universal is the truth of sensuous-certainty, and language only expresses this truth, it is, in that way, not possible at all that we could say what we *mean* about sensuous being" (Hegel 2018, 62).

lying" is obviously also a metaphor, namely a metaphor revealing to us something about the overall metaphorical nature of language as suggested by Nietzsche. The resulting *autopoietic* generalization is rather straightforward: it is this *metaphor* of language as a lie and its crooked "truth", i.e. our thinking in language about language and ourselves, that brings us closer to a better understanding of what not only language but what we ourselves, in fact, are. What we see in this example is "uroboros" at work, moving forward by feeding on the tail of its previous differences, treating what was false both as true *and* false in a certain, more complex sense.

3 The World Is Split

Autopoiesis, or self-creation, is a term serving several purposes of which I would like to mention two. The first or broader one is connected to the concept *self-reference* as a means of distinguishing the *sapient* creatures from merely *sentient* ones and the inanimate objects. Philosophers in the tradition of German idealism, particularly Hegel, captured this purpose by embedding us into the "system", the so-called Spirit, that develops according to its own *immanent* rules, simply because the transcendent rules are, by definition, not available. As such, the Spirit, despite some stereotypical readings, is not a mysterious, "spiritual" entity floating above our mortal bodies, but a fully developed *society*. Thus, it is both *more* than a set of social atoms and *less* than something beyond them or next to them, some other entity of the same order. One can describe it rather in *structural terms*, as based on the relation that the individuals take to each other and, codependently, to themselves. The individual, hence, is a mirror of society and *vice versa*.

The self-reference, accordingly, is the relation one achieves *via* his or her position within the whole, which is the Spirit or the "I that becomes the We" (Hegel 2018, 108). Hegel describes this achievement as a process of *mutual acknowledgment*, to be fully developed in a society democratic by nature, in which the given relations are more or less *symmetric* or *balanced*. It is this ability to develop itself into a certain kind of stability and to sustain this condition that provides for Spirit's autopoietic nature. This is not to say that there is nothing beyond that, such as society's environment or the universe of which this society inhabits only a small part, but that without society these differences, including the very concept of environment, does not make any sense.

The second, or narrower, concept of autopoiesis stems from this broader one, endowing it, through close contact with the specialized sciences, with a more detailed *heuristics* and *methodology*. It started in the biological context of Maturana and Varela (1980; 1984) only to be later, despite Maturana's original intention, transferred to the social sciences in the *systems theory* of Niklas Luhmann.[3] For us, understandably, this latter version is of a larger importance and I will, in the following passage, focus almost exclusively on that. Despite the many similarities between Luhmann and Hegel that will come forth later, there is a rather systematic difference in their autopoietic concepts in that, according to Luhmann, there is never only one system, or the Spirit, but always a plurality of them. All of Luhmann's systems, though, – and here we see the unity again – demonstrate an underlying "circular" or rather "fractal" feature: they are divided into *two* interrelated parts, the system itself and its environment which, by definition, is outside the system and, at the same time, defined exactly by means of it. See Fig. 1.

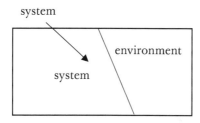

Fig. 1.

The media, being one of the systems particularly studied by Luhmann, treat everything as something that one can report about, thus making all that is reportable into its environment. It is this ability of a system to operate, e.g. to report about something, that leads to the given differentiation that we can schematize *via* the recursive operation of "$x = x + y$". This is not to say that the environment (y) does not interact with the system (x): just think here of media being influenced by the advertisement opportunities and influencing their environment

---

3   See Luhmann 2013 as a kind of quick introduction to the subject, but also Tereza Matějčková's and Tomáš Klír's contributions to this volume.

by publishing the voter preferences; but that this all depends on their *operative function* of reporting. The environment (y) affects the system (x) only by means of what Luhmann called "irritations" or "shocks", i.e. impulses that must be ordered or systematized so that one can even talk about them. Thus, the new facts to be reported about (and the fact that "y" adopts new values) are connected to the reporting as media's defining operating activity that is here to produce further reporting, *ad infinitum* (this is the recursively developed "x" in "$x = x + y$"). It is in this sense that the autopoietic system is both *operatively closed* and *environmentally open*.

To give a more friendly, visual illustration, let us think of our ways of representing the space. On the one hand, there is always a *system of such representations* (such as the circle and ruler, as in ancient geometry, or the methods of the central projection as known from the invention of the linear perspective in Renaissance paintings), and there is the *represented environment*, that, however, is accessible only by the given representational system. Thus in the tradition of the linear perspective, what is discussed is not merely reality, which, in fact, cannot answer the most elementary questions concerning its spatial order (such as the exact distances between the horizontal lines of the square pavement – see my contribution to this volume for the further details), but the previous attempts at picturing it which, in fact, lead always to some kind of "picture within a picture", as is known from Albrecht Dürer's woodcuts.

These "pictures in pictures" not only provide an easily accessible visualization of what "$x = x + y$" might mean, but also an additional insight that the given differentiation must further develop in a kind of infinite loop. The consideration is as follows: what one has here is not only *the environment*, represented via the established ways of representing, as, e.g. in the pre-Renaissance paintings of things without the perspective shortening, but also the environment's *appearance* according to the new system of representation, as given, e.g. by the perspectival rules. Thus, it is not these pictures *per se*, but their comparison by which the relation of the system to its environment is made explicit, or, as Luhmann phrased it, *re-enters* the original system as the new difference between the self-reference and reference to the other: "The world is divided, cut, split, or torn asunder into system and environment, and the observer is himself also a system that observes other systems by means of the distinction between system and environment" (Luhmann 2013, 107).

This is, of course, a *paradox*, but a *real* one which we cannot postpone or "solve" but can merely accept as already given, responsible not only for our troubles, but our development as well, adequately captured exactly in the autopoietic concept of experience. In this context, Luhmann (2013, 112–13) quite consequently mentions Brunelleschi's perspectival experiments as a means of discovering the "blind spots" of every representation by combining various perspectives, i.e. observations of higher order.

4 A Straight Line Is Boundless

Idiosyncratic as it is, Luhmann's theory of systems provides a complex reading of experience as *circular* which, at the same time, deals with the problem of the *viciousness* of such a circle as typically posed by traditional logic and its analysis of classical antinomies. These antinomies are, of course, in a sense vicious, but if looked at not as mere incidents that somehow happened to our reason and might be avoided, but as an intrinsic part of our experience, the situation changes, as already suggested in the previous section.

This very idea of paradox as something "reasonable", i.e. stemming from reason itself, goes back to Kant and his transcendental idealism that sees the roots of the so-called *antinomies of pure reason* in our inherent tendency to *self-reflection*. We cannot help but to observe *ourselves* not because we are so conceited but because it is the pre-condition of having an experience at all, i.e. something that transforms mere unconnected data or *Erlebnisse* into a unified account of the *world* or our *Erfahrung* of it.

In this, however, reason behaves in a way which is both *too short* and *too long* (Kant 1998, A529/B557), always fixing some account as given, and, at the same time, seeing its limits, i.e. seeing such an account as something that can be surpassed. If we apply this observation to some ultimate totality – such as the final explanation of the world, or, for that sake, the world itself – the antinomy arises: the explanation or the given totality are too short, because they always can be extended, and too long, because this extension is at variance with their final nature. Similarly, the idea of the world as something *definite* requires this world has an end, but the very idea of such an end leads to the possibility of its prolongation.

The fine *visualization* of this basic antinomic situation, in all its variants and displays – let us mention here Zeno's paradox of plurality (according to which one cannot give a definitive number of all things because this could be always increased) and Cantor's paradox of set theory (according to which the set of all sets cannot even exist because its power set, i.e. the set of all subsets, would be necessarily bigger, which is impossible) – is provided by a line segment. This segment is both finite, i.e. bounded, *and* indefinitely expandable, i.e. unbounded corresponding to the thesis and antithesis of the first two antinomies of pure reason. See Fig. 2.

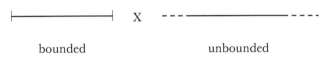

bounded   unbounded

Fig. 2.

Against this picture, I would like to claim, the problem of Kant's presentation of antinomies is, ironically, identical with his own analysis of them, namely too short and too long for the argument to work. Let me explain what I mean by that.

Using Luhmann's terminology, one can say that Kant knows one can observe her or his own environment only by means of some (rational) system, which he specifies as the system of *logical categories*. For Kant, these categories are heavily influenced by *Newtonian physics*, as the *a priori* tools of our measuring and quantifying the world. As such, his approach is necessarily *too short*, as he treats these categories as something forever fixed and given, which has (in)famously prolapsed with respect to the Euclidian geometry as part of Newton's explanational system. Once the given geometry was replaced or rather contrasted with its alternatives, Kant's original position became untenable. At the same time, Kant sometimes talks about his system's environment in terms of "the thing in itself", i.e. in absolute terms of something beyond that system and thus unreachable by its immanent means. In this sense, his explanation is simply *too long*, reaching not only beyond the given limit, which, by definition, can always be surpassed, but beyond any possible extension of it. Luhmann (2012, 50) alternatively phrases this second fallacy as a system's illusion to operate with a direct contact with the environment, while being directly connected only to itself.

The dilemma between "too short" and "too long", however, can be resolved if we appreciate the given geometrical visualization and the proper role of the Euclidian geometry in it. Just let us limit ourselves to

Euclid's five postulates,[4] particularly the second one according to which a finite straight line can be produced continuously in a straight line. What has happened with the invention of the non-Euclidian alternatives was not a simple *replacement* of one postulate by another, piece for piece, as in Hilbert's later metamathematical investigations or in the formal treatment of geometry in general, but rather the deep conceptual revision of the whole system, or the "paradigmatic switch". This switch might look harmless at first, consisting merely in Riemann's rephrasing of the second postulate as "a straight line is boundless". But it is more than once that one realizes that in this rephrasing, the very concepts of bounded and unbounded are fusing and, as such, lead to the hidden alternative to the given dilemma of the straight line and its infinite prolongation, namely their conceptual *reconciliation* in a circle. See Fig. 3.

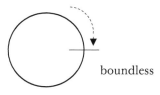

boundless

Fig. 3.

Such a switch is not formal if only because it requires a lot of mediating steps, in this case, as Kvasz (2008, 122–3) suggested, the phenomenon of *projective geometry* including the previous invention of the linear perspective. In these, geometrical forms are treated as *situated*, i.e. as seen from a certain point of view which, by means of projection, provides new conceptual identities, even *inconsistent* ones, as in the case of parallels, i.e. lines that by definition do not meet but are now intersecting each other at the horizon.

---

4 Their wording, according to the Heath edition, is: "(1) To draw a straight line from any point to any point. (2) To produce a finite straight line continuously in a straight line. (3) To describe a circle with any center and distance. (4) That all right angles are equal to one another. (5) That, if a straight line falling on two straight lines make the interior angles on the same side less than two right angles, the two straight lines, if produced indefinitely, meet on that side on which are the angles less than the two right angles" (Euclid 1968, 154–5).

If one takes the situatedness seriously, one can easily replace the Euclidian surface with the curved surface of a sphere, such as our Earth's, and check that the first four postulates are still fulfilled. The second postulate, particularly, holds because the straight line now, boundless as it is, becomes the sphere's *great circle*, both finite and infinite at the same time. The paradigmatic change proper, though, occurs with respect to the fifth postulate, according to which – or rather according to its more famous rewording, the so called Playfair axiom[5] – in a plane, one and only one parallel can be drawn to the given line through the given point. Unlike the previous postulates, the parallel postulate is violated, because any two sphere's great circles obviously intersect each other. Thus, the phenomenon of non-Euclidian geometry arises. What I am suggesting now is that Hegel's solution of Kant's paradoxes follows the same conceptual pattern, treating both antinomic sides as valid by giving reality a paradoxical form of a circle, or, *the circle of circles*, as Hegel calls the Absolute, i.e. the fully developed version of the Spirit.

The transfer from Euclidian to non-Euclidian geometries illustrates in which sense this "circle" parable can be used; namely, not as a simple label for some radically new solution to the old problems, but as an insight that this solution consists exactly in comparing the old solutions with the new ones, in a way corresponding to Dürer's self-referential pictures. The difference between the "new concepts", such as straight line or circle, is as important as their continuity, and, in fact, it is their difference that constitutes this continuity in the same way in which Euclidian geometry constitutes the intelligibility of the non-Euclidian systems. If read adequately, they do not just represent a new evolutionary stage in the scientific development, but also "the eternal return" to the original meaning of geometry as an operative part of our spatial orientation in the environment. The "irritations" and "shocks" behind this development are easily identifiable with the focus on both micro- and macro-cosmoses instead of the traditional environment of medium-sized objects, times, and distances.

In this rather complex sense the given circle is not vicious, i.e. explaining the same by the same, but *hermeneutical*, returning to its beginning, yet this time enriched by the journey undergone which, in a sense, is part of the goal and, as such, somehow identical with it.

---

5   Both axioms are not equivalent as such, but with respect to the whole of Euclidian geometry. See Heath's commentary in Euclid 1968, 312–14.

5 The Friendly Devil

So far, my goal has been to indicate in which sense the reference to the "curved truth" metaphor is not only some poetic innuendo, but has some real conceptual ground, the ultimate purpose of which is to establish a framework for the explanation of *who we are*. So, for Hegel, the dilemma of "straight" vs. "circular" is not just a logical wordplay, but most importantly the symbol of the *tragedy* of our lives which repeatedly strive for something new, replacing one thing by another, be it the scientific theory or any other goal, without the promise of arriving at some definitive solution and finding the final rest. This *Golgotha of Spirit*, as Hegel (2018, 467) calls it, is a natural part of our lives, or these lives themselves, and not uncommonly leads to ultimate skepticism or resignation, if not despair. The belief in the transcendent solutions, be it the objective world of the positive sciences or the unreachable beyond of the traditional religions, does not usually help here and even amplifies the resulting despair. This is particularly because it leads us away from a true solution of a certain kind of *cautious, moderate optimism* in which one does not want to replace desperation by false promises of other-worldly certainty, but to capture the true meaning of what Hegel calls the *Speculative Good Friday*,[6] or the moment of history in which the *death of God* stands for the possibility of a *new life*. It is exactly this moment of transforming the negativity into something relatively positive in which, for Hegel, our experience circumscribes the full circle.

The religious metaphor used here, obviously, has some ambivalent, double-faced meaning, standing both for the unhappy, transcendent concepts of life and for the essential steps that the Spirit has to take to its

---

6   The relevant and extremely enigmatic passage is this: "But the pure concept or infinity as the abyss of nothingness in which all being is engulfed, must signify the infinite grief purely as a moment of the supreme Idea, and no more than a moment. Formerly, the infinite grief only existed historically in the formative process of culture. It existed as the feeling that 'God Himself is dead,' upon which the religion of more recent times rests; the same feeling that Pascal expressed in so to speak sheerly empirical form: 'la nature est telle qu'elle *marque* partout un Dieu *perdu* et dans l'homme et hors de l'homme.' By marking this feeling as a moment of the supreme Idea, the pure concept must give philosophical existence to what used to be either the moral precept that we must sacrifice the empirical being, or the concept of formal abstraction. Thereby it must re-establish for philosophy the Idea of absolute freedom and along with it the absolute Passion, the speculative Good Friday in place of the historic Good Friday. Good Friday must be speculatively re-established in the whole truth and harshness of its Godforsakenness. Since the more serene, less well grounded, and more individual style of the dogmatic philosophies and of the natural religions must vanish, the highest totality can and must achieve its resurrection solely from this harsh consciousness of loss, encompassing everything, and ascending in all its earnestness and out of its deepest ground to the most serene freedom of its shape" (Hegel 1977, 190–1).

own socialization. The death of God, thus, does not represent only the end of the traditional religions and "superstitions" connected to them, as in one of Nietzsche's most famous gnomons, but also the death of the divine individual in favor of the Spirit which is wherever two or three are gathered in God's name (Matt. 18:20). In this sense, for both Hegel and Luhmann, religion is a mode of speech, or system, which brings the very fact of differentiation to its utmost limit. By dividing the world into an immanent and a transcendent part, it advocates the latter while belonging to the former, thus arriving at an explicit version of the above-mentioned paradox.

For Hegel, this paradox stems from the basic logic of *differentiation* connected, as here, with the utmost *generality*, or, one might say, with the very concept of a difference. If determination is negation – or, in Luhmann's setting, the system splits into the system and its environment –, then to determine some totality, be it the world, God, or the set of all sets, one must delimit it with respect to something else, which, however, by definition, cannot exist. The modern antinomies, starting with those of Kant and proceeding to those of Cantor and Russell, are based on this elevation of *nothing*, or the inherent negativity of being, to *something*.

Theo-logically speaking, this is to say that God does not admit differentiation, which either jeopardizes his omnipotence or further indicates his intrinsic contradictoriness. The latter option leads directly to the figure of a *friendly devil*, the first schismatic not by his own will but by being deputized by God. As Nietzsche put it: "The devil has the broadest perspective for God; therefore, he keeps so far away from God – the devil being the most ancient friend of wisdom" (Nietzsche 1966, 87).

Mephisto's self-definition in Goethe's *Faust* programmatically plays with the same idea in a significant detail:

FAUST: But still I ask, who are you?
MEPHISTOPHELES: A *part* of that force which, *always* willing evil, *always* produces good.
FAUST: That is a riddle. What does it mean?
MEPHISTOPHELES: I am the Spirit of Eternal Negation.[7] (Goethe 2004, 36; my italics)

---

7 Faust: Nun gut, wer bist du denn? Mephistopheles: Ein Teil von jener Kraft, die stets das Böse will, und stets das Gute schafft. Faust: Was ist mit diesem Rätselwort gemeint? Mephistopheles: Ich bin der Geist, der stets verneint!

The focus rightly put on the *combination* of negativity and generality, continues with stressing the relation of the whole to its part, which is elaborated on later:

> FAUST: You call yourself a part, yet stand before me whole?
> MEPHISTOPHELES: I only speak the sober truth.
> You mortals, microcosmic fools,
> may like to think of yourselves as complete,
> but I'm a part of the Part that first was all,
> part of the Darkness that gave birth to Light.[8] (Goethe 2004, 36)

Accordingly, God is not seen merely as one part of the basic difference, as the good opposed to the bad, but he is this *whole* itself which, by means of the devil, makes all the relevant differences. As the Book of Isaiah says: "I *am* the Lord, and *there is* none else. I form the light, and create darkness: I make peace, and create evil: I the Lord do all these *things*" (Isa. 45: 5–6). This inner differentiation of the original good into the good and the bad is, in fact, what all Luhmann's systems do, but religion does that more radically, treating division of the non-divisible as its proper task.

It is due to this metatheoretical form of the given discourse that one cannot read the previous considerations as a mere *relativization* of evil, but rather as an appreciation of the fact that the source of our creativity is the same as that of our destruction. As such, they mutually amplify their potential, of which Faust is a prominent example. Thomas Mann's variations on this theme in *Doktor Faustus* are nicely summed up in his lecture "Germany and the Germans", delivered at the Library of Congress three weeks after the surrender of Nazi Germany on 29 May 1945:

> The story I told you in brief outline, ladies and gentlemen, is the story of German "inwardness". It is a melancholy story, – I call it that, instead of "tragic", because misfortune should not boast. This story should convince us of one thing: that there are *not* two Germanys, a good one and a bad one, but only one, whose best turned into evil through devilish cunning. Wicked Germany is merely good Germany gone astray, good Germany in misfortune, in guilt, and ruin. For that reason it is quite impossible for

---

8   Faust: Du nennst dich einen Teil, und stehst doch ganz vor mir? Mephistopheles: Bescheidne Wahrheit sprech ich dir. Wenn sich der Mensch, der kleine Narrenwelt, gewöhnlich für ein Ganzes hält: Ich bin ein Teil des Teils, der anfangs alles war, ein Teil der Finsternis, die sich das Licht gebar.

one born there simply to renounce the wicked, guilty Germany and to declare: "I am the good, the noble, the just Germany in the white robe; I leave it to you to exterminate the wicked one." (Mann 1945, 18)

It is exactly this double-faced or *fragile* nature of humanity that is the topic of the religious discourse, warning us that we are not only passive products of *evolution*, of the survival of the fittest, as the positive sciences would like to say, excusing us easily from anything we do, or justifying these doings by transferring the guilt to the others, but that we are also essentially *creative* beings, accommodating ourselves to our environment *and* accommodating this environment to our ever-changing needs. This creativity, our ability to destroy or deform what there positively is by reading it in some new, "creative" way, is what defines us as cultural beings as opposed to the merely natural ones, such as brutes and animals.

As cultural beings, we might call ourselves *beyond good and evil*, not just by rejecting the conventional morals of our fathers and forefathers, but in a more radical, and, in fact, contradictory way of being *co-responsible* for what we do, including the consequences that our deeds had, no matter whether these consequences were intentional or not. This codependency of good and evil, of good intentions and evil deeds, is completely neglected and misunderstood in all the positive accounts of humanity in their hedonistic and utilitaristic approach to the world. Just consider Nietzsche's outcry:

What? The aim of science should be to give men as much pleasure and as little displeasure as possible? But what if pleasure and displeasure were so tied together that whoever *wanted* to have as much as possible of one *must* also have as much as possible of the other [...]? And that is how things may well be. (Nietzsche 1974, 85)

Along these lines, to be moral is to not to be *amoral* in a conventional sense of the word, but to be moral more radically, according to Hegel's concept of *heroic* consciousness (Hegel 2018, 385). It is while acting, as Hegel says, that one becomes necessarily *guilty*, not because we are subjects to some *natural* law of guilt, but because the guilt is one of the constitutive features of our *culture*, of our autopoietic ability to make things what they are not, or, more importantly, to become someone else. This guilt is something, for which we must always take responsibility, not only as individual agents, but also as belonging to the society that acts.

6 Lying as a Work of Art

In discussing the autopoietic worldview, I started with an example of language, both (1) as an exercise which, in its metaphorical reading, leads us from one metaphor to another, being in fact itself a metaphor of a metaphor, and (2) as a medium through which negativity enters the world. Now, after what has been said, I can repeat the same move by maintaining that it is our *language*, with its ability to both invent and corrupt, or lie in both the positive and negative sense of the word, through which, as Eagleton (2010, 30–1) put it in his essay *On Evil*, "man is Faustian Man, too voraciously ambitious for his own well-being, perpetually driven beyond his own limits by the lure of the infinite".

This "lure", or the language's "death drive", lies exactly in the metaphor's ability to *abstract* from certain finite differences, be it from the different phenomena (all these different creatures will be named "snake") or from the different cognizing subjects (I call them "snake" because you call them "snake" too), i.e. in drawing a linguistic meta-difference between things that matter and things that do not. Only in this way does objective knowledge as something *universal* become possible. The sinister consequences are part of that:

> Those who try to leap out of their finite situation in order to see more clearly end up seeing nothing at all. Those who aspire to be gods, like Adam and Eve, destroy themselves and end up lower than the beasts, who are not so plagued by sexual guilt that they need a fig leaf. Even so, this aberration is an essential part of our nature. It is a permanent possibility for rational animals like ourselves. We cannot think without abstraction, which involves reaching beyond the immediate. When abstract concepts allow us to incinerate whole cities, we know we have reached too far. A perpetual possibility of going awry is built into our capacity for sense-making. Without this possibility, reason could not function. (Eagleton 2010, 32–3)

The identification of the source of all division, as well as of autopoiesis, with language, is not a mere accidental observation, but also a retrospection of what we have been doing so far, namely using our language to draw differences, including the *difference of the difference*. In this retrospection, what might be noticed is that such a possibility of both creating something and destroying it by "reaching too far" expresses itself in a particularly self-conscious way in the *indirect* forms of language, such as metaphor, irony, or jokes, in which one problematizes or even undermines our relation to the world and to ourselves. As such, these "crooked" narrative forms are the true tools of the devil, as opposed to the straight forms of Godly or "objective" discourse of positive sciences. In the end, of course, everything is a "matter of difference".

The true domain of the "crooked" forms of our discursive practices is undoubtedly the *art*, as the most powerful and, at the same time, dangerous realm of the spirit. This is, in fact, how I read Hegel's famous delimitation of beauty as the sensuous shining or manifestation of truth, which, in this reading, is not some specific truth, but the *truth about truth*. The indirect forms of speech, I would suggest, are adequate to that goal by capturing – by their broadly semantic form – the universe that is divided not only into us and our environment, but mainly into us that is I and us that is the others, as any social concept of knowledge requires. My previous short presentation of metaphor as *topos* requiring the scene in which the addressee knows that I – the speaker – know that what I am saying is not true in order that it could be true is an example of what I mean by that.

Against this background, art is never only an appendix to the more serious and straightforward matters such as science, but both its devilish counterpart and its *spiritus agens*, not only in capturing the original sense of treating the difference as creating something new, at variance with how things positively are or have been so far, but in its being at the same time aware of experience's destructive powers. This starts with mere *stipulations* such as "A is A" to be read as "this will be called A", which is trivially true, yet completely vacant, not being a claim proper but rather a preparation for it. Transformation of "A is A" into the more informative "A is B" is what matters here and can easily start with the observation that "A is A" also presupposes the difference, not only of A on the left side from the A on the right side, but also of A as such against all other possible differences. Thus, any claim is and even must be, in a sense, a lie, based on the identification of what is different, e.g. different individuals, as what is the same, e.g. by being named "snake". But it is exactly this lie, and its *crooked* way of dealing with things, that represents a way to the truth, consisting in joining the different ends A and B as one, thus forming a basic circle of *conceptual* explanation.

As a means of such unnatural or counter-natural combination of two unrelated concepts A and B in the judgement of "A is B", language might represent the corruption that "society imposes in order to exist". Accordingly, truths rooted in metaphors are lies, or "illusions which we have forgotten are illusions, [...] metaphors that have become worn out and have been drained of sensuous force" (Nietzsche 1979, 84). But this focus on the original force reflects the positive side of the whole story, namely the primordial creative process:

> The drive toward the formation of metaphors is the fundamental human drive, which one cannot for a single instant dispense with in thought, for one would thereby dispense with man himself. The drive is not truly vanquished and scarcely subdued by the fact that a regular and rigid new world is constructed as its prison from its own ephemeral products, the concepts. It seeks a new realm and another channel for its activity, and it finds this in *myths* and in *art* generally. (Nietzsche 1979, 88–9)

If read in the Freudian manner, in which the channel – or the release of the surplus energy – just leads back to the original happiness of the pre-cultural state, simply by avoiding, though temporarily, the *barriers* and *differences* built around us by culture, the art and its treatment of metaphors seem to be only an analgetic to our eternal state of pain. But one can pursue a more radical goal, close to the final redemption of humanity by the reconciliation of experience's creative and destructive powers. Oscar Wilde phrased this point, in a double-ironic way, like this:

> CYRIL: Lying! I should have thought that our politicians kept up that habit.
> VIVIAN: I assure you that they do not. They never rise beyond the level of misrepresentation, and actually condescend to prove, to discuss, to argue. How different from the temper of the true liar, with his frank, fearless statements, his superb irresponsibility, his healthy, natural disdain of proof of any kind! After all, what is a fine lie? Simply that which is its own evidence. If a man is sufficiently unimaginative to produce evidence in support of a lie, he might just as well speak the truth at once. (Wilde 2010, 5)

The true liar, of course, is an *artist* who sees that at the beginning of any truth there is a creative act of lying which, as "the telling of beautiful untrue things, is the proper aim of art" (Wilde 2010, 37). This does not separate the artist, as a mere believer in fiction, from the scientist, as a mere believer in hard facts, but, on the contrary, makes them compatible, the artist being even superior to the scientist because he or she makes the underlying metaphorical sources of all our truths explicit.

The artistic message to humanity is as follows: to read any *"A is B"* as a *metaphor* is a risky, yet rewarding, enterprise if one captures the metaphor right, i.e. reveals, with respect to the obvious untruth, or "dissimulation", some deeper layer leading to a new insight or truth. That is why the "good" metaphor, like the "true" cognition, as Scruton (1997, 86) repeatedly points out, is not based on a mere similarity, but just the opposite, on overcoming the obvious difference by a connection that somehow leads to the *transformation* of reader's experience.

7 Backdoor to Paradise

What this transformation of our experience looks like is the very heart of the whole problem in which all the above-mentioned areas of experience – i.e. science, art, or religion – meet and prospectively adjust each other. They all agree, at least in their autopoietic setting, that there is some defining *difference*, true vs. false, beautiful vs. ugly, or grace vs. sin, and that we are falling prey to the latter while aspiring to the former. The idea now is to take this differentiation as well as our oscillation between the given poles as a stimulating rather than destructive one, defining the whole enterprise of experience as a double-movement starting with our propensity to fall and reading our successes only as relative improvements on these failures once they did happen.

The biblical story of the First Fall captures our situation quite well by connecting the original sin and the loss of naivete with the very emergence of humanity. The next step, though, is a complicated one, belonging to the true meaning of autopoiesis, namely whether the goal of mankind is to return to the original state of grace in which one is not aware of the ridge between the man and his environment, or whether there is some way of keeping the difference yet being reconciled with it. Or, as Hegel put it, whether one can achieve the state in which "the wounds of the spirit heal and leave no scars behind" (Hegel 2018, 387). Kleist's enigmatic essay "On the Marionette Theatre" offers the following ingenious solution:

> Such mistakes, he mused, cutting himself short, are inevitable because we have eaten of the tree of knowledge. And Paradise is bolted, with the cherub behind us; we must journey around the world and determine if perhaps at the end somewhere there is an opening to be discovered again. I laughed. Indeed, I thought, the spirit cannot err where it does not exist. (Kleist 1972, 24)

The return to the Paradise, as Kleist claims, is possible, yet not identical with the previous *unconscious* state of God's marionette. Rather it is the state of somebody who achieved a balance in his life, and, as such, discovered paradise's new opening. In my reading, this is the lesson to be taken from Kleist's substory of the young man who by observing himself in the mirror, i.e. by the gift of self-reflection, loses his previous grace to the vice of vanity.

Due to self-reflection and the knowledge built on it, so my reading goes, we are deprived of the life in the given moment. We become divided – or, as Nietzsche put it, we are *dividua*, not individua (Nietzsche 1996, 42) – and, as such, feel discontent with what we currently are. The insight into the impossibility of mirroring the world exactly as it is can even bring us to the verge of despair, in which we proceed from one failure to another without some satisfaction in sight. But then, suddenly, the new possibility arises, stemming from the second insight that the goal of our experience is not to mirror anything *as it is*, if only for the reason that by such a mirroring one will duplicate the world and thus make it, as in the seemingly trivial sentence of "*A is A*", what *it is not*. What we typically do is something else, namely enlarging the original state of affairs by new possibilities of expression and, accordingly, new varieties of grace.

Thus, e.g., by playing a musical instrument, one necessarily starts with the state of discontent, the unpleasant moments of exercising and failing to play it right, in which we have to constantly think about ourselves, about the coordination of our body with the requirements of the score. But if everything goes right, one might arrive at the state in which one does not have to think about what one does, being in the original state of identity with the world, i.e. in the state of grace unknown to the world before. This is how I read the final words of Kleist from the already discussed essay:

> We can see the degree to which contemplation becomes darker and weaker in the organic world, so that the grace that is there emerges all the more shining and triumphant. Just as the intersection of two lines from the same side of a point after passing through the infinite suddenly finds itself again on the other side – or as the image from a concave mirror, after having gone off into the infinite, suddenly appears before us again – so grace returns after knowledge has gone through the world of the infinite, in that it appears to best advantage in that human bodily structure that has no consciousness at all – or has infinite consciousness – that is, in the mechanical puppet, or in the God. Therefore, I replied, somewhat at

loose ends, we would have to eat again of the tree of knowledge to fall back again into a state of innocence? Most certainly, he replied: That is the last chapter of the history of the world. (Kleist 1972, 26)

Accordingly, the last chapter of mankind is not the state in which we achieve godlike qualities but in which we realize that reconciliation and grace is possible, together with the insight that it is never definitive. We are not immortal and cannot be immortal because immortality is the state in which *no differences* matter –, but we are defined by them. The state in which we can do anything we want is the state in which nothing matters. The original idea of Paradise is a chimera based on the de-relativization of the positive side of every difference, including truth, beauty, and grace. We know these concepts only in their relative meaning which makes their de-relativization impossible and even corrupting both in the conceptual and moral sense.

8 Synoptic Visions

The particularly powerful and influential *synoptic vision* of paradise in which the autopoietic concepts of art, religion, and science meet is to be found in Dante's *Divine Comedy*. It is of some importance here that Dante's vision of the universe goes back to Aristotle's *Physics* in which the conceptual primacy of circular movement is argued for, not only because it does not have a determinate beginning and end, which is why "a sphere is both moving and at rest", and as such finite, unlike the infinite – and thus non-existent – straight line (Aristotle 1996, 265a) but because it is also "a measure of change" (Aristotle 1996, 265b), be it in the regular movement of planets or the clocks as we know them. The modern physics of Galilei and Newton famously contradicted this, taking linearity as the most natural shape, which led to what is known as Newton's *law of inertia*: everything perseveres in a straight line (with a uniform, i.e. "straight" motion) unless compelled to change this state by the effect of external forces.[9]

---

9   It is appropriate to say that Galileo's "discovery" of inertia differs from that of Newton's in the sense that it is not phrased in opposition to Aristotle's preference for circular movement but to his supposition that the Earth, as the center of universe, is at rest. Galileo's ingenious justification of inertial movement via the experiment with the inclined plane goes like this: "So there could be a plane with so little inclination that, to gain a given degree of velocity, a body would

It is still commonplace to read the critique of Aristotle in the works of Galileo and Newton as a clash of the scientific approach with the philosophical one. What one has here is allegedly the straight thinking of self-evident experiments (*hypotheses non fingo*), on the one hand, and the vicious circles of the metaphysical philosophy, on the other. In the light of the autopoietic approach to the experience, we are probably wiser now, taking the relevant lesson from modern physics itself, including the conceptual shifts and emergence of the former conceptual "impossibilities" such as the non-Euclidian geometry or the relativistic concepts of space and time. This lesson does not say that Aristotle's was right (anyway, it was he who introduced linearity as the measure of conceptual exactness in his organon of logic, particularly in his concept of direct proof), but that the circularity of our experience has a more nuanced, generalized sense in which the truth does not consist in a mere stating of the straight facts, be it those of Aristotle, Newton, or Einstein, but by "crooking" these facts along the lines of some bold theory. This theory, in the course of time, will be necessarily "straightened out" by other theories in a kind of infinite, hermeneutical circle. This is, in fact, what Hegel's solution of Kant's antinomies asks us to realize.

In this context, the specific significance of Dante's synoptic vision is not only that it illustrates why the geometrical solution of Kant's paradoxes described above is a rather *intuitive* one, not delimited to the highly abstract and specialized realm of mathematics, but that it shows how it can be embedded into a bigger picture of our moral and cultural lives, of which the description of our orientation in time and space is only a small part – or rather metaphor. As such, it puts Hegel's idea of the Absolute as the "circle of circles" into a new perspective. Starting with physics, or rather geometry, one can argue, as has been repeatedly done,[10] that Dante pushes the above-mentioned idea of reconciliation of

---

have to move a very great distance over a very long period of time; and on a horizontal plane it would never naturally gain any velocity at all, as the body would not move. But motion along a horizontal line which is not inclined either upwards or downwards is circular motion around a center. Therefore, circular motion can never be acquired naturally unless it is preceded by rectilinear motion; but once required, it will continue perpetually at a uniform velocity" (Galileo 2012, 148). This obviously contrasts with Newton's concept of circular motion as reducible to infinitesimal, yet straight shifts caused by the body's inertia, on the one hand, and the pull of some other force, such as the gravity of the Sun, on the other.

10   There is plenty of representative literature to this reading, to the extent that it became rather colloquial. One can find it, e.g., in Rovelli's recent (2020) book of popular essays; see also Peterson 2011 or Egginton 1999 for further references. For mathematical details, as mentioned further, the rather popular explication might be found in Rucker 2007, 15–20. For a more

the finite with the infinite, or bounded with the unbounded, by means of a boundless circle, even further – from the surface to space. Accordingly, what he describes is a situation, well-known from modern models of universe based on non-Euclidian space, in which one can, by proceeding strictly forward, come around to one's own back.

In *The Divine Comedy*, this possibility is suggested at the very end, where Dante, leaving the sphere of primum mobile, sees, through the reflection in Beatrice's eyes, the same picture of concentrically rotating spheres twice, in front and behind him, with the centers being Satan and God (Dante 2017, Canto XXVIII, 22–39). In the crucial passage, then, the uniformity of the outermost terrestrial sphere is given by claiming that no matter at which point it is left, the same picture, i.e. the rotating spheres around the God, is seen:

> All of it is so lively and so high
> And uniform, I do not know which part
> Beatrice selected as the place for me.[11] (Dante 2017, Canto XXVII, 100–2)

Geometrically, this easily corresponds to the representation of the 3-dimensional sphere, such as our Earth, by means of two circles or 2-dimensional spheres, the Earth's hemispheres, connected by their circumference. Now, we have to think of the situation as transferred "metaphorically" into the higher dimension, with the hypersphere,

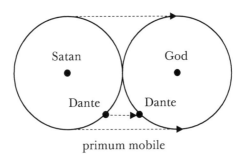

primum mobile

Fig. 4.

---

technical approach, see Peterson 1979, which is probably the first paper devoted to this very subject.

11 Le parti sue vivissime ed eccelse / sì uniforme son, ch'i' non so dire / qual Bëatrice per loco mi scelse.

i.e. 4-dimensional sphere of our boundless universe represented by two 3-dimensional spheres as in the Fig. 4, the surface of the primum mobile being the connecting surface.

Hence, the new entry to paradise is, in fact, the old one which was, obviously, the original exit from it, marking the loss of our innocence as the start of our experience's journey. This picture stands for a metaphor that ceased to be a *mere* metaphor once we revealed its deeper meaning of standing both for what it expresses and for itself, or, as Oscar Wilde put it, for that which is its own evidence.

This double-meaning of metaphor is not easy to grasp, because the *synoptic visions*, such as those given by Dante (in which both Aristotle's circular cosmology and ethics plays a role) or Goethe's *Faust* (written and re-written within the long span of 60 years of Goethe's active life) are accessible to us only after we have already set out for such a journey, i.e. come to us in their full meaning when we are "halfway along our journey to life's end". This is not to say that one is to wait for the journey to be over but rather the opposite: one has to set out as soon as possible despite *and* because of the fact there is no guarantee that it will lead to something at least remotely satisfying. As William James (1997, 86) put it, we are living in the universe that does not respond to us unless we are willing to meet it half-way, and it is exactly this feature of the universe that makes it good in the one and only sense we have.

9 Contents of the Volume

The task of this volume, one might say, is to provide a synoptic vision of its own. Unlike the above-mentioned works, particularly those of Niklas Luhmann, it cannot nor does it want to cover the whole of our experience, but rather the central concepts according to which it, in the given autopoietic settings, develops itself, including the terms of negativity, creativity, and self-reflection. Being interdisciplinary in its very nature, the volume necessarily oscillates between conceptual exposition, on the one hand, and its application to the specific field of research and topics, on the other, arching from literature to archeology, from religion to cognitive linguistics, from the theory of art to the role of the university and education today. Accordingly, it is divided into four interconnected parts.

In the first one, *Methods of Self-Creation*, the general problems of autopoiesis are addressed, including the relations of creativity to destruction, the concepts of boundary, self-organization, complexity, and others. Thus, in his essay "The Method Is Justified by Its Outcome", **Miroslav Petříček** compares the main feature of modern thinking, namely its openness to the unexpected, with the double-faced nature of autopoietic systems that are both open to the interpretation of outer inputs and closed by means of self-organizing principles. For philosophy and thinking in general, Petříček claims, these inputs are problems to be solved but as their solution leads to the change of the existing system, the problems of modern philosophy become, in an autopoietic recourse, the very topics of becoming, change, and process. The first part continues with **Martin Procházka**'s study "From Boundaries to Interfaces: Autopoietic Systems and the 'Ontology of Motion'", that explores the dynamic quality of autopoiesis against the background of Thomas Nail's procedural philosophy. The essay's main stress is put on the "autopoietic" concept of "boundary" or "border" with a suggestion to interpret it, for autopoiesis' sake, as "interface": "If borders are modelled as interfaces, cultures do not have to be approached as closed systems with specific identities but described in functional terms, as interfaces of transcultural communication which engender dialogue and use fictions to enable and facilitate sharing knowledge, emotions, attitudes, beliefs and values". The first part closes with the essay "'I *am* the Combat: Hegel's Dramatic Theory of Knowledge". Here, **Vojtěch Kolman** elaborates on an autopoietic image of Hegel's philosophy, according to which the Spirit or society self-feed on the tail of our own failures, in terms of epistemological fallibilism. Hegel, Kolman claims, not only fits into the standard fallibilist picture, but enriches it with what might be called a dramatic twist, famously known from the dialectics of the master and slave parable.

The second part *Narratives of Self-Creation and Self-Destruction* takes literature as the most natural point of departure for the proper autopoietic enterprise. It begins with **Josef Vojvodík**'s essay, "Autopoiesis and the 'Pure Culture of Death Instinct': Creativity as a Suicidal Project", in which the negative, or even suicidal aspects of creativity are explicitly dealt with in regard to the figures of Paul Celan and Péter Szondi. It is the "unsettling symmetry" of their fates that illustrates, as Vojvodík says, that "danger, risk, the proximity of death, [...] bestow a special character on every act of courage, on every adventure, including the creative act". The following paper, "The Dark Side of the End of Art" by **Tomáš Murár**, shares Vojvodík's general reference to Luhmann's idea that "the self-negation of art is realized at the level of autopoietic operations in the form of art, so that art can continue". But Murár contrasts it explicitly with Danto's thesis about the end of art according to which art self-consciously freed itself from the master narratives of art history. Based on the theoretical works and tragic life of Robert Klein, Murár proposes a new reading of the thesis, in which art not only dies so that it can live, but "after its end [it] is substituted by life itself, thus it is no longer secured by social (artistic) forms, the vitality of art is replaced by the tragedy of life". In the next essay, "The Author in the Making: Ethos, Posture, and Self-Creation", **Josef Šebek** addresses the relations of author and the work in an autopoietic sense in which the author is, in fact, created by the literature rather than *vice versa*. Against the detailed polemic with the broad tradition of the Western concept of literary authorship (Pierre Bourdieu, Ruth Amossy, Dominique Maingueneau, Jérôme Meizoz, and Liesbeth Korthals Altes), Šebek tests this theory of authorship against the "autobiographical" novel of Édouard Louis, as "an extreme example of self-creation through literature". Finally, **Eva Voldřichová Beránková** deals with the reception of the great autopoietic system of Hegel in French philosophy and literature, discussing in great detail the basic contrast between the negativity of our experience and our persistent striving for some positive closure. In her paper "A Negative Autopoietic Principle in French Interpretations of Hegel – Breton, Sartre, Bataille", she demonstrates that the positive side of Hegel's philosophy, criticized by the revolutionary ideas of Breton or Sartre, is in fact mimicked in their treatment of negation as "both unlimited and yet in the service of a determinate end (the dissolution of opposites, the end of capitalism) which gives it an ambiguous character".

The third part, *Religion and Education as Autopoietic Projects*, begins with **Tereza Matějčková**'s essay "Luhmann's Religious Carnival and the Limits of Communication" that discusses the specific features of Luhmann's philosophy of religion. Based on a short, yet detailed and informed introduction to his systems theory, Matějčková argues that despite some limitations of Luhmann's approach to religion as a form of communication, religion's function in modern society is secured by its role of embracing the paradox contained in every system's distinguishing itself from itself. By picking up the otherworldly, inaccessible, and thus negative side of this division, "religion doubles the world but continues on the re-valuation of the negative side, and thus provides means for re-evaluating failures." "These failures," Matějčková continues, "can be thoroughly real and material, such as illness, poverty, or social exclusion. But they can also be subtler – for example, the inability to understand oneself and others". In a related way, **Tomáš Halík**, in his essay

"Historical Transformations of Christianity and Luhmann's Theory of Autopoietic Systems", draws on Luhmann's claim that the modern process of secularization is not necessarily at variance with the influence of religious thinking, but they, in fact, strengthen each other if captured in an adequate way. In a system of short paragraphs, Halík sketches his idea of what this adequate way is with reference to his recently published book, *The Afternoon of Christianity. Courage for Transformation*, that is devoted to the transformations of Western Christianity and the possibilities of the further development of it in postmodern pluralist culture. In the final paper of this part, **Jakub Jirsa** reflects on the role of university and the higher education in modern society. In his essay, "On Universities and Contemporary Society: The Issue of Trust", he argues it is the autopoietic nature of the university – going back to Hegel's concept of *Bildung* as work on itself, as opposed to the authoritative and instrumentally conceived methods of education – which, in fact, stands behind the degradation of universities in the modern world governed by the managerial, i.e. instrumental, approach to the world and to others.

The fourth and final part, *Society in an Autopoietic Perspective*, covers several case-studies from a variety of research fields. In his study, "An Autopoieticist Vision of Society: Luhmann's Social System Theory and the Understanding of Medieval Transformation", **Tomáš Klír** provides a comparison of Luhmann's systems theory with the concept of medieval transformation in a bold attempt to extend the scope of Luhmann's autopoietic methodology to the world of historical sciences. His idea is to use the autopoietic vision of society as an extremely effective tool for description, analysis, and understanding of the dialogical relationship between people and their artefactual world, particularly between the organization and interactions in pre-industrial peasant communities and the geographical patterns of field systems in which these communities operated. After that, **Jakub Jehlička**'s and **Eva Lehečková**'s contribution "Participatory Sense-Making through Bodies: Self-Organizing Principles in the Continuity of Life and Mind" brings us to the field of cognitive linguistics and language philosophy. Based on the idea of language as something that both individually and socially embodies a broadly conceived concept of linguistic gesture, Jehlička and Lehečková – based on an analysis of performative gestures employed in Petipa's productions of Adam's *Giselle* – describe how new forms arise from the old, familiar ones and how they can sediment. **Josef Šlerka**, in his essay "Conspiracy Theories and Disinformation as Viruses in Social Media", addresses the negative concepts of disinformation, conspiracy, and lies, treating them as kinds of viruses (or according to Richard Dawkins, memes) of the human mind. In his reading, the human mind thus becomes not the centre, but the environment, and the rules of how the viruses spread and mutate come to the fore. The part as well as the whole volume is concluded by **Ondřej Slačálek**'s paper "Aspiring Autopoiesis and Its Troubles: What Else Is Produced When the Nation Is Reproduced". Starting with the explicit goal "to understand the nation as a construct that reconstructs itself and thus to understand how elements of spontaneity and elements of construction are present", Slačálek explores what he calls "the myth of self-constitution" of a nation. Based on a discussion of the ideas of Rousseau, von Clausewitz, Benda, and Arendt, he arrives at a moderate conclusion in which such a constitution is possible but only via the nation's relation to other nations and the permanent growth caused by its own endeavor. "The nation is a Uroboros devouring its tail," he concludes, "however, this tail is much fatter at some times than it is at others."

References

Aristotle. 1996. *Physics.* Translated by Robin Waterfield. Oxford: Oxford University Press.

Dante Alighieri. 2014. *Inferno.* Translated by J. G. Nichols. Richmond, VA: Alma Classics.

Dante Alighieri. 2017. *Paradise.* Translated by J. G. Nichols. Richmond, VA: Alma Classics.

Eagleton, Terry. 2010. *On Evil.* New Haven, CT: Yale University Press.

Egginton, William. 1999. "On Dante, Hyperspheres, and the Curvature of the Medieval Cosmos". *Journal of the History of Ideas* 60 (2): 195–216.

Euclid. 1968. *The Thirteen Books of the Elements. Volume I.* Translated by Sir Thomas L. Heath. Cambridge: Cambridge University Press.

Galileo Galilei. 2012. *Selected Writings.* Translated by William R. Shea, and Mark Davie. Oxford: Oxford University Press.

Goethe, Johann Wolfgang von. 2004. *Faust.* Translated by Stuart Atkins. Princeton, NJ: Princeton University Press.

Hegel, Georg Wilhelm Friedrich. 1977. *Faith and Knowledge.* Translated by Walter Cerf, and H. S. Harris. Albany: State University of New York Press.

Hegel, Georg Wilhelm Friedrich. 2018. *The Phenomenology of Spirit.* Translated by Terry Pinkard. Cambridge: Cambridge University Press.

James, William. 1997. "The Will to Believe". In *Pragmatism. A Reader*, edited by Louis Menand, 69–92. New York: Vintage Books.

Kant, Immanuel. 1998. *The Critique of Pure Reason.* Translated by Paul Guyer, and Allen W. Wood. Cambridge: Cambridge University Press.

Kleist, Heinrich von. 1972. "On the Marionette Theatre". Translated by Thomas G. Neumiller. *The Drama Review* 16: 22–6.

Kvasz, Ladislav. 2008. *Patterns of Change. Linguistic Innovations in the Development of Classical Mathematics.* Birkhäuser: Berlin.

Luhmann, Niklas. 2012. *Theory of Society. Volume 1.* Translated by Rhodes Barrett. Stanford, CA: Stanford University Press.

Luhmann, Niklas. 2013. *Introduction to Systems Theory*. Translated by Peter Gilgen. Cambridge, MA: Polity.

Mann, Thomas. 1945. *Germany and the Germans*. Washington, D.C.: Library of Congress.

Maturana, Humberto, and Francisco Varela. 1980. *Autopoiesis and Cognition. The Realization of the Living*. Dordrecht: D. Reidel.

Maturana, Humberto, and Francisco Varela. 1984. *The Tree of Knowledge. Biological Roots of Human Understanding*. Translated by Robert Paolucci. Boston, MA: Shambhala.

Nietzsche, Friedrich. 1966. *Beyond Good and Evil*. Translated by Walter Kaufmann. New York: Random House.

Nietzsche, Friedrich. 1974. *The Gay Science*. Translated by Walter Kaufmann. New York: Random House.

Nietzsche, Friedrich. 1979. "On Truth and Lies in a Non-Moral Sense". In *Philosophy and Truth. Selections from Nietzsche's Notebooks of the Early 1870's*, edited by Daniel Breazeale, 77–97. Jersey City, NJ: Humanities Press.

Nietzsche, Friedrich. 1996. *Human, All Too Human. A Book for Free Spirits*. Translated by R. J. Hollingdale. Cambridge: Cambridge University Press.

Nietzsche, Friedrich. 2006. *Thus Spoke Zarathustra*. Translated by Adrian del Caro. Cambridge: Cambridge University Press.

Peterson, Mark A. 1979. "Dante and the 3-sphere". *American Journal of Physics* 47 (12): 1031–5.

Peterson, Mark A. 2011. *Galileo's Muse. Renaissance Mathematics and the Arts*. Cambridge, MA: Harvard University Press.

Rovelli, Carlo. 2020. *There Are Places in the World Where Rules Are Less Important Than Kindness*. London: Allen Lane.

Rucker, Rudy. 2007. *Infinity and the Mind. The Science and Philosophy of the Infinite*. Princeton, NJ: Princeton University Press.

Scruton, Roger. 1997. *The Aesthetics of Music*. New York: Oxford University Press.

Wilde, Oscar. 2010. *The Decay of Lying and Other Essays*. London: Penguin Books.

Wittgenstein, Ludwig. 1958. *The Blue and Brown Books*. Oxford: Blackwell.

Part I
Methods of Self-Creation

The Method Is Justified by Its Outcome

Miroslav Petříček

Section 1

Over the last half century or so, thinking has been characterised by an openness that accentuates the event-based nature of time (i.e. does not exclude the unpredictable), non-hierarchisation and de-centralization. This has been both a period of general transformation, and yet a significant period in its own right, since it also represents the thinking through of change, namely modification, refashioning, i.e. action/event.

And this is why even so much as describing this transformation is difficult: it does not have a single cause, and it is not impossible that the search for causes is itself something that this transformation bequeaths us in the sense that it problematises the classical notion of causality. It would thus perhaps be more accurate to say that this transformation arises from a certain constellation of aporias culminating in a general problematisation of the current way of thinking, in the light of which certain theoretical problems appear as paradoxes, as something that is irresolvable in respect of the dominant "image of thought" (Deleuze's term), since the only solution would be to change the framework.

One of the striking features of this transformation (and not merely modification) is how it undermines a concept of order hitherto accepted without question, comprising unquestioned operative concepts such as *system* and, until the 1960s, *structure*, the common denominator of which was an endeavour to abstract from historicity. However, during the 1960s we also see the assertion of a new element, namely, the concept of auto-poietic systems or self-organisation. This changes everything. We are now speaking of a *processual* order, and what we mean by *system* is now a process in which the dynamic relationship between the various components or instances of said system allows them to self-organise without any external or internal cause (as classical thinking would have it) in the form of *responses* to changes in their environment; the system moves to a level of higher complexity, in which new properties are created or appear (both are implied in the word *emergence* in the sense of spontaneous generation) that cannot be explained as being the product of some force external to the system in question. The 1970s and 1980s then saw a number of books published that now enjoy the status of classics, which interpret (within a broader context) this process of self-organisation. Ilya Prigogine, Henri Atlan, Stuart Kauffmann and Michel Serres (Prigogine and Stengers 1984; Atlan 1999; Atlan 2003; Kauffmann 1983; Serres 1969–1980) are but a few of the authors to deal with this question. A key to understanding the internal dynamic of autopoietic systems is by examining how they interact with their environment. The system reacts to what is happening in its environment (which can often not be predicted by the system and thus has the character of an event in the strict sense of the word: it is *historical*) by means of its internal transformation in such a way that it is able to decode these *errors* (*noise*) as information. Hence the principle *order from noise* (which is considerably at odds with the traditional notion of the formation of order): hence, too, another of the possible *definitions* of an open, processual order.

Henri Atlan summarises this concept briefly and precisely in his essay "Noise as a Principle of Self-Organization" of 1972, which it suffices to quote:

> it does not seem correct to characterize them entirely as errors. The noise provoked in the system by random factors in the environment will no longer be truly noise from the moment it is used by the system as a factor of organization. This is to say that factors in the environment are not random. But, of course, they are. Or more exactly, it depends on the subsequent reaction of the system in relation to which, a posteriori, these factors are recognized as either random or as part of the organizing process. A priori, they are in effect random, if one defines randomness as the intersection of two independent chains of causality: the causes of their occurrence have nothing to do with the chain of phenomena that has constituted the prior history of the system until then. It is thus that their occurrence and their encounter with the system can constitute noise from the viewpoint of the exchanges of information in the system, where these

encounters are susceptible to producing only errors. But from the moment the system is capable of responding to these "errors", not just so that it does not disappear, but rather so that the system uses them to modify itself in a way that benefits it or at least ensures its subsequent survival – in other words, from the moment the system is capable of integrating these errors into its own organization – then these errors lose, a posteriori, a little of their character of error. They retain this only from a viewpoint exterior to the system, in that the effects of the environment on the system do not themselves correspond to any preestablished program contained in the environment and destined to organize or disorganize the system. On the contrary, from the interior perspective, insofar as organization consists precisely in a series of recaptured disorganizations, they do not appear as errors except at the instant of their occurrence. The thermodynamic mechanisms of order through fluctuation seem to put the accent on the internal character of organizational noise. This distinction is not a real one, and in relation to a maintenance of the status quo (which would be as unfortunate as it is imaginary) of the organized system, which one pictures to oneself as soon a static description of it can be given. Indeed, after this instant, the errors are integrated, recuperated as factors of organization. The effects of noise then become events in the history of the system and its process of organization. They remain, however, effects of noise inasmuch as their occurrence was unforeseeable.

It thus might be sufficient to consider organization as an uninterrupted process of disorganization and reorganization, and not as a state, for order and disorder, the organized and the contingent, construction and destruction, life and death, to no longer be really distinct. However, this is not at all the case. The processes in which this unity of oppositions realizes itself (this realization not being a new state, a synthesis of thesis and antithesis, but a movement of the process itself – the "synthesis" being nothing besides this) cannot exist except inasmuch as errors are a priori true errors, inasmuch as order at a given moment is truly perturbed by disorder, inasmuch as destruction, while not total, is real, inasmuch as the irruption of the event is a real irruption (a catastrophe, a miracle, or both at once). In other words, the processes that appear to us as one of the foundations of the organization of living beings, as results of a sort of collaboration between what we are accustomed to calling life and death, cannot exist except to the degree that they are never really about collaboration but always about radical opposition and negation. (Atlan [1972] 2011, 111–12)

Here's a little thought experiment: read the lengthy quote above as if it were describing the relationship of philosophy to (historical) reality, and bear this in mind when looking back over the changes that have taken place in thinking over the last half century or so. This is not merely a mechanical task, but involves a rigorous search for other concepts and models. In this thought experiment the *system* (in a sense autopoietic) will be philosophy, or rather philosophical discourse, the environment of which is unfolding reality and the unexpected *perturbations* occurring in it (*problems* that must be resolved even though we have no proven way of dealing with them, as Adorno would say), to which thinking reacts by means of its own transformation, after which it is able to incorporate these perturbations or *irritations* (events) in itself (to grant them significance, to turn them into *information*). However, all of this must now be illustrated in the work of specific writers, and the inspiration behind their work revealed. At the same time, the broader context must be borne in mind (the relationship of philosophical discourse to tradition) and similar considerations undertaken on the basis of a comparison of the system we call philosophy and the system we call artistic creation.

Section 2

However, things are made somewhat more complex by the fact that not even the term *environment* is as clear cut in this context as it might appear at first sight. At this point it might be useful to introduce another term, namely *model*, above all in the sense that it is used by the semiotician Yuri Lotman. This will also help us answer the question of why the experience of and reflection upon artistic creation participates to such a significant extent in the transformation of the notion of order, and why so many philosophers have addressed the topic of aesthetics from the mid-20th century onwards, from Adorno's *Aesthetic Theory*, via the existentialists and structuralists, to Lyotard, Derrida, Nancy, Marion, et al. Moreover, the concern displayed by philosophers not to restrict the subject of their enquiries to books often takes a hitherto unusual form. They now participate fully in the planning of exhibitions, they write introductions to catalogues, they devote more of the energies to the topic of aesthetics (albeit taking issue with philosophical aesthetics of the past), and the creative process becomes part of philosophical argumentation. Why is this? It is because the meaning of art seems to reside in the fact that the artwork somehow interprets reality, while at the same time anticipating it. In other words, the artwork *models* reality.

Yuri Mikhailovich Lotman, who takes art to be a "secondary modelling system" (Lotman 1981), adopts a description of the model from cybernetics and information theory. This is completely logical, since his semiotics develops in association with a theory of text within the framework of culture, while at the same time conducting a polemic with an understanding of text as merely the carrier of non-textual structures or pre-textual (pre-semiotic) meanings. Lotman criticises classical and certain modern theories of the text for merely bumping up against the text that is supposedly the object of their investigation, since they always end up behind it, in front of it or outside it. In contrast, Lotman asserts that the text does not embody meaning, nor does it manifest it: the text *produces* meaning, it is the active generator of meaning.

According to Lotman, the texts of a given culture fall into one of two categories. The first contains texts whose function is to impart information in the most appropriate way. The ideal text in this category would be one written in an artificial language guaranteeing maximum concordance between addresser and addressee. The second category contains texts traditionally referred to as *artistic*. Such a text *generates* meaning, above all because it is a *game of different languages*, which also happens to be the most general description of the creative process. We find a somewhat sophisticated analogy to these two *limits* to the communication and generation of meaning in Barthes' distinction between readerly texts and writerly texts (*lisible*, i.e. a readable text; *scriptible*, i.e. a text that can only be read by virtue of each reader themselves rewriting it, in other words, writing it) (Barthes 2002, 119–341; Barthes 2007). The general semiotic definition is less poetic, though precise: "The text appears as a unity composed of at least two subtexts, which have a fundamentally different organization, and of some meta-level mechanism that connects the two subtexts and guarantees their mutual translatability" (Barthes 2007, 15).

However, this meta-level is not a given, but is a place where *secondary* codes are forever being constructed, by which the equivalence is made possible of initially completely diverse languages or differently coded texts. In other words, texts arise from languages (and because of that we have, for instance, a constant supply of new novels), but likewise languages arise from texts.

> The processes of sense-making emerge both as a result of the interaction of semiotically heterogeneous layers of the text, which are in a relationship of mutual untranslatability, and as a consequence of complex sense-creating conflicts between the text and the heterogeneous context. (Lotman 1981, 15)

Confirming or verifying these theses would involve a detailed investigation of what happens when, for instance, a certain culture takes receipt of a *foreign* (in the sense of incomprehensible) text that, precisely because of its incomprehensibility, sets in motion all the semiotic mechanisms of said culture, in which the whole point is to create some secondary code or language on the basis of which it would be possible to accept this foreign text (i.e. to concede that it speaks intelligibly, to grant it credibility, etc.). Based on this concept we can now link the mechanism of semiosis with energetics, providing we adopt a thermodynamic definition that says that energy is the general equivalent of transformation, because we are now in a position to say that the indecipherability of a heterogeneous text or context represents the energy that sets in motion the process of creating meaning (*Sinnbildung* rather than *Sinngebung*), i.e. the transformation of *noise* into a message.

However, the reference to heterogeneity as an energy source of the dynamic process of *Sinnbildung* (sense formation) means that it is impossible to consider the text (and any semiotic system in general) in *isolation*, outside its relationship to the *environment* (which from the point of view of text is always to some extent or other *non-text*). Lotman's language, a highly original import of cybernetics, systems theory and the theory of self-organisation autopoiesis, thus thermodynamics, would frame things thus:

> while a description that eliminates from its object all extrasystematic elements is fully justified when constructing static models, and needs only certain correction coefficients, it presents difficulties of principle for the construction of dynamic models. One of the chief sources of the dynamism of semiotic structures is the constant process of drawing extrasystematic elements into the realm of the system and of expelling systematic elements into the area of non-system. A refusal to describe the extrasystematic, placing it beyond the confines of science, cuts off the reserve of dynamism and presents us with a system in which any play between evolution and homeostasis is, in principle, excluded. (Lotman 1981, 93)

What in this context does "extra-systematic" mean? What it does not mean, though it might appear to, is without further realism, *reality*. From the point of view of the system as a certain (textual) culture, in the extra-systematic *environment* there is to be found everything that this culture, during its development, has postponed, displayed, rejected, proscribed, etc. For in some respects, the system-environment relationship seems to be duplicated within the system in the form of a *core-periphery* relationship, with the periphery as both the boundary of the system and a site of ambiguity within it; if the periphery is negated, the system becomes non-existent and moves into a position relative to the external system. A simple illustration: from the point of view of philosophy as a certain system, medicine (at a certain moment in its development) represents a different system, i.e. medicine is an *extra-systematic environment* in respect of philosophy. However, historically speaking we know that medicine was both *displaced* and that it found itself in this place thanks to its own, autonomous development. Yet both the energetic gesture of its elimination from philosophy on the one hand, and its autonomy on the other, seemed to give it a certain *potential* energy that was even capable of accumulation over time, which might prove to be a very powerful energy source at that moment when we attempt to bring *medical science* from the outside or periphery closer to the core of *philosophy*. One might think in a similar way about *pre-Cartesian physics* in relation to biology, as philosophy of the latter half of the 20th century addresses this topic, for instance in the form of French epistemology. And above all this idea of the "extra-systematic" legitimises an interest in the history of science, including the so-called exact sciences.

The role of heterogeneity in the generation of meaning is best illustrated by what Lotman calls "stereoscopy" and also the elementary example of the genesis of semiosis, in connection with which the term "extra-systematic" appears in both senses of the word: as a foreign system and as a non-system par excellence. The rudimentary basis of semiosis can now be imagined as the "communication" (in inverted commas) of two beings that only exchange disorganised signals that are simply unconscious symptoms of their psycho-physiological processes. Their "code" (in inverted commas) has only the trivial form "edible fruit – satisfaction", and so their "communication" regarding the world consists in an exchange of identical meanings, without there existing any *content* that could be communicated outside this mechanism. Both are actually a single being united by a common code. However, it is for this reason that we cannot *strictu senso* speak of communication either, since in (what we call) communication only that which establishes the *individuality* of the partner as Other possesses informational value (this individuality being manifest, for instance, when its involuntary signalling cannot be deciphered on the basis of a common code). It is to this polarity that on a higher level the typological polarity of two "limit" texts corresponds: however, in this simple illustration it is clear how the "extra-textual", i.e. the *environment* of the system, can be understood as reality (the individuality of the Other is presented as a reality).

But what does *stereoscopy* actually mean? Communication itself leads to the division therein of the individual pole and the general pole, yet the opacity of the individual is not a barrier, but, on the contrary, a need (an energy source). It is only thanks to the heterogeneity of the individual that the information has a stereoscopic character, since it is generated as the irruption of the heterogeneous. Hence the elementary imperative of communication: that it comprises both equivalence and difference. Without the first there is no possibility of exchange: without the second, the information exchanged is not new, it has no meaning.

> The potential possibility of hypertrophy of both aspects, the fact that one could be completely overwhelmed by the other, as well as the possibility that partial untranslatability will become complete, are all already inherent in the initial scheme, just as the possibility of malfunctions is potentially hidden in the normal functioning of the mechanism. [...] disharmony between these subsystems is a source of pathological phenomena if we consider culture from a synchronic point of view, while diachronically it works as a source of dynamism for the system as a whole. (Lotman 1981, 113)

The stereoscopic nature of information is the result of cultural multilingualism. The model is therefore a far more complex apparatus, as we see from the terms "meta-level" and "meta-language". The model models reality by generating meaning, since every description of the extra-systematic transforms this extra-systematic into a fact of the very system in question.

Multilingualism leads to an attempt to create equivalences between the heterogeneous. We might say that the outcome of these *secondary* processes (from the point of view of individual languages) is always a certain model of *models*, which, however, is always a self-description of the semiotic system in question (implying multilingualism) and functions as its self-organisation. It is a *subgroup* of texts, which, however, function as a *meta-language* of this self-description. The meta-language does not come from outside, but is one of the subsystems of the system in question. Incidentally, one of the *products* of this self-description, which also has a *regulating* character, is the relocation of certain texts to the sphere of the extra-systematic. An example would be Boileau, *L'Art poétique*. Another more complex example would be the Surrealist manifestos, which initiate complex movements between the periphery and the core, while at the same time refining the "extra-systematic" itself. Self-description regulates and simultaneously shapes the history of its object from the point of view of its own model (Lotman 1981, 98). Culture cannot be understood as anything other than a model of an open system.

Section 3

Adorno's "definition" of art in *Aesthetic Theory* says much the same thing, albeit using a different language:

> The definition of art is at every point indicated by what art once was, but it is legitimated only by what art became with regard to what it wants to, and perhaps can, become […] It is defined by its relation to what it is not. The specifically artistic in art must be derived concretely from its other […] Art acquires its specificity by separating itself from what it developed out of; its law of movement is its law of form. It exists only in relation to its other; it is the process that transpires with its other. (Adorno 2002, 2–3)

At the same time, however, it is clear at first glance that this definition, as though from the other side, i.e. from the side of philosophy, repeats the basic operations of Adorno's negative dialectics, which transmit impulses from the pre-war period (Walter Benjamin) to the 1960s, while at the same time formulating them within another context, i.e. that of thinking as being permanently *in statu nascendi*, characterised by an element of experimentation (all the characteristic features of openness). It is for this reason that the starting point of negative dialectics is a postulation of the irrevocable divergence of the concept and the intended thing that the concept grasps. And it is necessary to think through this divergence, i.e. to open conceptual thinking to that which escapes it, to the non-identical moment in the process of identificatory thinking, but still within the realm of the discursive. This is why, as Martin Seel has shown (2018), a necessary complement to negative dialectics is *constellational* thinking, which, while working with concepts, works against them.

General concepts coined by means of abstraction or axiomatically by individual sciences form the material of representation no less than the names of individual objects. Opposition to general concepts is absurd. There is more to be said, however, about the status of the general. What many individual things have in common, or what constantly recurs in one individual thing, needs not be more stable, eternal, or deep than the particular. The scale of categories is not the same as that of significance. That was precisely the error of the Eleatics and all who followed them, with Plato and Aristotle at their head.

The world is unique. The mere repetition in speech of moments which occur again and again in the same form bears more resemblance to a futile, compulsive litany than to the redeeming word. Classification is a condition of knowledge, not knowledge itself, and knowledge in turn dissolves classification. (Adorno and Horkheimer 2002, 182)

That which the concept (as generality) eliminates is everything *special* (*das Besondere*). However, this elimination necessarily leads to contradictory implications in the *system of knowledge* (in rational discourse) and to internal deformations caused by the fact that conceptual thinking has become the basic tool of *instrumental* thinking. The eliminated, non-identical then survives to one side in the form of traces and fragments, which Adorno has already pointed out in his inaugural lecture "The Actuality of Philosophy":

Whoever chooses philosophy as a profession today must first reject the illusion that earlier philosophical enterprises began with: that the power of thought is sufficient to grasp the totality of the real. No justifying reason could rediscover itself in a reality whose order and form suppresses every claim to reason; only polemically does reason present itself to the knower as total reality, while only in traces and ruins it is prepared to hope that it will ever come across correct and just reality. Philosophy which presents reality as such today only veils reality and eternalizes its present condition. Prior to every answer, such a function is already implicit in the question – that question which today is called radical and which is really the least radical of all: the question of being (*Sein*) itself, as expressly formulated by the new ontological blueprints, and as, despite all contradictions, fundamental to the idealist systems, now allegedly overcome. This question assumes as the possibility of its answer that being itself is appropriate to thought and available to it, that the idea, of existing being (*des Seienden*) can be examined. The adequacy of thinking about being as a totality, however, has degenerated and consequently the idea of existing being has itself become impervious to questioning, for the idea could stand only over a round and closed reality as a star in clear transparency, and has now perhaps faded from view for all time, ever since the images of our life are guaranteed through history alone. The idea of being has become powerless in philosophy; it is nothing more than an empty form-principle whose archaic dignity helps to cover any content whatsoever. The fullness of the real, as totality, does not let itself be subsumed under the idea of being which might allocate meaning to it; nor can the idea of existing being be built up out of elements of reality. It [the idea of being] is lost in philosophy, and thereby its claim to the totality of the real is struck at its source. (Adorno 1977, 120)

Negative experience (the *murmure* of remains) must be transformed into positive, which presupposes a critique of the current image of rationality. Thinking, in other words, must be capable of thinking against itself without surrendering itself, by somehow attempting to grasp *appropriately* the *physiognomy* of the object (a thing or event) that it is concerned with. The current concept of order must be supplemented by one that eludes this order, one might say. Concepts need to be put together in such a way that they become an appropriate *model* of that thing, so that they correspond to the thing. And it is clear that this constellating of concepts is also, and above all, a matter of experience, experimentation or strategy.

A more careful reading of Adorno's texts will then divulge a fairly close connection between "constellation" and "model". For example, in *Negative Dialectics* (the final section of which is entitled "Models") we read: "a model covers the specific, and more than the specific, without letting it evaporate in its more general super-concept" (Adorno 1973b, 29), i.e. without understanding what is *special* about the object with respect to concept or category, resp. the hierarchy of genus, species, exemplar (*differentia specifica et genus proximum*), since specificity here clearly refers to the unique features that determine the *physiognomy of the object or event* and which are beyond the reach of a concept. And so the following sentence states ambiguously: To think philosophically means to think in models. Such thinking is characterised by *obligation*, without this obligation being guaranteed by any system.

The smallest intramundane traits would be of relevance to the absolute, for the micrological view cracks the shells of what, measured by the subsuming cover concept, is helplessly isolated and explodes its identity, the delusion that it is but a specimen. There is solidarity between such thinking and metaphysics at the time of its fall. (Adorno 1973b, 408)

The model is characterised by a specific *mimesis*, but for this very reason also by openness: it is forever transcending philosophical discourse. However, with the term mimesis we again enter the realm of Adorno's *Aesthetic Theory*. I shall restrict myself to a single quote from his essay on Paul Valéry, which also sheds light on the context of *knowledge, strategic rationality* and the openness of thought: "'The beautiful demands perhaps the slavish imitation of what is indefinable in things', reads the finest sentence in Rhumb. The indefinable is the inimitable, and aesthetic mimesis becomes a mimesis of the absolute by imitating this inimitability in the particular" (Adorno 2019, 172). This of course has far-reaching implications (and not only in Adorno: many such implications only come to light by radicalising this critique of concepts in other writers). Strategic rationality is not exact, but is characterised by obligation (Adorno very often uses the term *Stringenz*), i.e. its measure is its commensurability to the thing we are thinking. Hence another method of providing proof (or winning an argument) in philosophical discourse, which consists in striving to ensure for the obligation expressed that it is commensurate with the means of discursive thinking, without deriving therefrom. Hence, too, the well-known statement by Adorno from the preface to *Negative Dialectics*: "The procedure will be justified, not based on reasons" (Adorno 1973b, xix). Justification, meaning *result* – it makes sense, it is a response. A model of order is a *model*, an equivalent corresponding to reality. The model is a response to an event that is an encounter with reality – it is a response to this event. In Adorno's words: thinking is mediated by art and art by thinking, without it ever being possible to achieve any synthesis.

Section 4

Adorno's relationship to the concept and to what is unidentifiable by conceptual thinking and thus non-identical within the framework of the dialectic, can be understood as a certain threshold. It is both a radical modification of the classical (Hegelian, Marxist) dialectic, and a form of thinking that points beyond itself to the other side of this threshold. This is especially so when Adorno's thinking encounters art, where thinking (in that which he calls "spiritual experience") turns to its own form and, in a more precise way and following up on Walter Benjamin, he pays increased attention to his own method of presentation (*Darstellung*). In "The Essay as Form" he makes it clear that content is not indifferent to its own presentation even in philosophy, and that the form of the essay is something that ensues directly from the critique of the (closed, history-eliminating) system, since it incorporates the anti-systematic impulse into its own procedure. However, this is exactly where its principal openness is to be found:

> The essay becomes true in its progress, which drives it beyond itself, not in a treasure-hunting obsession with foundations. Its concepts receive their light from a *terminus ad quem* hidden from the essay itself, not from any obvious terminus *a quo*, and in this the method itself expresses its utopian intention. All its concepts are to be presented in such a way that they support one another, that each becomes articulated through its configuration with the others. In the essay discrete elements set off against one another come together to form a readable context; the essay erects no scaffolding and no structure. But the elements crystallize as a configuration through their motion. The constellation is a force field, just as every intellectual structure is necessarily transformed into a force field under the essay's gaze. (Adorno 2019, 13)

If we look upon Adorno's negative dialectics from the perspective of the thinking that has appeared from the mid-20th century onwards, we are justified in stating that its "non-identical" is now becoming either an *irreducible remainder* (for example in the form of Derrida's *restance non présente*) or – which is the same thing – that which transcends absolutely the boundary of the identifiable and representable (beginning with Levinas's "face" and the asymmetric relationship with the Other, via Nancy's excessiveness as an infinite *ex-positio*, to Deleuze's disjunctive synthesis and Derrida's *à-venir*). Everywhere we look there is an openness and an accent not on being, but on events, i.e. on processualism (see, for example, the *Dílo jako dění smyslu* [The Work as a Process of Meaning] by Milan Jankovič), which has as its necessary complement the relationship of thinking to the event, to its *emergence* and unpredictable arrival, and therefore also to history. Inasmuch as a problem particular to philosophy relates to the remainder or that which transcends thinking (i.e. as something *unthought*), then philosophical discourse itself – its discursive strategies and its relationship to that which comprises the *environment* of every discursive practice – will find itself foregrounded.

One might formulate this more generally thus: that which is external in relation to the existing image of thought and its dominant concept of order must somehow be incorporated into this image, though in such a way that its radical exteriority does not disappear during this operation. Here there is a paradox: in the coexistence of that which is identical to itself, with that which is incompatible or incommensurable with this identity, it is necessary to reveal an order that, from the perspective of the hitherto dominant philosophical discourse, simply cannot be an order. And since the solution to this paradox is to change the framework, we need to look for other *models*. Or perhaps looking differently at old models would suffice as a first step, e.g. catching a glimpse of *écriture* or a dynamic system from the genus of *dissipative* systems within *text* and *discourse*. This is a philosophical approach inspired by literature, an approach made necessary by the realisation that the *content* of thinking cannot be separated from the method of its presentation. The inspiration of literature is the inspiration of its speech, which, as Maurice Blanchot points out, gives rise to the world and at the same time leads us to realise that its reality is inaccessible through language, since language is the language of common nouns. Hence the well-known paradox, albeit expressed differently and in another *medium*: this Other in respect of language (singularity, or being itself in its concreteness) cannot be expressed by (ordinary) language, and yet at the same time language (somehow) relies on this Other, regarding which it wishes constantly to speak, as in a precursory presence that I must exclude in order to speak – in order to speak of said presence. Literature resolves this paradox by describing its own ability to name. It records in language the distance that separates us as speakers from the reality of the world, and as such literature becomes a special place for showing that which is not shown. This place is exactly what the word *écriture* refers to. Of the innumerable examples of this, it suffices to quote from the well-known essay by Roland Barthes "The Death of the Author" of 1968:

> In the multiplicity of writing, everything is to be *disentangled,* nothing *deciphered;* the structure can be followed, "run" (like the thread of a stocking) at every point and at every level, but there is nothing beneath: the space of writing is to be ranged over, not pierced; writing ceaselessly posits meaning ceaselessly to evaporate it, carrying out a systematic exemption of meaning. (Barthes 1977, 147)

Jean-Luc Nancy calls this simultaneous extrusion and intrusion *exscription*. A referencing via itself to a meaning that can never become a given. However, the concept of *écriture* evolved into this form. Its genesis is in linguistics, literary theory and philosophy (Mikhail Bakhtin, Julie Kristeva, Roland Barthes), as is evident from the fact that it gradually incorporated within itself the concept of *intertext* or *intertextuality*. This is not an object, but a field of events that is activated both within the text and between texts, a field of incalculable referentiality; it is a process that is non-instantiable as such, because it is akin to virtuality, which is always actualised differently and in a unique way with each reading and by each reader differently, without any actualisation being able to exhaust it. It is, to use 1960s parlance, a *game*, and it is this that allows us to claim that it is an open order, since at least intuitively we feel that not everything can refer to each and all, without mediating articles and long detours through other forms of mediation. This order is already open because it implies an irreducible non-calculability and randomness, though in some sense also a necessity. This is why, for example, Barthes characterised the "text" not as "work", but as a field of productivity or creation, as a theatre of creation, in which the creator encounters the reader. And so the words *significance, signifier* and *signified* (the latter two as components of the sign) are now joined by the word *signifiance* (the event of sense/meaning, often with an echo of "jouissance", ecstasy, as Roland Barthes use the term in his book *The Pleasure of the Text*, and by which he wishes to intimate the pleasure in multiplicity and simultaneously non-discovery, a game of disclosure and concealment).

> But once the text is conceived as Production (and no longer as product), "signification" is no longer an adequate concept. As soon as the text is conceived as a polysemic space where the paths of several possible meanings intersect, it is necessary to cast off the monological, legal status of signification, and to pluralise it. (Barthes 1981, 37)

Thinking in general and philosophy in particular cannot stand outside this game. Philosophical discourse is not able to reduce this dimension of "signifiance", even if the phrase "conceptual thinking" would like to suggest otherwise. The *substance* of concepts is not only the materiality of a text, but also the text *qua* intertext or (here almost synonymous) *écriture*; the event of articulation, differentiation, a game in which each actualisation is exposed to virtuality and thus radical *otherness* in respect of concept, discourse and meaning. As regards the concept and discursiveness, this Other is that which *compels thinking*, thinking is a reaction to this otherness. Thinking is a transformation of discourse in a response to otherness such that discourse is able to make the *Other* communicable and conceivable, albeit at the cost of a reduction of its sense to meaning, which is why there is always a remainder, and we always come across something that makes us think again, perhaps think the same thing.

Inasmuch as it is impossible for philosophy to dream of closing in on itself and somehow extricating itself from this game, there is no alternative but for *philosophical* texts also to possess the character of *performative* texts, which endeavour to do something with the reader, to lead them to something, to force them to answer for themselves and, in their own way, to force them to think and somehow engage with the philosophical text (discourse) in this way.

However, this also means that concepts such as intertextuality and *écriture* are a parallel to the concept of the dynamic or dissipative system, autopoiesis.

Section 5

From various writers who have investigated autopoietic, dynamic or dissipative systems in different spheres of science and culture (Francesco Varela, Humberto Maturana, Ilya Prigogine, Isabelle Stengers, Michel Serres, Katherine Hayles, William Paulson, et al.), we know – to simplify matters somewhat – that the environment or surroundings of a system, which we tend to understand as its *exterior*, is always the exterior of *this* system. If we assume, therefore, that each self-organising system is characterised by *operational closure*, i.e. that its relationship to its surroundings or environment is not direct, then what the system understands as exterior is something like a model of this exterior inside the system in question.

According to systems theory, systems exist by way of operational closure and this means that they each construct themselves and their own realities. How a system is real depends on its own self-production. By constructing itself as a system, a system also constructs its understanding of the environment. And thus a systematic world cannot suppose any singular, common environment for all systems that can somehow be "represented" within any system. Every system exists by differentiation and thus is

different from other systems and has a different environment. Reality becomes a multitude of system-environment constructions that are in each
case unique. (Moeller 2006, 16)

The relationships are far more complex (it is by no means mere coincidence that this involves systems with a higher level of complexity).
Nevertheless, this preliminary image suffices to begin with. In any case,
the openness of systems is always the product or effect of their internal
activity (their differentiation, which establishes them by setting their
boundaries) – they always understand their exterior in their own way.
A different perspective, e.g. that of the view of a cosmic observer (as it
was called by Maurice Merleau-Ponty), is unavailable to them. Thus we
are always speaking of a somehow reduced exterior, and yet dealing with
this exterior leads to a higher complexity of the system through the work
of its self-organisation.

In this reflection upon the complexity and relationship of a dynamic
system to its surroundings/environment, let us now take another step,
without making any claims to terminological accuracy, in the direction
of the possible transposition of the elementary differentiations of systems
theory into contemporary philosophy. The environment or surroundings
of thought would (generally speaking) represent a problematicity that
cannot be reduced by any model that would necessarily simplify their
complexity and contingency. However, reduction brings with it the fact
that thinking is more often than not irritated, i.e. something resonates
in it from its surroundings that it is unable to interpret as information.
However, thinking's possible reaction will not be a causal effect (since
we already know that the basic characteristic of every system is its *operational closure*); the fact that it is irritated shows that, in the given situation, it is unable to react appropriately and must transform itself, all the
while retaining its identity *qua* system (even, for instance, at the cost of
declaring itself to be non-philosophy, as in the case of François Laruelle).
Thinking will work on such models that are able, within certain limits,
to predict the unpredictable (events, origins, emergence), and its evolution to a higher level of complexity will be an evolution to models of an
open order. If we call the *irritation* of philosophical discourse a *problem*,
this means that only a change in discourse can be an appropriate and
commensurate reaction to it. And if so, as is basically in line with the
general tendencies of 20th-century philosophy to thinking of the *event*
and the order that relies on the event, then we can say that what thinking during this period was irritated by above all as a problem was the

phenomenon of event and origin and understanding processual identity or the order of events inside and out, i.e. the problem of *history* as the surroundings or environment of philosophical thinking. Therefore, if we speak, for example, of the unpredictability of history, then this is a characteristic inherent in how history is understood by a certain philosophical system, and not a characteristic of history in and of itself. However, it follows that, inasmuch as the event or emergence (*becoming, devenir, Werden*) or contingency is at present becoming a privileged theme of philosophical thinking, and inasmuch as there is a trend towards a study of the genesis of structures (as in the case of the phenomenology of late Husserl), and inasmuch as philosophy is devoting its attention to the phenomenon of the event in its irreducibility to existing horizons of expectation – this could mean that philosophy has understood to what extent its current conception of history was the correlate of an ideal of philosophy as a closed system, which was also the determining framework of its relationship to empirical history. The transformation that is at the same time a change to (not a modification of) this framework then begins with a reassessment of the relationship between narrative and history, the most striking manifestation of which is the three-volume work by Paul Ricœur *Time and Narrative*. Ricœur understands narrative as a medium in which an empirical event not only acquires its meaning as a historical event, but acquires meaning full stop, this from the moment it is placed within the context of a narratively reconfigured time. This operation then reveals an important feature of the event, which has been studied in detail by Claude Romano in particular, namely, that the event that is occurring still awaits an awareness of its own meaning (it never coincides with the meaning we ascribe to it). As Burkhard Liebsch says: the event seems to be holding out for the time that it will be able to enter into a context that makes it significant in some way. However, in itself it is ambiguous or significatively polymorphous. Narrativity guarantees its significance by indicating how that which took place followed on from that which had both taken place previously and anticipated that which was yet to take place. It thus gives rise to a certain, specifically narrative *order*, which emerges from the pre-narrative multiplicity of events and their irreducible disorder. However, this order comes at a price:

> Any "synthesis of the heterogeneous" pays for the transformation of wild contingency into ordered contingency by an unsmoothable contingency of itself, which again leads to a trace of other possibilities that would make the events narratively intelligible in a different, again heterogeneous, way.

It is therefore fallacious to judge that only the narrative order establishes the event as an event. While events can be embedded in different narrative orders, at the same time, their signifying polymorphism resists being cancelled (*Aufhebbarkeit*) in any narrative order. And it is in this resistance that the "narrative event-ness" of the event is revealed. The event is far from merely contributing in some traceable way to the progress of a story (*Geschichte*), because in the light of the contingency of narrative it shows itself precisely as that which can never be extinguished (*aufgehen*) in any narrative intelligibility. Not only can it not be reduced to some sufficient reason and causal determination without exhaustion; not only does it not enter into any succession without exhaustion, but as narrative it also defies reduction to something else to a narrative order that arises through the "synthesis of the heterogeneous". The heterogeneity of the event as an event lies, from the perspective of narrative, precisely in the fact that it cannot be wholly embodied in any "synthetic" order. (Liebsch 2004, 194–5)

Section 6

However, such a synthesis of the heterogeneous is also that which is referred to as tradition, a theme dealt with in Gadamer's *Wirkungsgeschichte*. On the one hand, tradition *qua* sedimented memory is a grid allowing us to read that which we encounter (the historically generated or generating horizon of understanding). On the other hand, it is a grid that is flexible within certain limits, inasmuch as understanding is not a mere reproduction of tradition but is also productive (a point made by Gadamer's model of dialogue as game). The word *effect* then refers to the fact that we are always already somehow situated in tradition and that what we experience as new is always *mediated* by tradition, i.e. integrated within certain limits into the existing horizon of understanding. However, it might be said that Gadamer's hermeneutics approaches the determination of the meaning of an event analogically to narrative: likewise, tradition is a medium incorporating the new into what has already occurred. However, it is precisely the relationship to tradition that can become an important key to changing the framework, as long as we understand the idea of *connecting with* or *taking on* tradition or, as Derrida would put it, accepting our heritage. Derrida says that "we must do everything we can to appropriate a past that we know at its core remains unassignable" (Derrida and Roudinesco 2003, 11), but also that it is a heritage that we must embrace, a tradition which, whether we like it or not, we must somehow connect with, because the concept of obligation makes no sense outside the experience of heritage (Derrida and Roudinesco 2003, 13). The logic of this reasoning is not clear at first glance: one of the reasons is probably that, in Derrida's understanding of tradition as heritage, we hear an echo of one of Benjamin's theses "On the Concept of History": "The past carries with it a secret index by which it is referred to redemption" (Benjamin 2006, 390), by which he means that everything individual can only be brought to justice at the end of history, only when a life will not be judged from the perspective of its function in historical events. Benjamin continues: "There is a secret agreement between past generations and the present one. Our coming was expected on earth" (Benjamin 2006, 390), expected by virtue of the disappearance of its uniqueness in historicity. It is up to us to ensure that this lost uniqueness does not fall into oblivion (for instance, by virtue of history always being written by the victors and not the losers), or – to put things more soberly – that which could not be recognised in the past can be recognised in the light of the present. For Derrida this means an inheritance is never a given, because it is always a task.

> That we are heirs does not mean, that we have or that we receive this or that, some inheritance that enriches us some day with this or that, but that the being of what we are is first of all inheritance, whether we like it or not, know it or not. (Derrida 1994, 54)

This profound transformation in relation to tradition has no less profound consequences. It combines lines that are somehow close and that intersect in this transformation as soon as it turns out that the concepts of tradition, historical experience and history are almost synonymous, thus illuminating the event as the basic characteristic of historical time and historical memory. For if inheritance is a task and not a given, then its acceptance is the acceptance of the responsibility for its *traditionalisation* in the name of the future. And it is a call for responsibility because, as Derrida also says, every acceptance of the past is necessarily its re-affirmation.

> What does it mean to reaffirm? It means not simply accepting this heritage but relaunching it otherwise and keeping it alive. Not choosing it (since what characterizes inheritance is first of all that one does not choose it; it is what violently elects us), but choosing to keep it alive.

Life – being-alive – is perhaps defined at bottom by this tension internal to a heritage, by this reinterpretation of what is given in the gift, and even what is given in filiation. This reaffirmation, which both continues and interrupts, resembles (at least) an election, a selection, a decision. [...] It would be necessary to think life on the basis of heritage, and not the other way around. It would be necessary therefore to begin from this formal and apparent contradiction between the passivity of reception and the decision to say "yes", then to select, to filter, to interpret, and therefore to transform; not to leave intact or unharmed, not to leave *safe* the very thing one claims to respect before all else...[1] (Derrida and Roudinesco 2003, 13)

There exists no guide on how to take receipt of the past, just as there is no guide on how to live. Neither history nor life is teleological, no matter how much they attempt to obscure the narrative order and push to one side the suspicion that building on tradition and the past is always about an original *response* to history. Walter Benjamin had already observed that this was the basic imperative of human life as historical, in which the relationship to the past opens up a relationship to the future, when in his theses he strongly recalled the debt of the present to the past. Paul Ricœur subsequently returned to this idea, writing in the third volume of *Time and Narrative*:

As soon as the idea of a debt to the dead, to people of flesh and blood to whom something really happened in the past, stops giving documentary research its highest end, history loses its meaning. [...] The scientific use of data stored in and manipulated by a computer certainly gives birth to a new kind of scholarly activity. But this activity constitutes only a long methodological detour destined to lead to an enlargement of our collective memory in its encounter with the monopoly exercised over speech by the powerful and the clerisy. For history has always been a critique of social narratives and, in this sense, a rectification of our common memory. (Ricœur 1988, 118–19)

---

1   Cited in Naas 2008, 31.

Section 7

The transformation of philosophical discourse is not a one-way operation; *irritation* also mobilises its past, in which it is possible right now to update what could not be updated at the time or was pushed aside as being of secondary importance. But all of this is shown in a completely different light in a different present, including, for instance, Benjamin's understanding of history. The accent on responding without predetermined rules of connection can then be understood as a moment of self-reflection or self-reference on the part of philosophical discourse, which, in various texts by very different authors, states that its *condicio sine qua non* is its openness, that the order it needs is possibly something for which it can seek inspiration not only in science, but also in art. A closer look appears in literary texts regarding which we cannot decide conclusively whether they belong to the prose narrative of a fictional story, to scientific considerations, or to philosophical reflections on the theme of order, which from the point of view of existing models is non-order. But non-order is not something that cannot somehow be described (description always already anticipates some kind of arrangement), and the same is true of the synonym of non-order, namely chaos, since it is quite useful to imagine chaos as a maximum of information, a maximum of informativeness. Or like what happens when a complex system collapses, which is a frequent theme of various anti-utopias. However, it is possible to imagine it in other ways, as, for example, Stanislav Lem did in his book *His Master's Voice* (whose fictional author is a philosophical mathematician). In what was supposed to be *pure noise*, i.e. complete chaos, scientists identified a message seemingly sent from extraterrestrials (a neutrino letter from the stars). The message is undoubtedly structured, as various attempts to decipher it show, but is structured in such a way that we cannot deem structure. What is order in the message is non-order for us. Or in other words: we come across a level of complexity that we are incapable of infiltrating or fathoming if we start from that level of complexity that we are still able to understand.

A slightly ironic commentary is provided by Roland Barthes, who, in addition to texts intended for reading and texts requiring transcription by the reader, proposes another category, namely illegible texts:

> I now conceive (certain texts that have been sent to me suggest as much) that there may be a third textual entity: alongside the readerly and the writerly, there would be something like the receivable. The receivable

would be the unreaderly text which catches hold, the red-hot text, a product continuously outside of any likelihood and whose function – visibly assumed by its scriptor – would be to contest the mercantile constraint of what is written; this text, guided, armed by a notion of the unpublishable, would require the following response: I can neither read nor write what you produce, but I receive it, like a fire, a drug, an enigmatic disorganization. (Barthes 1994, 118)

In his novel *The Crying of Lot 49*, Thomas Pynchon systematically subverts the reader's expectations. Nonetheless, he continues to arouse such false expectations in the reader no less systematically, which he apparently confirms over and over again by means of various symbols and indexes. Like the central character Oidipa Maas, the reader attempts to unveil the conspiracy that must lie behind everything that is happening. Perhaps in time he will arrive at the conclusion that the book itself is a conspiracy against his concept of order.

Translated by Phil Jones.

References

Adorno, Theodor W. 1973. *Ästhetische Theorie*, edited by Gretel Adorno, and Rolf Tiedemann. Frankfurt am Main: Suhrkamp.

Adorno, Theodor W. 1973a. "Aktualität der Philosophie". In *Gesammelte Schriften I. Philosophische Frühschriften*, edited by Gretel Adorno, and Rolf Tiedemann, 325–44. Frankfurt am Main: Suhrkamp.

Adorno, Theodor W. 1973b. *Negative Dialectics*. Translated by E. B. Ashton. London, New York: Routledge.

Adorno, Theodor W. 1977. "The Actuality of Philosophy". Translated by Benjamin Snow. *Telos* 31: 120–33.

Adorno, Theodor W. 1981. *Noten zur Literatur,* edited by Rolf Tiedemann. Frankfurt am Main: Suhrkamp.

Adorno, Theodor W. 1994. *Negative Dialektik*. Frankfurt am Main: Suhrkamp.

Adorno, Theodor W. 1997. *Estetická teorie*. Translated by Dušan Prokop. Praha: Panglos.

Adorno, Theodor W. 2002. *Aesthetic Theory*. Translated and edited by Robert Hullot-Kentor. London, New York: Continuum.

Adorno, Theodor W. 2019. *Notes to Literature*. Translated by Shierry Weber Nicholsen. New York: Columbia University Press.

Adorno, Theodor W., and Max Horkheimer. 2002. *Dialectics of Enlightenment*. Translated by Edmund Jephcott. Stanford, CA: Stanford University Press.

Adorno, Theodor, W. 1966. *Negative Dialektik*. Frankfurt am Main: Suhrkamp.

Atlan, Henri. 1999. *Les Étincelles de hasard*, tome I: *Connaissance spermatique*. Paris: Seuil.

Atlan, Henri. 2003. *Les Étincelles de hasard*, tome 2: *Athéisme de l'écriture*. Paris: Seuil.

Atlan, Henri. 2011. "Noise as a Principle of Self-Organization". In *Selected Writings. On Self-Organization, Philosophy, Bioethics, and Judaism,* edited by Stefanos Geroulanos, and Todd Meyers, 95–113. Fordham: Fordham University Press. Original edition, 1972.

Bachtin, Michail Michajlovič. 1980. *Román jako dialog.* Translated by Daniela Hodrová. Praha: Odeon.

Barthes, Roland. 1994. *Roland Barthes by Roland Barthes.* Translated by Richard Howard. Berkeley: University of California Press.

Barthes, Roland. 1977. *Image-Music-Text.* Translated by Stephen Heath. London: Fontana Press.

Barthes, Roland. 1981. "Theory of the Text". In *Untying the Text. A Post-Structuralist Reader,* edited by Robert Young, and Kegan Paul, 31–47. Boston, MA, London: Routledge.

Barthes, Roland. 2002. *Œuvres complètes III,* edited by Éric Marty. Paris: Seuil.

Barthes, Roland. 2002a. *Œuvres complètes IV,* edited by Éric Marty. Paris: Seuil.

Barthes, Roland. 2007. *S/Z.* Translated by Josef Fulka. Praha: Garamond.

Barthes, Roland. 2015. *Roland Barthes o Rolandu Barthesovi.* Translated by Josef Fulka. Praha: Fra.

Benjamin, Walter. 2006. "On the Concept of History". In *Selected Writings, 4: 1938–1940,* edited by Michael W. Jennings, and Howard Eiland, 390–7. Cambridge, MA: Harvard University Press.

Benjamin, Walter. 2010. *Über den Begriff der Geschichte. Werke und Nachlass. Kritische Gesamtausgabe, Bd. 19,* edited by Gérard Raulet, Frankfurt am Main: Suhrkamp.

Benjamin, Walter. 2011. "O pojmu dějin". In *Teoretické pasáže. Výbor z díla II.* Translated by Martin Ritter, 307–16. Praha: OIKOYMENH.

Derrida, Jacques. 1994. *Specters of Marx.* Translated by Peggy Kamuff. London, New York: Routledge.

Derrida, Jacques, and Elisabeth Roudinesco. 2003. *Co přinese zítřek?* Translated by Josef Fulka. Praha: Karolinum.

Derrida, Jacques. 1993. *Spectres de Marx.* Paris: Galilée.

Hayles, Katherine et al. 1991. *Chaos and Order. Complex Dynamics in Literature and Science.* Chicago, IL: The University of Chicago Press.

Kauffmann, Stuart. 1983. *The Origins of Order: Self Organization and Selection in Evolution.* Oxford: Oxford University Press.

Kristeva, Julie. 1969. *Semeiotikê. Recherches pour une sémanalyse.* Paris: Seuil.

Liebsch, Burkhard. 2004. "Ereignis – Erfahrung – Erzählung". In *Ereignis auf Französisch. Von Bergson bis Deleuze,* edited by Marc Rölli, 183–200. München: Wilhelm Fink Verlag.

Lotman, Juri M. 1981. *Kunst als Sprache.* Leipzig: Reclam.

Luhmann, Niklas. 2006. *Sociální systémy.* Translated by Pavel Váňa. Praha: Centrum pro studium demokracie a kultury.

Moeller, Hans-Georg. 2006. *Luhmann Explained. From Souls to Systems.* Chicago, IL, La Salle: Open Court.

Naas, Michael. *Derrida from Now On.* New York: Fordham University Press.

Nancy, Jean-Luc. 1994. *Les Muses. Edition revue et augmentée.* Paris: Galilée.

Nancy, Jean-Luc. 2009. *Le Plaisir au dessin.* Paris: Galilée.

Paulsom, William. 1988. *The Noise of Culture: Literary Text in a World of Information.* Ithaca: Cornell University Press.

Prigogine, Ilya, and Isabelle Stengers. 1984. *Order Out of Chaos: Man's New Dialogue with Nature.* London: Heinemann.

Pynchon, Thomas. 2004. *Dražba série 49.* Translated by Rudolf Chalupský. Praha: Volvox Globator.

Ricœur, Paul. 1988. *Time and Narrative 3*. Translated by Kathleen Blamey and David Pellauer. Chicago, IL, London: The University of Chicago Press.

Ricœur, Paul. 2008. *Čas a vyprávění III*. Translated by Věra Dvořáková, and Miroslav Petříček. Praha: OIKOYMENH.

Seel, Martin. 2018. "Versionen der Negativität konstellativen Denkens". In *Negativität. Kunst – Recht – Politik*, edited by Thomas Khurana, Dirk Quadflieg, Juliane Rebentisch, Dirk Setton, and Francesca Raimondi, 424–34. Frankfurt am Main: Suhrkamp.

Serres, Michel. 1969–1980. *Hermès I–V.* Paris: Editions de Minuit.

Stanislav Lem. 1981. *Pánův hlas*. Translated by Stanislav Jungwirt, and Pavel Weigel. Praha: Svoboda.

Varela, Francesco, and Humberto Maturana. 1980. *Autopoiesis and Cognition*. Boston, MA: Reidel.

From Boundaries to Interfaces: Autopoietic Systems and the "Ontology of Motion"

Martin Procházka

1 Introduction: Perspectives on Autopoiesis

In this study, autopoietic systems are not viewed as "autonomous [...] unities" having "individuality" and emerging "in the process of self-production" (Maturana and Varela 1980, 80–1) from specific material conditions (Maturana and Varela 1980, 91). Although Maturana and Varela have tried to apply a similar approach to the society, being aware of "political and ethical implications" of their considerations (Maturana and Varela 1980, 118; Maturana 1980, xxiv–xxx), their theory runs into problems, when it presupposes that systems' boundaries emerge as results of the growing complexity of systems' organization. Moreover, their view does not take into account novel information produced in the interaction of autopoietic systems with their environment: "The notions of acquisition of representations of the environment or of the acquisition of information about the environment in relation to learning, do not represent any aspect of the operation of the nervous system" (Maturana and Varela 1980, 133).

If, on the other hand, autopoiesis is defined in terms of information exchange "as the ratio between the complexity of a system and the complexity of its environment" (Gershenson 2014, 4), the reciprocal flow of information between the system and its environment limits the possibility to predict the system's autopoietic functioning. As a result, "a priori assumptions are of limited use, since the precise future of complex systems is known only a posteriori" (Fernández, Maldonado and Gershenson 2013, 20).

The reassessment of the concepts of "autopoiesis" and "dynamic system" has been typical of a number of recent approaches in natural sciences, but it also becomes necessary in the social sciences and the humanities. What happens if autopoietic systems are seen from a different perspective than that of "the phenomenology of the living systems" (Maturana and Varela 1980, 73) based on "the characterization of living systems [...] in the physical space" (Maturana 1980, xviii–xix) and their "autopoietic unities" (Maturana and Varela 1980, 96)? One of these recently discussed perspectives is that of the "ontology of motion" (Nail 2018, 6).

2 The Ontology of Motion

Thomas Nail's ontology posits motion as "a unique dimension of reality, irreducible to space or time" (Nail 2018, 37). This understanding of motion is incompatible with autopoiesis, which presupposes a "topological unity" of a dynamic system in a "self-contained" space, "a network of productions of components which realizing the network that produced them constitute it as a unity" (Maturana and Varela 1980, 89, 80). According to Maturana and Varela, "autopoietic systems are homeostatic systems which have their own organization as their variable that they maintain constant" (Maturana and Varela 1980, 80). As a result, movement in autopoietic systems is restricted in several ways: by their topological unity, homeostasis and their fixed organization, which is "variable" only with respect to a general model of "living machines" (Maturana and Varela 1980, 78–9).

If, as Nail assumes, bodies can be studied "as movements" (Nail 2018, 37), the point of departure changes: instead of homeostasis resulting from the adaptation to the environment, the basic conditions of the dynamic system become those of "the kinetic flux of matter" (Nail 2018, 61) including "an open multiplicity of flows" (Nail 2018, 77) and "an indeterminate fluctuation that comes to be determined through its interaction with other flows" (Nail 2018, 82). As Nail points out, referring to Prigogine: "Chaos theory [...] has shown that the flux, turbulence, and movement of energy are more primary than the relative or metastable fixity of classical bodies" (Nail 2018, 2).[1]

---

1   Although Nail refers to Prigogine (1980), the vagueness of his reference precludes identification of corresponding passages in Prigogine's book, which is chiefly about "time", the transition "from being to becoming", and "complexity" (Prigogine 1980, i–xix).

Rather than adaptation leading to greater complexity and homeostasis, the condition of the system's development is, according to Prigogine, the state of non-equilibrium, where fluctuations can lead either to the transformation of the system by means of the bifurcation of its flows (Prigogine and Stengers 1984, 160–70), or to its dissipation into chaos (Prigogine and Stengers 1984, 206).

3 Motion as "Flux"

A problematic aspect of Nail's theory of motion is his rather vague use of the term "flux", which overlaps not only with "flow" and "fluctuation" but also with "turbulence and movement of energy" (Nail 2018, 2). Unfortunately, the vagueness of the term reaches beyond analogies with physical processes. Nail uses it to describe "our present" as "the flux of things and dates in the twenty-first-century so far" (Nail 2018, 16), which raises a question: How can "the flux" be restricted by formal temporal and historic divides, such as the beginning of a century? This question is left unanswered in the conclusion of the passage, which reveals that Nail's phrase has been used to describe his approach as "a specific view from the early-twenty-first-century" (Nail 2018, 17).

Evidently, in Nail's argument "flux" serves as a vague metaphor of the dynamic nature of "the present". Other uses of the word in *Being and Motion* can be traced back to Deleuze's notion of a process leading to change ("there are fluxes and variations in nature"; Deleuze [1968] 1994, 2). A reference to Lucretius' philosophy, where, as Deleuze and Guattari contend, "ancient atomism is inseparable from flows, and flux is reality itself, or consistency" (Deleuze and Guattari [1980] 1987, 361) are slightly more specific. Yet, Nail's loose interpretation of *De Rerum Natura* (in particular of II. 292) confuses the minute swerve of atoms ("exiguum clinamen principiorum"; Lucretius 1916) with "the continuous and turbulent flow [...] of movement" (Nail 2018, 41), which makes the meaning of "flux" even vaguer.

In spite of this, Nail's use of the term can be understood in contrast to *Anti-Oedipus* (Deleuze and Guattari [1972] 1983), where "flux" is used in multiple and overlapping meanings, which may be called, with a good deal of simplification, ontological, epistemological, existential and semiotic.

4 "Flux" and Complexity of Motion in *Anti-Oedipus*

Ontologically, "an endless flux" is an ideal quality of the Greek *hyle*, designating "the pure continuity that any one sort of matter ideally possesses", which extends "to the very limits of the universe" (Deleuze and Guattari [1972] 1983, 36). However, the "ideal" nature of this continuity results from its "relative" (or rather relational?) character: flows of energy are "broken" by organ-machines, which produce flows in relation to an infinite network of other machines. Their relations produce "a continuous, infinite flux" (Deleuze and Guattari [1972] 1983, 36) – a dynamic open structure.

In epistemological terms, "flux" refers to "the perspective" from which an "organ-machine" interprets "entire world", namely "from the point of view of the energy that flows from it" (Deleuze and Guattari [1972] 1983, 6). While in Nail's theory "flux" vaguely describes the "kinetic" nature of "the present", in *Anti-Oedipus* it is associated with the flows of energy produced and broken by individual organ machines.

In existential terms, "flux" characterizes the Nietzsche's "men of desire" who "ceased being afraid of becoming mad" and whose desire, affirming life in its fundamentally tragic nature (Nietzsche [1901] 1968, 852), is "a flux that overcomes barriers and codes" (Deleuze and Guattari [1972] 1983, 131).

This leads to the semiotic meaning of the term: the flux is opposed to "the code" as a shorthand for "the graphic system", and to the code's lack of expressivity. Following Leroi-Gourhan ([1965] 1993), Deleuze and Guattari characterize the voice, which has subordinated the graphic system, as a source of "a deterritorialized abstract flux that it retains and makes reverberate in the linear code of writing" (Deleuze and Guattari [1972] 1983, 202). However, the "deterritorialization" of graphic systems produces "a sign of a sign, the despotic sign [...] [t]he sign made *letter*" (Deleuze and Guattari [1972] 1983, 206). "The signifier implies a language that overcodes another language, while the other language is completely coded into phonetic elements" (Deleuze and Guattari [1972] 1983, 208). This process generates "a despotic signifier", a "repressing representation" which encodes language "into phonetic elements" or "alphabetic script" and reduces the flux into a "linear [...] graphic flux", transforming the unconscious and appropriating "reality in the operation of despotic overcoding" (Deleuze and Guattari [1972] 1983, 208–10). The convergence of "code" and "flux" is accomplished under capitalism, which "decodes" all kinds of social and economic flows – "of property [...], money [...], production [...], workers" and brings them to "conjunction" (Deleuze and Guattari [1972] 1983, 223–4), transforming *"the surplus value of code into a surplus value of flux"* (Deleuze and Guattari [1972] 1983, 228) and subsuming knowledge, specialized education and culture under a single heading of capital (Deleuze and Guattari [1972] 1983, 234).

Although "the great mutant flow of capital is pure deterritorialization, [...] it performs an equivalent reterritorialization when converted into a reflux" (Deleuze and Guattari [1972] 1983, 372). The reflux has numerous forms of economic operations such as regulation of capital markets and interest rates, distribution of employee incomes, influencing consumers' purchase power, military and security expenses of the state, its bureaucratic apparatuses, etc. (Deleuze and Guattari [1972] 1983, 229, 235). In this way the capitalist deterritorialization is being constantly reterritorialized and the flux always coincides with the reflux and "afflux [...] of raw *profit*" of corporations (Deleuze and Guattari [1972] 1983, 238). Simultaneously, "as capitalist deterritorialization is developing from the centre to the periphery, [...], [e]ach passage of a flux is a deterritorialization, and each displaced limit, a decoding" (Deleuze and Guattari [1972] 1983, 232).

Nonetheless, the process of "deterritorialization" is not limited to production and representation within a specific socioeconomic order ("decoding and deterritorialization of flows"; Deleuze and Guattari [1972] 1983, 244). It never exhausts itself by the oscillation between "deterritorialization" and "reterritorialization" (Deleuze and Guattari [1972] 1983, 260). There is also a different deterritorialization, which "must produce a new earth" (Deleuze and Guattari [1972] 1983, 299). It connects flux with the ontological (and existential) term "line of flight" which rearranges and transforms "multiplicities" (Deleuze and Guattari [1980] 1987, 9–10),[2] as well as "an unconscious libidinal investment of desire", which "does not bear upon the regime of the social syntheses, but upon the degree of development of the forces or the energies on which these syntheses depend" (Deleuze and Guattari [1972] 1983, 345).

---

2   The term is anticipated in *Anti-Oedipus* as "a chain of escape": "The function of the chain is no longer that of coding the flows on a full body of the earth, the despot, or capital, but on the contrary that of decoding them on the full body without organs. It is a chain of escape, and no longer a code. The signifying chain has become a chain of decoding and deterritorialization, which must be apprehended – and can only be apprehended – as the reverse of the codes and the territorialities" (Deleuze and Guattari [1972] 1983, 328).

It can be concluded that in Deleuze and Guattari the notion of "flux" is always connected with the interaction of human bodies and the forms of power, production and communication. Flux can be called "material" only in its simplest and most general ontological form, as the "pure continuity that any sort of matter ideally possesses" (Deleuze and Guattari [1972] 1983, 36). However, it always exists in its specific social forms related to semiotic aspects of communication ("codes" as well as "decoding"). Which implies that different forms of flux indicate the complexity of the representation of dynamic social processes: their oscillation between "deterritorialization" and "reterritorialization", unconscious desire and regimes of "social syntheses". In contrast to Nicolis's and Prigogine's attempt to model a society as a dynamic system (Nicolis and Prigogine 1989, 238–42), Deleuze and Guattari consider the interaction of more diverse and complex "actors" than environmental constraints, economic activities, social stratification, etc. (Nicolis and Prigogine 1989, 240–1). Their understanding of complexity implies, in Nicolis' and Prigogine's words, a greater degree of "randomness [...] switching on different evolutions, different histories" (Nicolis and Prigogine 1989, 241).

5 "Flux" vs. "Fluxes": Nail's "Historical Materialist Ontology" against Complexity

Nail misunderstands Deleuze when he tries to reduce the complexity of his term "becoming" (Deleuze [1969] 1990, 1–3) to a binary opposition of "continual flux, matter, and motion" and "difference, thought, and stasis" (Nail 2018, 45). This is an important cause of the vagueness of his uses of "flux" and "ontology of motion": "There can be all kinds of fluxes: fluxes of time, fluxes of space, fluxes of force, and so on. The ontology of motion is strictly the flux of matter" (Nail 2018, 44). The problem here is not that "[t]ime, space, and force do not transcend matter in motion" (Nail 2018, 44) but that the complexity of motion does not directly depend on its material nature but rather on flows of information, products and capital, as well as on their "codes" and "decoding". Although Nail refers to Deleuze's and Guattari's use ([1972] 1983, 202) of Leroi-Gourhan ([1965] 1993, 113), he does not seem to realize the importance of representation and communication for understanding the complexity of motion. According to Nicolis and Prigogine, the process of decoding can be interpreted in general terms as *"selection* [...] that allows the transfer of complexity from one level to another" (Nicolis and Prigogine 1989, 143).

Even in physical terms Nail does not reflect on the complexity of motion which can be expressed in terms of "fluxes" as "the rates of irreversible processes [...] such as heat transfer or diffusion of matter" (Prigogine and Stengers 1984, 135). Evidently, complexity is characterized by different "fluxes", but Nail can accept this only in terms of the absolute primacy of material motion: "If there is truly an ontological equality of fluxes, then history and matter are fully capable of becoming other than themselves through their *own flux*: motion" (Nail 2018, 49). This eliminates the difference of "fluxes" as specific "rates of irreversible processes".

In order to establish the authority of his reductive approach, Nail repeats the dogmatic treatment of Hegel's dialectic by Marx:

> Just as Marx extracted a "rational kernel" of the dialectic from the "mystical shell" of Hegel's speculative philosophy, [...] so the ontology of motion extracts from the speculative ontology of becoming the "rational kernel" of flux, resulting in a new historical materialist ontology of motion. (Nail 2018, 50)

It can be concluded that Nail's use of the term "flux", reveals the weakness of his philosophy, which sacrifices the notion of complexity to authoritarian positing of being as "matter in motion". The acknowledgement of its "*historical and regional*" (Nail 2018, 50),[3] limitations does not mitigate the authoritarian reductionism of Nail's ontology.

---

3   The term "regional" points back to Heidegger's "fundamental ontology" of *Dasein* as "the kind of Being we have" (Brandom 1983, 388). See Heidegger's explanation of the term "region" (*Gegend*) in *Being and Time*: "Something like a region must first be discovered if there is to be any possibility of allotting or coming across places for a totality of equipment that is circumspectively at one's disposal. [...] Thus the sun, whose light and warmth are in everyday use, has its own places – sunrise, midday, sunset, midnight; these are discovered in circumspection and treated distinctively in terms of changes in the usability of what the sun bestows. [...] But this spatiality has its own unity through that totality-of-involvements in-accordance-with-the-world [*weltmässige Bewandtnisganzheit*] which belongs to the spatially ready-to-hand. The 'environment' does not arrange itself in a space which has been given in advance; but its specific worldhood, in its significance, articulates the context of involvements which belongs to some current totality of circumspectively allotted places" (Heidegger [1927] 1962, 136–8). Nail does not seem to be familiar with Heidegger's use of the term, when he claims that his "ontology of motion [...] includes the largest possible region of being, excluding only the future" (Nail 2018, 24). This statement ignores the key role of the "totality" or "network" of "involvements" as a context of "everyday equipmental practice" (Wheeler 2020) in Heidegger's determination of "region". The superficiality and inconsistency of Nail's use of "regional" is also evident from

This shows itself in Nail's treatment of motion which focuses on "some minimal kinetic attributes" of "historical being [...], flow, fold and field" (Nail 2018, 31, 52). All of them "form the theoretical framework" of Nail's theory of motion (Nail 2018, 30–1). Especially "the flow" is important for understanding Nail's theories of migration, social mobility and borders (Nail 2015; 2016).

6 Social Flows and Their Circulation: A Challenge to Autopoietic Systems

Despite its reductionism, Nail's ontology of motion can be said to open a new perspective on social dynamics of migrations and borders. Research of these areas has a foremost importance for the study of societies as autopoietic systems (Echeverría 2020). In contrast to the approaches to migration as a result of "the complex and dynamic interaction between all social systems" (Echeverría 2020, 122), whose inclusivity poses an alternative to "the exclusive logic of states that insists on regulating human mobility on the basis of a membership principle" (Echeverría 2020, 119), Nail bases his theory on "social motion" (Nail 2015, 7), which in terms of his approach, called "kinopolitics" or "a politics of movement" (Nail 2015, 8, 21–38), exists prior to social systems. This motion is caused by "territorial, political, juridical and economic expulsion" (Nail 2015, 6) and has two major forms: migration and circulation. While the latter establishes "social formations" and "regimes" (Nail 2015, 3–4), the former generates "its own forms of social motion in riots, revolts, rebellions, and resistances" and demonstrates "the capacity of contemporary migrants to pose an alternative to the present social logic of expulsion that continues to dominate our world" (Nail 2015, 7).

Social flows result from "expansion", which can be "territorial" (e.g. the enclosures in early modern England) and include "warfare, colonialism, and massive public works" (Nail 2015, 22–3). However, it can also manifest itself in a more complex way, as an "intensive or qualitative growth in territorial, political, juridical, and economic kinopower" (Nail 2015, 36). All these forms of expansion engender "expulsion", which is "not simply the deprivation of territorial status (i.e., removal from the

___
his claims that "ontological practice itself is historical and kinetic" and that "regional ontology" is "rooted in the present, and thus can at most lay claim to a single dimension or historical trajectory in being leading up to a certain region of the present (Nail 2018, 32–3).

land)", but "includes three other major types of social deprivation: political, juridical, and economic" (Nail 2015, 35). As a result, "expulsion" is primarily not a spatial or temporal movement, but a "kinetic concept" presupposing both intensive and extensive understanding of movement (Nail 2015, 35). These flows cannot be modelled as movements of material points: they can be grasped only in statistical terms as "variable data flows" (Nail 2015, 25). As "a continuous process", "a multiplicity", they cannot be unified or totalized (Nail 2015, 26).

Social flows bifurcate, which can lead to their "redirection" back onto themselves "in a loop or fold" (Nail 2015, 27). The repetition of this movement creates "junctions" which differ from a mere "confluence [...] of overlapping and heterogeneous flows" (Nail 2015, 27). Though the folding of the flow on itself is arbitrary, it "constitutes a point of self-reference" because of "the haptic circularity" of the process (Nail 2015, 27). Junctions may produce "relatively immobile" points where "the flow intersects with itself" (Nail 2015, 28) and from where it can be controlled. In social terms, these points are moments of "relative stability" of territorial, political or economic character (e.g. house or city), or border walls (with watchtowers and patrol cars, etc.) with respect to migration (Nail 2015, 28).

"A series of junctions" is linked in the process of circulation, which regulates the flows "into an ordered network of junctions" (Nail 2015, 29). Each form of circulation, e.g. the movement of migrants across a border, includes a number of "circuits" ("border", "detention" and "labor" circuits; Nail 2015, 31–2). As a result, not only a flow but also its circulation is a dynamic process of considerable complexity.

Circulation increases the power and variability of a system of interconnected flows, thus causing their "expansion" (Nail 2015, 35). The movement of expansion is always connected with "expulsion" and has several distinct historical forms. The "centripetal" movement is linked with the territorialisation of earth and the rise of first centers of settlement. It leads to the arrival of agriculture and the expulsion of nomads from cultivated territories (Nail 2015, 39–47). The "centrifugal" movement gives rise to the old empires and their administration (Nail 2015, 48–58). The "tensional force [...] held between legally bound persons" is generating a movement among numerous local centers of power "linked through a web of juridical connections" which bind lords and their subjects "to a piece of land and its cultivation" (Nail 2015, 59–60). As a result, the major "form of kinopolitical expansion by expulsion in the Middle Ages is juridical" (Nail 2015, 60). Finally, the expansion achieves predominantly economic character of kinopower, distinguished by "elasticity", the capacity of "a network of junctions to return to its normal shape after contraction or expansion" (Nail 2015, 82). Important features of elastic circulation are a quick "redistribution of people" (especially workforce), "oscillations" of a social system and "a surplus of motion [...] to fill a deficit or displace an excess to avoid social decline or collapse" (Nail 2015, 82). Each of these forms of circulation and expansion by expulsion corresponds to a specific form of "the figure of the migrant": "nomad", "barbarian", "vagabond" and "proletarian" (Nail 2015, 8, 130–78). These forms do not have "a fixed identity": each of them is "a mobile social position or spectrum that people move into and out of under certain social conditions of mobility" (Nail 2015, 8).

7 From Social Flows to Borders

Nail's theory of social flows, their junctions, circulation and expansion is also relevant for the understanding of borders, which are part of this movement. Borders are not lines demarcating state territories. Also, they are not parts of these territories, since they lie "'between states" (Nail 2016, 2). They are "fuzzy zone-like" phenomena of "inclusive disjunction" (Nail 2016, 3). States infinitely approach borders as their limits but can never entirely reach them, "because the limit is a process that infinitely approaches the point of bifurcation, like the slope of a tangent" (Nail 2016, 3).

Borders are zones of division of a specific nature. In contrast to a division as a break or a cut, the division performed by borders is called "bifurcation" (Nail 2016, 3). It "adds a new path to the existing one", "diverges from itself" and produces "a qualitative change" of the flow of population as "a continuous system" (Nail 2016, 3). As a result, border is perceived as a continuity by some participants in social flow and as a discontinuity by others (Nail 2016, 3).

Borders are in a constant motion due to migration, circulation, geomorphological processes, negotiations between states or ethnic groups and changes of technologies of border protection and control. They can be seen as "motors, the mobile cutting blades of society" (Nail 2016, 7). Their dynamic functions manifest themselves chiefly with respect to social flows.

Nail does not understand borders territorially, but as "a process of social division" (Nail 2016, 2). The border is in motion not only in spatial terms (in spite of geomorphological divides or "border regimes" and technologies enforcing them) but also, and chiefly, as a moment of bifurcation, junction and circulation producing social division (Nail 2016, 2–8). Circulation of social flows is changing its course and intensity depending on the number and character of their junctions (Nail 2016, 29). It also changes the conditions and nature of exclusion and inclusion, because

> [i]t is a multifolded structure creating a complex system of relative insides and outsides without absolute inclusions and exclusions, but the insides and outsides are all folds of the same continuous process or flow. Each time circulation creates a fold or pleat, both a new inclusion and new exclusion are created. (Nail 2016, 29)

Due to the circulation of social flows borders escape full control of state power. The divisions they make are not based on static binary oppositions but on dynamic multiplication of differences (Nail 2016, 8). Borders are limits of social flows and their circulation. They circulate social divisions and order the society spatially (Nail 2016, 8–9). Moreover, they can be said to "define" society by giving it "limits" (Nail 2016, 9).

8 Nail's Theory of the Border

Nail describes his theory as a framework for a study of *"the historical conditions* in which empirical borders emerge across different social contexts" (Nail 2016, 12). This methodological assumption is supported by a reference to Kant's philosophy, which however does not seem to work in the wider context of Nail's allegedly "materialist" approach. In Nail's account, the problem addressed by his methodology is similar to that of the relationship between metaphysics and empiricism described in the introduction to the second edition of Kant's *Critique of Pure Reason*. Instead of assuming that "all our cognition must conform to objects" (Kant [1787] 1996, 21), which prevents us from discovering "more general (a priori) conditions of knowledge" under which objects appear to us (Nail 2016, 12), we should identify these conditions as rules "expressed in a priori concepts", to which "all objects of experience must necessarily conform [...] and agree with them" (Kant [1787] 1996, 22).

This speculative basis of Nail's methodology is problematic because of its claims of generality and objectivity. These become more resolute in the context of his ontology of motion (Nail 2018, 55), which develops a methodology called by Nail "transcendental realism, [...] the study of the real minimal ontological conditions for the actual emergence of the historical present" (Nail 2018, 52). The vague statement of the purpose of Nail's methodology – "to give a description of what previous being must *at least* be like given that it appears as it does today: in motion" (Nail 2018, 52) – reads like a clumsy attempt to revise Kant's apriorism by an approach remotely resembling Hans Vaihinger's neo-Kantian "philosophy of 'as-if'" (Vaihinger [1911] 2000). However, in contrast to Nail's colloquial use of "like" ("must *at least* be like given"), which in present-day American English may acknowledge "the discomfort" as well as the "reinforcement" (McWhorter 2016, 218–19), Vaihinger's use of "fiction" (Vaihinger [1911] 2000, 274) is based on a consistent interpretation of Kant's *Critique*, e.g. the "Appendix to the Transcendental Dialectics: On the Final Aim of the Natural Dialectics of Human Reason" (Kant [1787] 1996, 638–62), where Kant almost regularly uses the adverbial construction "as if" which denotes a specific methodological principle.[4] The vagueness of the basic assumption of Nail's methodology is increased by his idiosyncratic use of "transcendental" in connection with "regional" (e.g. "regional transcendental structure of our time – motion"; Nail 2018, 52) and defined as "a minimally real ontological structure of historical being – but not the *only* one. There are multiple coexisting real transcendentals; motion has simply emerged today as a relatively dominant and undertheorized one, thereby making possible a new ontological description of the present from this perspective" (Nail 2018, 52). It can hardly be justified by the reference to "the hybrid nature of ontological practice today" (Nail 2018, 53).

The determination of historical conditions in Nail's theory of the border is based on his knowledge and understanding of history which have

---

4 "Although in reason's empirical use this idea can never come about [as realized] completely, the idea yet serves as a rule as to how we are to proceed in regard to these series of conditions – viz., in explaining given appearances (i.e., in regressing or, in other words, ascending), we are to proceed *as if* the series were in itself infinite, i.e., we are to proceed in indefinitum. But where (viz., in [the realm of] freedom reason itself is regarded as determining cause, i.e., where we deal with practical principles, we are to proceed *as if* we had before us an object not of the senses but of the pure understanding. There the conditions can no longer be posited in the series of appearances, but can be posited outside this series; and the series of states can be regarded *as if* it began absolutely (through an intelligible cause). All of this proves that the cosmological ideas are nothing but regulative principles, and are far from positing – constitutively, as it were – an actual totality of such series. The remainder of these considerations can be found in its place under the Antinomy of Pure Reason" (Kant [1787] 1996, 649).

a generalizing and speculative character. Although presented as "minimally real", Nail's claims of generality and objectivity of his theory are problematic compared with pragmatic methodologies in social sciences, for instance the use of "frame analysis" (Goffman 1974; Ogien 2015, 6–9).

Nail's theory distinguishes "four major social and material types of borders: territorial, political, juridical, and economic" (Nail 2016, 12). This tetradic structural and functional scheme of "border kinopower" (Nail 2016, 43) is based on the previously developed typologies of expansion by expulsion" and migrants (Nail 2015, 39–124; 130–77).

Territorial borders are represented by "the fence" as "a border regime that produces a centripetal social motion: the movement of flows from the periphery toward the center" (Nail 2016, 47). Importantly, fence, or rather "fencing", is "not a border that emerges from a centralized power", it is a process of "centripetal segmentation that creates the conditions for a socially central power" (Nail 2016, 63). The fence is "a vertical junction" (Nail 2016, 62) delimiting settlements, pastures, tribal or sacred areas (the last mentioned can be marked, e.g. by megaliths). It expels "the wild flows of the earth inward toward [...] the pen, garden or a village" (Nail 2016, 62). It defends the "centripetally accumulated stock" and "binds several social junctions" (e.g. houses) "into a single circulatory social system", e.g. village community (Nail 2016, 62).

Political borders are represented by "the wall", which "transforms" the functions of the fence and "creates a new form of dominant social circulation" (Nail 2016, 64). It "consolidates the centripetal accumulations of the previous fence regime into a central point" (Nail 2016, 64), the city as an "urban center", and generates centrifugal flows of economic and military expansion establishing an empire. Moreover, the wall directs the circulation of social flows within cities and becomes an important force transforming the society "into a mechanism of transport" (of goods, armies, colonists, etc.) "in the service of centralized rule" (Nail 2016, 65).

Juridical borders are represented by "the cell", which was originally a monastic space of individuation and identification. These processes of the separation of individuals from social flows were dividing "human life into individual lives" (Nail 2016, 88). Historically, the cell can be seen as an outcome of the problems of mobility caused by the downfall of ancient empires. Its "juridical" kinopower stems from the "network of binding laws", which in medieval Europe "replaces the central power of the emperor" (Nail 2016, 89). Nail refers to Perry Anderson who shows that under feudalism "political sovereignty was never focused in a single center" and "the functions of the feudal State were disintegrated"

(Anderson 1974, 148). The social circulation is caused by "*a dynamic tension* [...] within a centrifugal State" leading to its "disintegration in the vertical allocation" of power and feudal bonds "downward" (Anderson 1974, 151). In kinopolitic terms, the cell represents the basic form of processes producing not only prisons, asylums and hospitals, but leading to the invention of travel letters and passports (from the French phrase *passe porte* – "authorization to travel through the country"), quarantine measures and scheduling ("*horarium* or timetable matrix") as the chief means of organizing human activities (Nail 2016, 97–102, 105).

Economic borders are represented by "the checkpoint" dividing the individuals into "collections of data [...] age, height, weight, location, status" (Nail 2016, 110). These checkpoints do not only exist at privileged locations in space (gates of cities, monasteries, border crossings). They can emerge anywhere, thus making border regimes "far more polymorphic [...]. Any space-time point can become a border" (Nail 2016, 110). Rather than to regulate specific social flows, the new concept of mobile borders is used to "maintain a dynamic equilibrium (homeorhesis) and, when possible, expand this equilibrium" (Nail 2016, 111).

These "new elastic borders" rely on security forces and flows of information. "Instead of blocking movement", they order these forces and flows "according to the multiple and competing ends of dynamic social oscillation" (Nail 2016, 112). "Everything must be set into economic circulation" whose main purpose is "the redistribution of a surplus to whatever point needed" (Nail 2016, 112). Nail quotes Foucault (2007, 314–15) to demonstrate how this significant change of border kinopolitics produced a new academic discipline (*Polizeiwissenschaft*) in the second half of the 18th century. In the 19th century, the theory of the police became seminal for the constitution of modern police apparatuses (Nail 2016, 119, 121). As a result, the regulation of social flows has become connected with the "practice of prevention" which "actually destroys the fixed borders and all limits to police motion" (Nail 2016, 121).

Simultaneously with these internal border regimes, modern border technologies were emerging, which became a synthesis of all the previous ones. The basic type of modern border technology is "the security checkpoint", which "protects, defends, and enforces the institutions defined and ordered" by the system of mobile police checkpoints (Nail 2016, 138). Nonetheless, "security checkpoint" is no mere gate, through which territorial borders are crossed. Nail shows how "private property", oscillating among owners according to their purchase power, also functions as a "security checkpoint", since it "offers the owner some security – the security of subsistence or future productivity" (Nail 2016, 139–40). It introduces new divisions into the social flow (between the owners and the workers, and between poor workers and needy, destitute people) and "acts as a limit junction within an oscillating social flow to secure a social division between those who can circulate freely via ownership and those who cannot" (Nail 2016, 140).

These differences influence the traffic at "national security checkpoints" (Nail 2016, 143) which can be relatively freely crossed by well-to-do individuals and citizens of rich countries, while the citizens of poor countries, travelling in search of better paid employment, often become criminalized as illegal migrants. In this way, "divisions between global elites and underclasses" come into existence (Nail 2016, 161). Apart from bifurcating social flows and creating new limiting junctions, national security checkpoints define, by means of ideologies of the sovereign state, the nation as the "new bordering technique" (Nail 2016, 144). Nonetheless, national security checkpoints are no mere means of regulating and centralizing social mobility. They are also means of freeing it and controlling it only occasionally, first by photo passports and later, e.g., by cameras and surveillance systems. Their operation is thus based on the oscillation between the increased freedom of movement and the increasing control of it (Nail 2016, 147).

National security checkpoints may also function as "information checkpoints" which gather information about individuals, "binding and bounding data sets together into discrete assemblages" – archives – "for criminal, private, and national management" (Nail 2016, 157). Like the police checkpoints, these "information checkpoints are mobile and their chief function is to make "macrolevel statistical observations possible" (Nail 2016, 158). The purpose of information checkpoints is "to produce a kinetic environment such that data groupings (individuals) regulate themselves according to the boundaries of their informational complex, [...] following the path" of the least resistance (traffic) or greatest profit (trade) (Nail 2016, 155). This leads to "social landscaping based on an informational topography – no longer simply a coordinate matrix or cartography, but a topological surface with trajectories, slopes, and curves" (Nail 2016, 155).

These social landscapes are spaces of surveillance (capturing the data of individuals in social flows) which leads to the expansion and perfection of control. According to Grégoire Chamayou, the control exercised through information checkpoints consists in a reversal of the "temporal logic" of tracing individuals and their activities in the social flow

(Chamayou 2013, 5). Instead of reconstructing their traces aposteriori to establish evidence (as in the case of criminal investigation), the control based on information checkpoints replaces these material traces "by prefabricated traces captured by means of automatic recording apparatuses integrated into activity itself, every material flow now being coupled with a production of a flow of data" (Chamayou 2013, 5). This advanced technology of control makes the movements of individuals both predictable and manipulable. As Nail points out, "social flows are now recorded, deported, criminalized, redirected, restricted, slowed down, sped up, and modulated at any point within a network of oscillating flows punctuated with checkpoints" (Nail 2016, 161). Information checkpoints transform social flows into "variable data flows" (Nail 2015, 25). Though these cannot be unified or totalized (Nail 2015, 26), they can be efficiently controlled and manipulated, which poses a great threat to present-day democracies.

In spite of its apriorism, Nail's methodology can not only lead to understanding "borders as regimes of concrete techniques" and their specific "historical conditions" (Nail 2016, 13), but also to exploring the complexity of motion within each of the four major types of borders. Even though the tetradic structure of these types may resemble the patterns based on cycles major tropes (Vico [1744] 1948; Frye 1957, 158–239; White 1973, 7–11), Nail's tetrad of the border regimes is neither cyclical, nor does it represent a linear movement of evolution and progress. As Nail points out,

> the transformation and advent of the forms of border kinopower [...] is not linear, evolutionary, or progressive. Their transformation is not linear because kinopower is always a mix of its different types: emerging, receding, and re-emerging in history. Their transformation is not evolutionary in the sense that the new form does not abandon the previous one. Finally, their transformation is not progressive because there is no end or goal that kinopower strives for. (Nail 2016, 42)

The four types of border regimes do not form an abstract, speculative pattern, reflecting, as in the case of Vico, White or Frye, the figurative powers of poetic language or archetypal imagery of myths based on the cycle of seasons. They are "rather coexistent in various degrees through history", but each of them "more strongly expressed" in a specific historical period (Nail 2016, 43).

The dependence of Nail's theory on traditional periodizations of history can be seen as its most problematic aspect. Although Nail makes an efficient use of Foucault's theories of power or surveillance, he does not take into account his theory of discourse and its role in the formation of historical knowledge, especially the contrast between "the historical a priori" and "the archive" (Foucault [1969] 1972, 126–34). In the light of Foucault's approach, Nail's methodology of border studies can be said to oscillate between the reliance on speculatively defined material processes and a differential analysis of modalities of discourse in search of "the system of discursivity" (Foucault [1969] 1972, 129).[5]

9 Borders as Interfaces

In contrast to Nail's "hydrodynamic" models of social motion based on the assumption of "expansion by expulsion" and describing the changes of social flows at their junctions and in the process of circulation, borders can also be modelled as "interfaces" – devices or applications enabling the transfer of information from one system to another. Although the term has been used in cultural and new media studies for a considerable time, it was most often focused on crossing and transforming the boundaries between humans, computers and internet (e.g. "graphical user interfaces" or web browsers; Johnson 1997), human bodies and virtual or "mixed" reality (e.g. "the sensory integration of or interface with a concrete virtual domain [...] transformative integration of the virtual"; Hansen 2006, 6), or on modelling perception as "an adaptive interface [...] a perceptual strategy favored by selection" (Hoffman, Singh and Prakash 2015, 1480).

Understanding border as an interface implies a different interpretive perspective from that chosen by Nail, who sees borders as products of bifurcations and junctions of social flows resulting in circulation, division and redistribution of forces (Nail 2016, 8). Although Nail never admits it, border regimes and technologies always tend to create (at least temporarily) closed systems: "the fence" captures "the flows of the earth", "the wall" transforms the society into "a mechanism of transport in the service of a centralized rule", "the cell" generates modern techniques

---

5   Interestingly enough, there is no reference to Foucault ([1969] 1972) in Nail 2016, and only a single, most general one in Nail 2018, 576.

of identification, confinement and scheduling, and "[n]ational borders" are "written on the body and can thus be inspected" (Nail 2016, 47, 65, 88–108, 148). Whereas Nail's theory of border traces the transformations of the open systems of social flows into the closed systems of border regimes, the use of the interface as a model of the border points to an opposite direction: seeing borders and their permeability as important means of opening up closed political, social and cultural systems of nation-states based on the nationalist ideologies of identity, sovereignty and homogeneity (Diener and Hagen 2012, 40). If borders are modelled as interfaces, cultures do not have to be approached as closed systems with specific identities but described in functional terms, as interfaces of transcultural communication which engender dialogue and use fictions to enable and facilitate sharing knowledge, emotions, attitudes, beliefs and values. This approach may be viewed as parallel to ecocriticism, complementing its nature-based and largely material notion of environment with a pragmatic understanding of culture as human-made habitable and sustainable surroundings.

In contrast to borders which are "in between" (Nail 2016, 2–5), interfaces are specific "contact zones". However, most recent approaches to "contact zones" follow their description by Mary Louise Pratt, who has coined the term. According to Pratt, "contact zone" is "the space of colonial encounters, the space in which people geographically and historically separated come into contact with each other and establish ongoing relations, usually involving coercion, racial inequality and intractable conflict" (Pratt 1992, 6). Despite her emphasis on coercion and conflict, Pratt admits the transcultural importance of contact zones, which are spaces of "interactive, improvisational dimensions of encounters [...] copresence, interaction, interlocking understanding and practices" (Pratt 1992, 7). Moreover, Pratt's emphasis on conflict in contact zones can be balanced by some "interculturalist" approaches which not only stress the possibility of "the recognition of common human needs across cultures" but also admit their "dissonance" and the need of "critical dialogue" (Nussbaum 1998, 80).

The main mode of communication facilitated by borders as interfaces is a "critical dialogue" based both on "dissonances" among them and on "the common human needs across" them. To describe inter- and transcultural cultural communication across borders, an analogy with computer interfaces based on specific protocols offers itself. In computer science "an interface refers to the connecting point between two adjacent network entities. A protocol defines rules to be complied with for exchanging information on the connecting point" ("Interfaces and Protocols" 2011). While in computer science this task is highly formalized, inter- and transcultural communication depends on human agency, transformation potential and intercontextuality.[6] The main means of generating protocols in cultural exchange are generally known fictions – narratives using symbols and myths –, which, among others, enable the transmission of emotions or value criteria.

Under certain circumstances, as in the Chicano Feminism, exemplified by the work of Gloria Anzaldúa (1987), these fictions can transform the border into a transitional and transcultural zone. Stressing the hybrid nature of cultural, gender and sexual identity, Anzaldúa and her fellow authors have effected changes on both sides of the Mexico-U.S. border. A well-known instance of these changes is the identification of the colonial symbol of Mexican identity, the Virgin of Guadalupe (*Virgen de Guadalupe*), and the power of the serpent deity of Mexican Indians. It can be said that the performative capacity of literature to create new hybrid fictions does not only contribute to destabilization of traditional identities but also to the emergence of protocols making the border work as an interface. Nowadays, Chicano feminism still poses a humanistic alternative to the grim repression epitomized by the U.S.-Mexico border wall and all forms of aggressive populist nationalism.

Apart from its foundations in the ontology of motion, Nail's theory of borders shows the powerful and often violent impact of "border regimes" on the quality of social life and cohesion. Nail's pessimistic perspective leads to the questioning of the adequacy of his model, which bears features of the "new materialism" (Gamble, Hanan and Nail 2019). Instead of the emphasis on social flows and border regimes, theories of borders as "contact zones" lead to the understanding of boundaries as connecting devices among originally closed cultural, social and political systems.

References

"Interfaces and Protocols". 2011. *All About Wireless and Telecommunication* 19 February 2011, http://allaboutwirelesstelecommunication.blogspot.com/2011/02/interfaces-and-protocols.html. Accessed 28 June 2021.

Anderson, Perry. 1974. *Passages from Antiquity to Feudalism*. London: New Left Books.

---

6 For a detailed analysis of computer protocols in relation to control, power and Internet art see Galloway 2004, 2–27.

Anzaldúa, Gloria. 1987. *Borderlands / La Frontera: The New Mestiza*. San Francisco, CA: Aunt Lute Books.

Brandom, Robert. 1983. "Heidegger's Categories in *Being and Time*". *The Monist* 66 (3): 387–409.

Chamayou, Grégoire. 2013. "Fichte's Passsport: A Philosophy of the Police". Translated by Kieran Aarons. *Theory and Event* 16 (2): 1–17.

Deleuze, Gilles, and Félix Guattari. 1983. *Anti-Oedipus: Capitalism and Schizophrenia*. Translated by Robert Hurley, Mark Seem, and Helen R. Lane. Minneapolis: University of Minnesota Press. Original edition, 1972.

Deleuze, Gilles, and Félix Guattari. 1987. *A Thousand Plateaus: Capitalism and Schizophrenia*. Translated by Brian Massumi. Minneapolis: University of Minnesota Press. Original edition, 1980.

Deleuze, Gilles. 1990. *The Logic of Sense,* edited by Constantin Boundas, translated by Mark Lester, and Charles Stivale. London: Athlone Press. Original edition, 1969.

Deleuze, Gilles. 1994. *Difference and Repetition*. Translated by Paul Patton. New York: Columbia University Press. Original edition, 1968.

Diener, Alexander, and Joshua Hagen. 2012. *Borders: A Very Short Introduction*. New York: Oxford University Press.

Echeverría, Gabriel. 2020. "Understanding Irregular Migration through a Social Systems Perspective". In *Towards a Systemic Theory of Irregular Migration: Explaining Ecuadorian Irregular Migration in Amsterdam and Madrid*, 95–125. Trento: Springer Verlag.

Fernández, Nelson, Carlos Maldonado, and Carlos Gershenson. 2013. "Information Measures of Complexity, Emergence, Self-Organization, Homeostasis, and Autopoiesis". In *Guided Self-Organization: Inception, Emergence, Complexity and Computation 9*, edited by Mikhail Prokopenko, 19–59. Berlin, Heidelberg: Springer Verlag.

Foucault, Michel. 1972. *The Archaeology of Knowledge*. Translated by A. M. Sheridan Smith. London: Tavistock. Original edition, 1969.

Foucault, Michel. 2007. *Security, Territory, Population: Lectures at the Collège de France 1977–78*. Translated by Alessandro Fontana. Basingstoke: Macmillan.

Frye, Northrop. 1957. *Anatomy of Criticism: Four Essays*. Princeton, NJ: Princeton University Press.

Galloway, Alexander R. 2004. *Protocol: How Control Exists after Decentralization*. Cambridge, MA: The MIT Press.

Gamble, Christopher N., Joshua Hanan, and Thomas Nail. 2019. "What Is New Materialism". *Angelaki* 24 (6): 111–34.

Gershenson, Carlos. 2014. "Requisite Variety, Autopoiesis, and Self-Organization". https://arxiv.org/ftp/arxiv/papers/1409/1409.7475.pdf. Accessed 28 June 2021.

Goffman, Erving. 1974. *Frame Analysis: An Essay on the Organization of Experience*. Boston, MA: Northeastern University Press.

Hansen, Mark B. N. 2006. *Bodies in Code: Interfaces with Digital Media*. London: Routledge.

Heidegger, Martin. 1962. *Being and Time*. Translated by John Macquarrie, and Edward Robinson. Oxford: Blackwell. Original edition, 1927.

Hoffman, Donald D., Manish Singh, and Chetan Prakash. 2015. "The Interface Theory of Perception". *Psychonomic Bulletin and Review* 22: 1480–506.

Johnson, Steven. 1997. *Interface Culture*. New York: Basic Books.

Kant, Immanuel. 1996. *Critique of Pure Reason*. Translated by Werner S. Pluhar. Indianapolis: Hackett. Original edition, 1787.

Leroi-Gourhan, André. 1993. *Gesture and Speech*. Translated by Anna Bostock Berger. Cambridge, MA: MIT Press. Original edition, 1965.

Lucretius Carus, Titus. 1916. *De Rerum Natura*. Translated and edited by William Ellery Leonard, http://data.perseus.org/catalog/urn:cts:latinLit:phi0550.phi001. Accessed 28 June 2021.

Maturana, Humberto R. 1980. "Introduction". In *Autopoiesis and Cognition: The Realization of the Living*, edited by Humberto R. Maturana, and Francisco J. Varela, xi – xxx. Dordrecht: D. Reidel.

Maturana, Humberto R., and Francisco J. Varela, 1980. *Autopoiesis and Cognition: The Realization of the Living*. Dordrecht: D. Reidel.

McWhorter, John. 2016. *Words on the Move: Why English Won't – and Can't – Sit Still (Like, Literally)*. New York: Henry Holt.

Nail, Thomas. 2015. *The Figure of the Migrant*. Stanford, CA: Stanford University Press.

Nail, Thomas. 2016. *Theory of the Border*. Oxford, New York: Oxford University Press.

Nail, Thomas. 2018. *Being and Motion*. Oxford, New York: Oxford University Press.

Nicolis, Grégoire, and Ilya Prigogine. 1989. *Exploring Complexity: An Introduction*. New York: W. H. Freeman and Company.

Nietzsche, Friedrich. 1968. *The Will to Power*. Translated by Walter Kaufmann, and R. J. Hollingdale. New York: Vintage Books. Original edition, 1901.

Nussbaum, Martha. 1998. *Cultivating Humanity: A Classical Defense of Reform in Liberal Education*. Cambridge MA: Harvard University Press.

Ogien, Albert. 2015. "Pragmatism's Legacy to Sociology Respecified". *European Journal of Pragmatism and American Philosophy* 7 (1): 1–19.

Pratt, Mary Louise. 1992. *Imperial Eyes: Travel Writing and Transculturation*. New York: Routledge.

Prigogine, Ilya, and Isabelle Stengers. 1984. *Order out of Chaos: Man's New Dialogue with Nature*. New York: Bantam Books.

Prigogine, Ilya. 1980. *From Being to Becoming: Time and Complexity in the Physical Sciences*. New York: W. H. Freeman.

Vaihinger, Hans. 2000. *The Philosophy of "As-If": A System of the Theoretical, Practical and Religious Fictions of Mankind*. Translated by C. K. Ogden. Abingdon: Routledge. Original edition, 1911.

Vico, Giambattista. 1948. *The New Science of Giambattista Vico*. Translated by Thomas Goddard Bergin, and Max Harold Fisch. Ithaca, NY: Cornell University Press. Original edition, 1744.

Wheeler, Michael. 2020. "Martin Heidegger". *The Stanford Encyclopedia of Philosophy,* edited by Edward N. Zalta, https://plato.stanford.edu/archives/fall2020/entries/heidegger/. Accessed 28 June 2021.

White, Hayden. 1973. *Metahistory: The Historical Imagination in Nineteenth-Century Europe*. Baltimore, MD: The Johns Hopkins University Press.

"I am the Combat": Hegel's Dramatic Theory of Knowledge

Vojtěch Kolman

I am the combat; I am not one of the conflicting terms but both the combatants and the combat itself. I am the fire and the water which make contact.
I am the contact and union of that which is utterly self-repelling.
Georg Wilhelm Friedrich Hegel: *Lectures on the Philosophy of Religion*

1 Introduction

George Steiner once wrote that the rarity of Hegel's style consists in his being "able to think against himself" or "to dramatize in the root sense of the verb, which is one of pure action" (Steiner 1984, 20–1). To illustrate this, he quotes the above-mentioned passage from Hegel's *Lectures on Religion* in which Hegel seems to describe the "state of war" as the true expression of the *conditio humana*.

Considering the role that Hegel's philosophy played in the stabilization of the Prussian state or,[1] via Marx, in the history of two consequent centuries of mankind, the suspicion might arise whether the terms used here do have dramatic value rather than some military quality. This would

---

[1] It is, of course, unfair to overemphasize the brief connection between Hegel and Prussianism. Hegel's career in Berlin began within a program of liberal reforms (including those of Humboldt) under the chancellor, Karl August von Hardenberg, and education minister, Karl vom Stein zum Altenstein, who offered Hegel the professorship there. The increasingly conservative tendency of the government following the defeat of Napoleon was by no means welcomed by Hegel, if only because he associated the idea of the state with the constitutional monarchy, by which the power of sovereign and estates was mediated. Hegel's importance lies elsewhere, in treating the state as something of essential value, not destroying an individual's identity but,

be in accord with Hegel's other "war-like" strategies, most importantly the dialectics of "master and slave" (and the primordial conflict this differentiation is a product of), or his very concept of war – as means by which "peoples are strengthened, nations, which are involved in civil quarrels, winning repose at home by means of war abroad" (Hegel 2001, 259). It is mainly because of them that he is often seen as a prototype of a philosophical cynic justifying negativity and violence instead of truth and peace.

At the same time, the given negativity plays an important role in what might be seen as Hegel's most *positive* achievement, namely his *autopoietic* worldview. Here, the concept of the human world, or the Spirit, develops immanently from its *own resources*, and these resources are in fact nothing other than his own *failures and mistakes*. This turns the negative delimitation of Hegel's philosophy inside out: the only thing by which we can *positively* measure the greatness of our victories and truths is the size of our previous failures and mistakes. It is exactly in this sense that, according to Hegel, Spirit arises from nothing and keeps growing while following rules of its own.

In my paper, I would like to elaborate on this *cautiously positive* side of Hegel's philosophy, going beyond the mere metaphor of legendary uroboros self-feeding on the tail of his failures in the more argumentative terms of *epistemological fallibilism*. Hegel, as I will claim, not only fits into the standard fallibilist picture, as represented particularly by C. S. Peirce and Ludwig Wittgenstein, but enriches it with what might be called a *dramatic twist*. This is famously known from the *dialectics* of master and slave, but the pattern pervades his whole philosophy, endowing it with a significant *quality* which is exactly that described by Steiner as a kind of dramatization. Its main benefit is that it avoids the "positivist" reading of Hegel's negative epistemology, as adopted famously by Marx and Engels. The direction I suggest, on the other hand, is one that keeps the dialogical, or "war-like" quality of Hegel's text intact, systematically entertaining the ambiguity of their readings for the sake of the continuity of our experience and its prospective unified approach. Scruton's differentiation between *allegorical* and *symbolic* readings will be of some importance here.

---

in fact, completing it. It is in this specific sense of Prussia as an example of a welfare state that one might say that "no individual did more to promulgate the dignity of the Prussian state after 1815 than Georg Wilhelm Friedrich Hegel" (Clark 2007, 431).

2 I Know What You Are Thinking

What *fallibilism* seems to say, at first, is a practical truism, or rule of thumb, rather than a deep philosophical insight: to learn something one must be prepared to make mistakes. This is captured in proverbs like "failure is the mother of success" (or "shit happens", for that matter). But the doctrine itself wants to say more than that. It is one thing to say that we should not give up just because we did not succeed straight away ("never give up, never surrender"), and another to say that failure and success are different sides of the same coin, i.e., one cannot have one without having the other, not because it is *often* so but for *conceptual reasons*.

It is already because of this that in fallibilism the negativity and fighting quality of knowledge has a more *positive* standing. Both Peirce and Wittgenstein ascribe to this, transforming what traditionally looked like a failure to be remedied into knowledge's essential feature. Our propensity to make mistakes *cannot* be remedied but only used to our own advantage, e.g., along the lines of Wittgenstein's intersubjective perception: "It is correct to say 'I know what you are thinking', and wrong to say 'I know what I am thinking. (A whole cloud of philosophy condensed into a drop of grammar)" (Wittgenstein 1958, 222).

It is easy to connect this doctrine with Hegel's concept of Spirit, defined as I that is We and We that is I, which is basically a community of individuals who, in its most developed form, completed what he calls the Golgotha of the Spirit or the journey of the infinite grief. But beyond the obvious interdependency of both concepts, knowledge and error, what Hegel stresses is the intensity of the previous pain that provides for the positive quality of the subsequent success. This success is in no way guaranteed, as in the famous "high risk, high gain" principle, but provides the *cautiously optimistic* or *realistic* reading of the originally negative autopoietic enterprise.

Thus, along the depictured dramatic lines, one can start with the idea that there is no absolute certainty in our lives and, as such, life is essentially tragic: we often fail and even must fail. But in this failing – and here comes the dramatic twist – sometimes the higher gain is won. It is only through this reversal that the *new certainty* arises, belonging to knowledge *proper* as opposed to its impoverished variants. It is along these lines that Hegel's claim "I am the combat" can be read as a dramatized alternative to the traditional concepts of knowledge based on unconditioned certainty, prominently Descartes' "cogito, ergo sum".

What Hegel's version claims is that there is still *certainty* of consciousness, but only a relative one achieved in an *epistemological combat* and its *dramatic reversal*. Here, consciousness risks its primordial subjectivity where no error is possible, and so is not *truth*.

The bigger good to be won is socially mediated knowledge, the *I that is We and We that*, where the "wrong" and "right" are the two sides of the same coin and the resulting certainty stems from the underlying self-corrigible structure of mutual acknowledgment. In my paper, I will not present Hegel's theory directly but arrive at it in Hegel's own method of *immanent* presenting, starting with standard approaches, such as Descartes' idea of individual certainty, and refuting them in the next step by their own means. What will be achieved will also be a concept of certainty, but this time resulting from the underlying fallible structure of our socially-based knowledge.

3 Seeing It Right

Newton says: "The errors are not in the art, but in the artificers" (Newton 1995, 3), i.e., in *the eye of the beholder*. And this is quite in accord with traditional epistemology and its distinction between mere belief (*doxa*) and real knowledge (*episteme*): One thing is to *see how things are* and another to *see them right*, according to the correct art. But what such an art is, is quite difficult to tell from the point of view of the beholder, who is supposed to have both *episteme* and *doxa* and who, as such, cannot be stronger than his or her *weakest* link, which is the intrinsic tendency to *err*. If reality has resources that make us fail, it is a vain effort to differentiate exactly what it is to see it right.

The option entertained by the modern philosophy of both Descartes and Kant is to retreat to the very *source* of our sight, to the *cognizing subject* itself. If I cannot infallibly know what things are, I can at least *know something about my knowing* them. And, maybe (just maybe), once I will be able to specify the indubitable example of knowledge about this knowledge itself, the rest will easily follow. This reflexive turn, trading the reality of the world for the reality of the subject, is almost didactically *foreseen* in the "discovery" of *linear perspective*, as the era which anticipated the dawn of the Cartesian certainty. Here, the things *as they are* are once and for all left to themselves and one starts with picturing them *as they might be seen* in the eye of the beholder, i.e., the *center of projection*. Brunelleschi's experiments with mirrors, with which the whole enterprise may have started, illustrate this focus on the *image* rather than, in some detail, *reality*.[2] As a result, we depict things as we see them in their perspective, through *foreshortening*, receding to the horizon, i.e., the line at the height of the spectator's eyes. But do we directly see how to see the things, or is there some doubt about this seeing itself?

Let us consider, by way of example, the elementary case of the square pavement, or *pavimento*, and the specific problem of drawing distances between the receding horizontal lines. How to get them right? Several "rules of thumb" have been devised providing approximative yet different results. Alberti's essay *Della Pittura* (where some of these approximative rules are mentioned) is of key importance here, resembling the replacement of Egyptian mathematics by a Greek one. In a similar way, it replaces rules of thumb by general truths that become *rules again* but that are based not (only) on some empirical observations but unifying reasons (Alberti 2014, 94–5).

What Alberti did was that he took a picture of the constructed pavement from the beholder's point of view *and* compared it with *another picture* of how this beholder looks at the pavement. In this, the projecting lines have been drawn, demonstrating both *where* the distances are to be drawn and *why* that is. See Fig. 1. Only now one can see why the parallel lines intersect at the horizon, the diagonal lines at the distance point, etc. These *phenomena* are not depicting something lying on the depicted pavement but belong to the given art of projection. As Wittgenstein would say, they provide a *scaffolding* for the world (Wittgenstein 2002, 76), present in the picture but not in the *re*presenting way: they do not *tell* us about the world behind the canvas but just show *themselves*.

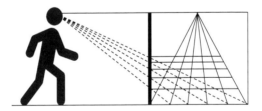

Fig. 1.

2   These experiments are hard to reconstruct because we must rely on Manetti's descriptions. But the point presented might be sustainable; see Edgerton 2009.

This scaffolding, though, is not something incorrigible or certain, as Newton and Kant suggested, but contains an element of arbitrariness already stemming from the fact that we are not one-eyed creatures with the fixed point of view. As the history of painting illustrates, once the art is settled, there is always a space for the alternative rules (such as orthogonal projection) and the underlying creativity. What Alberti showed us, accordingly, was not the *a priori* quality of some specific projective method but something deeper and more straightforward than that: namely, that the picture cannot be compared directly with reality, but only with another picture representing the other set of eyes.

4 Through Another's Eyes

The lesson, henceforth, is this: What I need to see something correctly is not a method of cleansing my eyes from *all* the prejudices and biases (as Descartes' *clarae et distinctae* and his universal doubt demanded), but just to subjugate my eyes to the eyes of another subject. The reality of the external world is always here but mediated by the reality of *another*. This another, in practice, might be another version of me, in the same sense in which I can correct myself retrospectively, but such a self-consciousness always depends on a previous encounter with another human being.

With this consideration, we meet the first form of the underlying *combat* in an epistemological setting. In theoretical terms, what one does is replace Kant's useless concept of a thing *in itself*, not by a thing as it is *for us*, but by a combination of both: the thing as it is for us and the thing in itself which, though, is again only for us. Together they form the thing "in and for itself" (Hegel 2018, 56), this time not guaranteed by the unifying powers of the transcendental subject but by this subject's overall socialization in the dialogical structure of the *I that is We and We that is I*.

This whole socialization, of course, might look like a rather useless step as the original subjectivity is not overcome but only replaced by a more complex one. But that is exactly the point: the objectivity arises only insofar as there is another man providing the independent *measure* by which my subjectivity is assessed as right or wrong – compare this to Wittgenstein, who states that "it is not possible to obey a rule 'privately': otherwise thinking one was obeying a rule would be the same thing as obeying it" (Wittgenstein 1958, 81). This measure is a relative one, but it has a certain *stability* with respect to what has been achieved, and this is the very distinction of what is (objectively) *right* or *wrong*.

In Hegel's dramatic choreography, one does not start with combat itself, but with an ambivalent concept of "desire" as a complex label for our *relation* to the world that we share not only with each other but also with other sentient creatures. This allows him to describe the emergence of culture from nature in rather naturalistic terms as a differentiation between *desires*, including *beliefs* as desires to know, in the immediate and mediated form. Brandom's key point is this:

> One way the difference that matters between things like itches and things like desires emerges concerns the possibility of *mistakes*. The notion of *felt satisfaction*, of relief from a motivating pressure, includes an element of immediacy as *incorrigibility*. The organism cannot be mistaken about whether its itch has been relieved. But I do not always and automatically know whether I have gotten what I want. (Brandom 2011, 75)

The difference between what I want and what I get is not sharply delineated, since I can easily persuade myself that I got exactly what I wanted no matter how I feel about it. But if I am about to achieve *knowledge* proper, this cannot be a typical option. The way out is to let my *desires* be mediated by another subject. The benefits of this resignation regarding the immediacy of my desires consists in *extending* what I can desire over the *immediate* moment. If I desire what you desire and take you as authoritative for what it is to satisfy this desire of mine, I can overcome my old sentient self. In this, as Hegel put it, "desire acquires the *breadth* of being not only the desire of a *particular* individual but containing within itself the desire of *another*" (Hegel 2007, 161). To this, I need *you*, *both* as *homogenous* with me, by being another *subject*, and as a subject *independent* of my immediacy.

The taming of the eye is, in fact, a case of taming subjective desires by social interaction, i.e., by making them subjective in a broader sense of the word. The *universality* of knowledge is nothing more than the generalization of my subjective point-of-view in this inter-subjective direction.

5 Tragedy's Transformative Powers

This brings us to the dialectics of *master and slave* as the founding act of *culture*. Here, one starts with the subject's desire to arrive at the right way of seeing how things are, for which the subjectivity of another represents a radical challenge. In this, I can well acknowledge that in specifying how the world is I need the help of others, but can still believe that, by using them cunningly, I will arrive at a certainty in which they play only the subordinate role of being the vehicles of my newly achieved knowledge or the satisfaction of my desire to know. In this sense, one is "certain of itself but not of the other, and for that reason its own certainty of itself is still without truth" (Hegel 2018, 111). As such, one must engage in a "life and death struggle" in which one's claim for certainty prevails.

Thus, it is the *presupposition* of the whole story rather than a lesson taken from it that one *must* engage in a *life and death* struggle if one wants to be a person in the full-fledged sense. Without such a risk, one will not be able to recognize the benefits of mediated desire and will merely live in the present as flowers and (lower) animals do. To be more than that, one must, in William James' words, meet the other people half-way in the same sense in which one cannot appreciate the company of gentlemen without starting to behave like one (James 1997, 69–92, 86, 89). James' "better risk loss of truth than chance of error" is a quite suitable (though ambivalent) motto for the whole presupposition (James 1997, 88), if only for the fact that to gain something here means also to lose something, namely the original certainty of immediately and unquestionably given.

The lesson proper of the whole dialectics, thus, is that of the person who risked his life and won, and, as such, wants to have the benefits of both the eyes of another (who is not killed but kept alive to serve) and the immediate certainty of the world which his new servant, in accord with the original demand, adapts to master's eyes' immediate desire. In this, the social, mediated nature of knowledge is already acknowledged, but in a *parasitic* way that somehow repeats the original idea of pure subjectivity being the true source of knowledge.

This is, let us say, for the fighting or military part of the whole story. Now, in a kind of *ironical twist*, the true dramatic part of Hegel's story comes forward when *for the master beholder* this part results in the old stage in which *he only thinks to be the measure* of all things while, in fact, he is, as such, only thanks to another subject, *the servant beholder*, who "works on the thing" and thus contributes to the immediate satisfaction of the master's desires. The old stage, however, does not repeat itself as such, because the master's old immediacy is his *private phantasy* defined with respect to the mediacy of the servant. Since the servant, unlike the master, is not immediately satisfied by the things he produces, his "work is desire *held in check*" (Hegel 2007, 115), which leads, *via* the thus discovered phenomenon of "deferred gratification", to the servant's *Bildung*.

The master's tragedy, though, turns out to be transformative since the very source of the servant's cultivation is the master's *original fancy* of having the world for himself. Thus,

> without having experienced the discipline that breaks self-will, no one becomes free, rational, and capable of command. To become free, to acquire the capacity for self-government, all peoples must therefore undergo the severe discipline of subjection to a master. [...] Bondage and tyranny are, therefore, in the history of peoples a necessary stage and hence something *relatively* justified. (Hegel 2007, 161)

Accordingly, it is not the mere results of the whole process, or the conflict that started it, but this result's overall dramatization, with all the *plot twists* and their inner structure, that allows us to explain what the knowledge is and in which sense it might be called certain or fallible: "it is only by the liberation of the bondsman that the master, too, becomes completely free" (Hegel 2007, 162). As a result, freedom, certainty, and fallibility are not mere individual qualifications of humanity but belong to its overall social structure in which some kind of symmetry, or mutual acknowledgment, has been achieved.

6 Hope without Optimism

After the previous passages, one can agree with Dewey who in his *Experience and Nature* says that "Greek reflection, carried on by a leisure class in the interest of liberalizing leisure, was preeminently that of the spectator, not that of the participator in processes of production" (Dewey 1929, 91). Indeed, it is this overall democratization of human thinking, which Peirce describes as a transfer from the methods of authority and apriority to the method of science, that is responsible for the massive ascent of science and culture in modern times.

As a part of this ascent, the individual mind must be *fallible* as it is a part of the enterprise that keeps the structure stable by questioning every individual's pretension to certainty, i.e., *authority* without corresponding *responsibility*, and *autonomy* without corresponding *dependence*. The given certainty is not the absolute certainty of final solutions but relative certainty that conflicts and doubts might be straightened out if addressed in a *democratic* rather than an *authoritative* way. In this new concept of knowledge, one does not start with universal doubt leading to the fixation of some unchangeable principles, but, as Peirce maintains *pace* Descartes, with all the prejudices which one actually has. This is because personal certainty is not an issue here, social agreement is:

> In sciences in which men come to agreement, when a theory has been broached it is considered to be on probation until this agreement is reached. After it is reached, the question of certainty becomes an idle one, because there is no one left who doubts it. (Peirce 1867, 141)

This new certainty is not a "provisional" state of "no doubt for now" but lies in the dialogical nature of the whole enterprise in which, in the case of doubt, one will strive for a new equilibrium not because there is some external guarantee for this, as Popper's version of Peirce's fallibilism suggests, but because there are no *external* obstacles to it, such as somebody's claim for authority. In this way, the original tragedy, or path of despair, as Hegel describes it in the introduction to the *Phenomenology of Spirit*, is transformed into a cautiously optimistic enterprise in which something positive can be achieved *because* it has been achieved before, though in an imperfect way.

This makes knowledge an essentially historic achievement. The historicity of knowledge in which past failures become an inherent part of today's truths cannot be itself positively given, but is only part of the whole dramatic *emplotment*, in which, as Terry Eagleton said in his *Hope without Optimism*, "we are responsible for the past as well as for the present". The reason is a rather pessimistic or tragic one, if we are dealing in absolutes. The point, of course, is that we should not deal in absolutes:

> The dead cannot be resurrected; but there is a tragic form of hope whereby they can be invested with new meaning, interpreted otherwise, woven into a narrative which they themselves could not have foretold, so that even the most inconspicuous of them will be, so to speak, mentioned in dispatches of the Last Day. (Eagleton 2015, 33)

By "dead", here, we can mean people as in the tragedy of the Holocaust, but "facts" as well, in the sense of beliefs we have held for true but do not hold them anymore because they turned out to be at variance with the body of socially moderated knowledge. This overall dramatization of our past shows why poetry, as Aristotle said, is more philosophical and graver than history in treating things as they might be rather than merely as they have been.

The standard and popular readings of Hegel's arguments, especially his master slave parable, as known influentially from Kojève's or Fukuyama's interpretations, are fine if understood as examples of such a dramatization. But read exclusively, in the allegorical way, in which the given combat stands only for another form of combat such as class or civilizational struggles, they become exactly that which Hegel's dramatic concept of knowledge, at least in my reading, tried to avoid: namely the pitfalls of *false positivity*. Marx and Engel's futuristic readings of Hegel's work as well as the false modesty of Popper's *falsificationism* that knows one cannot know (or, alternatively, knows that one is nearer the truth than those before him), are examples of such an approach that believes in the given method – or *art* – rather than the *socially subjugated* eye of beholder.

7 Conclusion

"O sun, clearing the clouds from troubled sight,
You make me so contented with your answers
That, much as knowledge pleases, so does doubt"
(Dante 2014, Canto XI, 91-3).[3]

My final suggestion is that to fully appreciate Hegel's dramatic theory of knowledge, one may follow Scruton's advice (in the similar context of reading Wagner's mythological tetralogy as a story of self-consciousness) and reject the *allegoric readings* of "I am the combat" because they add "nothing to our experience of drama", instead giving favor to more fruitful, *symbolic readings*. This is because, as Scruton puts it, "symbolism is distinguished from allegory in that the symbol both expresses a meaning and also adds to it, so that meaning and symbol are to a measure inseparable" (Scruton 2017, 188). What has been added to the very concept of combat, here, are the indirect, or figurative ways of reading quite in accord with how Hegel's original combat "to the death" is to be read. Rather than the biological death of an animal, what is meant here are the social or cultural variants of death, such as the possible loss of one's social status, job, self-respect, etc.

---

3   O sol che sani ogni vista turbata, / tu mi contenti sì quando tu solvi, / che, non men che saver, dubbiar m'aggrata.

It is no coincidence, I believe, that the parable of master and death occurs relatively soon in Hegel's text, in fact, almost too soon, before the Spirit is completely socialized, evoking doubts whether it deals with socialization itself.[4] The point, however, should not be that there are various conflicting readings, such as the psychological one (the combat of the mind and the body), the historical one (the conflict of slaveholder and slaves, be it in ancient Greece or on Haiti),[5] the political one (Marx's and Fukuyama's readings belong here), or the didactical one in which the role of master and slave correspond to that of the teacher and his pupil.[6] The point is that Hegel systematically entertains this variety of such readings throughout *Phenomenology*, thus meeting directly Scruton's definition of symbolic representation which by "condensing many meanings into a single symbol [...] enables each meaning to cast light on all the others, so that the symbol shows us the moral reality that unites them" (Scruton 2017, 188).

The series of other combats, as met by the Spirit on his path of desperation, such as between the knight of virtue and the way of the world, Antigone and Creon, or the hardhearted judge and the penitent doer are examples of this, with the "moral reality that unites them" being the renunciation of some immediate pleasure for the benefit of the bigger good. One of the most ultimate meanings of this is represented by the Savior's warning that those who wish to save their life will lose it (Matt. 16:25).

In fact, one should keep in mind that it was religious context in which Hegel's above quoted combat parable was introduced. Along these lines, of course, one can read the whole fallibility of knowledge as a symbolic sequel to the Biblical story of original sin and our desire to *know* rather than to stay in the primordial state of the unmediated certainty. The tragic path of our knowledge or, in Hegel's terms, the Golgotha of the Spirit, thus ends up with the magic of the *Speculative Good Friday* in which, via the *speculative sentence* of "God is Dead", one arrives at the insight that it is because of this death that he can be kept alive, at least two thousand years after that.[7]

---

4 See Stekeler-Weithofer 2008.
5 See Buck-Morss 2000.
6 See Kolman 2019.
7 According to Hegel, the speculative sentence is that in which "common opinion [...] learns from experience that it means something other than what it took itself to have meant, and this correction of its opinion compels knowing to come back to the proposition and now to grasp it in some other way" (Hegel 2018, 40).

Another layer belonging to the symbolic meaning of Hegel's words is the dramatic form itself, which, if we agree with Hegel that art is the sensuous manifestation (*Scheinen*) of truth, makes explicit that even in subjective matters of liking one cannot rely on the immediate feeling but must overcome the immediate pleasure for a bigger gain of the universal taste. One can, e.g., listen to music just to satisfy one's biological needs or simple desires for a regular beat or for established conventions such as traditional keys or cadences. Or postpone these direct satisfactions, as exploited *ad nauseam* in mass culture, by a variety of means such as syncopation, modulations, different progressions of chords, etc., thus arriving, by further opposition between the established canon and the (relatively) admissible exceptions, to true freedom within the limits of our immediate emotive nature and its continual transformation into the mediated immediacy of a healthy social life. As such, as Dewey put it, works of art would become both the "signs of a unified collective life" and the "aids in the creation of such a life" (Dewey 1934, 79, 81).

These aids might be a systematic way of postponing the combat itself by rehearsing it in relatively harmless ways where risks, at first, are relatively low, but the benefits grow the more one is prepared to invest in them. The main benefit here, one might say, is art's *condensing* quality which allows us to see things in interconnected, holistic ways, thus providing greater stability and certainty to the tragic occurrences of our lives. One of these benefits is art's ability to manifest experience's autopoietic features by being manifestly autopoietic itself, i.e., by having no other aims than to develop itself according to its own standards which include setting limits rich enough to be fruitfully violated later. This primordial conflict is, in fact, traditionally connected to the dramatic forms of tragedy and comedy that, in Hegel's system, thematize the inhering conflicts of our *conditio humana* as both necessary and contingent. But this is in accord with our previous treating of fallibility as a situation in which one can fail and even must fail if one ever wants to have knowledge.

References

Alberti, Leon Battista. 2014. *Della Pittura – Über die Malkunst*, edited by Oskar Bätschmann, and Sandra Gienfreda. Darmstandt: WBG.

Alighieri, Dante. 2014. *Inferno*. Translated by J. G. Nichols. London: Hesperus Press.

Brandom, Robert. 2011. *Perspectives on Pragmatism*. Cambridge, MA: Harvard University Press.

Buck-Morss, Susan. 2000. "Hegel and Haiti". *Critical Inquiry* 26 (4): 821–65.

Clark, Christopher. 2007. *Iron Kingdom: The Rise and Downfall of Prussia 1600–1947*. London: Penguin Books.

Dewey, John. 1929. *Experience and Nature*. London: George Allen and Unwin.

Dewey, John. 1934. *Art as Experience*. New York: Perigee Books.

Eagleton, Terry. 2015. *The Hope without Optimism*. New Haven, CT: Yale University Press.

Edgerton, Samuel Y. 2009. *The Mirror, the Window, and the Telescope: How Renaissance Linear Perspective Changed Our Vision of the Universe*. London: Cornell University Press.

Hegel, Georg Wilhelm Friedrich. 1986. *Vorlesungen über die Philosophie der Religion I*. Frankfurt am Main: Suhrkamp.

Hegel, Georg Wilhelm Friedrich. 2001. *Philosophy of Right*. Translated by S. W. Dyde. Kitchener: Batoche Books.

Hegel, Georg Wilhelm Friedrich. 2007. *Philosophy of Mind*. Translated by William Wallace, and A. V. Miller. Oxford: Clarendon Press.

Hegel, Georg Wilhelm Friedrich. 2018. *The Phenomenology of Spirit*. Translated by Terry Pinkard. Cambridge: Cambridge University Press.

James, William. 1997. "The Will to Believe". In *Pragmatism. A Reader*, edited by Louis Menand. New York: Vintage Books.

Kolman, Vojtěch. 2019. "Master, Slave and Wittgenstein: The Dialectic of Rule-Following". In *Wittgenstein and Hegel. Reevaluation of Difference*, edited by Alexander Berg, and Jakub Mácha, 227–42. Berlin: de Gruyter.

Mure, G. R. G. 1966. "Hegel, Luther, and the Owl of Minerva". *Philosophy* 41 (156): 127–39.

Newton, Isaac. 1995. *The Principia*. Translated by Andrew Motte. New York: Prometheus Books.

Peirce, Charles Sanders. 1867. "Some Consequences of Four Incapacities". *The Journal of Speculative Philosophy* 1: 140–57.

Scruton, Roger. 2017. *The Ring of Truth: The Wisdom of Wagner's Ring of the Nibelung*. London: Penguin Books.

Steiner, George. 1984. *Antigones: How the Antigone Legend Has Endured in Western Literature, Art, and Thought*. New Haven, CT: Yale University Press.

Stekeler-Weithofer, Pirmin. 2008. "Wer ist der Herr, wer ist der Knecht? Der Kampf zwischen Denken und Handeln als Grundform". In *Hegels Phänomenologie des Geistes. Ein kooperativer Kommentar zu einem Schlüsselwerk der Moderne*, edited by Klaus Vieweg, and Wolfgang Welsch, 205–37. Frankfurt am Main: Suhrkamp.

Wittgenstein, Ludwig. 1958. *Philosophical Investigations*. Translated by G. E. M. Anscombe. Oxford: Blackwell.

Wittgenstein, Ludwig. 2002. *Tractatus logico-philosophicus*. Translated by D. F. Pears and B. F. McGuinness. London, New York: Routledge.

Part 2
Narratives of Self-Creation and Self-Destruction

Autopoiesis and "Pure Culture of Death Instinct": Creativity as a Suicidal Project

Josef Vojvodík

> *Friend, let this be enough; if you wish more to read*
> *Go and become yourself the writ and that which is.*
> Angelus Silesius

> *It was a song from the abyss and once heard it opened an abyss in every*
> *utterance and powerfully enticed whoever heard it to disappear into that abyss.*
> Maurice Blanchot

Since Greek antiquity, philosophers and poets have known of a certain tension between the creative life and melancholy. In the *Problemata physica*, a fragmentary collection of short treatises attributed to Aristotle, philosophers and artists are characterized as melancholic heroes who lead a valiant but tragic existence, overshadowed by the eternal darkness of night, by the void:

> Why is it that all those who have become eminent in philosophy or politics or poetry or the arts are clearly of an atrabilious temperament, and some of them to such an extent as to be affected by diseases caused by black bile, as is said to have happened to Heracles among the heroes? [...] Any many others of the heroes seem to have been similarly afflicted, and among men of recent times Empedocles, Plato, and Socrates, and numerous other well–known men, and also most of the poets. (Aristotle 1984, 226)

This essay is an attempt to reconstruct the relationship between creative forms of self-realization and the suicidal "Pure Culture of Death Instinct" (Freud [1923] 1960, 54–5). In this sense, tragic autopoiesis figures as a lethal, sometimes fatal, vicious circle of self-construction and self-destruction, the kind of tragic symmetry of fates that unites Péter Szondi and Paul Celan. Péter Szondi (1929–71) was the son of Hungarian physician and psychiatrist Léopold Szondi, whose work in depth psychology led him to develop the theory and method of *fate analysis* (*Schicksalsanalyse*). A comparativist and theorist of literary hermeneutics and interpreter of *dark poetry*, Péter Szondi committed suicide in October 1971 in a manner identical to that of his friend, the poet Paul Celan (1920–70), with whose work Szondi was closely engaged. The links between Szondi and Celan that make up this *symmetry of fates* are numerous and unsettling: both were of Central European-Jewish descent; both experienced persecution during the war; both worked in a poetics characterized by aesthetic *passion*; both suffered from crippling depression; both died by drowning – a mirror – identical death.

At the beginning of Hermann Burger's novel *Die künstliche Mutter* (*The Artificial Mother*) from 1982, the protagonist, Wolfram Schöllkopf, learns he will be laid off from his job as associate professor of German literature and glaciology (the science of glaciers and natural phenomena involving ice) at the Institute of Technology in Zurich. He entertains the idea of committing suicide by jumping from the third floor over the university courtyard. In addition to the trauma of losing his job, he is plagued by a chronic illness that he characterizes as a *migraine of the genitals*, an illness that makes his sex life impossible and his daily existence miserable. A sudden heart attack turns Schöllkopf's mind away from suicide, and he decides, through various turns in the story, to subject himself to an (ultimately ineffective) psychotherapy treatment conducted by a secret society at the *Artificial Mother* clinic located in the abandoned Swiss Army tunnels of the Saint-Gotthard Massif. Schöllkopf's aim is to revive himself, or more aptly, reinvent himself under the literary pseudonym Armando, but what he discovers there are possibilities of creativity and ingenuity hitherto undreamed of, beyond the boundaries of ordinary linguistic expression. These open up a space for artistic self-determination – and, simultaneously, artificial reality – outside the natural world of social bonds and relations. Schöllkopf, alias Armando, will spend the last two summer months of his life in Lugano in a state of narcissistic-ecstatic intoxication where he alone is the subject, speaker, and audience of his monologues.

Most of Burger's works revolve around the question of death, a through line that begins with his very first prose text and continues to *Tractatus logico-suicidalis* (1988), a collection of aphorisms that was his last published work. It is as if the whole of his literary (self-) creation were simply a confirmation of Walter Benjamin's assertion in "The Paris of the Second Empire in Baudelaire":

> Modernity must stand under the sign of suicide, an act which seals a heroic will that makes no concession to a mentality inimical toward this will. Such a resignation is not resignation but heroic passion. It is the achievement of modernity in the realm of the passions. (Benjamin [1938] 2006, 104)

Just as Benjamin carries on the age-old tradition of heroizing death, identifying it as the "signature of modernity", so too does Burger carry on the Platonic tradition of philosophical existence as *ars philosophandi*, and with it the notion of *ars moriendi*.

While Schöllkopf-Armando never commits suicide by jumping from his university window, Burger himself, on 28 February 1989, would take his own life by overdosing on sleeping tablets. It was the death of a writer who understood his work not only as a form of existence, but as a process of self-creation through words, a process that carried with it both the opportunity and risk of becoming a "man made only of words". It is in these terms that Burger beckons to the reader in an essay of the same title ("Der Mann der nur aus Wörtern besteht", 1968): "Come with me! Come with me to the realm of words! Come with me and become a man who consists only of words!" (Burger 1983, 240).[1] In Hermann Burger (1942–89) were combined the sensibilities of a literary scholar, associate professor of German literature, poet and novelist. He was, we can safely say, the very model of *autopoietic* self-constitution by means of intense self-reflection, and by way of explicitly autobiographical subject matter. In this, of course, he was not alone, nor is it difficult to find similar examples: a literary scholar, for instance, who also produced literary works, or an art scholar who produced art. In Burger's semi-autobiographical fictional works, however, the theme of self-constitution is closely intertwined with that of self-destruction, in a manner reminiscent of the works

---

1   Komm mit! Komm mit ins Reich der Wörter! Komm mit und werde ein Mann, der nur aus Wörtern besteht!

of Heinrich von Kleist (his favourite author). If Burger seems particularly representative of this kind of gesture it is also by virtue of his intense reflections on the relationship between the literary text and its critical and scholarly reception. At the end of his lecture on "Poetic and Scholarly Language", delivered on 15 February 1983 at the *Hochschule für Wirtschafts- und Sozialwissenschaften* in St. Gallen, Burger states:

> Whether I base my work – and it's not so long ago one spoke of an "art of interpretation" – on a given text or on the non-linguistic reality of my experiences, emotions, memories, or dreams, creativity plays an equally important role. The discoveries of the writer correspond to the investigations of the scholar, the concept to the method – one takes its place in relation to the other. It is only primary and secondary literature that should never cross paths. The pursuit of understanding and interpretation are diametrically opposed to *poēsis*, which means creating, making. The ideal reader, writes Novalis, is an extension of the author, extending and illuminating that realm on whose darkness the *opus* is nourished.[2] (Burger 2010, 40)

The invitation that is extended to us by this "man made only of words" – "Come with me! Come with me to the realm of words!" – is also a challenge. It dares us to enter a space of seclusion between the extremes of life and death, an existence poised between painstaking virtuosity and loss of control, between the balancing act and the precipitous fall, between the loss of self and its creation in the written text. As author of a study on the poetry of Paul Celan (Burger 1974), Burger knew that the "realm of words" is also a treacherous domain of the unspeakable, of silence and enigma, into which the poet can only enter using his word-key. It is a key with which, as Celan writes in his poem *With a Variable Key* (*Mit wechselndem Schlüssel*), "you unlock the house in which drifts the

---

2 Ob ich bei meiner Arbeit – und es ist noch gar nicht so lange her, da hat man von einer "Kunst der Interpretation" gesprochen– von einem gegebenen Text oder von der außersprachlichen Realität meiner Erfahrungen, Emotionen, Erinnerungen, Träume ausgehe: Der Einsatz von Kreativität bleibt gleich hoch, der Sachermittlung des Wissenschaftlers entspricht die Recherche des Schriftstellers, der Methode die Konzeption, das eine hat neben dem anderen Platz, nur in die Quere kommen sollten sich Primär– und Sekundärliteratur nicht. Das Verstehen- und Deutenwollen ist der – was heißt das Machen, Verfertigen – diametral entgegengesetzt. Der ideale Leser, sagt Novalis, sei der erweiterte Autor. Er erweitert und erhellt ihn um jene Zone, von deren Dunkel sich das opus nährt.

snow of that left unspoken". Access to this house is invariably associated with the experience of injury and pain:

Mit wechselndem Schlüssel
schließt du das Haus auf, darin
der Schnee des Verschwiegenen treibt.
Je nach dem Blut, das dir quillt
aus Aug oder Mund oder Ohr,
wechselt dein Schlüssel.
Wechselt dein Schlüssel, wechselt das Wort,
das treiben darf mit den Flocken.
Je nach dem Wind, der dich fortstößt,
ballt um das Wort sich der Schnee. (Celan 2003, 74)

With a variable key
you unlock the house in which
drifts the snow of that left unspoken.
Always what key you choose
depends on the blood that spurts
from your eye or your mouth or your ear.
You vary the key, you vary the word
that is free to drift with the flakes.
What snowball will form round the word
depends on the wind that rebuffs you. (Celan 1972, 39)

In his analysis of Celan's poem, Burger writes:

With bleeding eye, ear and mouth, the poet also experiences and articulates, before even commencing with his poetic work, a kind of bleeding language – bleeding in the sense of an injured and "open" language. The variable key opens not only the house of the silenced, but also, as is clearly stated at the beginning of the second stanza, the house of language.[3] (Burger 1974, 89)

---

3   Mit dem blutüberströmten Auge, dem Ohr und dem Mund erfährt und artikuliert der Dichter, noch bevor er zur poetischen Gestaltung ansetzt, auch eine blutende Sprache, und zwar im doppelten Sinne: eine verletzte und eine "offene" Sprache. Der wechselnde Schlüssel erschließt nicht nur das Haus des Verschwiegenen, sondern auch, wie der Anfang der zweiten Strophe deutlich sagt, das Haus der Sprache.

Poetic creation, as a form of self-reconstruction by means of an aesthetic act based on language ("the house in which / drifts the snow of that left unspoken"),[4] engenders a form of mental space. However, this creative activity seems to be overshadowed at all times by the idea of self-destruction, and through it a consciousness of the agonistic Self. Snow drifts not only through this poem but through the whole of Celan's works (a collection of seventy poems from 1967–8 was given the title *Schneepart*, or *Snow Part*). Snow is a cipher standing not only for silence and ineffability, but also cold, mortality, lifelessness, death and the dead, as we find in the final poem *Inselhin* (22 June 1954): "masters of ice and stone" ("Meister vom Eis und vom Stein"; Celan 2003, 88). Silvio Vietta has shown how this is related to the characteristically romantic theme of nihilism (1992, 182–4), conveyed by metaphors of dormant light, cold and ice, as in Caspar David Friedrich's celebrated painting *The Sea of Ice: The Wreck of the Hope* (1823–4). The painting depicts a ship buried in huge ice floes, a terrifying symbol of human desolation and the glaciation of the world. In Celan's poem *Weggebeizt* (*Etched Away From*), the "realm of words" is imagined in geophysical terms as "the hospitable / glacier rooms and tables" (Celan 1972, 84),[5] a realm of unadulterated spirituality and words of crystalline clarity, a realm beyond the human. However, this *point suprême* of poetry is a non-human realm of pure negativity: "Whirled / clear, free / your way through the human shaped snow, / the penitents' snow" (Celan 1972, 84). The whiteness of snow becomes a signature of the nothingness and "cosmic negation", as Gaston Bachelard writes in *The Poetics of Space*: "snow covers all tracks, blurs the road, muffles every sound, conceals all colors. As a result of this universal whiteness, we feel a form of cosmic negation in action" (Bachelard 1994, 40–1). Bachelard quotes from Rimbaud's *Les déserts de l'amour*: "It was like a winter's night, with snow to stifle the world for certain" ("C'était comme une nuit d'hiver, avec une neige pour étouffer le monde décidément"; Bachelard 1994, 40–1).

In his renowned book *Abstraction and Empathy: A Contribution to the Psychology of Style* (*Abstraktion und Einfühlung. Ein Beitrag zur*

---

4   Jean Firges (1962, 263) interprets the motifs of "house" and "key" in Celan's poem in relation to Heidegger's proposition in his "Letter on Humanism": "Language is the house of Being. In its home man dwells. Those who think and those who create with words are the guardians of this home. Their guardianship accomplishes the manifestation of Being insofar as they bring the manifestation to language and maintain it in language through their speech" (Heidegger 1977, 193).

5   "zu den gastlichen / Gletscherstuben und "tischen" (Celan 2003, 180–1).

Stilpsychologie) – a book that would prove influential on the development of artistic modernism – Wilhelm Worringer considers a principle of
abstraction (the "urge to abstraction" or "Abstraktionsdrang") that aims
at the *purification* of life:

> the urge to abstraction finds its beauty in the life-denying inorganic, in
> the crystalline or, in general terms, in all abstract law and necessity. [...]
> The simplest formula that expresses this kind of aesthetic experience
> runs: Aesthetic enjoyment is objectified self-enjoyment. To enjoy aesthet-
> ically means to enjoy myself in a sensuous object diverse from myself, to
> empathize myself into it. (Worringer [1908] 1997, 4–5)

Abstraction as a principle of modernity finds its most intense expression in inorganic crystalline forms. According to Siegfried K. Lang, the
exclusionary aspect of the biosphere represents "a creative variant of the
instinct of death, one that, in fiction dealing with 'small deaths', anticipates the inevitable great death" (Lang 2002, 101).[6]

Even more radically, Maurice Blanchot considers the connection
between life and writing, between life and creation, to be a risky one.
He speaks of a certain ambivalence, and of the proximity of writing (and
creation) to death.[7] This is one of the main themes of his book *The Space
of Literature* (*L'espace littéraire*, 1955), especially the fourth chapter, *The
Work and Death's Space*. Here, the elementary experience and essence of
literature is this experience of nothingness, creeping continuously and
inescapably into the rift between speaker and the spoken, as Blanchot
writes in his essay "Literature and the Right to Death" ("La littérature et
le droit à la mort"):

> Language can only begin with the void; no fullness, no certainty can ever
> speak; something essential is lacking in anyone who expresses himself.
> Negation is tied to language. When I first begin, I do not speak in order
> to say something, rather a nothing demands to speak, nothing speaks,
> nothing finds its being in speech and the being of speech is nothing.
> (Blanchot [1948] 1999b, 381)

---

6   Der Abstraktionstrieb entpuppt sich als schöpferische Variante des Todestriebes, der in der
     Fiktion der "kleinen Tode" den unausweichlichen großen Tod vorwegnimmt.

7   It should be added that Blanchot's interpretation of the alliance between literature (as writ-
     ing) and death is influenced by Hegel's idea of the end of art – albeit in the form of a concept
     distinctly Blanchot's, especially in the essay "Literature and the Right to Death".

Perhaps writing, artistic creation, and artistic existence in the broadest sense are all connected to what Wilhelm Szilasi calls "dangerous being" ("gefährliches Dasein") in his book *Power and Powerlessness of the Mind* (*Macht und Ohnmacht des Geistes*). "The melancholy artist", he writes, "must endure the oppressive 'no further' with every completion and glimpse into the translucent incomprehensibility of being, which renders every completion incomplete" (Szilasi 1946, 302–3). At the end of the book, Szilasi returns to the melancholy of creators and philosophers and sees in it the intrinsic essence of both the philosophical and poetic existence. Melancholy places the philosopher, like the artist, in a situation of isolation and disappearance from the world ("Verschwinden für diese Welt"), or else it causes the world itself to disappear ("Verschwindenlassen der Welt"; Szilasi 1946, 302). Melancholy, however, plays a role in founding what Szilasi calls the "power of the spirit" ("Macht des Geistes"), a power that arises, paradoxically, from the very state of helplessness – or, more precisely, from the *renunciation* of one's own power. The idea that creativity has a potential, as it becomes more intense, to change into self-destruction – or more aptly, that it has a role in sublimating and delaying suicide (however futile) – are ideas that have a singular place in the philosophy of life of the 20th century. In the introduction to his book *Levels of Organic Life and the Human* (*Die Stufen des Organischen und der Mensch*), Helmuth Plessner writes, "Modern times culminated in the concept of life; [...] life, the demonically playful and unconsciously creative" (Plessner [1928] 2019, 1).[8]

There is another commonality that unites Burger, Celan, and Szondi. In addition to the fact that each of these authors chose to die by their own hand, they also prove quite difficult to classify, except perhaps for a common solitude, authenticity, personal charisma, and ultimately a tragic broken spirit. Burger's dissertation, which he wrote on Celan's poetry, as well as his own novels and poems in prose, reveal the extent of Celan's influence on his work. It was not only Celan's poetry or poetic language that shaped Burger, but also the world of his poetry: a closed and solipsistic *world concept*. Burger is also linked to Szondi through

---

8 The philosopher Alfred Seidel (1895–1924) writes on creativity as a "sublimation of suicide" in fragments published by his estate. After his suicide, Seidel's book *Consciousness as Doom* (*Bewusstsein als Verhängnis*, 1927) was published by Hans Prinzhorn. In a comprehensive introduction to Seidel's book, Hans Prinzhorn also deals with the context of the pessimistic philosophy of life ("Lebensphilosophie"), which was for Seidel – as for Schopenhauer – essential for his thinking, via Ludwig Klages, Georg Simmel, and initially Oswald Spengler (Prinzhorn 1927, 46–68).

Emil Staiger, the *Doktorvater* under whom Szondi completed his studies and dissertation *Theory of the Modern Drama* (*Theorie des modernen Dramas*, 1956). Burger too would complete his studies under Staiger, with a work on Celan's poetry (1973). Despite the fact that Szondi chose a different scholarly path, as he indicated in his dissertation, the trajectory of his career would diverge from Staiger's only in its ideological and methodological framework, and in terms of their mutual sympathy.[9] He mentions Staiger's habilitation thesis, *The Spirit of Love and Destiny: Schelling, Hegel and Hölderlin* (*Der Geist der Liebe und das Schicksal. Schelling, Hegel und Hölderlin*, 1935), in the first sentence of his own habilitation thesis, *An Essay on the Tragic* (*Versuch über das Tragische*). We might be inclined to see this as no more than a gesture of courtesy, except that the problem of destiny, of tragic fate, is also essential for Szondi's thinking – and not only in terms of his theory of the tragic.[10] It is this kind of tragic autopoiesis, as a lethal, sometimes fatal, vicious circle of self-construction and self-destruction that unites Szondi and Celan in a tragic symmetry of destinies.

1 Suddenness, Shock, Trauma: Between Self-Creation and Self-Destruction

"The main question underlying this research would be under what conditions can de-paradoxization be developed productively instead of pathologically or as a creative instead of a vicious circle" (Luhmann 1988a, 34).

Danger, risk, the proximity of death, these bestow a special character on every act of courage, on every adventure, including the creative act. In his study on the psychology of trauma, "Event and Experience" ("Geschehnis und Erlebnis"), neurologist and psychiatrist Erwin Straus offers the example of a climber who risks his life at every step, but who experiences his journey as a unique extension of the boundaries of his being. It is as if the proximity of death was a prerequisite for the possibility of such an experience – as if this awareness of impermanence compelled the artist to engage in acts of creative self-realization, cross borders, and

---

9   Andreas Isenschmid deals with the relationship between Péter Szondi and Emil Staiger (2006, 173–88).

10   Daniel Weidner (2015, 55–69) deals with Szondi's conception of the tragic in relation to that of Benjamin.

forge new ground. The flip side of this creative self-realization, however, is "a pure culture of the death instinct", as Sigmund Freud characterizes melancholy.[11] What is at stake here, in other words, is a strong propensity for depression that intensifies and transforms into self-destruction. According to Straus, this occurs because the creative process ultimately distances the creator from his creation, resulting in alienation, disappearance, and isolation, tearing the creator, at the moment of consummation, from the realm of "timeless being" (the creative act as such) and thrusting him back into the flow of life and time that imprison him:

> The realm of timeless being, which the individual touches in the moment of the deed, disappears from him as soon as the work has come into being and the deed has been accomplished. He remains imprisoned by life and by time. Just as the form is exposed to perishing and the work to destruction, so too the creative individual – already in the moment of consummation – sinks back into the flow of everyday events. His work leaves him behind; he cannot hold it. [...] It is inevitable that the creator outlives his work, that is, in the moment in which he completes the work he has already lost it. The good fortune of accomplishment and concentrated experiencing are followed by collapse. The whole of his own being, which he was close to in the one moment, vanishes again and leaves him in a state of doubt, of emptiness, and of disappointment. For this reason many drag out and delay the conclusion.[12] (Straus [1930] 1982, 82-3)

In Benjamin's allegory of modernity, the twin experiences of loss and shock together forge the physiognomy of modernity: its medium is cinema, which presents its own principle of shock, as well as the traces of an aura that has been lost. In Benjamin's theory, shock is a formal principle of film, as he argues in his essay "The Work of Art in the Age of Its Technological Reproducibility" ("Das Kunstwerk im Zeitalter seiner technischen Reproduzierbarkeit"):

---

11 "What is now holding sway in the super–ego is, as it were, a pure culture of the death instinct, and in fact it often enough succeeds in driving the ego into death, if the latter does not fend off its tyrant in time by the change round into mania" (Freud [1923] 1960, 54-5). According to Freud, the super–ego gains destructive power over the melancholic Self, transformed by narcissistic identification with a lost love object.

12 According to Maurice Blanchot in "The Essential Solitude", to write means "to surrender oneself to the fascination of the absence of time. Here we are undoubtedly approaching the essence of solitude" (Blanchot 1999a, 410).

It thereby fostered the demand for film, since the distracting element in film is also primarily tactile, being based on successive changes of scene and focus which have a percussive effect on the spectator. *Film has freed the physical shock effect – which Dadaism had kept wrapped, as it were, inside the moral shock effect – from this wrapping.* [...] Film, by virtue of its shock effects, is predisposed to this form of reception. In this respect, too, it proves to be the most important subject matter, at present, for the theory of perception which the Greeks called aesthetics. (Benjamin [1935] 2006a, 119–20)

Mortification precedes the return of the (seemingly) living image, as seen by the viewer. For Benjamin, cinema is therefore an eminently ambiguous and ambivalent medium, whose action – as a series of successive fragmented allegorical images projected by light onto the screen – performs the act of interpretation in the same terms as his theory of melancholy: the return and *resurrection* (of what is lost, of the past) must be preceded by death and loss. In his essay "On Some Motifs in Baudelaire" ("Über einige Motive bei Baudelaire"), which was published less than a year before his suicide (26 September 1940) and was his last publication during his lifetime, Benjamin returns to the principle of shock from a different perspective, this time in connection to the aura, the auratic gaze (in Baudelaire and Proust), and melancholy. After citing verses from Baudelaire's poem *Craving for Oblivion* (*Le Goût du néant*) – "Et le Temps m'engloutit minut par minut, / Comme la neige immense un corps pris de roideur" ("Moment by moment, Time envelops me / like a stiffening body buried in the snow"; Baudelaire 1982, 78) – Benjamin provides a few sentences of commentary that are now well-known: "In spleen, time is reified: the minutes cover a man like snowflakes. This time is history-less, like that of the *mémoire involontaire*. But in spleen the perception of time is supernaturally keen. Every second finds consciousness ready to intercept its shock" (Benjamin [1939] 2006b, 200–1).

Trauma and shock can have more universal, existential meanings. Erwin Straus, the psychiatrist mentioned above, was the first to point out the temporal dimension of traumatic experience in his study "Event and Experience". According to Straus, the experience of accidents and certain incidents is connected with the universal theme of death; it is this association that causes trauma. When trauma occurs, however, certain meanings enter into existence at the moment of the accident that will forever carry connotations of a distinctly existential nature. In such cases, Straus argues, the shock delivered by our experience of the world constitutes a historical modality, in the sense that something happens "for the first time". For Straus, the effect of trauma is produced only to the extent of the suddenness and immediacy with which a traumatic event enters our world, and transforms it in some fundamental way (Straus 1978, 21–2). Based on phenomenology, and with a focus on temporally structured experiences and suddenness as mechanism of the existential, Straus's theory of trauma and traumatization will remind us of the theory of shock presented by Benjamin in his essay "On Some Motifs in Baudelaire". Straus also captures the characteristic duality of suddenness: its prospective aspect that looks towards the future, in combination with a retrospective aspect that looks to the past (Straus 1978, 34). Straus's psychological-phenomenological theory of suddenness also seems to confirm the phenomenon of traumatic suddenness that Karl Heinz Bohrer identifies in the aesthetic mode of modernity.[13]

The notion that depression is intrinsically related to creativity may also have a bearing on the paradoxical tension that arises between states of autonomous self-creation and outside influences, such as the almost phobic "anxiety of influence" described by Harold Bloom (*The Anxiety of Influence: A Theory of Poetry*, 1973). What is at stake here, however, is not merely the anxiety of influence, but a confrontation with the Self – Pascal's "moi haïssable" ("The self is hateful"; Pascal 1999, 118), and with the Other. It is a paradoxical double bind between positivity and negativity, fullness and emptiness, passivity and activity, self-creation and self-destruction, in the same way that Niklas Luhmann characterises "self-reference" in relation to "external-reference" (Luhmann 2007, 137–58).

As Luhmann tells us, it is at the end of the 19th century that the "semantic career of the concept of creativity" ("Semantische Kariere des Begriffs der Kreativität") began. Creativity, he writes, is nothing more than "democratically distorted genius" (Luhmann 1988, 16), and thus:

> The trio new–significant–surprising remains, but the demands are reduced. Anyone who has talent and cares enough can lead a creative life. He needs a long breath and, of course, a fixed destination. With this

---

13 Karl Heinz Bohrer (1994) deals with the phenomenon of *suddenness* as an aesthetic category of modernity. As Bohrer shows, this notion dates back to Romanticism, and was given conceptual consistency by Nietzsche. It was conceptualized and aestheticised in literature by modernist writers of the 20th century (Joyce, Woolf, Kafka, Musil, Benjamin, Jünger, Breton, etc.). According to Bohrer, the suddenness associated with aesthetic negativity is interpreted by the category of the "negative moment", as an inversion of the emphatic moment (in modern texts) and an attempt to save eternity in the face of agnostic modernity.

transition to small formats, and renunciation of the peculiar and exclusive, questions concerning the recognition of creativity are all the more acute.[14] (Luhmann 1988, 16)

Creative originality relies in large part on a commitment to take risks associated with chance, unpredictability, and experimentation. According to Luhmann, creativity is about "using coincidences to build structures" ("die Verwendung von Zufällen zum Aufbau von Strukturen"; Luhmann 1988, 17). Coincidences are events that occur and immediately disappear, even if they "resonate" in the system. Coincidences cannot be captured, "they can only be made into something else, by virtue of their own system of combinatory possibilities" (Luhmann 1988, 17). Coincidences also carry risks that, as Luhmann writes, involve contingent phenomenon. We are exposed to risk when we make certain time-bound decisions capable of wreaking damage – the kind of damage that might otherwise be avoided. And while one should try to avoid damage, such a maxim severely limits the scope of action, which is why, according to Luhmann, actions that are "risky" should be permitted (Luhmann 1991, 21).

Part of the self-description of the art system, according to Luhmann, is the principle of tautology and iteration: "The history of modern self-descriptions of the art system, from romanticism via the avant-garde up to postmodernism, can be subsumed under one perspective, as variation on a single theme" (Luhmann 2000, 303). Instead of the "end of art", it is as if avant-garde and postmodern art had entered the endlessly repeating vicious circle of arbitrary ideas and mere "art productions" as a specific form of self-negation:

The point is not to declare the end of art on the basis of convincing arguments, thereby setting an end to art. The self-negation of art is realized at the level of autopoietic operations in the form of art, so that art can continue. (Luhmann 2000, 296)

---

14   Kreativität scheint nichts Anderes zu sein als demokratisch deformierte Genialität. Die Dreiheit neu–bedeutend–überraschend bleibt erhalten, aber die Ansprüche werden abgesenkt. Wer immer Talent hat und sich Mühe gibt, kann es zur Kreativität bringen. Man braucht langen Atem und natürlich Planstellen. Mit diesem Übergang ins Kleinformatige, gar nicht mehr so Seltene und Exklusive, wird aber die Frage nach der Erkennbarkeit des Kreativen erst recht akut.

Modern art in the avant-garde era was also compelled to enter the vicious circle under the pressure of originality and innovation, with the avant-garde widening the boundaries of art to such an extent that the distinction between art and non-art was ultimately blurred.

2 Péter Szondi, Tragic Irony, and Reflection of Destinies

"Who would not linger in death before mirrors?" (Celan 2002, 11).[15]

Szondi's name is directly connected to the theme of destiny through his father, Léopold Szondi (1893–1986), who, following Freud's psychoanalytic theories, developed a form of depth psychology during the second half of the 1930s, first in Budapest and later in Zurich, called *fate analysis* (*Schicksalsanalyse*). In fate analysis, human freedom and free choice – as found, for example, in the contexts of vocation, friendship, love, but also illness and death – occupy a semantically constitutive position. In November 1971, Szondi's notion of genotropic determinism would be tragically fulfilled in the case of his own son Péter, whose body was pulled from Lake Hallensee near Berlin after he had gone missing for several weeks without any message or letter of farewell. A notebook with the names and dissertation topics of his doctoral students was found in his cloak. Péter Szondi chose the same method of suicide as the poet Paul Celan,[16] whom he had met in person in 1959. Szondi had been a staunch supporter and interpreter of Celan throughout the 1960s,[17] and dedicated one of his last studies – originally written in French under the title "L'herméneutique de Schleiermacher" (Szondi 1970, 141–55) – to

---

15 "wer säumte im Tod nicht vor Spiegeln?" (Celan 2003, 31).
16 Celan probably jumped into the Seine in Paris on 20 April 1970 from Pont Mirabeau. His body was discovered on 1 May 1970.
17 In 1960, Claire Goll, widow of the poet Yvan Goll, accused Paul Celan of libel for accusing her husband of plagiarism. This affair marked the last decade of Celan's life until his suicide (1970). After many years of intensive research, Barbara Wiedemann, the editor of Celan's poetry, published documents on this *affair* showing how the campaign launched by Claire Goll in the German press was linked to her own ambitions and strategies for publishing Yvan Goll's estate, on the one hand, much in line with a mentality that still prevailed in Germany at the turn of the 1950s and 1960s (Wiedemann 2000). Péter Szondi appeared in Celan's defense in the newspaper *Neue Zürcher Zeitung*, 19 November 1960, with the article "Anleihe oder Verleumdung? Zu einer Auseinandersetzung über Paul Celan" ("Borrowing or Slander? On the Dispute over Paul Celan"), where he sufficiently proves the absurdity of Claire Goll's slander.

Celan. What accounts for the tragic symmetry of their fates? Was it their shared Central European-Jewish background, the Nazi persecution? Was it a shared aesthetic passion and awareness of the tragic dialectic of modernity? Or was it a crippling depression, culminating in their mirror-image suicides?

At the age of twenty-three Szondi's writings were focused on the dialectical conception of history as a tension between connection and unity (in antiquity), and between connection and fragmentation (in modernity). We find these preoccupations, for example, in his term paper from the summer semester of 1952 on "Friedrich Schlegel and Romantic Irony" ("Friedrich Schlegel und die romantische Ironie"). Emil Staiger considered it to be a pre-eminent work by a scholar whose ideas had already reached maturity, and he recommended it for publication in the renowned Germanist magazine *Euphorion* (1954). Szondi quotes from Friedrich Schlegel's letter to his brother August Wilhelm in 1793, in which Schlegel describes *Hamlet* as a work on "heroic despair, that is to say, an infinite derangement of the very highest powers. [...] The very innermost heart of his existence is a fearful nothingness, contempt for the world and for himself" (Szondi 1986, 59). In his interpretation of Shakespeare's play, Schlegel refers to his own situation and that of his time. The early romantic subject is, as Szondi writes, the isolated subject, "thrown back upon itself and becoming an object for its own contemplation" (Szondi 1986, 61). The subject of romantic irony, which Schlegel defines as the "continuously fluctuating of self-creation and self-destruction" ("steter Wechsel von Selbstschöpfung und Selbstvernichtung"; Schlegel 1991, 24), is a subject divided between the world and the self, between a desire for unity and a desire for an infinite world, between *self-creation* (*Selbstschöpfung*) and *self-destruction* (*Selbstvernichtung*), between the will and disbelief. Already in this early treatise, we find the central theme of Szondi's life and literary work: not only a fascination with fragments and fragmentation,[18] but also a keen sensitivity for the tragic moment when self-confidence and self-reflection intersect, when the philosopher's thought comes face to face with poetic sensibility. Szondi's *An Essay on the Tragic* is also written in fragmentary form. In it, the author offers his analyses of the tragic in the form of brief comments, rather than elaborating them into full interpretations. Similarly,

---

18   In a letter to Emil Staiger dated June 1967, Szondi wrote: "the fascination with fragments has not left me since I wrote a paper for your seminar fifteen years ago" (Szondi 1993, 226).

Szondi's *Introduction to Literary Hermeneutics* as well as his *Celan Studies* were left as unfinished fragments.

The notion of tragic irony also plays a role in Szondi's theory and philosophy of the tragic. He understands it rather as a dialectical phenomenon, namely as a modality of impending and actual destruction, a modality of dialectical nature. This is the moment of tragic-ironic reversal, when the tragic hero, in order to secure his salvation, embarks on a journey that will ensure his destruction. In the chapter devoted to Georg Simmel's reflection on "The Concept and the Tragedy of Culture" ("Der Begriff und die Tragödie der Kultur"), Szondi quotes a passage in which he sees a convincing formulation of tragic dialectics:

> In contrast to a sorrowful fate or one whose destructive force is external, we characterise a tragic fate as follows: The destructive powers directed toward a being arise from the deepest strata of this very being and, with its destruction, a fate takes place that is moored in the being itself and, so to speak, is the logical development of the very structure with the being constructed its own positivity. (Szondi [1964] 2002, 44)

Simmel's concept of culture is wedged between fixed forms of existence and the "flowing liveliness" ("strömende Lebendigkeit") that opposes them, which is to say between, on one hand, a subjective life constrained by time, and on the other, its contents: the motionless but timeless creations of the human spirit (*zeitlos*). In the midst of this dualism lies the idea of a culture that Simmel understands as "the soul's path to itself" ("der Weg der Seele zu sich selbst"; Simmel [1911] 2001, 194). This division of man between the *objective culture* of his material creations and works of art, but also religion, law, norms, science, technical achievements, and the *subjective culture* of human self-cultivation, constitutes a discrepancy between material meaning and values on one hand, and cultural meaning and values on the other. In modern times, this rift between objective culture and the subject has begun to widen, and Simmel also sees this as a tragic moment in modern culture: its self-destruction in the form of a boundless multiplication of its creations and achievements, one that can no longer be mastered. This is also due to the fact that "the inorganic purchase [...] of a book for a book, a work of art for a work of art, an invention for an invention" (Simmel [1911] 2001, 219), is not compatible with an individual life that is constrained by time. The motif of tragic culture, which Simmel expands into the "pathology of culture" towards the end of his life (Simmel 1999, 40), is similar to Benjamin's idea of modernity as a suicidal project.

The moment of the tragic belongs not only to modernity, but also to the life of modern man, which has a fragmentary character – in the same sense that Simmel means by the title of his 1916 reflection "Der Fragmentcharakter des Lebens". This is no longer simply a conflict between objective and subjective culture, between unity and plurality, but a process of fragmentation, a levelling down, which Simmel argues are symptomatic of modern life. The world is given to man as a sum of fragments (Simmel 1916/17, 29–40) and this fragmentation, as Simmel wrote in *The Philosophy of Money* (*Philosophie des Geldes*), means "that the core and meaning of life always slips through one's hand, then this testifies to a deep yearning to give things a new importance, and deeper meaning, a value of their own" (Simmel [1900] 2004, 407). Life in modern times is a fragment, for it has become a mere "cut-out of the metaphysical absolute" ("herausgeschnittenes Stück einer metaphysischen Absolutheit"; Simmel 1916/17, 32). Simmel is also concerned about the tension between fragment and totality, part and whole, which he deals with in his essay "The Ruins" ("Die Ruine"). In Simmel's conception, the ruin is both the "present form of the past" and a proof of nature's victory over the artefact, born of the activity of the creative spirit. As a fragment of the former whole, the ruin is a sign of a collapsed totality. Human creation eventually becomes a natural "product" again, a part of nature that triumphs over the idea that its human creator "imposed" on the material (Simmel [1911] 1958, 371–85).

Szondi's sentence in his essay on Schlegel's romantic irony that "the essence [...] of modernity is its dismemberment" (Szondi 1986, 58–9) foreshadows the tragic fragmentation of Szondi's own work and life. His interpretation of Celan's poem *You Lie* (*Du liegst*), which has provoked lively discussion and controversy to this day, also remains a fragment (Burdorf 2014, 409–26; Brandes 2003, 175–95; Scheuer 1995, 1–15). Originally with the title *Winter Poem* (*Wintergedicht*; Szondi 2003, 85), Celan wrote it during his visit to Berlin on 22–23 December 1967. It would later be included in the posthumously published collection *Snow Part* (*Schneepart*, 1971).

DU LIEGST im großen Gelausche,
umbuscht, umflockt.
Geh du zur Spree, geh zur Havel,
geh zu den Fleischerhaken,

zu den roten Äppelstaken
aus Schweden—
Es kommt der Tisch mit den Gaben,
er biegt um ein Eden—
Der Mann ward zum Sieb, die Frau
mußte schwimmen, die Sau,
für sich, für keinen, für jeden—
Der Landwehrkanal wird nicht rauschen.
Nichts
stockt. (Celan 2003, 315)

YOU LIE amid a great listening,
enbushed, enflaked.
Go to the Spree, go to the Havel,
go to the meathooks,
to the red apple stakes
from Sweden—
Here comes the gift table,
it turns around an Eden—
The man became a sieve, the Frau
had to swim, the sow,
for herself, for no one, for everyone—
The Landwehr Canal won't make a murmur.
Nothing
stops. (Celan 2001, 329)

In April 1971, one year after Celan's suicide, Szondi began working on his interpretation of the poem, which would remain unfinished. After Szondi's death, the piece was first published in the literary supplement *Neue Zürcher Zeitung* (15 October 1972), and subsequently in his posthumously published *Celan Studies*. This would be the last text he worked on – Szondi called it *Eden* – before committing suicide. If Szondi holds a special place in Celan scholarship and in the hermeneutics of modern poetry broadly speaking, it is because he based his interpretation on biographical events – namely, on Celan's trip to Berlin, on which Szondi himself accompanied the poet. Szondi recalls Celan's visit to the prison in Plötzensee to see the room where, on 20 July 1944, an officers' plot to assassinate Hitler was foiled. Those involved in the plot were caught and executed, hanged on butcher's hooks ("go to the meathooks"). Celan also walked through the Christmas market, where he saw Swedish

Advent wreaths decorated with red apples ("to the red apple stakes / from Sweden –"; small wooden stakes for affixing apples to the wreath). Having neglected to bring a book, he asked if Szondi had one he could borrow; Szondi lent him recently published documents on the shooting of Rosa Luxemburg and Karel Liebknecht in January 1919. After the shooting, Luxemburg's body was thrown into the Landwehrkanal ("the Frau / had to swim, the sow"),[19] which appears at the end of the poem ("The Landwehr Canal won't make a murmur"). Szondi brought Celan to see the building of the former Eden Hotel, which had once housed an officer staff and military unit that took part in the liquidation of Luxembourg and Liebknecht (Szondi 2003, 87).

It is on the basis of this kind of biographical contextualization that Szondi builds his interpretation of Celan's poem, in this way provoking a debate over the hermeneutic *legitimacy* of such an approach in the interpretation of a literary text. Hans Georg Gadamer asked how much we must know "to feel that the poems have been in any way 'addressed'", and whether the interpretation of the poem depends on special biographical information and knowledge (Gadamer 1976, 124). Szondi's intention was not to reduce the aesthetic and poetic complexity of Celan's poetry to mere biographical events, but rather to stylize reality on the basis of mythical, biblical, and intertextual allusions, as well as paraphrases and quotations that move the relationship with reality to an anti-realistic level. It is clear from the typewritten manuscript of Szondi's work how cautiously he worked through these biographical contexts. In the published version of *Eden* he notes:

This biographical report (others could no doubt make similar remarks apropos of other Celan poems), is not intended as the justification for a reading of the poem "Du liegst im großen Gelausche". Rather, we might ask whether such information can serve to support any reading at all. To what extent does understanding the poem depend on a knowledge of the biographical/historical framework? Or, in more general terms, to what extent is the poem determined by things external to it, and this determination from without invalidated by the poem's own internal logic? [...] Yet Celan also saw, read, and experienced many other things during the same few days that left no traces in the poem. But the poem's determi-

---

19 According to the documentation Celan read, one of the soldiers uttered these words just after Luxemburg was shot.

nation by everyday coincidence is already limited – indeed precluded – by the process of selection, which, no less than these more or less chance occurrences themselves, was a necessary precondition for the poem, part of its generis. We might ask whether the determination from without, the real-life referent, is not balanced out by the poem's self-determination: the interdependence of its various elements, by means of which even the real events referred to are transformed. (Szondi 2003, 88–9)

For Szondi, however, something else was at stake: the invocation of the two days he spent with Celan in Berlin, the invocation of "the experiences of his stay in Berlin" (Szondi 2003, 88). Szondi postulates a balance between *external-determination* (*Fremdbestimmung*) and *self-determination* (*Selbstbestimmung*), between the sum of real personal (non-textual) events and the artistic constellation they form in the literary work. Szondi's text as a whole, as Jürg Berthold points out, was written in such a way so as to evoke an atmosphere of intimacy (Berthold 1992, 94), and as a mutual reflection between two different experiences: the author-poet on one side, the reader-interpreter on the other. They are divergent yet analogous experiences, not least in the way they reflect the threat of Nazi terror and persecution. It is the same for the text of the poem itself, as if it were mirrored on the surface of Berlin's two rivers ("Go to the Spree, go to the Havel"), and on the surface of the Landwehrkanal at the end of the poem. At the same time, the ominous spectre of historical and political events is mirrored – as a strange kind of *mirror paradox* – in the "red apple stakes" at the Christmas market. Equally paradoxical and ambivalent is the motif of *Eden*, which brings together the biblical-mythical *locus amoenus* with a specific *locus terribilis* in relation to historical events – events that, in 1967, were still lingering in a not-so-distant past. We find the same paradoxical logic in a rapprochement of the Christmas market and Plötzensee Prison – the site (masterfully evoked in the text) where members of the foiled 20 July plot were brought to be executed. Both locations are projected metonymically into the material motifs of "meat-hooks" and "apple stakes".[20] Finally, we discover a historical-political

---

20 In 1956, Paul Celan was asked to translate comments into German for Alain Resnais' documentary *Nuit et brouillard / Night and Fog* (1956) about the Nazi extermination camps. The film features footage in which the SS celebrates the Christmas holidays in Auschwitz, in the immediate vicinity of the gas chambers. In his book *Hitler in uns selbst* (*Hitler in Our Selves*), Max Picard interprets this phenomenon as a consequence of the complete discontinuity of the modern world. Only in such a world, where peace can no longer be found among humans, only the peace of inhumanity, instruments, laboratories, and factories, was such a thing possible.

nexus at the intersection of two other images: on one hand, the man riddled with bullets ("the man became a sieve"; and "the Frau – the sow"); on the other, the "meathooks" used to suspend the steel wires on which the Plötzensee prisoners were brutally hanged. These images are associated, respectively, with the events of January 1919 and July 1944, which can be read in turn as a reference to the *Second Thirty Years War* (1914–45), the memory of which had been imprinted on the architecture of the city: the Plötzensee prison and the *Eden* hotel.

The gifts that appear in the poem ("Here comes the gift table") are also "gifts of death" (Berthold 1992, 17). "War is a further experience of the gift of death [la mort donnée]", as Derrida writes in his essay *The Gift of Death* (*Donner la mort*) in reference to Jan Patočka's *heretical essay* "Wars of the Twentieth Century and the Twentieth Century as War" (Patočka 1996, 119–37). For Derrida,[21] death, mystery, and the gift form a unity. The gift is at first a paradoxical "gift of death" – paradoxical

---

"Murder and Mozart, the gas chamber and the concert hall are next to each other. Or rather, they're in one and the same space, at one end furnished like a gas chamber, at the other like a concert hall. They share a single entrance, and it's just a coincidence that they hustle behind its door for a moment. Mozart after or before people are gassed, Hölderlin in the knapsack of an SS man, Goethe in the library of the concentration camp guards – this is only possible in a world where things are no longer here in their actuality, except without a context: they are valid only by virtue of their incoherence" (Picard [1946] 1969, 58, 64). In his famous *Death Fugue* (*Todesfuge*, 1944), Paul Celan captured this monstrous discontinuity of music and killing that Max Picard writes about. It came as a shock when in 1980 the original title of Celan's poem was discovered: *Death Tango* (*Todestango*). However, the name refers to the appalling reality that Jews had to dig their own graves in extermination camps and others had to play the "death tango" (Felstiner 2001, 27). Here Picard develops the speculative philosophy of German "discontinuous history" – but he was not the only one. As early as 1935, Helmuth Plessner published an analysis of National Socialism as a consequence of the "belated nation" (*The Belated Nation / Die verspätete Nation*, 1935/1959). According to Plessner, Germany, unlike England, France or even the Netherlands, failed to integrate the legacy of humanism and the Enlightenment. England's "political liberalism" and France's "democratic rationalism" remained something foreign to Germany, so that, according to Plessner, it fell victim to the ideology of Great German nationalism, which was strongly resistant to the process of modernisation. Plessner considers the suppression of Catholicism by the Reformation and "spiritual homelessness" ("geistige Heimatlosigkeit") of the Reformed Church to be a particularly unfortunate obstacle to the integration of a political Enlightenment in Germany. And – as one of the most serious causes of the slowing down of the liberal contents of German political thought – the radicalization of philosophy in the destructive thinking of Karl Marx and Friedrich Nietzsche. Plessner speaks directly of "the destruction of philosophy at the hand of Marx, Kierkegaard, and Nietzsche" (Plessner 2015, 185).

21 Péter Szondi was one of the first to introduce Derrida to German literary studies. Shortly after taking over the professorship of comparative studies at the Freie Universität in Berlin in 1965, Szondi began inviting literary scholars and philosophers from Europe and the United States to give guest lectures. Derrida lectured twice in Berlin at Szondi's invitation. It was also Szondi who introduced Paul Celan to Derrida in Paris (Riechers 2020, 163).

because death escapes the give–take relationship, and yet only death allows this exchange. According to Derrida, this is the initiation scene of Western Christian culture, which Derrida interprets as "the economy of sacrifice":

> For this is not just one theme among others: a history of secrecy as history of responsibility is tied to a culture of death, in other words to the different figures of the gift of death or of putting to death [la mort donnée]. What does donner la mort mean in French? How does one give oneself death [se donner la mort]? How does one give it to oneself in the sense that putting oneself to death means dying while assuming responsibility for one's own death, committing suicide but also sacrificing oneself for another, dying for the other, thus perhaps giving one's life by giving oneself death, accepting the gift of death, such as Socrates, Christ, and others did in so many different ways. [...] What is the relation between se donner la mort and sacrifice? Between putting oneself to death and dying for another? What are the relations among sacrifice, suicide, and the economy of this gift? [...] the possibility of dying of the other or for the other. Such a death is not given in the first instance as annihilation. It institutes responsibility as a putting-oneself-to-death or offering-one's-death, that is, one's life, in the ethical dimension of sacrifice. (Derrida [1992] 1996, 10, 48)

Victims for whom? "For herself, for no one, for everyone"? It could be said that Celan and Szondi are also connected by what Jan Patočka calls "the solidarity of the shaken": "the solidarity of those who are capable of understanding what life and death are all about, and so what history is about" (Patočka 1996, 134). *Du liegst im großen Gelausche*, however, is also a poem that anticipates death. Both the poet and his interpreter would choose a death by drowning, Celan in the Seine and Szondi, one and a half years later, in Hallensee near Berlin. How to explain their mirror-image suicides? Despite some mutual differences, which emerge in the correspondence (Celan and Szondi 2005), Szondi found his friendship and correspondence with Celan very important during the last decade of the poet's life. For Szondi, Celan was a poet whose words created the world anew, as Szondi writes in his interpretation of Celan's poem *Engführung* for the French journal *Critique* (Szondi 1971, 387–420), edited by Jacques Derrida. According to Szondi, the poem as a whole is a repetition of the creation of the world, a gesture made in the face of – and in this sense because of – the death camps: "The reality of ash, of the death camp and its crematories, only seems to prevent the advent of the word, of the re-creation of the World through language" (Szondi 1983, 259–60). Szondi writes about "the identity of word and being, and points to the accord between poetic reality and poetic text" (Szondi 1983, 250).

The "re-creation of the World through language". It is a notion that raises the clamour of the word *against* the lethal silence of the extermination camps – a vocalization and medicalization of the world (the word *Engführung*, or *stretto*, refers to the composition of a fugue). But it also raises its sound against the metaphysical horror and terrifying silence of "the endless cosmos" ("The eternal silence of these infinite spaces terrifies me"; Pascal 1995, 73). Along with the word, the world is recreated as *a millicrystal* (*ein Tausendkristall*). Once more, the word can be seen in semantic proximity to crystal structures: as a word enveloped in snow crystals ("What snowball will form round the word"), as a *crystal of breath* (*Atemkristall*), as *glacier rooms* (*Gletscherstuben*), *alveolate ice* (*Wabeneis*), and other motifs semantically related to crystals and crystallisation.

The flip side of the creation of the world is its glaciation and petrification.[22] Geometric-crystalline forms evoking lucidity, symmetry, transparency, and purification are extra-temporal, impersonal, and counter to life. Crystallization is synonymous with symmetry.[23] The poet of this anti-naturistic "will to crystallize" is Baudelaire;[24] his poem *Rêve pari-*

---

22 As Hedwig Conrad–Martius shows by comparing crystal and plant, the most complex attribute of all living things is self–regulation, autopoiesis, and self–creation: "It is not creation but self–creation that characterizes life. That is why life reaches its end where self–creation ceases (Nicht die Gestaltung, sondern die Selbstgestaltung macht das Leben aus. Deshalb ist das Leben aber auch zu Ende, wo die Selbstgestaltung aufhört). Atoms and crystals are subject to design potencies (Gestaltungspotenzen), which create and control them. They are formed by their own potential from formless matter (formloser Stoff) as shaped units (Gestaltseinheiten). Living being (lebendiges Sein) means self–creative autonomy (selbstschöpferische Autonomie)" (Conrad–Martius 1934, 60).

23 According to Niklas Luhmann, paradoxes produce symmetries that disrupt communication and remove differences. In this context, Luhmann speaks of the importance of asymmetrization: "Only with the help of such punctualization and asymmetrization can an autopoietic social system form" (Luhmann 1995, 169).

24 In his essay, Sartre very accurately describes the poet's intention: "It was because for him metal and, in a general way, minerals reflected the image of the mind. One of the results of the limits of our imaginative powers is that all those who, in their endeavors to understand the opposition between the spirit and life and the body, have been driven to form a non–biological image of it, have necessarily had to appeal to the kingdom of inanimate things - light, cold, transparency, sterility. Just as Baudelaire discovered that his own evil thoughts were realized and objectified in "foul beasts", so steel - the most brilliant, the most highly polished of metals and the one which offers least grip - always appeared to him to be the exact objectification of his Thought in general. If he felt a tenderness towards the sea, it was because it was a mobile

sien,[25] a vision of the transformation of the organic world into an inorganic-crystalline artefact, culminates in the Pascalian notion of the terrifying "eternal silence of these infinite spaces":

Et sur ces mouvantes merveilles
Planait (terrible nouveauté!
Tout pour l'oeil, rien pour les oreilles!)
Un silence d'éternité. (Baudelaire 1975, 102)

And on these marvels as they moved
there weighed (without a sound –
the eye alone was master here)
the silence of the Void. (Baudelaire 1982, 108)

However, the crystal is an ambivalent motif in Celan. As a homogeneous elementary and structured cell, it represents a microcosmic building block, an analogon of inwardness, interiorization, and crystallization of time. It is a protective monadic microstructure for "I" and "You", as in the poem *Schneebett* (*Snowbed*). Crystals represent the process of emergence, a growth from within, from a depth; yet it is a form of emergence that comes to an end within – that is terminated by – the process of crystallization. By combining the substance and the form, the homogeneous chemical unit of the crystal is always already finished. It can be formed again, but only by layering already existing particles of the same substance. It represents, however, the highest form of this process. With Celan, the world of crystals has a special affinity for death: *Glacier rooms* close the word and time, simultaneously prefiguring the grave, as in *Snowbed*:

---

mineral. It was because it was brilliant, inaccessible and cold with a pure and, as it were, an immaterial movement. Because it possessed those forms which succeeded one another, that changed without anything which changed, and sometimes that transparency, that it offered the most adequate image of the spirit. It was spirit. Thus Baudelaire's horror of life led him to choose materialization in its purest form as a symbol of the immaterial" (Sartre 1967, 108–9).

25 This poem by Baudelaire could be read as a poetic conceptualization of Alois Riegl's program *Kunstwollen*: "Only in inorganic creation does man manifest himself fully equal to nature; he also creates purely from internal excitement without any external patterns. Once it crosses this limit, it enters into an external dependence on nature; its creation is no longer completely independent, but imitative. (Nur im anorganischen Schaffen erscheint der Mensch völlig ebenbürtig mit der Natur, schafft er auch rein aus innerm Drange, ohne alle äußern Vorbilder; sobald er diese Grenze überschreitet, gerät et in äußere Abhängigkeit von der Natur, ist sein Schaffen kein völlig selbständiges mehr, sondern ein imitatives)" (Riegl 1966, 76).

Das Schneebett unter uns beiden, das Schneebett.
Kristall um Kristall,
zeittief gegittert, wir fallen,
wir fallen und liegen und fallen. (Celan 2003, 100)

The snowbed beneath us both, the snowbed
crystal by crystal
latticed time-deep, we fall,
we fall and lie and fall. (Celan 2002, 97)

The idea of ice graves is developed by the writer Jaroslav Durych in his novel *In the Mountains* (*Na horách*):

> Snow rang, fell underfoot, and as it tore and collapsed it formed long shadowy tracks. At its perimeter, the snow beckoned us treacherously to its glittering edge, then broke apart and caved in on its prey, singing and ringing joyfully to the icy graves that looked from above like an enchanted kingdom, crowded with sleeping naked bodies that stretched out towards some unknown celebration.[26] (Durych [1919] 1993, 79–80)

In Durych's text, the aesthetics of glittering snow, crystals, icy bushes – echoing the morphology of crystalline structures in Cubism – intertwines with the aesthetics of the sublime and with modern *thanatopolitics* (Durych's novel was written on the front of WWI). Icy graves, "crowded with sleeping naked bodies" are similar to the "glacier rooms" and "snowbeds" of Celan's poem *Weggebeizt* (*Etched Away From*), presenting a spatialised image of the sedimentation of time, as well as its *glaciation*. In Durych's text, as in Celan's poem *The Snowbed*, this image is connected to that of a fall ("we fall, / we fall and lie and fall"). It is a fall not only into the depths of time, but into a timelessness – as if into an icy eternity – where nothing is subject to transformation and expiration.

Hermann Burger characterizes *The Snowbed* as "a poem about a silent conversation with the dead" (Burger 1974, 124). The crystal wraps around the "I", forming a *protective layer*, while simultaneously closing it off from the surrounding world, confining it to a space of complete isolation.

---

26 Sníh zvonil, padal pod nohama, a jak se trhal a sesýpal, tvořily se dlouhé, stínové stopy. Okraje sněhu vábily záludně na své oslnivé ostří, aby se pak utrhly a zřítily se svou kořistí za zpěvu a radostného zvonění do ledových hrobů, které se z výše zdály jako zaklété království, přeplněné spícími nahými těly, která táhnou někam k neznámé slavnosti.

According to Oskar Becker,[27] the symmetrical structures of crystals and pure mathematics are without time or factual events. As Erwin Panofsky has pointed out in his well-known interpretation of Dürer's engraving *Melencolia I* (1514), there is a close connection between geometry and "Saturnian melancholy" (Panofsky, Klibansky and Saxl 1979, 327–38), which, aside from this work by Dürer, can be found in the crystalline structure of stereometric polyhedra.

3 "The Poetry of Constancy": Close Reading as the Work of Mourning

"Only that which is nourished by one's own life experience can appeal to someone else's life experience; only a bitter drink sensitizes disappointment. Pain is the eye of the spirit" (Plessner 1983, 95).[28]

Creativity as disaster? According to Maurice Blanchot, writing as a creative act involves what he calls "essential solitude". The writer no longer belongs to himself, ceases to be his own "I", and becomes a stranger to himself. "I" transforms into "He". To write means to disappear, to dissolve into speech: "Language has within itself the moment that hides it. It has within itself, through this power to hide itself, the force by which mediation (that which destroys immediacy) seems to have the spontaneity, the freshness, and the innocence of the origin" (Blanchot 1982, 39–40). The moment we speak the word, we invoke absence, non-existence. In a letter of 1952 to his friend Count Mario von Ledebur, Szondi writes: "You must know the fear, emptiness and solitude I live in" (Du mußt die Angst, Leere und Einsamkeit kennen, in der ich lebe; Riechers 2020, 55). In a brief note *On a verse from Romeo and Juliet* (*Über einen Vers aus Romeo und Julia*, 1957/1958), Szondi writes:

One of the essential constants of tragic poetry is the scene in which the hero turns into a foreigner. The moment he recognizes the path that fate

---

27 Becker writes: "Nature does not appear either as a divine animal or as a God–created horology, but as a formed crystal (Die Natur erscheint weder als divinum animal noch als von Gott geschaffenes horologium, sondern als ein gewachsener Kristall)" (Becker 1960, 25).
28 Nur was aus eigener Lebenserfahrung gespeist wird, kann auf fremde Lebenserfahrung ansprechen, nur der bittere Trank der Enttäuschung sensibilisiert. Der Schmerz ist das Auge des Geistes.

has shown him, the human realm lies behind him. It is an insight into the tragic nature of his situation: that he must do what he must not do, this alienates him from the world [...] However, he accepts the incompatibility that prevails between his "duty" and "power", following the only path left to him: the path of death. Yet the sight that death hurls back into the world from her doorstep is not clouded by tears of farewell. The world he once inhabited is no longer a place of desire for him, but the target of his criticism.[29] (Szondi 1978a, 133–4)

Szondi relates to Romeo's conversation with a pharmacist (V, 1), who secretly sells him the fatal poison:

> There is thy gold; worse poison to men's souls,
> Doing more murders in this loathsome world,
> Than these poor compounds that thou mayst not sell.
> I sell thee poison; thou hast sold me none. (Szondi 1978a, 134)

Romeo turns away from the world; at that moment he becomes as one who already stands outside the world, so that poison is not, as Szondi points out, a means of delivering him to death, but a kind of payment for access to life. Here, too, it is a question of the *economy* of paradoxical exchange, of the relationship between worth and worthlessness.[30] This will draw our attention to another motif essential to Szondi, that of authenticity – a kind of purity best expressed by the protagonist of André Gide's novel *Les Faux-Monnayeurs* (*The Counterfeiters*, 1925), Bernard Profitendieu:

---

29 Zu den wesentlichen Konstanten tragischer Dichtung gehören die Szenen, in denen sich der Held zum Fremden wandelt. Sobald er den Weg erkennt, den ihm das Schicksal weist, liegt der Bezirk der Menschen hinter ihm. Die Einsicht in die Tragik seiner Lage: daß er tun muß, was er nicht tun darf, entfremdet ihn der Welt [...] Er aber nimmt die Unvereinbarkeit an, die zwischen seinem Sollen und Können waltet, und geht den Weg, der ihm als einziger bleibt: den in den Tod. Doch der Blick, den er von dessen Schwelle auf die Welt zurückwirft, ist von keiner Träne des Abschieds getrübt. Worin er selber bislang gelebt hat, wird ihm nun nicht zum Ort der Sehnsucht, sondern zur Zielscheibe der Kritik.

30 Coins and gold simulate a value they do not themselves possess: appearances can never replace real being. As Jacques Derrida shows in "White Mythology: Metaphor in the Text of Philosophy", a coin, like a word sign, has the property of representing something else (the value of work), without, however, being itself. At the semiotic level, there is confusion in the sense that the invisibility of the sign leads to identification with the sign. It is a metonymic identification of the invisible with the visible; the symbolic representation of meaning is "absorbed" by metallicity, by the sound "quality" of the signifier (Derrida 1974, 14–17).

I should like all my life long, at the very smallest shock, to ring true, with a pure, authentic sound. [...] To be worth exactly what one seems to be worth – not to try to seem to be worth more... One wants to deceive people, and one is so much occupied with seeming, that one ends by not knowing what one really is... (Gide [1925] 1966, 180)

Insofar as Szondi's interpretations are both a form of self-interpretation and a means for self-understanding,[31] we see this play out especially in the case of his short text on *Romeo and Juliet*, and for Szondi's characterization of the tragic hero. "The hero as such", as Franz Rosenzweig writes, "has to be ruined only because his ruination makes him capable of the supreme heroic consecration: the closest self-realization of his Self. He longs for the solitude of disappearance, because there is no greater solitude than this one" (Rosenzweig 2005, 87). For Rosenzweig, the prototype of the tragic hero is Gilgamesh, whose tragic fate is to witness the death of his friend Enkidu. Through this encounter, he experiences all the horrors of death, which then become the central preoccupation of his existence:

It is all the same to him that death ends by taking even himself; the essential thing is already behind him; death, his own death, has become the event that dominates his life; he himself has entered into the sphere where the world, with its alternation of cries and silences, becomes a stranger to man; he has entered into the sphere of pure and sovereign muteness, the sphere of the Self. (Rosenzweig 2005, 85)

Mirroring is one of the basic figures of melancholy, often – particularly with Romanticism – in connection with (romantic) irony. "The Self is the lonely man in the hardest sense of the word", says Franz Rosenzweig (2005, 80). It is precisely this loneliness "in the hardest sense of the word" that characterizes the fundamental experience of both Celan and Szondi, and with respect to both life and death, as well as their experience of Nazi persecution. In December 1970, seven months after Celan's death, Szondi wrote the first of his Celan studies, dedicated to Celan's translation of one of Shakespeare's sonnets: "The Poetry of Constancy: Paul Celan's Translation of Shakespeare's Sonnet 105". The work lays

---

31 Riechers (2020, 17) quotes a sentence from Szondi's letter to Mario von Ledebur: "You know that, in a sense, I always deal only with myself (Du weisst, dass ich mich in einem gewissen Sinn immer nur mit mir beschäftige)".

out many of the concepts central to Szondi's studies on Celan, such as ambiguity, repetition, and chiasmus. Szondi speaks of *mirror symmetry* (*Spiegelsymmetry*) with regard to the chiastic structure in Shakespeare's verse "Kind is my love to-day, to-morrow kind" (Szondi 1986a, 167). According to Szondi, Celan foregoes this chiasmus in his translation ("Gut ist mein Freund, ists heute und ists morgen") in order to bring the semantic core of Shakespeare's sonnet to the fore: a constancy that is not subject to the passage of time between today and tomorrow. Rather than the linear flow of time, what Celan's translation emphasizes is a return of the same. According to Szondi, it is not merely that Celan bases his translation of this sonnet on the notion of constancy, but that his poetics taken as a whole is the poetics of constancy:

> Constancy, the theme of Shakespeare's sonnet, becomes for Celan the medium in which his verse dwells and which impedes the flow of his verse, imposing constancy upon it. Constancy becomes the constituent element of his verse, in contrast to Shakespeare's original, in which constancy is sung about and described by means of a variety of expressions. Celan's intention toward language, in his version of Shakespeare's sonnet 105, is a realization of constancy in verse. (Szondi 1986a, 174)

The theme in each of these texts – Shakespeare's sonnet, Celan's metatext, and Szondi's interpretation – is the constancy of friendship in spite of death. The theme can be found as well in Shakespeare's Sonnet 3 – "Look in thy glass, and tell the face thou viewest" – , which Celan also translated.[32] The fact that *Celan Studies* features an interpretation of the poem *Du liegst im großen Gelausche* (*Eden*) based on Szondi's "biographical report" of his meeting with Celan in Berlin, and that it returns to this fragmentary interpretation in its third and final section, gives an indication of what his friendship with Celan meant to Szondi. Shortly after Celan's death, Szondi began writing the first of these studies, "The Poetry of Constancy". Inaccessibility and loss are the primary forces driving these interpretations – a communication with the absent other –, but they are also the driving force of a process of self-construction in and by the text. It is this text, in turn, that constitutes the medium of self-interpretation. In *Celan Studies*, Szondi creates a space in which

---

32 These and other translations were included in a collection of twenty–one of Shakespeare's sonnets, which Celan translated as a young poet. They were published under the title *William Shakespeare, Einundzwanzig Sonnette* (1975).

this communication would be allowed to continue as a special form of *Spiegelsymmetry*: between the poet on one hand, and his interpreter and friend on the other. In Celan's texts, and especially in *Du liegst im großen Gelausche*, it is as if Szondi's meticulous reading culminated in a redis-covery of the dead, and by that same token, himself. In Husserl's fifth *Cartesian Meditation* we read:

> The "Other", according to his own constituted sense, points to me myself; the other is a "mirroring" of my own self and not yet a mirroring proper, an analogue of my own self and yet again not an analogue in the usual sense.[33] (Husserl 1960, 94)

As Jean Starobinski has pointed out,[34] this form of mutual mirroring as hermeneutic strategy of (self-) knowledge and (self-) interpretation is the opening gesture of Montaigne's essays, which he wrote in response to the death of his friend Étienne de La Boétie (to whom he dedicated his well-known essay *De l'amitié*).

> La Boétie's death robbed Montaigne of his only mirror: the loss of his friend effaced forever the image that La Boétie possessed. [...] In place of the faithful mirror reflecting the "true image", which enabled Mon-taigne to live two lives, one in himself and one in his friend's regard, there remains only white page on which the aging Montaigne must tell about himself (se dire soi-même), in words that will remain forever in-adequate compared with the reciprocity of life. The perfect symmetry wherein friendship is explained by its individual cause [...] has become forever impossible. The friend's death has destroyed this tautology [...] To perpetuate what one cannot resign oneself to having lost is commit oneself to a work of replacement, substitution, translation. (Starobinski 1985, 37–9)

---

33   Christian Lotz (2002, 72–95) deals with the phenomenon of "mirroring" in Husserl's phenom-enology of intersubjectivity.

34   When, in 1964/5, Petr Szondi became director of the Institute of Comparative Literary Studies at the Freie Universität in what was then West–Berlin, Jean Starobinski was one of the first guests. He gave a lecture there on Irony and Melancholy, 15 June 1966, and Szondi introduced Starobinski as a researcher who, in his words, ideally represented comparative studies as an interdisciplinary field that was neither exhausted by observation of influences nor a field of pure speculation, but which combined "ideas and history, theory and literary empiricism" (König and Isenschmid 2004, 77).

The space of the poem, in this case Celan's *Engführung*, is the space into which the reader has been *verbracht* starting with its opening verses: he is "'driven' into a strange and unfamiliar landscape" (Szondi 1983, 232). According to Szondi, the reader does not take the poem as object of his reading, "rather, he is transplanted to the interior of the text in such a way that it becomes impossible to distinguish between the one reading and that which is being read; the reading subject coincides with the subject of the poem being read" (Szondi 1983, 232). The reader does not merely *read* the text of the poem or *look* at its images so as to be able to describe them; rather "the poet desires that he and the reader 'go' forward into the 'terrain' which is his text" (Szondi 1983, 333–4). "Read no more - look! / Look no more – go!" (Szondi 1983, 233).[35]

We might read these lines as a challenge to the reader to repeat the author's own gesture: in this way, the reading of a text, its analysis and interpretation, may reflect the interpreter's personal style on a new level. As Starobinski shows in his interpretations of Rousseau and Montaigne, their autobiographical texts implement a specific strategy of self-reflection based on the *reading* of gestures: a strategy that is repeated in the work of criticism. Starobinski understands this gestural strategy and experience as a process of self-knowledge and – in the case of Montaigne's *Essays* – a gestural self-experience. In the end, he tries to turn awareness in on itself ("I roll about in myself"), or unravel it like a scroll (Starobinski 1985, 225). The reader-interpreter of the *Essays* repeats these gestures internally so that, at the end of his work, he may unravel the texture of his own kinaesthetic self-experience and self-knowledge, according to Montaigne's idea that "Every movement reveals us (Tout mouvement nous découvre)".

However, Szondi's *Celan Studies* are also a remarkable result of the *work of mourning* by which Szondi dealt with the death of Paul Celan, the endeavour to build a bridge to one who has disappeared, an endeavour that remained unfinished. More precisely, the interpreter's creative gesture results in a repetition of the poet's radical suicidal gesture. A mutual friend of Celan and Szondi, Jacques Derrida, wrote an aphorism about *Romeo and Juliet* that could well refer to the relationship between the poet and his interpreter: "Both are in mourning – and both watch over the death of the other, upon the death of the other. Double death sentence. [...] They both live, outlive the death of the other" (Derrida 2008, 132).

---

35 Lies nicht mehr - schau! / Schau nicht mehr - geh!

4 Epilogue

Eva Veronika Szondi, Petr Szondi's sister, published her work in psychiatry in 1975, *Suicide Among Melancholics and Schizophrenics in the Light of Psychoanalysis, Fate Analysis and Daseinsanalysis* (*Selbstmord bei Melancholikern und Schizophrenen im Lichte der Psychoanalyse, der Schicksalsanalyse und der Daseinsanalyse*). Based on these three psychological models (psychoanalysis, fate analysis and *Daseinsanalysis*) it reconstructs the hermeneutical horizon of knowledge on suicide in melancholics and schizophrenics. Unlike psychoanalysis and "genotropic" theory, the *Daseinsanalysis* created by Ludwig Binswanger and his school examines the analysis and hermeneutics of forms of existence and the position of a person in the world. From the point of view of psychiatry, Binswanger understands psychosis as a transformation of Being-in-the-world (In-der-Welt-Sein). The primary themes of melancholy, for example, are loss, feelings of guilt, and self-blame. Time is not experienced as a movement towards the future but on the contrary as something dying away. In severe forms of melancholy, and similarly in schizophrenia, the past is overwhelmed by the present: the meaning of life seems to be cut off from the future. The space afforded to the movement of Being (Dasein) is progressively constricted, so that Being begins to revolve tautologically around itself, as in a circle. From the point of view of *Daseinsanalysis*, suicide is the last attempt to break this rigidity of Being (Eva Szondi 1975, 94–5). In the essay "Hope in the Past: On Walter Benjamin" ("Hoffnung im Vergangenen. Über Walter Benjamin") Peter Szondi interprets Benjamin's memories of childhood *Berlin Childhood around 1900* (*Berliner Kindhiet um Neunzehnhundert*) as an attempt to save the past in the present, a paradoxical *Futurum der Vergangenheit*:

> Benjamin's tense is not the perfect, but the future perfect in the fullness of its paradox: being future and past at the same time. [...] Thus his understanding of utopia is anchored in the past. This was the precondition for his projected primal history of the modern age. The task is paradoxical, like the joining of hope and despair to which it gives voice. The way to the origin is, to be sure, a way backwards, but backwards into a future, which, although it has gone by in the meantime and its idea has been perverted, still holds more promise than the current image of the future. (Szondi [1961] 1978b, 499, 502)

This seems to restore the arrow of time towards the horizon of the future – but only seemingly. It is significant that Szondi refers to Benjamin's *Origins of German Tragedy* (*Ursprung des deutschen Trauerspiel*) in this essay, and to one of its motifs in particular, namely the allegory of the Baroque. Melancholy (*Schwermut*) and sadness – another of these key categories of Benjamin's thinking – return not only in Szondi's *Essay on the Tragic*, but also in "Walter Benjamin's City Portraits" ("Benjamins Städtebilder"), where Szondi comments on Benjamin's episode trip along the North Sea: "Melancholy sees only the dark side of everything" (Szondi [1963] 1986b, 140). From here, a direct path will lead to "a particular manner of destruction that is threatening or already completed" (Szondi [1964] 2002, 55), as Szondi himself tragically understands: "But it is also the case that only the demise of something that should not meet its demise, whose removal does not allow the wound to heal, is tragic" (Szondi [1964] 2002, 55).

Translated by Peter Gaffney.

References

Aristotle. 1984. *The Complete Works of Aristotle Vol. II.*, edited by Jonathan Barnes. Princeton, NJ: Princeton University Press.

Bachelard, Gaston. 1994. *The Poetics of Space*. Translated by Maria Jolas. Boston, MA: Beacon Press.

Baudelaire, Charles. 1975. *Les Fleurs du mal*. In *Oeuvres complètes. Vol. I.*, edited by Claude Pichois. Paris: Gallimard.

Baudelaire, Charles. 1982. *The Flowers of Evil*. Translated by Richard Howard. Boston, MA: David R. Godine Publisher.

Becker, Oskar. 1960. "Die Aktualität des pythagoreischen Gedankens". In *Die Gegenwart der Griechen im neueren Denken: Festschrift für Hans-Georg Gadamer zum 60. Geburtstag,* edited by Heinrich Dieter, Walter Schultz, and Karl-Heinz Volkmann-Schluck, 7–30. Tübingen: J. C. B. Mohr (Paul Siebeck).

Benjamin, Walter. 2006. "The Paris of the Second Empire in Baudelaire". In *The Writer of Modern Life. Essays on Charles Baudelaire,* edited by Michael W. Jennings, translated by Harry Zohn, 46–133. Cambridge MA, London: The Belknap Press of Harvard University Press. Original edition, 1938.

Benjamin, Walter. 2006a. "The Work of Art in the Age of Its Technological Reproducibility". In *Selected Writings. Volume 3, 1935–1938*, edited by Howard Eiland, and Michael W. Jennings, 101–33. Cambridge, MA, London: Harvard University Press. Original edition, 1935.

Benjamin, Walter. 2006b. "On Some Motifs in Baudelaire". In *The Writer of Modern Life. Essays on Charles Baudelaire*, edited by Michael W. Jennings, translated by Howard Eiland,

Edmund Jephcott, Rodney Livingstone and Harry Zohn, 170–210. Cambridge, MA, London: The Belknap Press of Harvard University Press. Original edition, 1939.

Berthold, Jürg. 1992. "Wir müssen 'wohl leiden': Formen 'autobiographischen' Schreibens: Paul Celan, Du liegst / Peter Szondi, 'Eden'." *Poetica* 24 (1/2): 90–101.

Blanchot, Maurice. 1982. *The Space of Literature*. Translated by Ann Smock. Lincoln, London: University of Nebraska Press.

Blanchot, Maurice. 1999. "The Song of the Sirens". In *Blanchot Reader*, edited by George Quasha, translated by Lydia Davis, Paul Auster, and Robert Lamberton, 443–50. Barrytown: Station Hill Press.

Blanchot, Maurice. 1999a. "The Essential Solitude". In *Blanchot Reader*, edited by George Quasha, translated by Lydia Davis, Paul Auster, and Robert Lamberton, 401–15. Barrytown: Station Hill Press.

Blanchot, Maurice. 1999b. "Literature and the Right to Death". In *Blanchot Reader*, edited by George Quasha, translated by Lydia Davis, Paul Auster, and Robert Lamberton, 359–99. Barrytown: Station Hill Press. Original edition, 1948.

Bohrer, Karl Heinz. 1994. *Suddenness: On the Moment of Aesthetic Appearance*. New York: Columbia University Press.

Brandes, Peter. 2003. "Die Gewalt der Gaben: Celans 'Eden'". In *Die Zeitlichkeit des Ethos. Poetologische Aspekte im Schreiben Paul Celans*, edited by Martin Jörg Schäfer, and Ulrich Wergin, 175–95. Würzburg: Königshausen & Neumann.

Burdorf, Dieter. 2014. "Der letzte Textgelehrte. Bemerkungen zu Peter Szondi". In *Textgelehrte. Literaturwissenschaft und literarisches Wissen im Umkreis der Kritischen Theorie*, edited by Nicolas Berg, and Dieter Burdorf, 409–26. Göttingen: Vandenhoeck & Ruprecht.

Burger, Hermann. 1974. *Paul Celan: Auf der Suche nach der verlorenen Sprache*. Zürich, München: Artemis Verlag.

Burger, Hermann. 1982. *Die künstliche Mutter*. Frankfurt am Main: Fischer Verlag.

Burger, Herman. 1983. *Ein Mann aus Wörtern*. Frankfurt am Main: Fischer Verlag.

Burger, Hermann. 2010. "Poetische und wissenschaftliche Sprache". In *Hermann Burger: Zur zwanzigsten Wiederkehr seines Todestages,* edited by Magnus Wieland, and Simon Zumsteg, 23–40. Wien, New York: Springer Verlag.

Celan, Paul. 1972. *Selected Poems*. Translated by Michael Hamburger, and Christopher Middleton. London: Penguin Books.

Celan, Paul. 2001. *Selected Poems and Prose of Paul Celan*. Translated by John Felstiner. New York: W. W. Norton & Company.

Celan, Paul. 2002. *Poems of Paul Celan. A Bilingual German/English Edition*, *Revised Edition*. Translated by Michael Hamburger. New York: Persea Publisher.

Celan, Paul. 2003. *Die Gedichte: Kommentierte Gesamtausgabe,* edited by Barbara Wiedemann. Frankfurt am Main: Suhrkamp.

Celan, Paul, and Peter Szondi. 2005. *Briefwechsel,* edited by Christoph König. Frankfurt am Main: Suhrkamp.

Conrad-Martius, Hedwig. 1934. *Die 'Seele' der Pflanze. Biologisch-ontologische Betrachtungen*. Breslau: Franke.

Derrida, Jacques. 1974. "White Mythology: Metaphor in the Text of Philosophy". *New Literary History* 6 (1): 5–74.

Derrida, Jacques. 1996. *The Gift of Death*. Translated by David Wills. Chicago, IL: University of Chicago Press. Original edition, 1992.

Derrida, Jacques. 2008. *Psyche. Inventions of the Other. Volume II*, edited by Peggy Mamuf, and Elisabeth G. Rottenberg. Stanford, CA: Stanford University Press.

Durych, Jaroslav. 1993. *Jarmark života. Na horách. Cikánčina smrt. Laň a panna*. Praha: Road. Original edition, 1919.

Felstiner, John. 2001. *Paul Celan: Poet, Survivor, Jew*. New Haven, CT: Yale University Press.

Firges, Jean. 1962. "Sprache und Sein in der Dichtung Paul Celans". *Muttersprache* 72 (9): 261–9.

Freud, Sigmund. 1960. *The Ego and the Id*. In *The Edition of the Complete Psychological Works of Sigmund Freud*. Translated by Joan Riviere. New York, London: W. W. Norton & Company. Original edition, 1923.

Gadamer, Hans Georg. 1976. *Wer bin Ich und wer bist Du? Ein Kommentar zu Paul Celans Gedichtfolge "Atemkristall"*. Frankfurt am Main: Suhrkamp.

Gide, André. 1966. *The Counterfeiters*. Translated by Dorothy Bussy. London: Penguin Books. Original edition, 1925.

Heidegger, Martin. 1977. "Letter on Humanism". Translated by Frank A. Capuzzi. In *Basic Writings*, edited by David Farrell Krell, 193–242. New York, San Francisco, CA: Harper & Row.

Husserl, Edmund. 1960. *Cartesian Meditations. An Introduction to Phenomenology*. Translated by Dorion Cairns. The Haague: Martinus Nijhoff Publ.

Isenschmid, Andreas. 2006. "Emil Staiger und Peter Szondi". In *1955-2005: Emil Staiger und die 'Kunst der Interpretation' heute*, edited by Joachim Rickes, Volker Ladenthin, and Michael Baum, 173–88. Berlin, Bern: Verlag Peter Lang.

König, Christoph, and Andreas Isenschmid. 2004. *Engführungen. Peter Szondi und die Literatur*. Marbach am Neckar: Deutsche Schillergesellschaft.

Lang, Siegfried K. 2002. "Wilhelm Worringers Abstraktion und Einfühlung. Entstehung und Bedeutung". In *Wilhelm Worringers Kunstgeschichte,* edited by Hannes Böhringer, and Beate Söntgen, 81–117. München: Wilhelm Fink Verlag.

Lotz, Christian. 2002. "Mitmachende Spiegelbilder. Anmerkungen zur Phänomenologie der konkreten Intersubjektivität bei Husserl." *Zeitschrift für philosophische Forschung* 56 (1): 72–95.

Luhmann, Niklas. 1988. "Über 'Kreativität'". In *Kreativität: Ein verbrauchter Begriff?*, edited by Hans-Ulrich Gumbrecht, 13–9. München: Wilhelm Fink Verlag.

Luhman, Niklas. 1988a. "Tautology and Paradox in the Self-Descriptions of Modern Society." *Sociological Theory* 6 (1): 21–37.

Luhmann, Niklas. 1991. *Soziologie des Risikos*. Berlin: De Gruyter.

Luhmann Niklas. 1995. *Social Systems*. Translated by John Bednarz, Jr., and Dirk Baecker. Stanford, CA: Stanford University Press.

Luhmann, Niklas. 2000. *Art as a Social System*. Translated by Eva M. Knodt. Stanford, CA: Stanford University Press.

Luhmann, Niklas. 2007. "Autopoiesis als soziologischer Begriff". In *Aufsätze und Reden,* 137–58. Stuttgart: Reclam.

Panofsky, Erwin, Raymond Klibansky, and Fritz Saxl. 1979. *Saturn and Melancholy. Studies in the History of Natural Philosophy, Religion and Art*. Nendeln, Liechtenstein: Kraus Reprint.

Pascal, Blaise. 1999. *Pensées and Other Writings*. Translated by Honor Levi. Oxford, New York: Oxford University Press.

Patočka, Jan. 1996. "Wars of the Twentieth Century and the Twentieth Century as War". In *Heretical Essays in the Philosophy of History*. Translated by Erazim Kohák, edited by James Dodd, 119–37. Chicago, IL: Open Court Publishing Company.

Picard, Max. 1969. *Hitler in uns selbst*. Erlenbach, Zürich and Stuttgart: Eugen Rentsch Verlag. Engl. *Hitler in Our Selves*. 2010. Translated by Heinrich Hauser. Whitefish, MT: Kessinger Publishing LLC. Original edition, 1946.

Plessner, Helmuth. 1983. "Mit anderen Augen". In *Gesammelte Schriften VIII: Conditio humana*, 88–104. Frankfurt am Main: Suhrkamp.

Plessner, Helmuth. 2015. *Die Verführbarkeit des bürgerlichen Geistes. Politische Schriften. Gesammelte Schriften VI*. Frankfurt am Main: Suhrkamp.

Plessner, Helmuth. 2019. *Levels of Organic Life and the Human. An Introduction to Philosophical Anthropology*. Translated by Millay Hyatt. New York: Fordham University Press. Original edition, 1928.

Prinzhorn, Hans. 1927. "Persönlichkeit und Werk". In Seidel, Alfred. *Bewusstsein als Verhängnis. Aus dem Nachlasse herausgegeben von Hans Prinzhorn*, 46–68. Bonn: Verlag Friedrich Cohen.

Riechers, Hans-Christian. 2020. *Peter Szondi. Eine intellektuelle Biographie*. Frankfurt am Main, New York: Campus Verlag.

Riegl, Alois. 1966. *Historische Grammatik der bildenden Künste*, edited by Karl Maria Swoboda, and Otto Pächt. Graz, Köln: Böhlau Verlag.

Rosenzweig, Franz. 2005. *The Star of Redemption*. Translated by Barbara E. Galli. Madison: The University of Wisconsin Press.

Sartre, Jean Paul. 1967. *Baudelaire*. Translated by Martin Turnell. New York: A New Directions Paperbook.

Scheuer, Hans Jürgen. 1995. "Parallel=Stellung. Paul Celan – Peter Szondi". In *Am Ende der Literaturtheorie? Neun Beiträge zur Einführung und Diskussion*, edited by Torsten Hitz, and Angela Stock, 1–15. Münster: LIT-Verlag.

Schlegel, Friedrich. 1991. *Philosophical Fragments*. Transl. by Peter Firchow. Minneapolis, London: University of Minnesota Press.

Silesius, Angelus (Johannes Scheffler). 1986. *The Cherubinic Wanderer*. Translated by Maria Shrady. New York: Paulist Press.

Simmel, Georg. 1916/17. "Der Fragmentcharakter des Lebens. Aus den Vorstudien zu einer Metaphysik". *Logos. Internationale Zeitschrift für Philosophie der Kultur* 6 (1): 29–40.

Simmel, Georg. 1958. "Two Essays. The ruins". *The Hudson Review* 11 (3): 371–385. Original edition, 1911.

Simmel, Georg. 1999. "Die Krisis der Kultur". In *Gesamtausgabe, Band 16. Der Krieg und die geistigen Entscheidungen. Grundfragen der Soziologie. Vom Wesen des historischen Verstehens. Der Konflikt der modernen Kultur. Lebensanschauung*, 37–53. Frankfurt am Main: Suhrkamp.

Simmel, Georg. 2001. "Der Begriff und die Tragödie der Kultur". In *Gesamtausgabe, Band 12. Aufsätze und Abhandlungen 1909–1918 I*, 192–223. Frankfurt am Main: Suhrkamp. Original edition, 1911.

Simmel, Georg. 2004. *The Philosophy of Money*. Translated by Tom Bottomore, and David Frisby. London, New York: Routledge. Original edition, 1900.

Starobinski, Jean. 1985. *Montaigne in Motion*. Translated by Arthur Goldhammer. Chicago, IL, London: The University of Chicago Press.

Straus, Erwin. 1978. *Geschehnis und Erlebnis. Zugleich eine historiologische Deutung des psychischen Traumas und der Renten-Neurose*. Berlin, Heidelberg, New York: Springer Verlag.

Straus, Erwin. 1982. "Event and Experience". In *Man, Time, and World. Two Contributions to Anthropological Psychology*. Translated by Donald Moss, 3–142. Pittsburgh, PA: Duquesne University Press. Original edition, 1930.

Szilasi, Wilhelm. 1946. *Macht und Ohnmacht des Geistes. Interpretationen zu Platon: Philebos und Staat VI, Aristoteles: Nikomachische Ethik, Metaphysik IX und XII; über die Seele III; über die Interpretation C 1–5*. Bern: Francke Verlag.

Szondi, Eva Veronika. 1975. *Selbstmord bei Melancholikern und Schizophrenen im Lichte der Psychoanalyse, der Schicksalsanalyse und der Daseinsanalyse*. Bern, Stuttgart, Wien: Verlag Hans Huber.

Szondi, Leopold. 1965. *Schicksalsanalyse. Wahl in Liebe, Freundschaft, Beruf, Krankheit und Tod*. Basel, Stuttgart: Schwabe & Co.

Szondi, Peter. 1970. "L'herméneutique de Schleiermacher". *Poétique* 2: 141–55.

Szondi, Peter. 1971. "Lecture de Strette. Essai sur la poésie de Paul Celan". *Critique* 288 (5): 387–420.

Szondi, Peter. 1978. *Schriften I.* Frankfurt am Main: Suhrkamp.

Szondi, Peter. 1978a. *Schriften II.* Frankfurt am Main: Suhrkamp.

Szondi, Peter. 1978b. "Hope in the Past: On Walter Benjamin". Translated by Harvey Mendelsohn, *Critical Inquiry* 4 (3): 491–506. Original edition, 1961.

Szondi, Peter. 1983. "Reading 'Engführung': An Essay on the Poetry of Paul Celan". Translated by D. Caldwell, and S. Esh, *boundary 2* 11 (3): 231–64.

Szondi, Peter. 1986. "Friedrich Schlegel and Romantic Irony, with Some Remarks on Tieck's Comedies". In *On Textual Understanding and Other Essays.* Translated by Harvey Mendelsohn, 57–73. Minneapolis: University of Minnesota Press.

Szondi, Peter. 1986a. "The Poetry of Constancy: Paul Celan's Translation of Shakespeare's Sonnet 105". In *On Textual Understanding and Other Essays.* Translated by Harvey Mendelsohn, 161–80. Minneapolis: University of Minnesota Press.

Szondi, Peter. 1986b. "Walter Benjamin's City Portraits". In *On Textual Understanding and Other Essays.* Translated by Harvey Mendelsohn, 133–43. Minneapolis: University of Minnesota Press. Original edition, 1963.

Szondi, Peter. 1993. *Briefe,* edited by Christoph König, and Thomas Sparr. Frankfurt am Main: Suhrkamp.

Szondi, Peter. 2002. *An Essay on the Tragic.* Translated by Paul Fleming. Stanford, CA: Stanford University Press. Original edition, 1964.

Szondi, Peter. 2003. *Celan Studies.* Translated by Susan Bernofsky, and Harvey Mendelsohn. Stanford, CA: Stanford University Press.

Vietta, Silvio. 1992. *Die literarische Moderne. Eine problemgeschichtliche Darstellung der deutschsprachigen Literatur von Hölderlin bis Thomas Bernhard.* Stuttgart: Verlag J. B. Metzler.

Weidner, Daniel. 2015. "Reading the Wound. Peter Szondi's Essay on the Tragic and Walter Benjamin". In *Textual Understanding and Historical Experience. On Peter Szondi,* edited by Susanne Zepp, 55–69. Paderborn: Wilhelm Fink Verlag.

Wiedemann, Barbara. 2000. *Paul Celan – Die Goll-Affäre – Dokumente zu einer "Infamie",* edited by Barbara Wiedemann. Frankfurt am Main: Suhrkamp.

Worringer, Wilhelm. 1997. *Abstraction and Empathy: A Contribution to the Psychology of Style.* Translated by Michael Bullock. Chicago, IL: Ivan R. Dee Publisher. Original edition, 1908.

The Dark Side of the End of Art

Tomáš Murár

Art is now the absolute freedom that seeks its end and its foundation in itself, and does not need, substantially, any content, because it can only measure itself against the vertigo caused by its own abyss.
Giorgio Agamben: *The Man Without Content*

1 Introduction

In 1984, Arthur Coleman Danto famously formulated the end of art as the reach of the self-awareness of art becoming its own philosophy (Danto 1984). He showed that there was no more a need, on the one hand, to represent reality in an artwork, as had been common in early modern European art since the late 14th century, than to define art as art through its formal aspects, as was sought after in Europe as well as in the US in the early 20th century. The development of art in the second half of the 20th century newly pursued its philosophical meaning by transforming itself into a concept beyond the form. For Danto, the eye-opening experience for such consideration was an encounter with Andy Warhol's *Brillo Boxes* from 1964, at first sight indistinguishable from the Brillo boxes displayed in almost every grocery shop around the US. As Danto summarized it for *The A. W. Mellon Lectures in the Fine Arts*:

> To use my favorite example, nothing need mark the difference, outwardly, between Andy Warhol's Brillo Box and the Brillo boxes in the supermarket. And conceptual art demonstrated that there need not even be a palpable visual object for something to be a work of visual art. That meant

that you could no longer teach the meaning of art by example. It meant that as far as appearances were concerned, anything could be a work of art, and it meant that if you were going to find out what art was, you had to turn from sense experience to thought. You had, in brief, to turn to philosophy.[1] (Danto 1997, 13)

Warhol, according to Danto, made art that looked like a common commodity, therefore it looked like the outer world, but it was not representation thereof. The *Brillo Boxes* were also based on their formal determination as ordinary store bought Brillo boxes, but that did not determinate their meaning as art either. Therefore, neither representation nor formal aspects, according to Danto captured the meaning of Warhol's artwork. Rather, the being of the artwork gave the meaning to its form and to its relationship with the outer world. In other words, the art made its own meaning outside any narrative secondarily given to it (Danto [1984] 1986, 111–12). Such self-awareness of art, according to Danto ended the master narrative of art history as the authority making the meaning *for* art. Thus the end of art meant the end of art history, because its ending allowed art to thrive outside its corrective narratives.

Art history that ended was, in Danto's view a coherent narrative evolving its methodologies in the same manner as Hegel or Marx considered historical development, which meant pursuing its own end (Danto 1985, 184–6; Caroll 1998, 18–21; Agamben 1999, 40). Danto formulated the beginning of this process in the writings of the 16th century Italian painter Giorgio Vasari, with continuation in texts of the 20th century art historian Ernst Hans Gombrich, born in Vienna and active in England, who was subsequently surpassed by American art critic Clement Greenberg (Danto [1984] 1986, 86–99). Gombrich in continuation of Vasari, as Danto stated, tracked the improving representation of reality in art as it gradually gained its purpose, which reached its peak at the end of the 19th century. This, at the beginning of the 20th century led toward non-representational – abstract – art, omitting the need to represent the outer reality, but still built on the thought of the formal improvement of art as its own meaning. In Danto's view the formal innovation remained, only the representational orientated search was replaced by the purification of art turning into its own principles, thus was Gombrich's art history

---

1   Danto dealt with such a problem for the first time in 1981, in his book *The Transfiguration of the Commonplace.*

surpassed by Greenberg's concern about the Abstract expressionism of the US avant-garde of the 1940s and the 1950s.

With Warhol's art of the early 1960s this concept of art's meaning as embedded in its form was nevertheless, according to Danto revealed as only a path toward the main goal in reaching the true essence of art, that being its existence beyond its formal existence. In Danto's view, the end of art that occurred in Warhol's work enabled understanding art outside its historical development, revealing its true essence without the need to create secondary narratives according to its formal aspects. In other words, the historical development, how it was created by art history, facilitated its own end by revealing the master narrative based on the research of the form as inefficient for pursuing its goal, that goal being to understand the meaning of art in general, because this lay outside the material understanding of art.

When we take Danto seriously in his account that art history governed (falsely, according to Danto) the essence of art, shouldn't we also ask what art history pursued by its clarification of art? Shouldn't we, before saying that art history wrongly constructed the meaning of art, ask what was the meaning of art produced by art history? If we start from this premise, we can ask not only what is the meaning of art without art history (Snyder 2018, 205–10), but also what is the meaning of art history for art's existence in order to reach its own meaning. Can we really say that art exists as itself only after the end of art history? Or does the possibility exist that this realization is only an outcome of the art historical narrative, changing not according to art's own purpose to realize itself, as Danto suggested (Snyder 2018, 153–67), but according to the society producing the art historical explanation, thus how Niklas Luhmann understood the function of the end of art: as determined by the need to secure art's own existence by denying its own meaning to gain it outside its premises?

At the same time Arthur Danto diagnosed the end of art, Hans Belting gave thought to the end of art history (Belting 1984). He took a similar approach as Danto by observing how the change of social structures gradually affected the abandonment of the traditional concept of art as a form. Due to this process art history lost its privilege to explain art, whereas its methodologies were limited to grasping art only as a form. When form was not the primary interest of art, art history did not provide a general approach to understanding art and accordingly, it started to be replaced by other methods, based on non-formal aspects of art, as can be traced in Danto's art critical texts as well as in Belting's new approaches to historical art (Danto 1992; Belting 2001; Rampley 2012).

Thus the answer to what Danto's end of art for art history means can be found in Belting's argumentation. However, it can be extended by understanding the end of art in Luhmann's notion of art as a social system (*die Kunst der Gesellschaft*). It is true that Luhmann's concept has already been adapted for comprehending art after its end (Schinkel 2010). Nevertheless, some problems are still unresolved, such as the possible dark side of the end of art. Neither Danto nor Belting or other commentators on the end of art grasped art history as an essential part of every social system, in which art exists as always recreating its own meaning *through* art history in order to make itself understandable despite the changing circumstances (social, cultural, ideological). This so far neglected aspect of the autopoietic mechanism of art – as unrealizable in its own meaning because it exists in social structures to which the meaning is constructed by art history – can reveal its negativity not only as needed for art's existence, but also as an actually negative outcome for the emergence of art's meaning in art history, especially when the art becomes life, as happened in the 1960s, as Danto as well as Belting simultaneously agreed on the result of the end of art and art history (Danto 1997, 5–14; Belting 1995, 53–9).

2 Niklas Luhmann's End of Art and Art History as Emergence

"The self-negation of art is realized at the level of autopoietic operations in the form of art, *so that art can continue*. The much debated "end of art" does not necessarily imply stagnation; art can continue to move along – if not as a river, perhaps as an ocean. The end of art, the impossibility of art, the final sellout of all possible forms assumes a form that claims to be self-description and artwork at once, and this secures the reproduction of art as a perfectly autonomous system, a system that includes its own negation." (Luhmann 2000, 296–7)

Luhmann, in his project to set out a new theory of society included art as an autopoietic system, realizing its own prerequisites and its own ends as the problematic not issued to the art system from outside, as suggested by the cultural history of the 19th century (Prange 2007, 9–15), but by its own means, therefore closely to the way art was comprehended at the beginning of the 20th century by its scientific reading, generally called *Kunstwissenschaft* (Kleinbauer 1971, 124–64; Wood 2019, 252–71). As an intentional intellectual project, the *Kunstwissenschaft* can be traced back to the German journal *Zeitschrift für Ästhetik und allgemeine Kunstwissenschaft* founded by Max Dessoir in 1906, in order to distinguish the rigorous study of art from its narrative – cultural as well as bibliographical – histories, thus from the *Kunstgeschichte* (Karge 2010).

What Luhmann in his theory implicitly reveals for such distinction of art research at the turn of the 19th century is that both projects, *Kunstgeschichte* (history of art) as well as *Kunstwissenschaft* (science of art), were variables of art as a social system, thus results of art creating its own meaning by the conditions of the given social structures. In other words, not art itself, but the social circumstances of its interpreters were managing how and when art began and with it, also how and when art ended, because when the *Kunstgeschichte* was replaced by the *Kunstwissenschaft*, art as an historical narration ended and started to be a scientific investigation. However, art as a self-sufficient system in itself (Luhmann 2000, 298–300) remained: what changed was how society perceived it.

This means that art had to be changed in its meaning within the given society, but the meaning of art as art remained constant: the end of art as the *Kunstgeschichte* and its beginning as the *Kunstwissenschaft* was defined by the self-sufficiency of art in capturing its essence for the given social structures. In this view, the substitution of the past by the present, which means explaining the history of art in the contemporary research of art history (whether as *Kunstgeschichte, Kunstwissenschaft* or other methods), was created in order to enable art to secure its existence in the future – what was created as the contemporary meaning of historical art was meant to persist as its general essence for forthcoming generations. Those, however, because their social, cultural and ideological circumstances had changed, altered the meaning of art by producing another way to understand it – and this understanding was again secured by new, different methodologies of art history.

Thus art can be understood – in the notion of art as a social system proposed by Luhmann – as needed to be present(ed) as understandable in the given social structures to confirm its existence as art, for which purpose different art histories, created in different social systems initiate new meanings of art and end those no longer relevant because they are not related to contemporary social conditions. This shows that art, to be able to secure its own self-sufficiency (Luhmann 2000, 297–8), needs art history to produce for art an explication of its meaning in order to be understood in changing social structures. Therefore, the meaning of art can be understood as an emergence of the self-sufficiency of art and the given social circumstances: social structures enable art to create its own self-sufficiency and this self-sufficiency bestows upon the given social structures the right to produce their own meaning of art. The negation of the general meaning of art in order to secure its existence by producing a meaning according to the social structures is the vital force here for art's autopoietic existence.

Luhmann's parable on art as an ocean is, for such a comprehension of art history extremely suitable – the meaning of art is to sustain its vital, vast surface powered by its nether life varying in shapes, motions and destinations, thus its own existence without formal, content or even temporal borders. There is no need for anything outside for the existence of such a system. However, at the same time it cannot exist separately from the outer world. Thus when the general conditions change, the change is required in its own being in order to negate its self-sufficiency to be able to control its own ends and beginnings. Such changes can lead to the end of one type of form or content, however when one such variable in the self-sufficient system ends and even affects other variables included in the system, the constant remains the same, because it is not governed by a linear (historical) flow, as might be suggested by a Hegelian concept used by Danto, but by its own premises securing its existence by negating itself, thus as an open structural emergence of the meaning in the given time and place. Therefore, the end of art does not mean a disappearance of art's meaning, but it provides vitalizing shifts in order to retain art's meaning; the ends of art are stipulations of art's existence in a given social system governing art's possibility to exist as art.

When Danto ended art as art history, he revealed his own position in the social system in which the need occurred to retrieve not the essence of art, but its social comprehension. Danto's end of art, viewed from the perspective of the way Luhmann understood the concept, can thus be taken as only another inevitable end produced by art in order to validate its own continuation by its social comprehension. When Danto thought about art's historical development from Vasari to Gombrich and Greenberg as not capturing the essence of art, it was not that these concepts were unable to grasp the essence of art in general – which is unrealizable until art exists in any social structures giving it its meaning – rather, they were unable to show what art meant in Danto's social conditions in the mid-1980s.

The role of an art historian and other commentators on art such as Danto can hence be understood similarly to the role of an artist (Luhmann 2000, 297–9). Both artist and art historian create the essence of art in their shared social structures. An art historian's interpretation of art, despite his or her methodology of research – as, to Luhmann, it is unimportant whether the form or meaning of art is the primary interest of the artist – should be understood as an emergence of, on the one side, the system of art; on the other side, of art in the given social system in which the research is happening. Art history, regardless of its methodology in use, can therefore in general be understood as a specific cultural phenomenon revealing the meaning of art in the given social structures, thus as Wolfgang Iser understood the concept of emergence: variables of art-as-art and art-as-social-existence are intertwined in the manner in which art as a constant should be understood in its meaning as a variable, thus in the pursuit of its continuation overcoming its ends as its vitalizing stimuli to define itself in the given social, cultural or ideological conditions now and here (Iser 2013, 227–45). An art historian's approach as creating such emergence varies according to art's own individual meaning abbreviated by contemporary social, cultural or ideological premises. An art historian as given the authority by society to produce the meaning of art pursues his or her goal of research in order to resume the concept of art as art for his or her own social, cultural or ideological values. Thus an art historian participates in the self-sufficiency of art by negating its general meaning in giving it the meaning important for the social structures of his or her own, which are at the same time needed for resuming art as art in its generality. This process of negating art's essence to secure its existence needs to be constant in order to secure the comprehension of art in different social conditions. However, when this negation inherent in art's autopoietic mechanism shifts to life as the emergence of art's meaning instead of to the form (Luhmann 2000, 296) – as, according to Danto this happened in the 1960s (Danto [1984] 1986, 113–5) – it can have tragic consequences.

3 Robert Klein's "Notes on the End of the Image"

In 1962 Enrico Castelli organized one of his famous international colloquiums, titled *Demitizzazione e immagine*, bringing into the Italian milieu the then important questions of philosophy, theology and, last but not least, the arts. Among the important philosophers participating in the colloquium were Paul Ricœur and Umberto Eco (Castelli 1962, 13–18, 131–48;

Giannini 1962, 628–30); the problematic of art and its demystification were dealt with by art historian Robert Klein, who presented his "Notes on the End of the Image" (Castelli 1962, 123–7; Giannini 1962, 631).

Klein opened his talk by showing that when art changes outside its own meaning, that means when its significance was given to it secondarily, it becomes its own parody. On examples from ancient art to Dadaism to Tachist art, Klein showed that what survives time is only the form, not its meaning, which is embedded in the structures in which it was created. In his words, at the moment when an artwork is put into a glass display case of a museum instead of a church altar, "all art that has outlived its time becomes self-parody" (Klein [1962] 1979, 171). However, Klein continued, art becoming its own parody was inevitable for the process of art's existence in general: "desacralization and misreading are the motors of artistic life, as inseparable from creation as from judgement" (Klein [1962] 1979, 171).

When art loses its meaning and the form survives over time, the academic – art historical – consideration enters into the process of art's existence, solving the task of understanding art that has lost its primary significance. Therefore, according to Klein, secondary concepts (which we have seen as the specific cultural emergences of art's meaning) were developed in order to secure the meaning of art in its surviving forms – according to them, the academic examinations abbreviated art's general meaning into particular exemplifications of its importance for contemporary judgements. Therefore, Klein continued, the formulas of the "right" art varied from confronting the work of art with the external reality to considering works of art as executed in order to emotionally conquer the viewer and so on. This variability was rooted in the fact that the "rightness" of art was not judged in the context of art's meaning, but within society and its prerequisites that approached the surviving forms of art. Every society was structuralized in itself, thus Klein spoke about subtler "correctives" as regulations of genres, more generally about the need of "a certain element of style" that was considered as historically changing in order to satisfy the period demands on the meaning of art – not art itself, but its correctives as the concept of style evident in the changed forms (Klein [1962] 1979, 172).

In Klein's view, this abbreviation of the meaning of art according to the surviving form ended at the beginning of the 20th century with Impressionism, Symbolism and Expressionism. In these artistic conceptions the form of an artwork gave art its timeless character, because the form was newly the meaning of art, not its survival proposed to become its own parody in its examination: "a Tachist canvas is nothing more than itself, and cannot be measured against anything" (Klein [1962] 1979, 172). This shift produced the meaning of art not in its examination, but in its visibility *as visibility*. For art it meant that: "the death of criticism brings in its wake the death of the work of art as a possible object of aesthetic appreciation" (Klein [1962] 1979, 173). Klein in this argumentation referred to the philosophy of Edmund Husserl and took the act of looking *as such*, realizing the artwork *as such* – the gaze bracketed the artwork as the intentional act made for seeing and thus by its reconstruction the meaning without its additive commentary could have been revealed: "it is [...] the conclusion of the act of looking that constitutes it as such" (Klein [1962] 1979, 174). Thus art, as Klein continued, can actually create its own meaning, but it is a meaning without intentionality – the meaning of art as existing in the given social structures is lost: "art as intention or act (of the artist, or the public, or both together), at once the foundation and the negation of its products" (Klein [1962] 1979, 173).[2] To reveal what is art in such structures, a "relativization" of art's meaning must have taken place: the art's visibility had to be negated as the general essence of art in order to understand art's existence in the given cultural surroundings. As Klein pointed out:

> At present art is elsewhere than within that which serves as its pretext – but it is before, and not behind, the work: in the glance that poses it, in the mechanism that produces it, in the invention of such mechanisms, and so on. That is where we are now: on one side the "ideal model" posited by the academic dichotomy, unreal but in the end inseparable from all art criticism and every work. (Klein [1962] 1979, 173)

If we put Klein's "Notes on the End of the Image" in comparison with Danto's "The End of Art", we can see the key distinction in their consideration of the importance of art's materiality. Danto showed that the meaning of art was *beyond* the art form. The form negated the meaning of

---

2 Klein elaborated such argumentation one year later, when he pointed out the impossibility of criticism to grasp the meaning of art without intentionality: "Once 'reference' is abandoned, the work can measure itself only against itself; criticism is no longer possible, since commentary, however understanding or faithful, places alongside the painting something with which it is compared; there is no longer any effect, since effect is aimed at a third party and thus introduces an alien point of view into the intentionality of the creator; there is no longer any work, since the work is, despite everything, a reality opposed to the consciousness that poses it" (Klein [1963] 1979a, 191).

art as such, because the indistinguishability of Warhol's *Brillo Boxes* from Brillo boxes in stores revealed the nonsense of art as existing only as the form. According to Danto, this negation was created as a reaction to the master narrative of art history preferring the meaning of art as form (representational or non-representational). Klein understood the form of art as securing the existence of art as its own meaning *before* it was given into the social structures. The form became the meaning because art for its existence needed the interpretation of the society in which it existed as form. When the form did not become the work of art by its affirmation in its examination and remained only as the surviving form coming from different historical, cultural or ideological contexts, it became its own parody. From the standpoint of art's meaning, form was a prerequisite to validate its existence in the outside word that secured it thanks to art's visibility according to which – as a validation of its existence – the art's meaning was produced in an examination appropriate to the social structures in art history. Thus the essence of art as art needed to negate itself by visualizing itself as a form, according to which meaning of art was created in social structures by art history. In Klein's words, the emergence of the essence of art "is beginning under our very eyes to substitute itself for the work of art", and therefore,

> the art work is no longer an in-itself; it is the end of a certain process that may, in the retrospective view [...] be called artistic creation. [...] In this way one suggests that any phenomenon has two sides, one natural, according to causes, the other artistic, according as it is seen. (Klein [1962] 1979, 173–4)

Klein therefore showed, in contrast to Danto, that the end of art did not destroy art's form in order to demonstrate it as secondary for the consideration of art's meaning, rather he understood the form as the outcome of the shift of the meaning happening before the making of the form of art: "contemporary art being what it is, the work only exists through a paradox, as if despite itself, by negating itself" (Klein [1962] 1979, 173). This means that the form is the emergence of art's meaning in its intersection of art-as-art and art-as-social-existence, thus form was for Klein the key existence securing art as art as well as art in changing social, cultural or ideological conditions. The paradox to which Klein gave thought was thus the process of the autopoietic existence of art built on the prerequisite to negate itself as the stipulation for preserving itself. Therefore, when form disappeared from this process and the existence of art had to be secured by life, life needed to become the emergence of this paradoxical autopoietic process, including its negativity.

4 The Dark Side of the End of Art

Arthur Danto saw the end of art retrospectively, thus in the way in which it was possible to see it as an artistic process, as Klein argued. Thanks to this retrospective comprehension Danto posited Warhol's art at the beginning of "Post-Historical" art as existing without any historical corrective (Danto [1984] 1986, 83–5). He was able to say what led to the end of art and what happened after it in order to make new art understandable for his own times (Danto 1997, 21–40). Robert Klein's end of art was formulated in a different way, because it was not defined from a retrospective standpoint – for him, the end of art was happening now. Witnessing the end of art, Klein did not pursue the strengthening of the structures of his contemporary society not understanding new art, he was rather searching for his own position in social structures by trying to understand the meaning of the end of art through the disappearance of its forms. This is evident in his text "The Eclipse of the Work of Art" written in 1967.

In the text Klein took seriously the avant-garde's attempt to destroy art. He pointed out – in a premise similar to Danto's – that the aim was not against art in general, but against the concept of an artwork. He showed that the need to destroy the materiality of art was caused by the consumption of works of art since the early 20th century, when art became a commodity that was technically reproduced to create the illusion of its accessibility to everyone. This process led to a deprivation of art's "aura", as Klein took up Walter Benjamin's argumentation from 1935 (Klein [1967] 1979b, 177); a work of art because of its high status as a rarity paradoxically lost its need to be presented as the form, because it was disseminated as its own technical reproduction (Benjamin [1935] 2006). In the 1960s, when art devoid of its aura in addition existed only in the closed "Artworld" – if we use Danto's concept for those participating in art's creation, display, examination and trade (Danto 1964) – it was newly eroded by the contemporary avant-garde as logically attacking the concept of the form as senseless, as shown by Warhol as well as Daniel Spoerri, as Klein pointed out (Klein [1967] 1979b, 178). Their art stripped down the relevance of the form as only an historical concept of art. Danto saw this process as finally getting beyond the form, which meant the liberation of art; Klein similarly indicated that the form was inevitably destined to be destroyed by "our repugnance at certain embodied values," because they were understood as "bourgeois" (Klein [1967] 1979b, 177). Thus we see the similarity of Klein's prognosis with Danto's diagnosis of the end of art in the 1960s. However, Klein in contrast to Danto – because he did not have the retrospective standpoint – asked what happens with art without the form as the emergence of its meaning between art-as-art and art-as-social-existence.

Klein showed that attempts to end art by creating "anti-art" already existed. As in the 1960s, they were not actually aimed against art *per se*, but against the society governing the meaning of art's forms. He stated examples in the works of Adrian Brower, Gustav Courbet and others, who were "showing indirectly, and sometimes despite themselves, that 'art' was elsewhere and could go on" (Klein [1967] 1979b, 177). However, as Klein observed, these attempts to end art in order to make it anew and by it support other than the dominant social structures were always expressed in forms, thus even though the art ended in the given society it always existed as a materiality that could have survived the end of art. The loss of form in the 1960s was therefore the fundamental difference from other ends of art.

Klein knew that form after the end of art had to be demystified of its historical values (Klein [1967] 1979b, 183). However, this was possible only when the values could have been taken from the surviving (although parodied) forms, as he showed in 1962. Therefore, according to him two questions must have been asked before the eclipse of the work of art was taken as the given outcome of the then happening end of art: "Can one imagine a state of affairs in which art could dispense with works of art? Or can one imagine works of art that would not be incarnations of values and congealed experience?" (Klein [1967] 1979b, 183). Klein posited these questions at the end of his text and did not answer them. Hypothetically speaking, the indirect answer can be found in his suicide few months after finishing the text.

We have seen that in Danto's argumentation the loss of the form in the end of art in the 1960s led to the possibility to consider everything in life as art, thus as a positive (and desired) outcome: the consequence of the end of art was a different life secured by its rightness as the new meaning of art. Klein, on the other hand, without the retrospective view that would be "after" the end of art, took life as the now happening emergence of the meaning of art without the existence of its form: at the moment life took on the role of art's meaning instead of the form, life had to secure art's existence. And at that instant:

> The inevitable came to pass: nowadays chance has full citizenship in the work of art, but a domesticated form of citizenship. A way has been found to limit the damage inflicted on the embodying work and to use tamed chance to disclose new aspects of art beyond the work itself. (Klein [1967] 1979b, 178)

Klein paraphrased here what he talked about in Rome – that the given society provides the meaning of the art even after it ends. However, when the "domesticity" of a work of art is lost, its meaning is lost as well. This means that without the surviving form that could gain other meanings in other structures as an emergence, the art as art is destined to end permanently. In other words, for Danto the replacement of the form with life was a liberation of the meaning of art, for Klein the loss of form meant an impossibility to give art its meaning as life, because of its negative autopoietic character happening at the end of art.

Klein's text from 1967 might thus refer to the overwhelming experience found by him in the late 1960s: art as newly embedded in life affected life with its impossibility to realize in itself because it was existing without an actual form. Thus life as newly giving the art its meaning instead of the form – from which life could have distanced itself and the form could have survived in different social, cultural or ideological structures – existed according to art's paradoxical need to find its meaning in social structures. When this meaning was not reached, art sought to end itself in order to secure its existence in different outward circumstances. This shift of art's meaning from form to life may have had a tragic outcome for Klein, regarding his own personal history: when in 1948 he proclaimed himself a political refugee in France with a result of losing his nationality, taken from him by the Romanian government he, as he wrote in his biographical note in 1965, "remained without nationality until the present day" (Klein [1965] 1979c, vii).[3] The following year Klein

---

3 Klein also mentioned other important events in his life: he was born on 9 September 1918 in Timisoara, in 1936–7 he studied medicine in Cluj, in 1937–8 philosophy in Prague, in 1938–9 sciences in Bucharest. During the WWII he did a military service in the Romanian army, then he was as a Jew forced to work in labor camps. After liberating Romania Klein joined the Allies during the liberation of Hungary and Czechoslovakia. In 1947 he finished his university studies with a degree in philosophy from the university in Bucharest and he was awarded a French Government Scholarship to study in Paris. There in the Spring of 1948 he proclaimed himself

received a prestigious research scholarship in Villa I Tatti in Florence, the Harvard Center of the studies on the Italian Renaissance (Chastel 1968, 200–1). Klein moved to Florence in 1966, and the following year, on 22 April, he committed suicide by overdosing on sleeping pills (Hendler 2018). The circumstances as to why Klein killed himself are still unresolved today – as is most of his contribution to art historical discourse of the late 20th century.[4]

However, due to Klein's lack of nationality to which he referred in 1965 and due to his witnessing the end of art of which he thought in 1962 and in 1967, we can see that he might have been caught in the paradoxical autopoietic process of art – Klein, without a nationality could have not found the possibility to give art, now becoming life, its meaning in the given social structures, because his life had none. Nor he could have found the meaning of art in particular forms of life as in his art historical research, because any form of materiality after the end of art lost its meaning.[5] Thus the only thing left was bare life as the emergence of art's autopoietic existence with its negative mechanics in denying itself in order to secure its existence. This process, at the moment when the emergence of art-as-art and art-as-social-existence became life instead of form, led to the tragic outcome in Klein's death by suicide, thus according to Klein only by Dadaists rightly understood way how to negate form in order to secure art's meaning:

The need to break with the work of art has been widespread since the beginning of this century; it has often been deep and sincere. Still, artists could not shake the feeling that it was a death wish. Only the Dadaists, attested specialists in suicide, endeavored to satisfy it directly. (Klein [1967] 1979b, 179)

---

a political refugee and the Romanian nationality was taken from him as well as the French scholarship. He then gave private lessons and took various jobs as washing dishes until he graduated from *l'Ecole pratique des hautes études, IVᵉ section* under the supervision of art historian André Chastel.

4 In 2018 the first attempt to research Klein's importance for art historical discourse of the 20th century took place in Florence in the form of an international conference. Interest in Klein's art history was initiated in 2013 when his estate was given to the library of French National Institute of Art History (INHA). Most of Klein's work was devoted to studies of Italian Renaissance art. In 1970 André Chastel published Klein's collected essays, titled *La forme et l'intelligible*.

5 As Klein pointed out in 1963: "Art cannot but end up as a presence, as a thing – while remaining meaning insofar as it is the living commentary of a living experience. To believe that meaning can fill that presence is an illusion, but a necessary one [...]" (Klein [1963] 1979a, 198).

5 Conclusion

Giorgio Agamben recently mentioned the above examined Klein's text from 1967 as an early example of the decomposition of the work of art (*l'opera d'arte*) by art as "devouring what had always defined its basis: its own work" (Agamben 2019, 3). Pointing out Alexandre Kojève's notion on the end of history in this context, Agamben inadvertently not only put Klein's thinking into the framework of *homo sacer*, thus as someone who was deprived from his social status as it happened to Klein in 1948,[6] but also into the context of the end of art opened by Arthur Danto in 1984.[7] Thus if we understand such reading as related to the interpretation proposed in this study, Klein's position in the discussion on the end of art – diagnosed by Danto as happening in the 1960s – can be comprehended in a speculative character helping us to understand its negative outcome.[8] That means when we are searching solely for the motives of Klein's suicide his other biographical circumstances need to be taken into consideration. These are so far, nevertheless veiled in mystery.[9] Thus for the time being what we can rely on when trying to understand Klein's suicide is his lack of nationality and his searching for comprehension of art's changes happening at the time of his death. These aspects – when taken from the standpoint of the self-sufficiency of art described by Niklas Luhmann and extended by understanding the role of art history as the basic instrument for securing art's existence – can show the dark side of the end of art, missing from the enthusiastic proclamation made by Arthur Danto.

Hence when we are considering the end of art, we need to see not only what it might bring for the future (for Danto the future was constructed retrospectively as an artistic process), but also what is lost in such a process, what is destroyed in order to secure the existence of the new. To put it another way, we need to ask what the end of art might mean for its art historical examination comprehended as a fundamental instrument of its autopoietic existence. From this standpoint the concept of the end

---

6   For the notion of *homo sacer* see Agamben 1998.
7   For the intellectual relationship of Kojève and Danto see Cascales 2018.
8   For the notion of speculation in art history see Vellodi 2017.
9   Klein did leave two pages long suicide note addressed to his friend, Renzo Federici. However, in the letter he did not explain reasons why he took his life apart from a cryptic sentence "I have many convincing reasons for getting off the train". In the letter Klein mostly left instructions who to inform about his death and what to say in which language. Klein even referred that his suicide note was rather "a business letter" (Hendler 2018).

of art can carry a tragic side when the meaning that should have been formulated in the given society by art history became embedded in life, as can be perceptible in Robert Klein's cryptic suicide at the time when the end of art occurred without a given retrospective development: Klein, in contrast to Danto saw only the end of art as the current emergence of art's meaning, no "after". In other words, when the emergence of the meaning of art became life, thus without any correction as a form, art as life negated itself as unrealizable in itself and led to its inevitable end.

Robert Klein's thoughts on the end of art from 1962 and 1967 thus *devour* Danto's positive take on the meaning of the concept, because they show that it can be taken as beneficial only until the meaning of art lies in the social structures. In such a premise art's autopoietic process generating negativity against itself is vital for the existence of art. However, at the moment when art, after its end is substituted by life itself, thus it is no longer secured by social (artistic) forms, the vitality of art is replaced by the tragedy of life.

References

Agamben, Giorgio. 1998. *Homo Sacer: Sovereign Power and Bare Life*. Translated by Daniel Heller-Roazen. Stanford, CA: Stanford University Press.

Agamben, Giorgio. 1999. *The Man without Content*. Translated by Georgia Albert. Stanford, CA: Stanford University Press.

Agamben, Giorgio. 2019. *Creation and Anarchy. The Work of Art and the Religion of Capitalism*. Translated by Adam Kotsko. Stanford, CA: Stanford University Press.

Belting, Hans. 1984. *Das Ende der Kunstgeschichte?* München: Deutscher Verlag.

Belting, Hans. 1995. *Das Ende der Kunstgeschichte: eine Revision nach Zehn Jahren*. München: Verlag C. H. Beck.

Belting, Hans. 2001. *Bild-Anthropologie. Entwürfe für eine Bildwissenschaft*. München: Wilhelm Fink Verlag.

Benjamin, Walter. 2006. "The Work of Art in the Age of Its Technological Reproducibility". In *Selected Writings. Volume 3, 1935–1938*, edited by Howard Eiland, and Michael W. Jennings, 101–33. Cambridge, MA, London: Harvard University Press. Original edition, 1935.

Caroll, Noël. 1998. "The End of Art?" *History and Theory* 37 (4): 17–29.

Cascales, Raquel. 2018. "The Development of the Sense of the End of Art in Arthur Danto", *Rivista di estetica* 68. http://journals.openedition.org/estetica/3542. Accessed 14 May 2021.

Castelli, Enrico. 1962. *Demitizzazione e immagine*. Padova: Cedam. Casa editrice Dott. Antonio Milani.

Chastel, André. 1968. "Robert Klein (1918–1967)". *Bibliothèque d'Humanisme et Renaissance* 30 (1): 199–201.

Danto, Arthur Coleman. 1964. "The Artworld". *The Journal of Philosophy* 61: 571–84.

Danto, Arthur Coleman. 1984. "The End of Art". In *The Death of Art*, edited by Berel Lang, 5–35. New York: Haven Publication.

Danto, Arthur Coleman. 1985. "The Philosophical Disenfranchisement of Art". *Grant Street* 4 (3): 171–89.

Danto, Arthur Coleman. 1986. "The End of Art". In *The Philosophical Disenfranchisement of Art*, 81–115. New York: Columbia University Press. Original edition, 1984.

Danto, Arthur Coleman. 1992. *Beyond the Brillo Box. The Visual Arts in Post-Historical Perspective*. Berkeley: University of California Press.

Danto, Arthur Coleman. 1997. *After the End of Art: Contemporary Art and the Pale of History*. Princeton, NJ: Princeton University Press.

Giannini, Giorgio. 1962. "Demitizzazione e immagine, Atti del Convegno indetto dal Centro internazionale di studi umanistici e dall'Istituto di studi filosofici by Enrico Castelli". *Rivista di Filosofia Neo-Scolastica* 54 (6): 627–40.

Hendler, Sefy. 2018. "The Brilliant Jewish Art Scholar Who Survived WWII and Killed Himself Once His Career Took Off". *Haaretz* 28 November, https://www.haaretz.com /world-news/europe/.premium.MAGAZINE-the-brilliant-art-scholar-who-killed-himself -once-his-career-took-off-1.6697052. Accessed 4 April 2021.

Iser, Wolfgang. 2013. *Emergenz. Nachgelassene und verstreut publizierte Essays*, edited by Alexander Schmitz. Konstanz: Konstanz University Press.

Karge, Henrik. 2010. "Stilgeschichte versus Kulturgeschichte: Zur Entfaltung der kunsthistorischen Methodik in den Jahrzenten ab 1850". In *Die Etablierung und Entwicklung des Faches Kunstgeschichte in Deutschland, Polen und Mitteleuropa*, edited by Wojciech Bałus, and Joanna Wolańska, 41–59. Warszawa: Instytut Sztuki Polskiej Akademii Nauk.

Klein, Robert. 1979. "Notes on the End of Image". Translated by Madeline Jay, and Leon Wieseltier. In *Form and Meaning. Essays on the Renaissance and Modern Art*, edited by Henri Zerner, 170–5. Princeton, NJ: Princeton University Press. Original edition, 1962.

Klein, Robert. 1979a. "Modern Painting and Phenomenology". Translated by Madeline Jay, and Leon Wieseltier. In *Form and Meaning. Essays on the Renaissance and Modern Art*, edited by Henri Zerner, 184–99. Princeton, NJ: Princeton University Press. Original edition, 1963.

Klein, Robert. 1979b. "The Eclipse of the Work of Art". Translated by Madeline Jay, and Leon Wieseltier. In *Form and Meaning. Essays on the Renaissance and Modern Art*, edited by Henri Zerner, 176–83. Princeton, NJ: Princeton University Press. Original edition, 1967.

Klein, Robert. 1979c. "Foreword". Translated by Madeline Jay, and Leon Wieseltier. In *Form and Meaning. Essays on the Renaissance and Modern Art*, edited by Henri Zerner, vii–xi. Princeton, NJ: Princeton University Press. Original edition, 1965.

Kleinbauer, Eugene. 1971. *Modern Perspectives in Western Art History*. New York: Holt, Rinehart and Winston, Inc.

Luhmann, Niklas. 2000. *Art as a Social System*. Translated by Eva M. Knodt. Stanford, CA: Stanford University Press.

Prange, Regine. 2007. *Kunstgeschichte 1750–1900*. Darmstadt: WBG.

Rampley, Matthew. 2012. *Art History and Visual Studies in Europe: Transnational Discourses and National Frameworks*. Boston, MA: Brill Publishing.

Schinkel, Willem. 2010. "The Autopoiesis of the Artworld after the End of Art". *Cultural Sociology* 4 (2): 267–90.

Snyder, Stephen. 2018. *End-of-Art Philosophy in Hegel, Nietzsche and Danto*. London: Palgrave Macmillan.

Vellodi, Kamini. 2017. "Speculation, Critique, Constructivism: Notions for Art History". In *Speculative Art Histories. Analysis at the Limits*, edited by Sjoerd van Tuinen, 203–24. Edinburgh: Edinburgh University Press.

Wood, Christopher. 2019. *A History of Art History*. Princeton, NJ, Oxford: Princeton University Press.

The Author in the Making: Ethos, Posture, and Self-Creation

Josef Šebek

When a literary text comes into being – a complex process that develops by stages from the initial project, through the act of writing, and on to publication and its reception by readers and critics – another entity simultaneously comes into being (or undergoes change). This other entity, no less complex, is called the *author*. In what sense does the work participate in *creating* the author? And how can this process of self-creation, or *autopoiesis* be made intelligible for others? In this study I will try to answer these questions with the help of several recent theories of authorship that explore the interrelationship between author, text, and social context.

1 Layers of the Author

The conceptual history of Western literary authorship can be conceived as a complex interweaving of notions originating in the ancient philosophy, rhetoric, and theory of poetry, spanning from *inspiration* to *techné*. In the early modern period, the development of the concept of the author would be influenced by certain key contexts, including the gradual formation of modern subjectivity, the notion of literature as an imaginative mode of writing, and the modern system of the arts (Burke 1995; Bennett 2005; Meizoz 2007, 33–46). From the 16th to 18th century the transformation of the author into the figure of individual creator and social agent was well underway, but other models remained firmly established: anonymous and collective authorship as well as forms of writing carried out on the part of *auctoritas* and precepts. In the second half of the 18th century, a number of new contexts – pre-romantic and romantic aesthetics, German idealist philosophy, and the new material, institutional, and legal frameworks of publishing – were integrated into the concept, so that the author figure was now seen as original creator and source of inspiration *vis-à-vis* the newly expanded reading public and growing class of critics and scholars (Abrams 1953; Tatarkiewicz 1980; Woodmansee 1994). By the post-romantic period of the 19th century, the centrality of the author had become firmly established. In the 20th century, however, the concept of the author came under attack from several critical positions, and the "struggle" against the idea of the biographical and expressive author has been one of the major tenets of literary criticism. One influential solution was to split the author into textual and extra-textual instances, with interest predominantly on the former, and theoretical focus gradually shifting from work to reader. Since the last decades of the 20th century this theoretical *doxa* has been undermined by scholars who believe, on the one hand, that it is imperative to reject the view of the author in the romantic tradition – or better, to historicize it –, and on the other that it is not particularly desirable (or feasible) to excise the author entirely from literary scholarship, and who therefore seek more sophisticated and layered models of authorship (Burke 1998).

As this brief outline of the history of the Western concept of literary authorship demonstrates, the author has been "in the making" – in literary texts as well as in theory – for quite some time. Yet this making of the author is carried out also in different, related and equally important sense: the author becomes himself in the process of writing and publishing, as an agent active in the literary field and a public persona, and also in a more general manner as someone who tries to achieve something and who is in turn formed by this endeavor. This applies to all arts and indeed any branch of human creativity; yet the author of literary texts – in complex and often indirect ways – achieves a specific form of visibility. It is this aspect, the reciprocity or even *retroactivity* of author and work, that has come into prominence in recent theories of authorship. Here, the author is a mediator between literary and social contexts, texts and publics, a locus where the literary and the social intersect and become intelligible.

The point of reference for this concept is Foucault's essay "What Is an Author?" (Foucault 1979). Despite its strongly "antiauthorial" reputation, it is this essay that originally set the agenda for the historical exploration of the "author function" and of the discursive shaping of the role of the author in particular eras and milieus. This agenda has been carried out by scholars like Roger Chartier (1994; 1995), Martha Wood-mansee (1994), and Alain Viala (1985), who have concentrated on the early modern period in French, British, and German contexts. Common to these approaches is the emphasis on frameworks that participate in constructing the role of the author in a given moment: the materiality and mediality of texts, the market, political and legal institutions, and the reading public.

However, the strongest impulse for reinstating the figure of the author came from the theory of the literary field formulated by Pierre Bour-dieu and summed up in his book *The Rules of Art* (Bourdieu 1996; 1993), one that – in spite of Bourdieu's express intention to bridge the internal and external reading of the literary work, thus forging a new "science of works" – launched a new sociology of authors, especially in the French context. If Bourdieu's theory did not accomplish the integration of text and social context as an approach to reading, it could be given credit for the renewed interest in studies that focus on the author.[1]

In Bourdieu's view, the author becomes himself by adopting positions available in the literary field (predominantly by writing and publishing literary texts); it is the sequence of these adopted positions that shapes the author's trajectory. This provides one model for the social creation of the author. The identity of the individual in the field, however, is more or less predetermined by field's internal pressures. Authorship is con-ceptualized here on the basis of the literary field, while its relationship to other fields and the wider social space is disregarded. Issues regard-ing the pre-literary or extra-literary habitus of the author are marginal-ized: aspects of his personal history, opinions, and behavior that are not directly related to the field are virtually irrelevant.

What matters for Bourdieu is the milieu of the author, narrowly conceived as other authors, critics, publishers etc. that are relevant as agents. The reading public is included in the model only as consumers of production in the heteronomous, commercial sector of the field. We might argue against Bourdieu that the genuine life of the literary work is shaped by the way it is read and interpreted in the wider social space (not just in the literary field). It is only with regard to these aspects of the work's reception that its full potential meaning is allowed to unfold,

---

1 Predominantly, but not exclusively, in the Francophone context; see among others: Viala 1985; Boschetti 1988; Sapiro 2011, 2014, 2018, 2020; Sapiro and Rabot 2017; Lahire 2006, 2010, 2010a, 2010b; Meizoz 2007, 2012, 2016; Casanova 2004, 2005, 2015; Lagasnerie 2011, 2011a; Dorleijn, Grüttemeier and Korthals Altes 2010; Martin et al. 2010.

relating it at the same time to other social discourses – politics, gender and sexuality, class, race, etc. The identities that matter are not just "literary identities" in the literary field but those constituted in the wider social space. A comprehensive research in this direction was carried out by scholars working in such fields as feminist, postcolonial, and gay and lesbian studies (though theoretical issues related specifically to authorship were at times left underdeveloped). Another important perspective on the author and authorship that is left out in Bourdieu's framework is the individual creative act, and a more nuanced view of author's own relation to the work (Lagasnerie 2011; 2011a).

In the analysis that follows, I will focus on a group of recent approaches that bring the author back into the discourse as a central figure, meanwhile dealing with some of the problems that Bourdieu's theory of the literary field largely neglects, re-conceptualizing the author as a central node in a complex interactional process. Their basic objectives are:

1. to bridge the gap between the textual and contextual, with the understanding that the literary field is only part of a bigger picture;
2. to conceive of the literary text as an act on the part of an author that is re-created (or rather co-created) by the reader;
3. to identify adequate models for the discursive framework in which this act takes place;
4. to understand the literary text in relation to the identity of the author, without thereby (re)introducing the notion of identity as a stable quality; identity is seen rather as a *work in progress* in which the (creation of) the literary text plays a role.

With an aim to understanding these objectives, our key questions will be: How does the author present himself in the discourse? How does this self-presentation relate to his identity? And how can the creation of a literary text be conceived as an act of self-creation? After discussing the concepts of authorship I will test this view of authorship in a reading of Édouard Louis' autofictional novel *The End of Eddy* published in 2014.

2 Ethos, Posture, and the Author's Identity

An Effective Speech

Our point of departure will be Ruth Amossy's theory of rhetoric, argumentation, and self-presentation in discourse, according to which "all verbal exchange rests on a play of mutual influences and on the effort, more or less conscious and acknowledged, to use speech to act upon the other" (Amossy 2008, 1). She focuses on the first and last in the ancient rhetorical triad *logos* – *pathos* – *ethos*. In her theory of argumentation in discourse, under the aegis of *logos*, she shows how this kind of exchange is at work in virtually all utterances, either in the form of a "persuasion aim" (*persuasion programmée*) or "argumentative dimension" (*dimension argumentative*). In the latter case, "the work of persuasion is indirect and often unacknowledged" and the argumentative aspect is present as "the tendency of all discourse to direct the way one's partner (or partners) sees a particular matter" (Amossy 2008, 3–4). This tendency is, according to Amossy, present also in "a large part of fictional narratives" (Amossy 2008, 4). Amossy thus advocates a "broader conception of argumentation, understood as an attempt to modify, influence, or simply reinforce, by means of language, an interlocutor's way of seeing things" (Amossy 2008, 2; Amossy 2021).

A related – and in our context even more pertinent – rhetorical dimension of every utterance is its *ethos*, by which Amossy means "the elaboration of a favorable image of oneself, one that conveys his authority and credibility" (Amossy 2010, 5). Again, according to Amossy, this image of the self is characteristic of all utterances, to the point that it is an "integrating dimension of discourse" (Amossy 2010, 7). Ethos is an image that the speaker must build in order to gain trust and win the favor of an audience. Yet the process of building ethos is always interactive, not only because it is subject to the interpretations of a particular audience, which necessarily implies a certain hermeneutic dimension, but in its very principle:

> the discursive construction of ethos is realised through a series of mirror reflections. The orator builds his own image as a function of the image he forms of the audience, that is to say, of the representations of what a trustworthy and competent orator is in the eyes of the public as the orator imagines it. (Amossy 2001, 6)

Constitution of ethos is dynamic and process-oriented:

> The act of self-presentation can be isolated only in an artificial way, by privileging one moment over others in a perpetual flow, a continuous movement. My image of myself is always subject to the reaction of the other and caught in the circulation of discourses. (Amossy 2010, 154)

In order for an ethos to be intelligible it must consist in social regularities and pre-existing images – in what Amossy calls "stereotypes": "The orator adapts his self-presentation to collective schemas which he believes are ratified and valued by the target public" (Amossy 2001, 8). This holds also for the "prior ethos" – the image that the audience already has of a speaker before encountering his utterance:

> the prior idea which one forms of the speaker and the image of self which the speaker constructs in discourse cannot be totally singular. To be recognised by the audience, both have to be bound up with a *doxa*, or linked to shared representations. (Amossy 2001, 7)

The idea of relying on "stereotypes" has important consequences for literary texts: in Bourdieu's view it is the literary field that shapes the relationship between author and text. Any relation to the wider social sphere, including the "reading public" (which does not belong to the literary field in the strict sense), is considered irrelevant. According to Amossy, ethos is mediated by stereotypes that are part of the "social imaginary", which means that the author's effective image (ethos) is based on sets of images and stereotypes that are not exclusively literary: "The discursive construction [the ethos as constructed in a text – J. Š.], the social imaginary [the socially shared images and stereotypes], and the institutional authority [the literary field] contribute [...] to construct a suitable ethos" (Amossy 2001, 21).

How exactly is the ethos constituted in literary fiction, where the speaking subject inevitably splits into more instances (the real author, the implied author, the narrator, the character)? Whose ethos is constructed there, and whose ethos is it that the reader and interpreter are trying to reconstruct? The overall ethos of the author, always connected to the "social imaginary" as well as the literary field, is constructed outside the text – by the author and by others – as well as within it, as an interplay of the narrator's ethos and the author's ethos (as it is shaped in the text). It is only by the convergence of these three aspects, in their mutual interaction, that the author is apprehended by the reader, and "the force of the discourse [...] strives to act on the other, and to influence, strengthen, or modify the other's representations" (Amossy 2009, 8).

One of Amossy's major assumptions is that the speaker establishes his social and individual identity precisely – and inevitably – in the dynamism of his self-presentation as it takes place throughout the discursive exchange. Identity does not appear there readymade, to be revealed as such by the act of self-presentation, but rather comes into being and is negotiated as the process unfolds (Amossy 2010, 42, 104):

> Identity is not an essence which translates itself in a more or less authentic fashion and which one can show or conceal for strategic reasons (although concealment and falsehood are not as such excluded) but a verbal construction achieved as a function of the exchange. By focusing on discourse, we see how subjectivity and identity fashion themselves through the use of language, how the subject emerges by saying "I" and how it gives itself an identity through the image it forms of itself, both in the act of utterance (the manner in which it speaks) and in its utterances (what it says about itself). (Amossy 2010, 210–11)

Effective speech does not imply a one-way influence but a complex interaction, not only in the case of literary texts but in all modes and genres of communication.

Incorporation, Scenography, and Paratopy

Dominique Maingueneau's theory of ethos,[2] largely consistent with Amossy's rhetorical approach, revolves around the aspect of *incorporation*: "[t]he text is not destined to be contemplated, it is an utterance stretched out to an interlocutor who must be summoned in order to make him adhere 'physically' to a certain universe of sense" (Maingueneau 2004, 203), therefore, "the concept of ethos permits us to interconnect body and discourse" (Maingueneau 2004, 207). It is not only oral discourse that is endowed with a certain "vocality" or specific "tone", but also written/printed texts. This vocality, however, can be actualized only in the process of reading, from which emerges "an origin of the utterance, an embodied subject instance that plays the role of guarantor" (Maingueneau 1999, 79). The reader builds this image on the basis of indicators in the text and the image of the "guarantor" is endowed with "a character

---

2   As the notion of ethos has made a "spectacular comeback" in contemporary theory (Amossy 2001, 2), it is now used by many scholars with varying signification, although Maingueneau and Amossy are the two sources most often referred to. For an overview, see Dhondt and Vanacker 2013; Korthals Altes 2014, 52–73; Maingueneau 2013; 2014. See also the no. 13, 2013, of the revue *COnTEXTES* dedicated to ethos (https://journals.openedition.org/contextes /5685) and no. 3, 2009, of the revue *Argumentation et analyse du discours* (https://journals .openedition.org/aad/656).

and a corporality whose degree of determinateness varies with particular texts" (Maingueneau 1999, 79). These are anchored in social and cultural representations and stereotypes (similar to Amossy's "social imaginary"); yet the image of the guarantor invites the reader into an "ethical world" and allows him to participate "physically" in this universe:

> The utterance of the text bestows "corporality" on the guarantor, giving him a body.
>
> The interlocutor incorporates and assimilates a set of schemes that correspond to a specific way of relating to the world by inhabiting one's own body.
>
> The two incorporations allow for the constitution of a body, an imagined community of those who adhere to the same discourse. (Maingueneau 1999, 80)

Evidently (and admittedly), Maingueneau's rhetoric leans on metaphor. His main concern is with the discursive ethos built within the utterance itself, as opposed to the potential pre-discursive ethos attached to the speaker/author. The ethos of the guarantor is thus manifested in the text and co-created by the reader, insofar as the "revitalization" of the author's ethos takes place in the act of reading. The text here signals the ethos and creates a "scenography" in relation to social and cultural representations and stereotypes. Since the reader is "incorporated", in the act of reading, he "gives flesh" also to the guarantor and the "ethical world" that thus emerges. For Maingueneau, incorporation is based on what is demonstrated in the text, and only secondarily on what is said in it, on the "tone", selection of words, and arguments, not on the statements about oneself (although they can and do appear): "the 'ideas' present themselves through a manner of speaking that refers to a manner of being, to the imaginary participation in a lived experience" (Maingueneau 1999, 80). What needs to be emphasized is the *inevitability* of the reader's projection of an ethos based on the characteristics of the text. Every text must include the image of *some* sort of guarantor, as it is only in relation to such a guarantor that it becomes intelligible, that it has credibility and "corporality".

Maingueneau dedicates much attention to literary discourse, where the act of enunciation is particularly complex. In relation to all types of texts, he emphasizes that ethos is always part of the whole "scene of enunciation", which encompasses three scenes with different levels of generality (Maingueneau 2004, 191–4). There is, first of all, the *global scene*, which is determined by the type of discourse to which the text belongs (religious, journalistic, philosophical, literary, etc.). Some discourses are "constitutive", offering a global view of the world, and cannot be legitimized by any other discourses than their own; as examples, Maingueneau cites religious, philosophical, and literary discourse. Second, there is the *generic scene*: a particular genre within a given discourse. The generic scene is especially rich and varied in literary discourse. The third scene, according to Maingueneau, is *scenography*. A text within a certain genre can be conceived in different ways – a love poem, for example, can be "staged" through complex allusion to the Petrarchan model, as a dialogue between two lovers or a reminiscence.

In relation to literature, Maingueneau elaborates a much cited triad of authorial instances: person, writer, and inscriptor (*personne, écrivain, inscripteur*). Person refers to civil life, or "flesh and blood" being; writer is the agent within the literary field; and inscriptor is the authorial subject of the text. Logically, ethos is linked primarily to the third instance, yet the three instances are mutually interdependent: "each of these three instances is permeated by the other two, none of them is a foundation or axis" (Maingueneau 2004, 108) and "none of these instances can be isolated from or reduced to the other two, their cleavage is the condition for the setting in motion of the creative process" (Maingueneau 2004, 108).

Furthermore, according to Maingueneau, literary discourse (as one of the constitutive discourses) is characterized by what he calls "paratopy". The notion of paratopy is based on the idea that "the literary institution cannot be fully subsumed by the social space, existing instead on the border between its inscription into a *topos* and yielding to forces that by their nature exceed all human economy" (Maingueneau 2004, 72). The author cannot be conceived either on the basis of belonging to the literary field (Bourdieu 1996), or on the basis of belonging to the general social space with its representations and stereotypes. On the other hand, the author is not entirely outside these social spaces, but exists inside and outside at the same time. This neither/nor position at the heart of the concept of paratopy is an original attempt to think social determinations in terms of both general social space and the literary field, on one hand, and on the other, the singularity of the creative act that eludes them.

In Maingueneau's view, the ethos of the author is shaped by the three scenes and embodied through the reconstructive activity of the reader. Amossy's emphasis on the *effective* ethos gains here substantial bodily dimension. In this way the author, embodied as a "guarantor" endowed with an ethos, *leads* the reader beyond the socially sanctioned into the paratopical, without ever completely transcending the social regularities of the literary field, or social stereotypes in the wider social space – indeed, it is precisely *in relation* to them that the paratopy is constituted.

Posture and its Retroactivity

We have observed the importance of stereotypes in the construction of the ethos: the "social imaginary" (Amossy) and the social regularities and stereotypes, as well as the scenography (Maingueneau) all play a role in shaping the ethos and in its re-constitution by the reader. The "image" of the author that circulates in texts, and outside of them, is central to the notion of "posture" coined by Jérôme Meizoz. Mezioz draws on Alain Viala's conceptualization of posture as the specific manner in which a position in the literary field is adopted (Molinié and Viala 1993, 216–17). Meizoz defines the concept more comprehensively, however, as the self-presentation of an author inside and outside the text, since "on the scene of literary enunciation, the author can only present and express himself by means of his *persona*, his posture" (Meizoz 2007, 19). The author's posture relates to a certain repertory: "The courtly or gallant poet, the libertine, the virtuous man, the dandy, the cursed poet, these postures can be considered as the historical repertory of the *ethos* as it has been incorporated, displayed, reversed, or imitated" (Meizoz 2007, 23). It is composed of two dimensions: "the rhetorical (textual) dimension and the behavioral (contextual) dimension" (Meizoz 2007, 17). The textual aspect is called ethos by Meizoz and the extratextual one consists in the behavior of the author (his way of speaking, clothing, etc.).

The process of posturing is always interactive, since the discourse surrounding an author plays a role in the construction of his image: "the author is not [...] only a cultural agent who signs the text. He is also literally the *product* of his work and of all discourses that play a role in this collective 'biographic creation'" (Meizoz 2007, 45). However, in Meizoz's view, the interactivity is conceived rather as a real act of creation and co-creation (in an interview, for example) of texts, audio-visual material, etc., and not as the "mere" reception and interpretation of these images by the reader (as we have seen, Amossy and Maingueneau hold a different point of view). Meizoz's various case studies present analyses of postures reconstructed from the text as something intelligible and relatively stable. He concentrates predominantly on non-fictional texts, such as prefaces written by the author, autobiographies, and various ego-documents. Fictional texts, according to Meizoz, pose specific problems for the study of postures because of the proliferation of speaking subjects. He tends therefore to focus on the ethos as it is explicitly presented – the presentation of the self by way of direct statements and self-descriptions –, rather than those instances in which it is conveyed by the "tone" of the text, as is the case in Maingueneau's conception. In any case, the author's posture is destined to interconnect all the three authorial instances defined by Maingueneau (person, writer, inscriptor) and it is "a constant mutual articulation of the singular and the collective in the literary discourse" (Meizoz 2007, 14).

As Meizoz stresses, the author's posture is the *persona*, a theatrical mask or character. It does not reveal the author's personal identity but hides it, allowing for the creation of a new, literary identity in relation to the historically developed – and ever changing – repertory of postures (Meizoz 2011, 82–3). On the other hand, posture is indeed a *kind of* presentation of the self, insofar as it could never be completely arbitrary in relation to personal identity. Authors *cannot but present themselves*, and postures may act retroactively on authors who are compelled to "be themselves", causing them to repeat certain patterns of behavior and manners of writing that their previously adopted postures have anchored in the literary field and public space (Meizoz 2007, 31–2). Meizoz thus emphasizes the retroactive effect of posture on the writer, since the posture projects back on the author in order to maintain an existing public image: "The discursive image of the author created in the discourse that imposes itself through the circulation of works, tends to become [...] a template for the public behaviour of the writer" (Meizoz 2011, 87).

Meizoz reflects on the terminological overlaps and differences between theories of authorship, in particular those drawing on rhetoric, analysis of discourse, and sociology of literature – he even offers a "scale" of terms that may be applied in the analysis of the author. It consists of seven "layers" pertinent to the study of the author (from the most general to the most specific): 1. social discourse in general and literary discourse in particular (see Maingueneau's analysis discussed above); 2. the literary field (Bourdieu); 3. genre (generic scene; Maingueneau); 4. materiality and mediality of the text (book, editing, typography; Chartier and others); 5. authorial scenography (José-Luis Diaz's "image of the author"); 6. posture (ethos plus behavior; Amossy, Maingueneau and Meizoz's own conception); 7. style. As we can see, it is a reworking of virtually all the notions we have discussed so far (Meizoz 2016, 45–6).

Hermeneutic and Narratological Frameworks

The last conception of the author I will comment on, that of Liesbeth Korthals Altes, transposes the problematic to the context of literary hermeneutics and narratology, both classical and cognitive, emphasizing the inevitable framing of the ethos in the acts of reading and interpretation. Her discussion is probably the most detailed to date. Unlike Meizoz, Korthals Altes does not hesitate to apply the concept of ethos to all genres of fiction – under two important conditions.

The first is to widen the purview of study to include the hermeneutic moment not only of the act of reading but also of scholarly analysis. In a literary text, she argues, neither ethos nor narratological categories can be "analysed" in any purely objective manner: "Posture, ethos, habitus, and their dynamic co-constructions require a hermeneutic and argued reconstruction rather than mere description of the codes on which such sign projections and readings rely" (Korthals Altes 2014, 56). Although literary texts themselves manifest certain characteristics and indications of an ethos, the actual ethos is largely dependent on the frameworks, scripts, and scenarios the reader and/or interpreter will mobilize. Often, it is precisely the ambiguity and interpretive openness of these characteristics that intensifies the reader's interaction with the text:

> Concepts such as posture and ethos might be understood as mental models, conventional paths along which writers classify themselves and in turn are classified by others, with consequences for the interpretation of their works. A posture, in this perspective, connects schemata (conceptions of literature, including ideas about its function in society and about constellations of roles; genres as macroframes, implicitly suggesting a communication contract), scripts (how to be – and behave like – a writer, on both the public and the private scene), and mental models (writer postures and ethos types: the writer as guide, prophet, outcast, genius, enfant terrible, etc.). (Korthals Altes 2014, 55–6)

Secondly, the necessary narratological tools must be applied to the "layers" of subjects who participate in a particular act of literary communication. In this regard, Korthals Altes asks (when discussing Christine Angot's works), "whose discourse, and whose ethos, do we read into the text, and how do we decide this, with what consequences?" (Korthals Altes 2014, 66). The ethos can be ascribed to a character, narrator, and/or the author (as we have already witnessed in Amossy's approach). In many cases, it is far from clear *whose* ethos it is, and a single text tends to produce several, each on a different level. Ascribing an ethos to a character or characters is a complicated process in itself. Drawing on Monika Fludernik's concept of experientiality, Korthals Altes points out that "[r]eaders would make sense of fictional narratives by drawing on their everyday experiences with people and their actions, stored in memory in schematized form (frames, schemata, scripts, and mental models)" (Korthals Altes 2014, 129). However, the "mimetic" reading is not the only one available: following James Phelan, Korthals Altes also considers *thematic* (ideological, allegorical, etc.) and *synthetic* readings (emphasizing the narrative constructedness of characters; Korthals Altes 2014, 131–2). Turning next to the question of how to ascribe an ethos to the narrator, Korthals Altes points out that we are confronted here as well with different types of narrators, and with the issue of the narrator's (un)reliability.

In the case of the author, Korthals Altes argues that ethos may be ascribed variously to six authorial instances: 1. to the biographic author; 2. to the author as social role (connected to posture); 3. to the image of the author based on his previous *oeuvre*; 4. to the image of the author, constructed on the basis of peritext and epitext; 5. to the image of the author based on the text (implied author); 6. to the author as narrator (Korthals Altes 2014, 157–9). All these instances are more or less co-created by readers and interpreters, since they are available only through social and cognitive frameworks or procedures that are hermeneutic by nature.

The Author's Presence: Identity and Self-Creation

How is the author present in discourse and in his text? Theories of authorship drawing on rhetoric, discourse analysis, and sociology of literature tend to answer this question in a rather complex way. On the one hand, they do not completely part with Roland Barthes's famous dictum that to enter writing means to enter a neutral space where voice, identity, and individuality disappear (Barthes 1977). On the other, they concede that to write inevitably means to present oneself in a discourse, to exert an influence, in such a way that this self-presentation tends, in turn, to exert a retroactive influence on the identity of the self.

The framework of self-presentation cannot be limited to the literary field. Ethos and scenography are shaped by the cultural imaginary and stereotypes that are not exclusively literary. The repertory of postures, the frames, scenarios, and scripts the authors and readers mobilize, together with the paradoxical status of paratopy – all point to the complexity of the "common ground" on which literary communication takes place.

The identity of the author is never "immediately" made available in discourse; identity is a process, not a product, and it is constantly negotiated in acts of communication. It might seem that an author produces a text and that this text is subsequently received by readers in this or that manner. Yet not only is it the case that the author has a certain image of the audience in mind, shaping his self-presentation accordingly; the author's own image – constituted in the text as well as circulating around it – is only partially under his control and exerts its influence on him. In this process, the person, writer, and inscriptor all interact in an exceedingly complex way.

As these three instances are intimately interrelated and interwoven, writing and publishing necessarily involve acts of both self-presentation and self-creation. As stated in the first section, this pertains to any artistic creation, and in the broader sense to any human creative activity, since the creation always creates the one who creates it; however, in literature the scenography of the self is particularly rich and intense.

3 Toward the New Self: *The End of Eddy*

Drawing on the approaches to the author discussed above, I will now sketch out an interpretation of the novel *The End of Eddy* (2014, English translation 2017) by Édouard Louis. In this *engagé* autofiction,[3] the narrator tells the story of his miserable childhood up to the moment when he left his native village to attend lyceum in the regional capital, with the vision that he would "get away [...] start over from the beginning [...] be reborn" (Louis 2017, 175). Although the author, narrator, and main character (the narrator's younger self) share biographic details, they do not share the same name. The main character throughout the novel goes by the name Eddy Bellegueule, but this is *no longer* the name by which the author – and perhaps also the narrator, since the story is narrated from an unspecified point in time after its "end" – refers to himself. In

---

3 For an interesting polemical discussion of the novel, see Meizoz 2016, 112–16. Unlike other commentators, Meizoz does not consider the novel an autofiction but an autobiography in the first place. For Meizoz, the novel is an example of a *miserablist*, quasi-sociological approach that blames the working class while parting with it. As will be evident, my interpretation of the text is different, although I partially draw on his theoretical concepts.

fact, the real life Eddy Bellegueulle legally changed his name to Édouard Louis in 2013, before the novel was published. By becoming Édouard Louis, the author symbolically "does away" with Eddy on two levels (of Maingueneau's triad): as a function of his *person* and of his identity as a newly "born" *writer*. The novel's narrative then prolongs and multiplies this act of "doing away" on the third level of *inscriptor*. The "end" of Eddy Bellegueulle and the meaning of this act are "staged" for the reader and presented as the key moment of the novel.

The narrator recounts his unhappy life as a gay youth in the impoverished working class environment of a small village in northern France in the 1990s and 2000s. The first paragraph establishes the tone of the process of remembering: "From my childhood I have no happy memories. […] suffering is all-consuming: it somehow gets rid of anything that doesn't fit into its system" (Louis 2017, 3). The narrative is arranged chronologically as well as thematically. In an almost panoramic fashion, it presents scenes of diverse forms of bullying, as well as physical and mental domestic violence, as Eddy tries and fails to deny his own emerging sexual identity, whose outer "symptoms" have been the cause of his inability to "fit in" with his family and community. The retrospective narration, in which the current self is telling the story of the self it had once been, allows the narrator's voice to be at once intimately personal and analytically distanced, and to expose working class lives from a personal point of view. Often a particular story or situation is put directly into a theoretical context: "I came to understand that many different modes of discourse intersected in my mother and spoke through her" (Louis 2017, 59). The narrator explicitly frames and comments on events and attitudes, frequently shifting from "then" to "now", to his present self, as in the excurses on the class politics of dental hygiene (Louis 2017, 8), visiting the doctor (Louis 2017, 103–4), and watching TV (Louis 2017, 48–9).

In the novel, the author's ethos is based on the significant and complex convergence of a real author, narrator, and main character, and the narrative act is stylized as a confession, accusation, and theoretical analysis. The reader is invited to accept the narrator as an honest guide and "eyewitness expert" to his past and to the past of his community. The situation is that of a very particular and rather "perverse" Gramscian "organic intellectual", who speaks for his community by denouncing it and pointing to social determinants that are at the root of systemic violence.

The ethos is constructed by way of a global scene of literary discourse, yet at the same time by a very distinctive generic scene of autofiction. The genre of autofiction helps to mobilize the framework of a (problematic) identity of subjects on the three levels discussed above, as well as a rich generic "memory". In the French context, autofiction is a notably productive genre, one that has been taken up by a range of authors, including Annie Ernaux, Pierre Michon, Hervé Guibert, Christine Angot, and Michel Houellebecq. The novel shares certain features especially with Annie Ernaux's "socioanalytical" novels, which explore her working class upbringing and trace the path of her ascent in the social hierarchy. Unlike in Ernaux's novels, however, *The End of Eddy* turns to the reader with a certain assertiveness, compelling him to take sides with regard to the represented social reality, and become more aware of his own social habitus. On the other hand, Édouard Louis presents his book with the subtitle *Novel*,[4] and does in fact mobilize the tools of fictional writing: the effective use of compression in the narrated sequences, studiously positioned voice of the narrator, and careful differentiation of register (the "high" language of literary prose vs. the "sociolect" of the village inhabitants, usually printed in italics).

The *tone* of the "guarantor" constituted in the text has an especially vocal quality, and key for the bond between the "guarantor" and the reader is the incorporation of the "voice" in Maingueneau's sense. The body of the narrator's younger self – which is historically continuous with the body of the narrator as he tells his story, though it has changed both physically and socially –, and bodies of his family members, are constantly exposed to the reader, revealing the most intimate details of corporal life as the source of "voice", as well as the effects of the social environment on the body – habitus and bodily *hexis* in the Bourdieusian sense. This technique is even reminiscent of the "humanitarian narratives" of certain realist writers of the 19th century, a concept that Thomas Laqueur (1989) has defined in terms of shocking representations of suffering bodies, with the aim of inspiring the reader, whose own corporality they attack, to act in favor of the poor and disadvantaged. Yet the body in this case is available both "from without" and "from within", since it is also the narrator's own body, evolving in time. In interesting contradistinction to the socially produced working class bodies, Eddy is confronted with his own body as the "organic" source of sexual desire – and identity – that he must make efforts, in vain, to resist, obsessively

---

4   In the English translation the subtitle was omitted. Some translations into other languages kept it, other left it out.

repeating to himself *"Today I'm gonna be a tough guy"* (Louis 2017, 170). These impulses play a decisive role in his feelings of becoming himself: "I obeyed his orders [of a boy Eddy is having sex with – J. Š.] with the sense that I was in the process of turning into what I have always been" (Louis 2017, 130; see also the chapter "The Body's Rebellion", 151–7).

The posture expressed in the text (that is, the *ethos* in Meizoz's conception) is that of an honest and *engagé* writer, staging his personal situation for the reader in order to convey a certain critique. However, the gesture remains ambiguous and open to interpretation. By exposing the male domination, racism, and homophobia both in his family and in the surrounding social world, does the novel serve to expose an unfair system, or is it itself an unfair portrait of real living people, violating their trust and privacy, so that it can be said to commit a kind of social injustice against them? And given the way in which he subjects his own family to such victimization, even pathologization and voyeurism, while capitalizing on it in the literary field, should we not feel compelled to question author's ethics (as does Meizoz 2016, 114–15)? This is a situation familiar to readers of autofiction. We may once more recall the novels of Annie Ernaux, in which the level of (auto)biographical detail is similar yet the images are much less drastic. In Louis' novel, it is the painful experiences themselves that give the speaking subject its credibility, legitimize the critical attitude towards the narrated events and characters, and ethically anchor the *engagé* stance. However, as Liesbeth Korthals Altes aptly points out in a discussion of two critical books on Michel Houellebecq, it largely depends on the value regimes and frames that readers and critics will mobilize whether this construction will prove convincing or whether it will be read as no more than an exploitation of the topic (Korthals Altes 2014, 77–86).

Since the publication of his first novel, Édouard Louis has constantly been in the spotlight of literary magazines and the media, in a manner reminiscent of other famous controversial debuts in French literature, such as Françoise Sagan's *Hello Sadness* (1954, published when Sagan was only eighteen). In numerous interviews in various media – journals, radio, TV, and live discussions available online –, he exposes his own experience in a manner similar to the narrator of the novel, adopting the posture of a sociologist and activist, and passing continuously from personal to expert register. He even provides the "evidence of body": recalling, for instance, that the narrator in the novel comments on Eddy's unhealthy teeth and the fact that he does not wear dental braces (a sign of his working class origin), readers may single out the fact that the real

Édouard Louis is wearing braces in a television interview – that there is a striking continuity between the autofiction and real life. The mutual entanglement of literary work and the person of the author then seems almost complete. The subsequent three books helped Louis establish himself in the literary field as an author and public intellectual with a mission, exploring over and over the problematic at the intersection of male domination, queer sexuality, race, and class by staging his own personal experience.

Jérôme Meizoz emphasizes the retroactive quality of the author's posture, which comes in fact to exert an influence on the life of the real person. As I hope is now clear, it is precisely this retroactive quality that can be found at the center of Louis' novel: the "end" referred to in the title of the book (even more pronounced in the original French *finir avec*, literally "to finish with") is performative in character. Published under the author's assumed name, he stylizes the book as an act of reckoning with his primary social environment and former identity. He also shapes the narrator as a critical intellectual and he maintains this image in his real life. At the same time, by publically exposing intimate details of the life of his family members and his attitudes in a literary text, Louis estranged himself in the literal sense of the word from his own family and community, embarrassing his parents and siblings.

The End of Eddy is an extreme example of self-creation through litera-ture, based on the sophisticated interweaving of the person, the writer, and the inscriptor, as well as the posture of the *engagé* writer and young leftist sociologist. In this novel, the author *persona* is socially mediated on many levels, attesting strongly to the relevance of the "social imagi-nary" (including the much contested areas of sexuality, race, and class) – besides the literary field – as a site for building ethos and posture. The author not only positions himself in the literary field by writing and pub-lishing such a piece of radical autofiction, he also literally transforms his life by the retroactive effects of his posture and "stages" this transforma-tion as exemplary for readers.

4 The Author in (and beyond) the Discourse

How is the author present in his text and at the same time created by it? The scholars discussed in this study offer a range of concepts that address this question, including: the creation of the author's *effective* ethos; the *incorporation* of this ethos on the scene of enunciation; the author's extra- and intratextual posture, retroactively changing his identity; and the framing of the whole process in reception and interpretation. Before concluding, I would like, however, to point out an omission or blind spot in these approaches – or better, to suggest their counterpart. Could we not also ask: What happens between the author and the text? How can we conceptualize the creative act from the point of view of the author? The theories we have been discussing focus on the discursive constitution of the author; however, by posing the question in the way I am suggesting here, we catch a glimpse of another side of the author's self-creation, one that seems to escape the purview of these theories. Derek Attridge's (2004; 2015) conception of the literary act, of the otherness that emerges in it and the singularity of the literary work (as inscribed in the philosophical tradition represented by such concepts as the "event" and "becoming", and by such names as Derrida, Lévinas, Lyotard, and Badiou), might be of particular interest here. This view of the creative act and its relation to the author, just briefly mentioned here, is not entirely incompatible with the one we have been discussing throughout this study; we may in fact consider these two views as dialectical counterparts. They offer two distinct registers through which we may think of the text not only as the creation of the author but also as creating the author, or rather as the locus of the author's self-creation.

References

Abrams, Meyer Howard. 1953. *The Mirror and the Lamp: Romantic Theory and the Critical Tradition*. New York: Oxford University Press.

Amossy, Ruth. 2001. "Ethos at the Crossroads of Disciplines: Rhetoric, Pragmatics, Sociology". *Poetics Today* 22 (1): 1–23.

Amossy, Ruth. 2008. "Argumentation et Analyse du discours: Perspectives théoriques et découpages disciplinaires". *Argumentation et analyse du discours* no. 1, September 6, http://journals.openedition.org/aad/200. Accessed 10 May 2021.

Amossy, Ruth. 2009. "La double nature de l'image d'auteur". *Argumentation et analyse du discours* no. 3, October 15, http://journals.openedition.org/aad/662. Accessed 10 May 2021.

Amossy, Ruth. 2010. *La présentation de soi: Ethos et identité verbale*. Paris: PUF.

Amossy, Ruth. 2021. *L'argumentation dans le discours*. Paris: Armand Colin.

Attridge, Derek. 2004. *The Singularity of Literature*. London: Routledge.

Attridge, Derek. 2015. *The Work of Literature*. Oxford: Oxford University Press.

Barthes, Roland. 1977. "The Death of the Author". In *Image Music Text*, translated and edited by Stephen Heath, 142–8. London: Fontana.

Bennett, Andrew. 2005. *The Author*. London: Routledge.

Boschetti, Anna. 1988. *The Intellectual Enterprise: Sartre and Les temps modernes*. Translated by Richard McCleary. Evanston, IL: Northwestern University Press.

Bourdieu, Pierre. 1993. *The Field of Cultural Production*. Cambridge: Polity Press, and Oxford: Blackwell.

Bourdieu, Pierre. 1996. *The Rules of Art: Genesis and Structure of the Literary Field*. Translated by Susan Emanuel. Stanford, CA: Stanford University Press.

Burke, Seán. 1995. *Authorship: From Plato to the Postmodern. A Reader*. Edinburgh: Edinburgh University Press.

Burke, Seán. 1998. *The Death and Return of the Author: Criticism and Subjectivity in Barthes, Foucault and Derrida*. Edinburgh: Edinburgh University Press.

Casanova, Pascale. 2004. *The World Republic of Letters*. Translated by M. B. DeBevoise. Cambridge, MA: Harvard University Press.

Casanova, Pascale. 2005. "Literature as a World". *New Left Review* 31: 71–90.

Casanova, Pascale. 2015. *Kafka, Angry Poet*. Translated by Chris Turner. London: Seagull Books.

Chartier, Roger. 1994. *The Order of Books: Readers, Authors, and Libraries in Europe between Fourteenth and Eighteenth Centuries*. Translated by Lydia G. Cochrane. Stanford, CA: Stanford University Press.

Chartier, Roger. 1995. *Forms and Meanings: Texts, Performances, and Audiences from Codex to Computer*. Philadelphia: University of Pennsylvania Press.

Dhondt, Reindert, and Beatrijs Vanacker. 2013. "Ethos: pour une mise au point conceptuelle et méthodologique". *COnTEXTES: Revue de la sociologie littéraire* no. 13, December 20, https://contextes.revues.org/5685. Accessed 10 May 2021.

Dorleijn, Gillis J., Ralf Grüttemeier, and Liesbeth Korthals Altes. 2010. *Authorship Revisited: Conceptions of Authorship around 1900 and 2000*. Leuven: Peeters.

Foucault, Michel. 1979. "What Is an Author?" In *Textual Strategies: Perspectives in Post-Structuralist Criticism*, edited by Josué V. Harari, 141–60. London: Methuen.

Korthals Altes, Liesbeth. 2014. *Ethos and Narrative Interpretation: The Negotiation of Values in Fiction*. Lincoln: Nebraska University Press.

Lagasnerie, Geoffroy de. 2011. *Logique de la création: Sur l'Université, la vie intellectuelle et les conditions d'innovation*. Paris: Fayard.

Lagasnerie, Geoffroy de. 2011a. *Sur la science des oeuvres: Questions à Pierre Bourdieu (et à quelques autres)*. Paris: Éditions Cartouche.

Lahire, Bernard. 2006. *La condition littéraire: La double vie des écrivains*. Paris: Découverte.

Lahire, Bernard. 2010. "Le champ et le jeu: La spécificité de l'univers littéraire en question". In *Bourdieu et la littérature*, edited by Jean-Pierre Martin, 143–54. Nantes: Éditions Cécile Defaut.

Lahire, Bernard. 2010a. "The Double Life of Writers". *New Literary History* 41 (2): 443–65.

Lahire, Bernard. 2010b. *Franz Kafka: Éléments pour une théorie de la création littéraire*. Paris: Découverte.

Laqueur, Thomas. 1989. "Bodies, Details, and the Humanitarian Narrative". In *The New Cultural History*, edited by Lynn Hunt, 176–204. Berkeley: University of California Press.

Louis, Édouard. 2017. *The End of Eddy*. Translated by Michael Lucey. London: Vintage.

Maingueneau, Dominique. 1999. "Èthos, scénographie, incorporation". In *Images de soi dans le discours: La construction de l'èthos*, edited by Ruth Amossy, 75–100. Lausanne: Delachaux et Niestlé.

Maingueneau, Dominique. 2004. *Le Discours littéraire: Paratopie et scène d'énonciation*. Paris: Armand Colin.

Maingueneau, Dominique. 2013. "L'èthos: un articulateur". *COnTEXTES: Revue de la sociologie littéraire* no. 13, December 20, http://journals.openedition.org/contextes/5772. Accessed 10 May 2021.

Maingueneau, Dominique. 2014. "Retour critique sur l'éthos". *Langage et société* 149 (3): 31–48.

Martin, Jean-Pierre et al. 2010. *Bourdieu et la littérature*. Nantes: Éditions Cécile Defaut.

Meizoz, Jérôme. 2007. *Postures littéraires: Mises en scène modernes de l'auteur*. Genève: Slatkine.

Meizoz, Jérôme. 2011. *La fabrique des singularités: Postures littéraires II*. Genève: Slatkine.

Meizoz, Jérôme. 2016. *La littérature « en personne »: Scène médiatique et formes d'incarnation*. Genève: Slatkine.

Molinié, Georges, and Alain Viala. 1993. *Approches de la réception: Sémiostylistique et sociopoétique de Le Clézio*. Paris: Presses Universitaires de France.

Sapiro, Gisèle. 2011. *La responsabilité de l'écrivain: Littérature, droit et morale en France (XIXe–XXIe siècle)*. Paris: Seuil.

Sapiro, Gisèle. 2014. *The French Writers' War, 1940–1953*. Translated by Vanessa Doriott Anderson, and Dorrit Cohn. Durham, NC: Duke University Press.

Sapiro, Gisèle. 2018. *Les écrivains et la politique en France: De l'affaire Dreyfus à la guerre d'Algérie*. Paris: Seuil.

Sapiro, Gisèle. 2020. *Peut-on dissocier l'oeuvre de l'auteur?* Paris: Seuil.

Sapiro, Gisèle, and Cécile Rabot. 2017. *Profession? Écrivain*. Paris: CNRS.

Tatarkiewicz, Wladyslaw. 1980. "Creativity: History of the Concept". In *A History of Six Ideas: An Essay in Aesthetics*, 244–65. The Hague: Martinus Nijhoff and Warsaw: PWN.

Viala, Alain. 1985. *Naissance de l'écrivain: Sociologie de la littérature à l'âge classique*. Paris: Minuit.

Woodmansee, Martha. 1994. *The Author, Art, and the Market: Rereading the History of Aesthetics*. New York: Columbia University Press.

A Negative Autopoietic Principle in French Interpretations of Hegel – Breton, Sartre, Bataille

Eva Voldřichová Beránková

> *Negativity is the very moment of a mind by which*
> *it always goes beyond what it is.*
> Jean Wahl: *Le Malheur de la conscience dans la philosophie de Hegel*

French philosophy and literature of the 20th century were deeply engaged with German thinkers such as Hegel, Marx, Nietzsche, Husserl and Heidegger. Of these, it is Hegel who most haunted French thought. Nowhere is French philosophy more ambivalent and conflicted in its attitudes toward a philosopher, strenuously resisting and *correcting* Hegel at the very moment it finds him most seductive. The Surrealists wanted negation, but without limits; Jean-Paul Sartre wanted negation, but without totality; Jacques Derrida and Georges Bataille wanted negativity, but not its recuperation in a positive result. Bruce Baugh, Professor of philosophy at Thompson Rivers University, argues in this regard: "It's as if French philosophy of the past century had to deny Hegel in order to affirm him, and affirm him in order to deny him" (Baugh 2003, 1).

After the 19th century which, evaluated from the point of view of how Hegel was received, was characterized by an immense misunderstanding followed by a deliberate ignorance of the German philosopher,[1] the

---

[1] In his book *Hegel in France*, Andrea Bellantone describes the enthusiasm of the eclectic school (formed around Victor Cousin in the 1830s) that saw in Hegel a liberal spirit capable of guiding the French administration on a "third way" between the conservatism of the *Ancien Régime* and the activism of modern socialists. After their shocking discovery of the existence of the *Young Hegelians* (proto-Marxist atheists claiming a social revolution), the French intellectual

Hegelian Renaissance of the 1920s and 1930s led in France to a true "century of Hegel" (Bellantone 2011a, 122) or, at least, to decades of a passionate relationship with the German thinker, which could be summed up by the famous slogan "Neither with Hegel, nor against Hegel" (Negri 1987, 5).

In this chapter, I will focus on *negative autopoiesis* as a common component of Hegel's French reception. Everything seems to have started in 1929 with Jean Wahl's famous book *The Misfortune of Consciousness in Hegel's Philosophy* that influenced all those French thinkers who were concerned with irreparable divisions and unbridgeable differences in human consciousness. Although this is only one aspect of the German philosopher's thought (moreover, not one always properly understood by his French followers), Hegel's description of how a reality divided against itself continually passes from one opposed term to the other, without finding repose or reconciliation, constitutes a dominant theme in French philosophy from the 1920s up to the present. Using examples from philosophical but also fictional works by André Breton, Jean-Paul Sartre and Georges Bataille, I will show the extent to which French Surrealists, Existentialists and *Postmodernists* used selected elements of Hegel's philosophy to develop their own negative autopoiesis.

1 Hegel with a Kierkegaardian Twist

Jean André Wahl (1888–1974), the author of *The Misfortune of Consciousness in Hegel's Philosophy*, was a French spiritualist and *proto-existentialist* philosopher of Jewish origin. A student of Henri Bergson and one of the first specialists in British and American pluralist philosophy (William James), Wahl became famous for inspiring a revival of Hegelian studies in the early 1930s, long before the legendary seminars of Alexandre Kojève at the *École des Hautes Études en Sciences Sociales*. His "non-systematic, innovative and concrete thinking" (Levinas, Tilliette, and Ricœur 1976, 73) has been enthusiastically followed by a multitude of philosophers (Vladimir Jankélévitch, Jean-Paul Sartre, Emmanuel Levinas, Paul Ricœur, Jacques Laurent, Xavier Tilliette, Gilles Deleuze) and writers,

---

scene of the years 1840–50 rejected the German philosopher for the rest of the century. From the 1870s, the intense fear of Prussian militarism only reinforced this negative appreciation of German idealism, so that Hegel came to be regarded as a "dead dog" (Bellantone 2011, 298).

both French (Pierre-Jean Jouve, André Breton, Georges Bataille, Pierre Boutang) and American (Wallace Stevens, Marianne Moore).

In his book, Wahl opts for a rather original approach to Hegel: "Behind the philosopher, we discover the theologian, and behind the rationalist, the romantic" (Wahl 1929, V). It is the young Hegel that the French philosopher admires, forsaking the works subsequent to the *Phenomenology of the Spirit*, which represents, according to him, the final point where the two tendencies of Hegelian thought would meet.

For Hegel, theological history begins with Hellenism (turned towards happiness) and continues with Judaism (embodying the unhappy consciousness). The history of the Spirit would consist in the assimilation of this separation, which is confirmed in the union of Hellenism and Judaism: Christianity. The last named represents the process of liberation from oppositions. The unity that Christianity promises is a true, real unity (as a daughter of the split), where, on the contrary, the unity of Hellenism would have been natural, still immature and undefined. Jesus promises this reunification and liberation, but unfortunately he does not realize it. Nevertheless, he shows the way: Hegel has discovered, through meditation on Christ, that the highest achievement could only be reached through suffering or misfortune. The synthesis presupposes sacrifice.

Thus, according to Jean Wahl's interpretation, the unhappy consciousness represents the very heart of the *Phenomenology* and Hegelian philosophy would be the first to express the experience of man's unhappiness in the form of a dialectical logic. Far from being an obstacle or, even, the main enemy of the rational, this negative experience only deepens and energizes reason: "Hegel's genius is therefore there: not to allow the intrusion of the negative into the positive to dethrone reason, but only to broaden it and set it in motion" (Wahl 1929, 152). In general, Wahl puts much more emphasis on the split than on the unity, the pillars of Hegelian philosophy being according to him: "negativity", "mediation", "time" (Wahl 1929, 157). He presents to the French a dynamic Hegel, Platonic to only a very small degree (contrary to what they had imagined until then) and so efficient that his dialectic and his "new rationality" could perhaps save reason and metaphysics from the modern mistrust that assails them.

Nevertheless, three years later, Jean Wahl published an article in the *Revue philosophique de la France et de l'étranger* entitled "Hegel et Kierkegaard" in which he rejected Hegel in favor of the philosopher's Danish critic. The themes addressed remain the same, but Wahl no longer believes in the possibility of resolving them in a logical synthesis. Instead of being restrained within the dialectical game of thesis and antithesis, the concept of negation would have caused "the collapse of any possible structure" (Bellantone 2011a, 171). From the idea of a dynamic reason that has integrated the negative into it, Wahl moves to the idea of a reason annihilated by the negative:

> For Hegel, negativity is not a pure force, but only the opposite side of the positive, and it is therefore introduced in a structural rhythm unable to make a turn to the empty, while in Kierkegaard, negativity is precisely this turn to the empty – It is a paradox. (Bellantone 2011a, 173)

According to Wahl, influenced by Kierkegaard, reality is chance and, as such, cannot espouse a logical structure. (The young Hegel would have sensed this, before succumbing to the pure speculation of his mature years.) Thus, Jean Wahl ended up playing a kind of double role: both that of being an innovator of Hegelian studies in France and that of being the founder of a radical critical attitude towards Hegel's thought.

2 Breton and His Marxist Big Brothers

Beginning in the 1920s, there was a flourishing of literature in which the unhappy consciousness was a central theme, and which related Hegel to Freud, Marx, Nietzsche and Kierkegaard. In Surrealism, Marxism, Existentialism and in the work of some Postmodern philosophers, the Hegelian unhappy consciousness assumed a key place in French thought. Inspired by the evolution of Jean Wahl's thought, most of the modern and contemporary thinkers refused the Hegelian solution of a speculative synthesis which could reconcile oppositions and differences in a higher unity. Nevertheless, if there is no synthesis, then there can be no dialectic, properly speaking, but only a sort of *anti-thetics*, a play of opposed terms that negate and pass into each other without ever coinciding in a meaningful whole.

Let us first look a little more closely at the case of Surrealism: in the first *Manifesto* of the movement, Hegel was mentioned only indirectly (in the citation of Nerval's letter)[2] and rather negatively, as an

---

2   "([Mes sonnets] ne sont guère plus obscurs que la métaphysique de Hegel ou les *Mémorables* de Swedenborg, et perdraient de leur charme à être expliqués, si la chose était possible...)" (Breton 1924, 11). ([My sonnets] are hardly more obscure than Hegel's metaphysics or

incomprehensible author, and his dialectic was in no way claimed as a method usable by the Surrealists.[3] Five years later, in the *Second Manifesto of Surrealism*, Breton gave Hegel markedly more attention, even if his explicit conclusions were hardly more favorable to the German philosopher.

The beginning of the text summarized the Surrealist effort as an ambition to demonstrate the "factitious character of the old antinomies" and to operate a kind of general synthesis of the real and the imaginary:

> Everything tends to make us believe that there exists a certain point of the mind at which life and death, the real and the imagined, past and future, the communicable and the incommunicable, high and low, cease to be perceived as contradictions.[4] (Breton 1929, 1)

However, this superior synthesis was not supposed to be realized thanks to a dialectic bringing into play theses and anti-theses, but by a free deployment of a negative and very violent anti-thesis:

> As it is the degree of resistance that this choice idea meets with which determines the more or less certain flight of the mind toward a world at last inhabitable, one can understand why Surrealism was not afraid to make for itself a tenet of total revolt, complete insubordination, of sabotage according to rule, and why it still expects nothing save from violence. The simplest Surrealist act consists of dashing down the street, pistol in hand, and firing blindly, as fast as you can pull the trigger, into the crowd.[5] (Breton 1929, 2)

Swedenborg's *Mémorables*, and would lose their charm in explication, if such a thing were possible...).

3   "Le surréalisme poétique, auquel je consacre cette étude, s'est appliqué jusqu'ici à rétablir dans sa vérité absolue le dialogue, en dégageant les deux interlocuteurs des obligations de la politesse. Chacun d'eux poursuit simplement son soliloque, sans chercher à en tirer un plaisir dialectique particulier et à en imposer le moins du monde à son voisin" (Breton 1924, 17). (Poetic Surrealism, which is the subject of this study, has focused its efforts up to this point on reestablishing dialogue in its absolute truth, by freeing both interlocutors from any obligations and politeness. Each of them simply pursues his soliloquy without trying to derive any special dialectical pleasure from it and without trying to impose anything whatsoever upon his neighbor).

4   Tout porte à croire qu'il existe un certain point de l'esprit d'où la vie et la mort, le réel et l'imaginaire, le passé et le futur, le communicable et l'incommunicable, le haut et le bas cessent d'être perçus contradictoirement.

5   Comme c'est du degré de résistance que cette idée de choix rencontre que dépend l'envol plus ou moins sûr de l'esprit vers un monde enfin habitable, on conçoit que le surréalisme n'ait pas craint de se faire un dogme de la révolte absolue, de l'insoumission totale, du sabotage en règle, et qu'il n'attende encore rien que de la violence. L'acte surréaliste le plus simple consiste, revolvers aux poings, à descendre dans la rue et à tirer au hasard, tant qu'on peut, dans la foule.

This attack on the Hegelian system went hand in hand with Breton's efforts in the second half of the 1920s to convince the Marxists of the subversive and revolutionary character of Surrealism (Lowy 2017, 86). Indeed, convinced of their monopoly over the youth of the time, the French Communists despised Breton's group, likening it to a club of bourgeois playing "harmless board games"[6] (collages, dream narrations, Exquisite Corpse game, public hypnosis etc.) (Reynaud-Paligot 1994, 4). Breton certainly felt obliged to harden his tone (as the passage about the pistol in hand testifies), but the situation made him hesitate about what strategy to adopt toward the Marxists. On the one hand, he proclaims his "adherence to the principle of historical materialism" (Breton 1929, 6) to gain their favor, and on the other, he affirms the independence and the relevance of the movement launched by him, dedicating several pages to answer Michel Marty's famous quip: "If you are a Marxist, you don't need to be a Surrealist" (Breton 1929, 6).

It is in this double perspective that Breton, inspired by Feuerbach and Marx, denounced the Hegelian system as a "colossal abortion" (Breton 1929, 5), declaring the dialectical method "inapplicable" (Breton 1929, 6) and confirming, in the name of the Surrealists, "the necessity to finish with the Idealism itself" (Breton 1929, 6). Nevertheless, this desire to please the Marxists was not just an artifice on Breton's part and a deeper affinity united the two movements. It is not for nothing that the founder of Surrealism declared in 1935: "Transform the world, said Marx. Change life, said Rimbaud. These two watchwords are one for us" (Breton [1935] 1992, 459). The Surrealists always agreed with the Marxists on the question of the necessary and liberating negation which must be torn from its recovery by the Hegelian dialectic:

> Despite the Party's mistrust of the Surrealist's "subjectivist tendencies", at the heart of this would-be "alliance" was the shared conviction that, through the proper use of negativity in destroying bourgeois society, a new society would be created where human beings would be able to realize or fulfill themselves as "total" and complete beings, more or less free from internal and social conflicts. (Baugh 2003, 54)

In this first Surrealist reading of the Hegelian dialectic, there is, of course, a certain contradiction, since negation is supposed to be both unlimited

---

6   Jeux de société inoffensifs.

and yet in the service of a determinate end (the dissolution of opposites, the end of capitalism), which gives it an ambiguous character. At the same time, Breton's later intuition that art could be in fact a kind of "free creative negativity" (Baugh 2003, 75), an activity not subordinated to any practical need or goal and therefore irrecoverable by a higher phase of the dialectic, seems to be much more stimulating for postmodern thinking.

In any case, from the moment Breton freed himself from Marxist domination, he began to re-evaluate the importance of Hegelian thought, so that in 1935 he exclaimed in a somewhat surprising way: "Even today it is Hegel whom we must question about how well-founded or ill-founded Surrealist activity in the arts is" (Breton [1935] 1969, 258).

3 A Very Bloody and Uncompromising Sartre

Negativity, as Sartre understood it, could be the subject of a whole book, as well as the interpretation that the French philosopher applied to the thought of his German predecessor. In order to illustrate this briefly, I will therefore base my analyses solely on a specific type of more *literary* sources, namely the prefaces that Sartre wrote to support the cause of African and Antillean authors and in which the Hegelian dialectic plays the crucial role. In the 1940s, 1950s and 1960s, Sartre's prefaces accompanied the publication of three works anticipating current postcolonial studies: Léopold Sédar Senghor's *Anthology of New Black and Malagasy Poetry in French* (1948), Albert Memmi's *The Colonizer and the Colonized* (1957) and Frantz Fanon's *The Wretched of the Earth* (1961).

In the first two texts, Sartre used the Master–Slave dialectic to draw a parallel between the fate of Blacks and that of other exploited people, particularly white proletarians and Jews:

> Like the white worker, the negro is a victim of the capitalist structure of our society. This situation reveals to him his close ties – quite apart from the color of his skin – with certain classes of Europeans who, like him, are oppressed; it incites him to imagine a privilege-less society in which skin pigmentation will be considered a mere fluke.[7] (Sartre 1948, XIII)

---

7   Le nègre, comme le travailleur blanc, est victime de la structure capitaliste de notre société ; cette situation lui dévoile son étroite solidarité, par-delà les nuances de sa peau, avec certaines classes d'Européens opprimés comme lui ; elle l'incite à projeter une société sans privilège où la pigmentation de la peau sera tenue pour un simple accident.

It should be pointed out here that, already in *Reflections on the Jewish Question* (1947), Sartre noted that black skin represents a much more serious handicap than belonging to the proletariat or to the Jewish community: while a proletarian can in certain circumstances become rich and an assimilated Jew is likely to melt into the majority society, the black person remains identifiable as a black person and his skin color is interpreted by the Western tradition as "pure negativity" (Sartre [1943] 1993, 219).

Another problem consists in the incompatibility of the original dialectical model with the colonial experience. In the first phase of the cycle governing the Master–Slave dialectic, Hegel assumes an equality of positions: two competing self-consciousnesses enter into a life-and-death struggle for recognition/truth. Having shown courage and being ready to risk its life, one of the consciousnesses wins the struggle, *proves* its truth and thus acquires the dominant position of the Master, while the other, more cautious or even cowardly, has to be satisfied with the submissive position of the Slave. From this first imbalance, a practice is established which makes the Slave work for the Master. The latter enjoys not only the products of the Slave's work, but also, on the ontological level, a recognition as a "being-for-itself," while the Slave is reduced to a "being-for-an-Other" (Berenson 1982, 81). However, as time goes by, the balance of power is reversed: while the Master becomes more and more passive and dependent on the Slave, the latter frees himself thanks to work, which represents both a means of social emancipation and a source of dignity on the psychological level. Unable to transform matter, the Master stagnates both physically and intellectually before regressing to a level dangerously close to that of the animal. The Slave, on the other hand, masters more and more the surrounding nature, which is accompanied by an awareness of his own professional and human value, as well as by the disappearance of the original fear. He evolves towards a higher level of humanity, unbalancing the system in the other direction and reversing the power relationships.

As Frantz Fanon reminded us in *Black Skin, White Masks* (1952), the colonial system does not function on the basis of this reciprocity assumed by Hegel.[8] The positions of real master and slave are not the result of an original struggle in which the master courageously risked his life, but are

---

8   Indeed, according to the German philosopher, a consciousness cannot be formed apart from a conflictual relationship with others. It is the confrontation with the other, it is the fight (not necessarily physical, but all the same engaging the life and requiring a great courage) which

given from the beginning by the historical context. Moreover, the white master has no desire to be recognized by the black slave, since the latter is, in his eyes, a kind of piece of furniture[9] or animal with no consciousness of its own.[10] The colonial slave, for his part, takes no pride in this drudgery which does not liberate him. Fanon noted that no "struggle" worthy of the name was provoked or subsequently instigated by a Slave thirsting for freedom. For decades, the ambition of the colonized was a timid imitation of the colonizer.[11]

Sartre was undoubtedly aware of this incompatibility of the colonial situation with the whole of the Hegelian model, which, let us emphasize, does not necessarily imply a historical-sociological reading and can be interpreted as an intrapsychic process, as a movement of consciousness within an individual.[12] This is probably the reason why Sartre's prefaces ended up focusing only on certain passages of Hegel, notably on those that develop the principle of the antithesis, while the idea of the synthesis disappeared at the beginning of the 1960s.

For example, the whole "Negritude" movement consists, according to Sartre, of a negative phase of dialectical evolution, of a kind of "anti-racist racism" (Sartre 1948, XIV, XL). The idea is very clearly stated in the preface to Senghor's anthology:

> In fact, Negritude appears like the up-beat [un accented beat] of a dialectical progression: the theoretical and practical affirmation of white

9   conditions the birth of a true consciousness. Without a certain degree of reciprocity, the dialectic does not even start.

9   According to article 44 of the *Code noir ou Recueil d'édits, déclarations et arrêts concernant la discipline et le commerce des esclaves nègres des îles françaises de l'Amérique*, a slave is "movable property". See https://gallica.bnf.fr/ark:/12148/bpt6k84479z/f218.item.r=Code+Noir.langFR. Accessed 11 May 2021.

10   "[T]he master laughs at the consciousness of the slave. What he wants from the slave is not recognition but work" (Fanon 2008, 172).

11   For an excellent exposition of the Fanonian reading of Hegel, see Mengozzi 2016, 182.

12   Out of the 900 pages of *The Phenomenology of Spirit*'s latest French edition, the Master–Slave dialectic occupies only 14 and a half. Moreover, it is inserted in chapter IV of the book, which deals with "The Truth of Self-Certainty". There is no explicit indication of Hegel's desire to have this passage interpreted historically or politically. It is true that, in the French context, Alexandre Kojève and his seminar at the *École Pratique des Hautes Études* (of which Sartre was one of the assiduous participants) imposed a Marxist reading of the dialectic that not only sees in the Master and the Slave two antagonistic actors of History, but that goes so far as to consider this passage as the main interpretive key to the *Phenomenology*. However, Kojève later admitted in his letter to Tran Duc Thao from 7 October 1948: "It was relatively unimportant for me to know what Hegel himself meant in his book; I gave a course in phenomenological anthropology using Hegelian texts, but saying only what I considered to be the truth, and leaving out what seemed to me to be an error in Hegel" (Jarczyk and Labarrière 1996, 64).

supremacy is the thesis; the position of Negritude as an antithetical value is the moment of negativity. But this negative moment is not sufficient in itself, and these black men who use it know this perfectly well; they know that it aims at preparing the synthesis or realization of the human being in a race-less society. Thus Negritude is for destroying itself, it is a "crossing to" and not an "arrival at", a means and not an end.[13] (Sartre 1948, XLI).

According to Sartre, the representatives of Negritude developed their particularism only as a way leading later to universal values, and they celebrated the violence/temporal negation only as a preparation for a final peace/positivity. In an analogous way, the French philosopher considered that Albert Memmi "tries to live his particularity by exceeding it towards the universal. Not towards the Man, that does not exist yet, but towards a rigorous Reason that imposes itself on all" (Sartre 1973, 24).[14]

It is only in his preface to Fanon's book that Sartre abandoned, at least in part, this universalist premise and formulated the unbearable paradox of the colonized vis-à-vis the colonizers: "you make monsters of us, your humanism pretends to make us universal and your racist practices make us particular" (Sartre 1961, 24).[15] (Even at this stage of the argument, Sartre ended up referring back to Hegel and Wahl, applying to Africans the concept of the "unhappy consciousness" that becomes entangled in its own contradictions.)

Nevertheless, contrary to the two previous prefaces, at the beginning of the 1960s, Sartre no longer dared to anticipate this third phase of the Hegelian dialectic which would bring a conciliatory and cathartic synthesis. While the propagators of Negritude basically aspired only to a non-conflicting recognition of their cultural specificity by the West, and Albert Memmi crowned his essay with an optimistic ending in which "the ex-colonized will have become a man like the others. With all the luck and misfortune of men, of course, but finally he will be a free

---

13 En fait, la Négritude apparaît comme le temps faible d'une progression dialectique : l'affirmation théorique et pratique de la suprématie du blanc est la thèse ; la position de la Négritude comme valeur antithétique est le moment de la négativité. Mais ce moment négatif n'a pas de suffisance par lui-même et les noirs qui en usent le savent fort bien ; ils savent qu'il vise à préparer la synthèse ou réalisation de l'humain dans une société sans races. Ainsi la Négritude est pour se détruire, elle est passage et non aboutissement, moyen et non fin dernière.

14 essaye de vivre sa particularité en la dépassant vers l'universel. Non pas vers l'Homme, qui n'existe pas encore, mais vers une Raison rigoureuse qui s'impose à tous.

15 vous faites de nous des monstres, votre humanisme nous prétend universels et vos pratiques racistes nous particularisent.

man" (Memmi 1973, 177).[16] Frantz Fanon considered the abyss that had opened up between the colonizer and the colonized, dehumanized for several centuries, to be so insurmountable and the extent of historical crimes so irreparable that he openly called for revolutionary violence, the only imaginable way out in the future. In his preface, Sartre took up this radical rhetoric and also stopped symbolically at the level of the second, negative, dialectical phase, which he pushed even further than Fanon:

> To shoot down a European is to kill two birds with one stone, to destroy an oppressor and the man he oppresses at the same time: there remain a dead man, and a free man; the survivor, for the first time, feels a national soil under his foot.[17] (Sartre 1961, 35)

The dialectic thus remained roughly in place, only its third utopian phase would be written with blood:

> The war, by merely setting the question of command and responsibility, institutes new structures which will become the first institutions of peace. Here, then, is man even now established in new traditions, the future children of a horrible present; here then we see him legitimized by a law which will be born or is born each day under fire: once the last settler is killed, shipped home or assimilated, the minority breed disappears, to be replaced by Socialism.[18] (Sartre 1961, 36)

The preface led to a revolutionary appeal to the French not to end up – like their colonial regime – in the dustbin of history. On the contrary, they should join the enemy camp, while there is still time: "But, as they say, that's another story: the history of mankind. The time is drawing near, I am sure, when we will join the ranks of those who make it" (Sartre 1961, 42).[19]

---

16 l'ex-colonisé sera devenu un homme comme les autres. Avec tout l'heur et le malheur des hommes, bien sûr, mais enfin il sera un homme libre.

17 Abattre un Européen, c'est faire d'une pierre deux coups, supprimer en même temps un oppresseur et un opprimé : restent un homme mort et un homme libre ; le survivant, pour la première fois, sent un sol national sous la plante de ses pieds.

18 La guerre – ne fût-ce qu'en posant la question du commandement et des responsabilités – institue de nouvelles structures qui seront les premières institutions de la paix. Voici donc l'homme instauré jusque dans des traditions nouvelles, filles futures d'un horrible présent, le voici légitimé par un droit qui va naître, qui naît chaque jour au feu : avec le dernier colon tué, rembarqué ou assimilé, l'espèce minoritaire disparaît, cédant la place à la fraternité socialiste.

19 Mais ceci, comme on dit, est une autre histoire. Celle de l'homme. Le temps s'approche, j'en suis sûr, où nous nous joindrons à ceux qui la font.

As we can see, at the beginning of the 1960s, Sartre abandoned all hope in the advent of a third conciliatory dialectical phase or, at least, he postponed it to a very distant future. In the name of loyalty to the historical and contemporary slaves, the philosopher persisted in making the antithesis last (even if very bloody) and in leaving the eventual synthesis to future (Socialist) generations.

4 Hegel Being Afraid of a "Limit Experience"?

Among all the French readers of Hegel and Jean Wahl, Georges Bataille probably went the furthest in the rehabilitation of negativity. It is true that the Surrealists and Sartre refused *a priori* the third phase of the dialectic, but their refusal was in fact only a postponement, and negativity, as they envisaged it, was to be put at the service of a higher good (art, creativity, freedom, the advent of a just and non-racist society). Far from subordinating it to an "idea", Bataille wanted a negativity that would be purely negative: not only destructive, but having no use at all:

> An inspiration to the generation of French philosophers who came to prominence in the 1960s, such as Foucault and Derrida, Bataille's thought prolonged and radicalized the Surrealist and Marxist reflections on Hegel's negativity. In the end, Bataille broke with both movements because he saw them as subordinating human negativity to its productive uses in work, and for Bataille, work constitutes a submission to the reality principle, including the reality of death, which work is meant to postpone. If the fear of death motivates work, as Bataille argues, then the only way of overcoming the fear is to release negativity from its connection to labor, which neither Marxism nor Surrealism succeeded in doing. To attain the Surrealist impossible, negativity must be unbound. (Baugh 2003, 71)

A "thinker of transgression and vertigo" (Sabot 2007, 87) who participated in all the intellectual, literary and philosophical movements of his time, "opening them up to each other beyond their limits" (Sichère 2006, 15), Bataille did not consider himself to be a conceptual thinker: "what I teach [...] is an intoxication, it is not a philosophy: I am not a philosopher but a *saint*, perhaps a madman" (Bataille 1973, 218).[20] In the wake of Nietzsche, he developed a paradoxical and heterodox philosophical discourse that disturbed traditional thought, questioning its unspoken, repressed, "Cursed part – *La Part maudite*" (Bataille 1967).

Although Bataille's interest in Hegel predated his participation in Kojève's seminars (1933–9),[21] for the purposes of my study I will focus on his peculiar reaction to the famous Russian professor. According to Kojève, the principle that animates the history of humanity is an "anthropogenic Desire". Driven by this Desire, man devotes himself to the Action (defined as a "negating negativity") which transforms him little by little from a natural being into an auto-poetic, self-constructed being:

> Its maintenance in existence will thus mean for this Self: "not to be what it is (as a static and given being, as a natural being) and to be (i.e. to become) what it is not". This Self will thus be its own work: it will be (in the future) what it has become by negation (in the present) of what it has been (in the past), this negation being carried out in view of what it will become. In its very being, this I [...] is the act of transcending this given which is given to it and which it is itself.[22] (Kojève 1947, 12–13)

Human life consists therefore in "annihilating" the present to project itself in the indeterminacy of the future. As a good Marxist, Kojève imagined that this negative action would be represented above all by Work and Struggle. As long as man runs after his Desire, works, struggles and is engaged in this process of self-creating negativity, we can speak of History. But History will have an end:

> If man is nothing other than his becoming, [...] if revealed reality is nothing other than universal history, this history must be the history of the

---

20 ce que j'enseigne [...] est une ivresse, ce n'est pas une philosophie : je ne suis pas un philosophe mais un *saint*, peut-être un fou.

21 Already in 1932, Bataille published in *La Critique sociale* an article (co-signed by Raymond Queneau) entitled "The Critique of the Foundations of the Hegelian Dialectic" in which he distanced himself from Hegel's "idealism" in favor of Marxist materialism. Not particularly original, the article has nothing to do with the later Bataillian theories.

22 Son maintien dans l'existence signifiera donc pour ce Moi : "ne pas être ce qu'il est (en tant qu'être statique et donné, en tant qu'être naturel) et être (c'est-à-dire devenir) ce qu'il n'est pas". Ce Moi sera ainsi son propre œuvre : il sera (dans l'avenir) ce qu'il est devenu par négation (dans le présent) de ce qu'il a été (dans le passé), cette négation étant effectuée en vue de ce qu'il deviendra. Dans son être même, ce Moi [...] est l'acte de transcender ce donné qui lui est donné et qu'il est lui-même.

interaction between Mastery and Servitude: the historical "dialectic" is the "Master–Slave dialectic". But if the opposition of the "thesis" and the "antithesis" has a sense only inside the conciliation of the "synthesis", if History in the strong sense of the word has necessarily a final term, if the man who becomes must culminate in the man who has become, if the Desire must lead to satisfaction, [...] the interaction of the Master and the Slave must finally lead to their "dialectical suppression".[23] (Kojève 1947, 16)

When man fulfills his own essence as negativity, his Desire will cease and he himself will disappear, giving way to beings of the Post-History. Their lives will no longer be governed by the will to recognition nor animated by the negativity of Work and Struggle. Living in a kind of quiet satisfaction, Post-Humans will devote themselves to non-lucrative and non-utilitarian activities: "art, love, play, etc., etc.; in short, everything that makes Man happy" (Kojève 1947, 435).[24]

Although very impressed by the Kojève courses,[25] Bataille pushed his customary provocation to the point of sending Kojève a letter on 6 December 1937, in which he opposed his own empirical experience (based on an assiduous frequenting of Parisian brothels in which the writer indulged in more and more extreme sexual practices) to the Hegelian system.

I admit (as a plausible assumption) that history is already finished [...]. My experience, lived with much concern, led me to think that I had nothing more "to do". [Now] if action ("doing") is – as Hegel says – negativity, the question arises whether the negativity of those who have "nothing left to do" disappears or remains in the state of "unemployed negativity": personally, I can only decide in one direction, being myself exactly this "unemployed negativity" (I could not define myself more precisely). [...] I imagine that my life – or its abortion, better still, the open wound that

---

23 Si l'homme n'est pas autre chose que son devenir, [...] si la réalité révélée n'est rien d'autre que l'histoire universelle, cette histoire doit être l'histoire de l'interaction entre Maîtrise et Servitude : la "dialectique" historique est la "dialectique du Maître et de l'Esclave". Mais si l'opposition de la "thèse" et de l'"antithèse" n'a un sens qu'à l'intérieur de la conciliation de la "synthèse", si l'Histoire au sens fort du mot a nécessairement un terme final, si l'homme qui devient doit culminer en l'homme devenu, si le Désir doit aboutir à la satisfaction, [...] l'interaction du Maître et de l'Esclave doit finalement aboutir à leur "suppression dialectique ".

24 l'art, l'amour, le jeu, etc., etc. ; bref, tout ce qui rend l'Homme heureux.

25 In his own words, he came out of class "broken, crushed, killed ten times" and completely under the spell of the charismatic teacher (Bataille 1973a, 146).

is my life – alone constitutes the refutation of Hegel's closed system.[26] (Bataille 1997, 131–2).

Indeed, Bataille considered himself to be a Sage at the end of the Hegelian-Kojèvian history who had already realized absolute knowledge and the integral accomplishment of the desire. However, his desire was not satisfied once and for all, but, on the contrary, it was exacerbated beyond any limit. As Philippe Sabot points out:

> To the Hegelian-Marxist schema imagined by Kojève which amounted to granting the negative a driving role in the historical dialectic of recognition, Bataille tends to superimpose the theme of a pure negativity according to which life resolves itself in activity in pure loss, without positive anchoring and without work to realize. Thus, in the margins of Kojèvism, the possibility of a reverse of the dialectic, of a form of non-dialecticizable negativity that engages man beyond his own completion (as Wisdom) and even in the contestation of this very completion, takes shape.[27] (Sabot 2012, 6)

From lack to excess, Desire thus changes sign (polarity), and so does the "death of man": it is no longer a matter of the completion of the human, but of its dissolution, as it is carried out, for example, in the "play of the limit and transgression" (Blanchot 1969, 308) within eroticism but also in the literary experience, identified as experience of the outside and of idleness.

In short, Bataille's philosophical and literary speculations on the "limit-experience" led him to *dedialectize* and, finally, to *deteleologize*

---

26   J'admets (comme une supposition vraisemblable) que dès maintenant l'histoire est achevée [...]. Mon expérience, vécue avec beaucoup de souci, m'a conduit à penser que je n'avais plus rien "à faire". [Or] si l'action (le "faire") est – comme dit Hegel – la négativité, la question se pose alors de savoir si la négativité de qui n'a "plus rien à faire" disparaît ou subsiste à l'état de "négativité sans emploi": personnellement, je ne puis décider que dans un sens, étant moi-même exactement cette "négativité sans emploi" (je ne pourrais me définir de façon plus précise). [...] J'imagine que ma vie – ou son avortement, mieux encore, la blessure ouverte qu'est ma vie – à elle seule constitue la réfutation du système fermé de Hegel.

27   Au schéma hégéliano-marxiste imaginé par Kojève qui revenait à accorder au négatif un rôle moteur dans la dialectique historique de la reconnaissance, Bataille tend à superposer le thème d'une pure négativité selon lequel la vie se résout en activité en pure perte, sans ancrage positif et sans œuvre à réaliser. Se dessine donc, dans les marges du kojévisme, la possibilité d'un revers de la dialectique, d'une forme de négativité non dialectisable qui engage l'homme au-delà de son propre achèvement (comme Sagesse) et même dans la contestation de cet achèvement même.

Desire and to substitute for the Kojèvian perspective of a post-historical Wisdom the theme of a transgressive eroticism that exacerbates the relation of man to the sacred, by maintaining, in an open and alive form, the dimension of an existence dedicated to the extreme, to the experience and to the diction of the extreme.

More than that: deeply influenced by Jean Wahl and his reflections on a romantic-existentialist Hegel, Bataille went so far as to accuse the German philosopher of cowardice and inconsequence. The young Hegel would also have ventured into borderline experiments (at least on the speculative level), but he would have become afraid of the danger of sinking into madness and would have turned back. His System would have been a kind of exorcism of the extreme, a will to tame it, to defuse it, even at the cost of self-mutilation:

> A little comic recap. – Hegel, I imagine, touched the extreme. He was still young and thought he was going crazy. I even imagine that he elaborated the system to escape (every kind of conquest, no doubt, is the fact of a man fleeing a threat). Finally, Hegel arrives at *satisfaction*, turns his back on the extreme. *The supplication is dead in him.* That one seeks salvation, still passes, one continues to live, one cannot be sure, it is necessary to continue to beg. Hegel won, alive, the salvation, killed the supplication, mutilated himself. Only a shovel handle remained of him, a modern man. But before mutilating himself, undoubtedly, he touched the extreme, knew the supplication: his memory brings him back to the perceived abyss, to cancel it! The system is the cancellation.[28] (Bataille 1943, 56)

It is interesting to observe to what extent these three intellectuals studied Hegel at crucial moments in their lives and needed his dialectic to affirm themselves: it allowed them to dream of a point where all binary oppositions would cease to be perceived as such (Breton), to imagine a society devoid of class and racism that would come about after the victory of

---

28 Petite récapitulation comique. – Hegel, je l'imagine, toucha l'extrême. Il était jeune encore et crut devenir fou. J'imagine même qu'il élaborait le système pour échapper (chaque sorte de conquête, sans doute, est le fait d'un homme fuyant une menace). Pour finir, Hegel arrive à la *satisfaction*, tourne le dos à l'extrême. *La supplication est morte en lui.* Qu'on cherche le salut, passe encore, on continue de vivre, on ne peut être sûr, il faut continuer de supplier. Hegel gagna, vivant, le salut, tua la supplication, *se mutila*. Il ne resta de lui qu'un manche de pelle, un homme moderne. Mais avant de se mutiler, sans doute, il a touché l'extrême, a connu la supplication : sa mémoire le ramène à l'abîme perçu, *pour l'annuler* ! Le système est l'annulation.

the Slaves (Sartre), or to meditate on the role of Desire in human history (Bataille). Would Breton have been a surrealist, Sartre an existentialist, and Bataille a postmodernist without Hegel? Perhaps yes, but their intellectual paths would have been much less dynamic and passionate.

Fascinated by the Hegelian dialectical system and at the same time deeply irritated by its third synthetic and conciliatory phase, the French intellectuals finally placed not only their thoughts, but also their auto-stylizations and autopoiesis under the sign of a perpetual polemic with Hegel. Indeed, although each of them proceeded in his own way, all three came to see themselves (and man in general) as a (self)creative negativity to which no limits should be imposed. To dream, to act or to desire without any limit, to yield nothing to the given, to fatality, to the natural, such seems to be the program of these modern French thinkers. It is true that, in practice, Breton subordinated the negativity to the art and Sartre saw its overcoming in a utopian future. Only Bataille made himself the propagator of extreme and eminently transgressive experiences, which – according to him – allowed the practice of an unlimited negativity, an expenditure of oneself in pure loss.

In any case, the French *century of Hegel* turns out to be much more a *century of negativity* (whether it ended up playing a positive role or not). A century which went very far in the affirmation of the human freedom: against the System, against nature, against the given, against the very limits of the body. For Breton, Sartre and Bataille, negativity equals freedom and that is why they fought for it with so much enthusiasm.

References

Bataille, Georges. 1943. *L'Expérience intérieure*. Paris: Gallimard.
Bataille, Georges. 1967. *La Part maudite*. Paris: Le Seuil.
Bataille, Georges. 1973. *Œuvres complètes V*. Paris: Gallimard.
Bataille, Georges. 1973a. *Œuvres complètes VI*. Paris: Gallimard.
Bataille, Georges. 1997. *Choix de lettres. 1917–1962*. Paris: Gallimard.
Baugh, Bruce. 2003. *French Hegel. From Surrealism to Postmodernism*. New York, London: Routledge.
Bellantone, Andrea. 2011. *Hegel en France I. De Cousin à Vera*. Translated by Virginie Gaugey. Paris: Hermann Éditeurs.
Bellantone, Andrea. 2011a. *Hegel en France II. De Vera à Hyppolite*. Translated by Virginie Gaugey. Paris: Hermann Éditeurs.
Berenson, Frances. 1982. "Hegel on Others and the Self". *Philosophy* 57 (219): 77–90.
Blanchot, Maurice. 1969. *L'Entretien infini*. Paris: Gallimard.
Breton, André. 1924. *Manifeste du surréalisme*. Paris: Éditions du Sagittaire.

Breton, André. 1929. "Second manifeste du surréalisme". *La Révolution surréaliste* 12, 15 décembre, 1–23.

Breton, André. 1969. "Surrealist Situation of the Object". Translated by Richard Seaver, and Helen R. Lane. In *Manifestoes of Surrealism*, 255–78. Ann Arbor: University of Michigan Press. Original edition, 1935.

Breton, André. 1992. "Discours au Congrès des écrivains". In *Œuvres complètes II*, edited by Marguerite Bonnet, 451–9. Paris: Gallimard. Original edition, 1935.

Fanon, Frantz. 2008. *Black Skin, White Masks*. London: Pluto Press.

Jarczyk, Gwendoline, and Pierre-Jean Labarrière. 1996. *De Kojève à Hegel : cent cinquante ans de pensée hégélienne en France*. Paris: Albin Michel.

Kojève, Alexandre. 1947. *Introduction à la lecture de Hegel*. Paris: Gallimard.

Levinas, Emmanuel, Xavier Tilliette, and Paul Ricœur. 1976. *Jean Wahl et Gabriel Marcel*. Paris: Beauchesne.

Lowy, Michael. 2017. *L'Étoile du matin : surréalisme et marxisme*. Paris: Éditions Syllepse.

Memmi, Albert. 1973. *Portrait du colonisé précédé du Portrait du colonisateur*. Paris: Petite Bibliothèque Payot.

Mengozzi, Chiara. 2016. "Lo sguardo e la colpa: Tempo di uccidere di Ennio Flaiano e la dialettica servo-signore alla prova del colonialism". *Modern Language Notes* 31 (1): 175–95.

Negri, Antimo. 1987. *Hegel nel Novecento*. Roma, Bari: Laterza.

Reynaud-Paligot, Carole. 1994. "Histoire politique du mouvement surréaliste (1919–1969)". *Les Cahiers du Centre de Recherches Historiques* 13: 1–7. https://journals.openedition.org/ccrh/2718#text. Accessed 18 May 2021

Sabot, Philippe. 2007. "Extase et transgression chez Georges Bataille". *Savoirs et clinique* 8 (1): 87–93.

Sabot, Philippe. 2012. "Bataille, entre Kojève et Queneau : le désir et l'histoire". *Le Portique. Revue de philosophie et de sciences humaines* 29 (2): 1–13. http://journals.openedition.org/leportique/2594. Accessed 11 May 2021.

Sartre, Jean-Paul. 1948. "Orphée noir". In *Anthologie de la nouvelle poésie nègre et malgache de langue française*, edited by Léopold Sédar Senghor, I–XLIV. Paris: Presses universitaires de France.

Sartre, Jean-Paul. 1961. "Préface". In *Les Damnés de la terre*, edited by Frantz Fanon, 23–42. Paris: Éditions François Maspero.

Sartre, Jean-Paul. 1973. "Préface". In Albert Memmi, *Portrait du colonisé précédé du Portrait du colonisateur*, 23–30. Paris: Petite Bibliothèque Payot.

Sartre, Jean-Paul. 1993. *L'Être et le néant. Essai d'ontologie phénoménologique*. Paris: Gallimard. Original edition, 1943.

Sichère, Bernard. 2006. *Pour Bataille. Être, chance, souveraineté*. Paris: Gallimard.

Wahl, Jean. 1929. *Le Malheur de la conscience dans la philosophie de Hegel*. Brionne: Gérard Monfort.

Part 3
Religion and Education as Autopoietic Projects

Luhmann's Religious Carnival and the Limits of Communication

Tereza Matějčková

Wer spricht von siegen?
Überstehen ist alles
Rainer Maria Rilke: "Requiem für Wolf Graf von Kalckreuth"

1 Introductory Remarks

The inability to fully adapt to modernity is religion's key advantage in contemporary society. Such is the provocative interpretation proposed by Niklas Luhmann. Why is religion maladapted to modernity? Like any other system in a functionally differentiated society, religion is autopoietic, which means that it creates itself out of its own operations. At the same time, it refutes its self-made operations and believes in God as its true creator. Accordingly, it is the only modern system that turns against itself and prefers its *beyond* over itself. Through this latter process, the religious system devises unique means of self-observation. The religious communication arising therefrom can be a source of inspiration for other systems to occasionally invert their values – and paradoxically, thus succeed in generating a more realistic external reference where, in fact, no external reference exists.

It is impossible to understand Luhmann's theory of religion independently of the outline of his systems theory as such. I will offer an outline in the first part of this paper. This section's key concepts are "difference" and "paradox," both of which are pivotal to Luhmann's understanding of religion. In the first part, I will as well remark that modern philosophers have understood religion as a key binding element in society. We encounter this attitude in such thinkers as Rousseau ([1762] 2002, 245–54), Hobbes ([1651] 1996, 99), and later, especially in Durkheim ([1912] 1995, 9). According to their point of view, religion and morality play either structurally equivalent roles, or are identifiable. One of Luhmann's key contributions is to break up this alliance, accept that "difference" is the last word of modernity, and understand religion not as a substantial structure but as a specific form of communication that, rather than sanctioning society's values, challenges these.

In many respects, however, Luhmann's perspective on religion is limited. Above all, it is obvious that for him, religious communication is a form of communication that proceeds from Western society, and thus, he is mostly concerned with Christianity. This criticism, often leveled against Luhmann (Pannenberg 1978; Helmstetter 2002), may be considered – at least from one perspective – misguided. Rather than viewing this limitation as a fault, one may claim that Luhmann is not interested in Buddhism any less than he is in Christianity. He does not observe these main traditions for a simple reason: he studies individual forms of communication classified as religious, irrespective of their tradition. This *limited* scope might prove particularly fruitful – especially during a time in which religious traditions, adapting to internet culture, interact and often coalesce (Roy 2008).

It is indubitable that Luhmann offers a highly specific observation of the religious system, especially in a time when the topos of a divided society is invoked ad nauseam. Rather than searching for ways to escape this situation, Luhmann embraces it. Rather than claiming that in modernity religion has lost its function, he notices that it is only now that it has freed itself from functions foreign to it – be it education, politics, or the economic system.

But what is it that is autochthonously religious? In the last part, I will comment on Luhmann's insights into mystical communication. This type of communication is a phenomenon that is surprisingly relevant in modern society – in a society where everyone understands that it is impossible to escape society, but that this very society is at the same time dependent on the existence of something *beyond* society. The communication of that which cannot be communicated can be considered mystical and represents for Luhmann the most insightful and relevant religious contribution in a functionally differentiated society.

2 The Modern Fight Against Religion and Its Unlikely Victor

With the term "secularization", sociology grounds and designates its own self-understanding (Luhmann 2002, 278). This insight points to at least two things. First, Luhmann emphasizes the social importance of the evolution of religion. Second, sociology has emerged once it has become apparent that religion no longer plays the role of a social "cement". Far from designating a mere change in infrastructure, or the transition from a religious to a secular base, secularization entails such a retreat by religion that it essentially transforms the social landscape as such.

Understood in this way, secularization thus finds its counterpart in the early philosophers of society who gradually established the discipline of sociology. Significantly, these philosophers did not consider their role to lie exclusively in reflecting on society. Instead, they actively sought new values that would bind individuals into a unitary whole. In many respects, they believed that it was science and its worldview that would eventually replace the religious infrastructure whose trustworthiness seemed outlived.

This was the idea of Auguste Comte – at least prior to encountering Clotilde de Vaux, the short-lived love of his life. In the first part of his career, Comte trusted wholly in rationality, trying to formulate a concept of society based on scientific rationality. Bearing a remote similarity to Plato's idea of philosophers on the throne, scientists would wield power over the social body. This worldview finds its best formulation in the *Course de philosophie positive*, a series of lectures published between 1830 and 1842.

As it happens, love altered the philosopher's worldview, and although interpreters do not agree on whether to read this change as a break or rather as a gradual shift in emphasis, it is beyond doubt that after falling in love with Clotilde, Comte's faith in science wavered. Henceforward he believed that the key to the lost unity in society lay in a shared sense of affection, as propounded in his second decisive work, *Système de politique positive, ou Traité de sociologie instituant la religion de l'Humanité*. In 1852, Comte used a phrase later identified as the "sacred formula of positivism": "Love as the principle, and Order as the base, Progress as the goal" (Comte 1929, title page).

Eventually, Comte chose love – a topic of some importance to Luhmann himself (1986; 2010) – as the foundation of his "religion of humanity". And it does not need reminding that love is a phenomenon that is not restricted to the intimate realm, but one that is *at home* in religious traditions too: to speak in the language of systems theory, love is God's observation of the world. For Comte, the cultivation of affectionate ties, the deliberate preference of the other's interest at the expense of one's self was the key means to avert a decomposition of the social body fatally endangered by modernity. In this respect, it is not accidental that Comte was the inventor of two terms: sociology and altruism.

Even later, social scientists did not abandon the search for a new social law to live by. In this respect, a peculiar normativity persisted in these writings authored before sociology as such existed. From Luhmann's point of view, the insight into the disintegration of the social body is an accurate one; what he deems questionable are the attempts to remedy this situation.

An apt illustration of this modern loosening of ties is the division of labor: people understand a tiny section of a certain process extremely well, while the process as a whole eludes them. This junction of minute attentiveness to details and blindness to the horizon is a phenomenon that extends beyond the workplace. Karl Marx has shown how the process of alienation from one's product results in one's alienation from the other human being, and eventually, the human species too (Marx 2015, 82–98). It is not necessary to speak about Karl Marx's "human species" in order to state that many theorists of modern society reflect on the individual's alienation from a shared realm, interest, or project.

For Luhmann, "division" is the key concept of secularization and, accordingly, of modern society and sociology as well. In modernity, people start identifying themselves with a severely limited "share" of reality. This provokes fear and uncertainty since this very specialization turns the environment into something unfathomable. In a vain attempt at self-defense against the unknown and inscrutable, people specialize even more and thus aggravate all of the aforementioned obstacles. In this perspective, modernity is, as William Rasch pointed out, "a force field of competing anxieties" (Rasch 2000, 127).

Durkheim, a philosopher who gradually lay the foundation of sociology, was not as much of an activist as Comte. Still, throughout his work, he pointed out that modernity is based upon certain values – key among them the dignity of the individual rather than the group. Thus, he claimed: "the collective conscience is becoming more and more a cult of the individual [...] we shall see that this is what characterizes the morality of organized societies, compared to that of segmental societies" (Durkheim [1893] 1964, 407).[1]

However, since this positive evaluation of the individual is itself a social achievement, it needs to be safeguarded at the political and social levels. Durkheim expressed his opinion for the need to politically guarantee individualism (which he convincingly distinguished from egoism) in his article "Individualism and Intellectuals". In this text, published in 1898, Durkheim stepped forward as an advocate of the unjustly accused and convicted Alfred Dreyfus, defending the right to a just trial and presenting the central tenets of his humanistic worldview.

Crucially, Durkheim considered this worldview itself to be a religious expression of sorts, and without meaning to diminish its worth, he even suggested that humanism is a form of prejudice. Every society is founded upon insights that are rationally difficult, even impossible to prove as right. For Durkheim, a "society without prejudices would resemble an organism without reflexes: it would be a monster incapable of living" (Durkheim 1886, 69). In this regard, humanism is a religion for modern people; its central axiom being that any person has inalienable rights. If these rights are infringed upon, the public sphere reacts with an irritation similar to the one provoked upon the profanation of a holy object in a traditional society (Durkheim [1898] 1973, 46).[2]

The expression of these principles led many contemporary sociologists to consider Émile Durkheim as a thinker with a strong theological spin. Hence, Robert Bellah named Durkheim the "high priest of civil religion" (Bellah 1973, x), pointing out that for Durkheim, "society" was less an empirical than a profoundly theological concept. While this theological twist sounds old-fashioned, in fact it is of central importance to Luhmann, and it discloses a surprising agreement between his systems-theory and classical sociologists. As a matter of fact, Luhmann also adopts key theological motives and concepts. However, he never wavers in his belief that division is – irredeemably – the last word of modernity. No system of shared values or morality can reverse this trend. That modern society is functionally differentiated means in other words that here, division rather than unity reigns. Every identity is already the result of a difference.

---

1   See also Luhmann 2008, 7–24.
2   Hans Joas's analysis of Durkheim's insight into the holiness of the person is relevant to today's strains of thought. See Joas 2011, 81–101.

Luhmann himself acknowledges his predilection for viewing society under the lens of theology which he considers a tradition more inspiring than modern philosophy, with its interest in epistemology. In fact, Luhmann claims that the structure of basic social issues – and thus the structure of communication – is best understood with the instruments of theology rather than the categories of modern thought, which he often deems impoverished in comparison to the theological heritage (Luhmann 1992, 529).

3 Outlines of Luhmann's Systems Theory

In the Beginning Was the Difference

Society consists of social systems; social systems consist of communication. The principal means of differentiation of communication into social clusters are specific codes. These codes proceed from a first distinction and are the central pillars of Luhmann's theory, as put forward in one of his major writings, *Social Systems*, published in 1984.

Its first axiom – *There are systems* – may strike one as naïve. According to Luhmann, this suggestion is right as such, but wrong if it were considered to be a criticism of his starting point. The naïveté of any beginning is inevitable. It is impossible for the first step or distinction to be a product of reflection. Accordingly, he considers it an intellectual parade to pretend that one starts with a thought or even doubt – this itself is extremely dubious, if not downright excluded. The first *stroke* is a blind decision, an act of sovereignty.

Subsequent steps from which the system unwinds itself are more or less successful attempts to hide the contingency of the original step and lend the initial decision the appearance of necessity. Thus, any theory, any human achievement is – eventually – a cover-up, an attempt to obscure the awkwardness of the preceding step.

How to capture the initial step more concretely? The origin of any system lies in a decision to observe a concrete, very narrow, part of reality while ignoring everything else. Such is, for instance, the distinction that separates reality into whatever is lawful and whatever is unlawful. Analogically, one can observe the world from the perspective of health versus illness or from that of transcendence and immanence. These distinctions are foundations of modern social subsystems: The first refers to the subsystem of law, the second to the healthcare system, and the third to religion. Rather than a unity that precedes individuals or one proceeding from individuals, society – meaning a plurality of systems – is a horizontal landscape of a plurality of systems, lacking a dominant center or summit.

Luhmann calls the aforementioned distinction "lawful/unlawful" a "binary code". This is the "fuel" of observation and, hence, every system has its own binary distinction. The economic system bases itself on the distinction between prosperity/poverty, the system of politics on government/opposition, and religion on immanence/transcendence. The main objective of these codes is to limit contingency, and thus limit possibilities that might occur, confining the realm one may refer to and the questions one may raise. In short, in choosing a very confined perspective on reality, these systems limit complexity. Hence, they are formulas of subtraction. Without these, communication would not be possible. Consequently, initial blindness is the very foundation of insight.

The code internal to the system relates to what Luhmann calls "operational closure". Under "operational closure", he means that the system's operations are based on self-observation, rather than on observing the outside. According to this Kantian insight (transposed onto the social plane), the economic system is unable to capture ecological problems, unless they lend themselves to an economic perspective. The system reacts to another system's problems if it senses perturbations in its inner structure. In the above example, this would occur if something in the economic system were to break down because of an ecological catastrophe. Accordingly, the term "closure" does not refer to complete isolation but rather the inability to interact directly with any other system. Every response proceeds from an irritation that needs to be sufficiently strong in order to make itself felt in the inner structure of another system.

So far, the most radical insight has not been mentioned. Luhmann himself called his theory a "Trojan horse". The impenetrable language and complexity of his theory were meant to disguise the radicality of his ideas. At least in one respect, Luhmann's theory surpasses the radicality of even revolutionary Marxism (Stichweh 2003, 208): Marxists still hold on to a conservative view of humans and of their relation to the social world. They assume that society is made of people and that it can be changed by human agents.

For Luhmann, this is a very naïve picture. Since society is of a qualitatively different nature than human beings, people cannot walk into society and start changing things. In fact, he maintains that society is not made up of people but of social systems. Social systems operate on communication. On the contrary, people do not communicate, only communication communicates (Luhmann 1988, 884). Luhmann does not deny that communication is conditioned by (or "structurally coupled" to) consciousness but this does not mean that any consciousness can directly engage in communication.

The "old-European prejudice" (Luhmann 1997a, 868–79) of people communicating grows out of the unwarranted assumption that consciousness enters communication. Against this, Luhmann argues that consciousness – in Luhmannian language, the "psychic system" – is itself not made up of communication but of thoughts. These thoughts observe other thoughts which give rise to further thoughts.

It is pivotal that no transfer between thought and communication take place. Thus, thought and communication are two structurally different systems. As to this, Luhmann – contrary to his anti-traditional rhetoric – takes up a very traditional European viewpoint but radicalizes it. Many would claim that Descartes' insight into the nature of the human mind, and accordingly, his dualism of mind and body have proven highly formative for early modern philosophy. Luhmann accepts this Cartesian dualistic conception.

Thus, the human brain belongs to the physical system, and while it apparently does condition the mind, the brain and the mind never intermingle. While the human body operates on chemical communication, the human mind is a cluster of cognitive communication. In this respect, Cartesian dualism does seem convincing to Luhmann. But he makes a significant addition: Human beings do not consist of two "parts", but of three. The mind and the body are both "coupled to" the system of social communication. Thus, mind, body, and communication are three co-existing, interrelated, but never intermingled systems.

As in the case of social systems, the closure of body and mind does not prevent them from influencing each other. But these interactions are never direct. What happens outside of oneself can be recorded only through one's inner self. The outside or the environment – which is communication for consciousness on the one hand, and chemical processes in one's body on the other – does enter the psychic system or the mind exclusively as something internal – as thoughts. Thus, communication "enters" the mind only in the form of thoughts. In other words, as thinking beings, people do not communicate; as thinking beings, they think. Consequently, Luhmann can claim that it is not people, minds, or the brain that communicate: only communication communicates (Luhmann 1997, 105).

Foundation and its Paradoxes

Proceeding from Spencer-Brown (1969), Luhmann claims that every observation represents a distinction of two sides. The very drawing of a distinction presupposes a "marked" and an "unmarked" side. Hence, I draw a distinction and refer only to one side of the distinction (the one which is the more relevant aspect). To speak in more concrete terms, the lawyer observes the world proceeding from the distinction of lawful/unlawful, while focusing on the side of "lawful", without ignoring the side "unlawful" completely. In other words, any observation includes the side of the observed and the non-observed.

Alternatively, we can explain the relevance of this distinction with an even simpler example. What is a human being? The meaning of the relevant side, of the marked state, will become clear once we know what the unmarked state is. Is it *animal*, *God*, *android*? While the marked state remains the same, the unmarked state changes and, with this, the marked state does not remain completely unchanged either. In this respect, Luhmann remarks, "whatever happens, happens multiple times, depending on the system-reference" (Luhmann 1997a, 599). Such concepts as the human being or the phenomenon of an earthquake have different significances depending on what we relate it to: do we relate it to the economic system, the system of law, or education? In this sense, the unmarked side of the distinction is not invisible. Yet invisibility plays a key role after all. Paradoxically, it is the very distinction that is invisible. In order to see it, another distinction – which would be in turn invisible – would have to be drawn.

Drawing a difference between system and environment is still not sufficient for the creation of communication. Communication depends on what Luhmann calls – again, in the wake of Spencer-Brown – "re-entry", or the re-introduction of the original distinction into the system itself. Thus, the system first differentiates itself from the extralegal realm and upon this, it distinguishes itself into lawful/unlawful, or it bases itself on observing what is in accordance with the law and what violates the latter. It is upon this re-entry that communication and, accordingly, the entire system, are built. For Luhmann, this is the very reason and grounds for the auto-poietic nature of the system: it creates or constructs itself.

With respect to the re-entry, Luhmann introduces the paradox as the foundational principle of his theory. In order to relate to itself, the system needs to distinguish itself from itself, and it achieves this by introducing the distinction of lawful/unlawful into law itself. This paradoxical distinction is akin to an open wound that can never heal since healing would be the system's death. The very foreignness in the midst of itself prevents the system from becoming fully what it wants to be. Thus, in the Luhmannian universe, nobody knows what he or she means and the longing for authenticity is considered a romantic excess.

The Individual: Saved and Banished

For Luhmann, the historical differentiation of the religious system is archetypal of a functionally structural society. This is not surprising. After all, traditional societies are defined by the inability to clearly differentiate between the social or the cultural on the one level and the religious on the other. The relevance of religion is omnipresent.

In the midst of the Western religious tradition, the forces of secularization have gradually awoken. Continuously, the differentiation within religious communication results in the formation of certain thoroughly non-religious segments that break away. This, in turn, leads to more differentiation, specialization, and, in this respect, secularization too. To anchor this point historically, Luhmann notices that the first step towards secularization is taken during the Renaissance when Machiavelli denies religion the right to set political agendas.

Differentiation is synonymous with closure, and thus in a way with individualization as well; differentiation, in turn, leads to secularization. Luhmann counts among the most momentous historical achievements two events, both tied to writing and reading. First, with writing and its propagation throughout society, new forms of creativity emerge; these gradually transform traditional religiosity. Second, writing strengthens the very role of the individual. Thanks to writing, ideas can be separated from the ritualistic context, which means, among other things, that people – at least, the educated elite – can think on their own. Thus arises the need for interpreters and an institution that curbs the danger of misinterpreting sacred texts. The vital need for instituting a controlling mechanism becomes evident during the time of the first Christian heresies. For Luhmann, these are intricately related to the new freedom provided by writing and reading (Luhmann 2002, 253–63).

Moreover, through writing, we influence the future and enliven the past: past thinkers become quasi-contemporaries who can transform the present. Writing opens the realm of potentiality as well: what is important, is set down, and thus secured from loss. Consequently, we do not fear its loss and freely engage in playing with alternatives. In this respect, writing is an inexhaustible "impregnation" of social processes (Luhmann 1997, 269).

There is yet another significant religious transformation linked to writing: Gutenberg's printing press. The advent of print placed the means of communication in the hands of people previously presumed to be silent. The spread of writing leads to a de-hierarchization of the religious system, to further differentiation in the form of religious fragmentation, and to the definitive – but ambivalent – victory of the individual. While this transformation is linked mainly to Protestantism, a parallel process occurs in Catholicism. Henceforward, belief stands above deeds and communication above rituals.

Gradually, legitimacy and the criteria of true belief take recourse in the human subject. The social transformation makes itself fully felt around the 18th century. During this time, the impotence of the religious realm to offer binding values throughout society becomes ever more apparent. This gives rise to fully autonomous social systems that base their existence on religious neutrality. Rather than communicating on the background of a shared, religiously infused horizon, they introduce their own codes. Thus, the finger of God, once central to the creation of hierarchies, is now substituted by the invisible hand of the market that creates its own social order in a wholly different manner (Luhmann 1997a, 1063). In the case of the state, the decisive criterium is national sovereignty and in the case of ethics, it is rationality – rather than divine revelation.

Not only did religion lose its dominant position, but it was also accorded a negative privilege. In modernity, religion is the only system one does not depend on. While it is impossible to live a life without taking part in the system of economy, education, or law, one is not obliged to communicate religiously. Henceforward, belief is an individual decision. And the fact that it is based on a personal decision transforms its nature very qualitatively. The human being knows that his or her belief is permeated by his or her sovereign decision, and accordingly, belief is accompanied by doubt, a sense of contingency, and a characteristically modern feeling of restlessness.

Religion shares this fate with the modern individual as such. If in the Middle Ages philosophers defined a human being by his or her ability to relate to universals, in modernity, a human is someone who is able to actively constitute themselves in the act of self-reflection, and is someone who reads, too. With reference to Dean and Juliet F. MacCannell,

Luhmann notes: "whenever one has the potential to read one has the potential to be uncertain" (Luhmann 1997, 269).

Still, this is the less interesting transformation related to human beings as subjects. While on the surface their role is strengthened – individuality, authenticity, and autonomy are the key values of the time – people are gradually evicted out of society. As differentiation proceeds, the systems become fully autonomous and start operating on their own respective codes. Moreover, they are specialized to such an extent that it becomes impossible *to live* in them. One cannot spend one's life in the system of education, law, or religion, and there is no place called "society" beyond the sum of these systems.

At the level of psychological and social systems arises an "endogenous unrest" provoked by the "hopelessness of self-reference" (Luhmann 1997, 291). Even though Luhmann does not wish to psychologize his theory, he acknowledges that this unrest is anything but comfortable. He links this diagnosis with a fairly opaque proposal: one can try to endure this situation, or one can take a leap of faith (Luhmann and Fuchs 1989, 98).

4 Religion in Luhmann's Thought

A Moral Unity?

Throughout his writings, Luhmann indeed refers to two possible responses to modern uprootedness. Firstly, religion can be turned into morality, and thus into a secular set of values and a cosmology based thereupon. The second option consists of relying on certain advantages of mystical communication. While the first option is, according to Luhmann, a mere pathology (he refers to it most often as an "infection" or "molestation"), the second is more promising (Luhmann 1997a, 1036–45).

Luhmann's own preferences notwithstanding, it was the first option that seemed more feasible to modern thinkers. Thus, in Kant's work, we witness the autonomous thinker proposing a thorough moralization of religion, claiming Jesus as the ultimate materialization of the categorical imperative and the "prototype of humanity" (Kant 1998, 80–1). On a not dissimilar level, Émile Durkheim adopted the view that religion is essentially tied to morality. But for him, morality's source lay neither in the noumenal world of the godly realm, nor was it embodied in a holy person; rather, society was its embodiment, as such (Durkheim [1912] 1995, 208, 221–2).

In fact, for Durkheim, the social world is not only the moral, but even the epistemological a priori: "men owe to religion not only the content of their knowledge, in significant part, but also the form in which that knowledge is elaborated" (Durkheim [1912] 1995, 8). It is as members of society that we learn to value certain phenomena or actions; more than that, society bestows upon us the very ability to experience in a coordinated way with others. Eventually, any piece of knowledge is based on robust presupposition as to what counts as knowledge – on the epistemic criteria in the first place. In this respect, knowledge and its significance are always correlated with a specific society.

For Durkheim, this means that society itself rests on forces and processes that do not lend themselves to thorough inquiry since this very inquiry is conditioned by society. Accordingly, as to its original epistemic opacity and as to its extra-rational foundation that secures coordination among its members, society has a religious status. It furnishes us with the very basics into which we are unable to inquire and which are at the same time essential for us and for our ability to co-exist with others. What do we look for? Where does our attention go to? What do we abhor? The answers to these questions are the basic tenets that comprise the fundamental values of a given society.

In this respect, Durkheim maintains that any society depends on such a set of fundamental values in order to be considered a society. For Luhmann, this is a questionable thesis, even mere wishful thinking, at least in a functionally differentiated society. Furthermore, he maintains that Durkheim's identification of religion and morality is anything but inevitable. Despite the arbitrariness of linking religion and morality, the fact is that this link has been bequeathed to sociology which, in turn, is hesitant to free itself from its grip (Reder 2018). And surely, in mainstream society, too, we encounter the conviction that religion is somehow linked to shared values.

Now if we are speaking about European culture, which Luhmann does, this is an odd thing to say, or it is at least a very superficial one. After all, there are few religious founders who have so adamantly fought the hypocrisy and merely formal fulfillment of religious duties as Jesus did. Assertions such as "likewise joy shall be in heaven over one sinner that repenteth, more than over ninety and nine just persons, which need no repentance" are more likely to raise doubts as to proper behavior rather than offer a clear set of moral directions. Jesus's problematization of everyday morality and intuitions is nowhere as apparent as in the so-called "immoral" parables (Pokorný 2005, 82, 87–8).[3]

However, the fact is that once religion has lost persuasiveness on the social level, it has been replaced by morality, which takes on the role of the cohesive function. Henceforward, secularized morality assesses the religious worldview and oftentimes condemns it, attempting to occupy the place of a faltering religious tradition. Yet, at least in Luhmann's interpretation, morality turns out to be the least successful candidate to fill the vacant position of social-religious ties.

Before inquiring into why this project fails, I will mention one important trait that seems to favor morality's gradual ascendancy and its ability to replace religion. Both morality and religion refer to the entire human being. While being a good or bad scientist does not prevent anyone from being successful in another subsystem, for instance, in the subsystem of the economy, politics, even education, being a bad person is considered a disqualification relating to one's entire existence (Luhmann 2008, 111). Therefore, communicating in the moral code is risky: it is totalizing. Yet, this risk is outweighed: moral communication potently and efficiently reduces contingency. To speak prosaically, calling someone a *bad person* is a reaffirming experience.

Yet, morality fails in exactly the same manner as does authoritative religion when confronted by modernity – it lacks a sufficiently robust foundation to counteract functional differentiation. The attempt to found religion on secular reason is as fragile as to tie morality to religion. In a functionally differentiated society, every system has a rationality of its own – and most importantly, one that is "amoral" (Luhmann 1990a, 24). The duty of the medical doctor is to make decisions according to the health of the patient without probing into the question of the patient's

---

3   The writer and essayist Francis Spufford captures this point nicely: "So of all things, Christianity isn't supposed to be about gathering up the good people (shiny! happy! squeaky clean!) and excluding the bad people (frightening! alien! repulsive!) for the very simple reason that there aren't any good people. Not that it can be securely designated as such. It can't be about circling the wagons of virtue out in the suburbs and keeping the unruly inner city at bay. This, I realise, goes flat contrary to the present predominant image of it as something existing in prissy, fastidious little enclaves, far from life's messier zones and inclined to get all 'judgemental' about them" (Spufford 2013, 47). In fact, this is, as I understand it, the point of Luhmann's conception of morality from the perspective of systems theory: it is not that morality is bad per se, but that moral communication errs constantly and, on top of this, triggers – rightfully – strong reactions. For an insightful interpretation of Luhmann's conception of morality. See Kirchmeier 2011, 141–56.

morality. Analogically, it is not acceptable to refuse a scientific article by pointing out that its author is a corrupted human being.

In trying to be in sync with modernity and believing that rationality is the right path, morality discloses its problematic – according to Luhmann, even pathological – nature. Precisely because it has the power to judge the entire human being, it is a medium of communication with a particularly polemic nature and thus creates unproductive differences. Contrary to this, while religion relates to the entire being, too, it is capable of irony, of accepting paradoxes, and thus of relativizing its own tenets. This is precisely what any system or type of communication needs to have if it wants to be able to be successful in modernity. Thus, even though religion needs to accept its inappropriateness in most regions of modern social communication, it is still better equipped to survive modernity than moral communication.

What morality was purported to achieve – social unity – could not have been achieved, since in a modern, functionally differentiated society, unity is firstly a highly questionable goal, and secondly, rather than furnishing unity, morality creates disunity of a pernicious kind. Once one starts communicating morally, one creates conflict, since most often, one does not rely on such communication in order to praise someone but in order to refuse them and claim for oneself the position of an arbiter. This is rarely a good communicative investment. Luhmann is never weary to spell out the burden morality posses for any form of well-being:

> Morality repels, quarrels, and impedes the resolution of conflicts – an experience that has resulted, among other things, in the separation of law and morality. In any event, the function of morality is not determined adequately by referring to the need for societal integration. Society, fortunately, is not a moral state of affairs. (Luhmann 1996, 236)

And in fact, the highest vocation of ethics is to warn against the (ab)use of moral communication (Luhmann 1990a, 41).

Transcendence Beyond Differences

As suggested in an earlier section, Luhmann is a sociologist with a profound knowledge of and interest in theology. In this respect, he might be thought of as following up on the tradition of Émile Durkheim, yet without relating religion in any form to morality. In this sense, he is a better theologian than Durkheim since, traditionally, theologians were reticent to identify God with a *morally* conceived good.

For Luhmann, religion – freed from morality, "beyond good and evil" – plays a double role. He notes that, for one thing, it is the only system whose traditional specialization is to formulate unity in difference, to even sketch a horizon beyond differences. This is an extremely attractive function in a society totally committed to differences, while at the same time incessantly invoking the need to overcome divisions, ripping it asunder.

In a functionally differentiated society, religious communication can take up its specialization and concentrate on communication that is autochthonously religious, and thus traditional, but – at the same time – highly relevant in contemporary society. First, from a religious perspective, salvation represents redemption from differences. Second, religious communication offers a means of alienation from oneself. This becomes central precisely – and paradoxically – once the system knows that there is in fact no exit out of one's system. Because of this inevitable knowledge, any system – social or psychic – needs to devise specific means to simulate such an escape, since, without this simulation, it loses touch with reality, it suffers a loss of the outside. In fact, the feat the systems need to perform is an intricate one: they are operationally closed off from the outside, yet their task is to generate an adequate picture of what surrounds them.

Before inquiring further into the second religious function, I want to delve into communication as a source of transcendent unity. Luhmann's procedure is traditional in founding *religion* on God as a unity in differences or a unity of differences. In fact, God has the prerogative to observe without dropping either side of the binary distinction. He observes in such a way as to distinguish transcendence (his position) and immanence (the world's position) while He, simultaneously, embraces both sides of this distinction. Contrary to this, as a created entity, the human being is incapable of holding on to both sides of the distinction.

So, what does God's perspective offer? First, let us be sure that religious communication does not abolish differences. Instead, religious communication makes it possible to handle them in a specific manner. I have already suggested that the defining feature of modernity is that humans no longer figure as parts of society. In this respect, religion's function could be interpreted to be traditional: it responds to the situation of exclusion. Of course, the specific point is that in modernity, everyone is excluded. As mentioned above, people are excluded from social systems which are excluded from direct communication between each other, and on top of it, both psychic and social systems are excluded from self-knowledge. As has been shown, the first distinction one draws is an act of sovereignty rather than of knowledge. Consequently, no system observes the position from which it currently observes the situation, and, accordingly, everyone is a "parasite of communication" (Luhmann and Fuchs 1989, 178).

That insight depends on an original blindness, constituting a heavy burden for both consciousness and system. Transcendence – that which inevitably escapes any system but which at the same time grounds it – descends from the realm of the "above" into the "midst" of the individual, into the immanence of social systems. Consequently, distance or "remoteness" are no longer convincing sites of transcendence. A more convincing one is the very inner structure of society and its communicational obscurity.

But this obscurity extends further. For every system, its environment is impenetrable, too. Accordingly, for any system, two forms of transcendence are constitutive: its inner self and its environment. Of course, these are not types of transcendence to which one would direct one's prayers. And exactly this is Luhmann's point: religious communication reveals the thoroughly banal insight that neither the transcendence of one's innermost constitution nor the transcendence of the environment is true transcendence, and should not be misinterpreted as absolutes of sorts.

This insight is crucial, especially for a functionally differentiated society. In such a society, systems tend to be incapable of responding adequately to the environment since they wrongly equate perfect functioning and absolute specialization. While specialization is necessary and the very principle of modernity, modernity's essence rests equally on the insight that there are no absolutes. After all, this was the lesson taught to religion by other systems. Now, they themselves need to follow its lead. William James has beautifully noted the reluctance to take the same steps that one expects from religion. Naturally, people are absolutists and when left to their devices, they "dogmatize like infallible popes" (James 1992, 446). The same holds true for social systems.

Eventually, the system of religious communication knows much more about fallibility, contingency, and finitude than any other modern system. Furthermore, it has practiced communicative strategies for managing one's fragility some time before modern social systems even came into existence. Most importantly, the system of religion knows that the true absolute lies beyond its system, in God. Thus, communicating religiously means de-valuing one's systematic point of view by observing God's observation. In other words, religion uses its binary code – the distinction between immanence and transcendence – to observe its immanent system from the perspective of transcendence. It is important that this transcendence is not affected by the contingency of surrounding systems. In this respect, the stability of the religious system is a stability unknown to any other systems that do not use transcendence positively but only endure it in the guise of the contingency of surrounding systems, knowing that modernity is a permanent revolution (Luhmann 1997, 197).

Mystical Communication

Curiously, Luhmann adopts his concept of God from Nicholas of Cusa. Thus, the Luhmannian God is *coincendentia oppositorum*. For both Luhmann and Cusanus, God is the highest of all paradoxes, and – being this paradox – he is the highest form of reality. The source of Luhmann's fascination with Cusanus stems not only from the latter's fondness for paradox but also his dialectic pair of "enfolding/unfolding" (*complicatio-explicatio*), which he used to specify God's relation to the world. As Cusanus observes: "God would, in the humanity, be all things contractedly, just as God is the equality of being all things absolutely" (Cusa 1997, 176–7).

Thus, according to Cusanus, God enfolds the oppositions and differences experienced as unfolded in the created world. From this perspective, differences themselves appear as a manifestation of a deeper unity – or, this observation uncovers a degree of necessity in contingency (Luhmann 2006, 111). In this sense, enfolding and unfolding are two aspects of God as the *coincidentia oppositorum*, in whom all differences are transcended without being negated.

While looking at oneself from God's perspective does not abolish divisions and differences, it nonetheless provides an indispensable service. Thanks to religious communication, the system is capable of changing perspective on its paradoxical constitution: This paradox is an expression of God's power, it is an immanent reflection of the highest reality; whatever is experienced as unfolded from the immanent perspective, is enfolded from the transcendent perspective of God's observation. From God's perspective, these differences are contemplated as harmonized infinity or simplicity.

Translating one's own paradoxes into divine paradoxes is not the only result achieved through religious communication. Crucially, this communication accomplishes a form of alienation. As Peter Berger has shown, religion is a grand undertaking that dispossesses from the human being its own world. From this perspective, religions are alienating, thus creating the productive illusion of solidity and (subject-independent) meaning. In this respect, in Berger's conception thereof, religion is a tremendous projection of human meanings that returns as a foreign reality (Berger 1969, 100). Accordingly, far from being only negative, in some of its forms, alienation can be understood as a liberation from the exclusively subjective dimension of one's existence.

Luhmann formulates a not dissimilar project of alienation. This undertaking itself might be considered a paradox. After all, the very idea of Berger's and Luhmann's theory is that meaning is constructed, rather than revealed. But, according to Berger – and in a sense, to Luhmann too – this very constructionism needs to turn against itself. Why is this need so vital? For Berger, systematic religious alienation has traditionally been one of the most effective bulwarks against anomy (Berger 1969, 87). Since Luhmann is not interested in man's well-being, he does not thematize anomy; instead, he reflects on the need to not lose the ability to communicate. This very ability depends on an openness to differences that might appear too risky for modern systems.

In other words, in a society in which every system has its own rationality, there exists the danger that operationally closed systems will surrender absolutely to their own perspective. They cease to see that their own viewpoint is relative and thus they lose the ability to productively resonate with the outer and instead will "dogmatize like infallible popes", to again borrow James's expression.

Religious communication offers the psychic and social systems to – occasionally – communicate in a very different manner than other social systems. This is the case because the code of the religious system works in a formally different manner. It has been shown that the system of law operates on the binary code of lawful/unlawful, or that of the health system on health/illness. In the case of these systems, the sides of lawful and health are positively evaluated while the system attempts to eliminate the respective codes' negative sides. Religious communication works differently: it too has a binary system – immanence and transcendence – yet it does not positively evaluate itself (immanence), but rather the other side of the code, namely, transcendence.

Accordingly, through religious communication, one can formally "connect" to the communication of other social systems. It offers a perspective that runs counter to the normal communication process and its expectation: Religion is able to relativize its code and analogically show that sometimes, lawlessness might be a positive value (for instance, in the form of mercy, mere justice – as the Bible shows – can be profoundly cruel), or, religion can as well offer an additional code of transforming illness into something that might bear potential. Eventually, the most painful events or moments of absolute failure are an occasion for formulating new life-bestowing possibilities that open up thus far unconsidered possibilities. Nor are these possibilities thwarted by the absolute defeat of death at the cross. Instead, this defeat is exactly what preserves them (Luhmann 1977, 169).

In this respect, the claim is warranted that, even in modern secularized societies, the religious system plays the role of inverting traditional social roles and values. Religion in modern society is an institutionalized carnival of sorts (Luhmann 1990, 159). Across the relativity of individual systems, across their amoral and polycontextual nature, there exists, in the words of Teresa of Ávila, an "unspeakable heart of all experience" (Luhmann and Fuchs 1989, 99).

Generations of mystics have bequeathed upon us the lesson that there is no reason why we should – as per Wittgenstein – fall silent when facing the inexpressible (Wittgenstein [1921] 2001, 89). Quite on the contrary, the inexpressible does invite communication – the reason for this is not that systems strive to find where the "unspeakable heart" of truth lies. Rather, for systems in a functionally differentiated society, the key information is not where to find truth but rather where *not* to look for it. This information is provided by religious communication – truth is not in your own system nor in its immediate environment.

But even the information that the system is not the center of reality can be communicated exclusively from one's own center. Any form of the exterior is accessible only through the interior. If it is the case that rather than being a substance, truth is a form of process or of exercise, it may be that this active self-distancing is the closest one can get. Truth is not something to be *known*. In a way it is simpler and more difficult at the same time: it is something *to be*.

5 Conclusion

"Yet communication is the only form in which society is capable of realizing itself. There is no other possibility for realizing meaning in society.
When it is necessary, then, one has to communicate incommunicability"
(Luhmann 2002, 168). While there is no way to reach outside of society,
the outside, even the beyond, is vital for any system. In this regard, religious communication offers a way to communicate that which is beyond
one's communication – in fact, beyond any communication. And eventually, that which is beyond communication is truth itself. Following in
Hegel's footsteps, we may claim that rather than being a partial perspective, truth is the whole; but, adding a Luhmannian twist, we conclude:
the truth is certainly the whole, but the whole is a paradox.

There are specific ways in which one can proceed if one wants to communicate the incommunicable and unattainable. Even in this endeavor,
one depends on one's code, and since it is binary, it can be used in two
ways only. Either one picks up on its positive or negative side. Communication in a religious genre entails picking up on the negative side and
thus establishing a different perspective on the system's situation. Religion doubles the world but continues on the re-valuation of the negative
side, and thus provides means for re-evaluating failures. These failures
can be thoroughly real and material, such as illness, poverty, or social
exclusion. But they can also be subtler – for example, the inability to
understand oneself and others.

Finally, in this context, the human being recovers a position after
being banished from society (Luhmann and Fuchs 1989, 77). Mysticism
is tied to the psychic system. Whoever enters the inner self realizes that
there exists no boundary, no clues, only a never-ending humming of
thought, the process of one thought observing another thought. Mystical communication devises strategies to communicate about autopoiesis, about ways to endure the fact that one originates out of one's own
observation. And once again, this enduring itself is nothing other than
a specific type of communication.

From communication, there is no escape. The idea that it is a means to
find reconciliation – even truth – is an expression of a thoroughly modern naïveté – of a "holy simplicity," even. Communication is purgatory;
mystical communication is the hope that while it cannot be defeated, it
might be worked through.

References

Bellah, Robert. 1973. "Introduction". In Émile Durkheim, *On Morality and Society*, ix–lv. Chicago, IL: University of Chicago Press.

Berger, Peter L. 1969. *The Sacred Canopy. Elements of a Sociological Theory of Religion*, Garden City, New York: Doubleday.

Comte, Auguste. 1929. *Système de politique positive ou Traité de sociologie. Vol. 1.* Paris: Au siège de la Société Positiviste.

Cusa, Nicholas of. 1997. *On Learned Ignorance*. In *Selected Spiritual Writings*. Translated by Lawrence Bond. New York: Paulist Press.

Durkheim, Émile. 1886. "Les etudes de science sociale". *Revue philosophique* 22: 61–80.

Durkheim, Émile. 1964. *The Division of Labor in Society*. Translated by George Simpson. New York: The Free Press. Original edition, 1893.

Durkheim, Émile. 1973. "Individualism and the Intellectuals". In *On Morality and Society*, edited by Robert Bellah, 43–57. Chicago, IL: University of Chicago Press. Original edition, 1898.

Durkheim, Émile. 1995. *The Elementary Forms of Religious Life*. Translated by Karen E. Fields. New York, London, Toronto: The Free Press. Original edition, 1912.

Helmstetter, Rudolf. 2002. "Einen Unterschied kann man nicht anbeten: Luhmanns Systemtheorie als negative Theologie?" *IASL Online*. http://www.iaslonline.de/index.php?vorgang_id=2138. Accessed 4 June 2021.

Hobbes, Thomas. 1996. *Leviathan*, edited by Richard Tuck. Cambridge: Cambridge University Press. Original edition, 1651.

James, William. 1992. *Psychology: Briefer Course, The Will to Believe and Other Essays in Popular Philosophy*. New York: The Library of America.

Joas, Hans. 2011. *Die Sakralität der Person. Eine neue Genealogie der Menschenrechte*. Frankfurt am Main: Suhrkamp.

Kant, Immanuel. 1998. *Religion within the Boundary of Mere Reason (and Other Writings)*. Translated and edited by Allen Wood. Cambridge: Cambridge University Press.

Kirchmeier, Christian. 2011. "Am Anfang war der Teufel ein Engel. Moral in systemtheoretischer Perspektive". In *Noch nie war das Böse so gut. Die Aktualität einer altern Differenz*, edited by Franz Fromholzer, Michael Preis, and Bettina Wisiorek, 141–56. Heidelberg: Universitätsverlag Winter.

Luhmann, Niklas. 1977. *Funktion der Religion*. Frankfurt am Main: Suhrkamp.

Luhmann, Niklas. 1984. *Soziale Systeme. Grundriß einer allgemeinen Theorie*. Frankfurt am Main: Suhrkamp.

Luhmann, Niklas. 1986. *Love as Passion. The Codification of Intimacy*. Translated by Jeremy Gains, and Doris L. Jones. Cambridge, MA: Harvard University Press.

Luhmann, Niklas. 1988. "Wie ist Bewußtsein an Kommunikation beteiligt?" In *Materialität der Kommunikation*, edited by Hans Ulrich Gumbrecht, and K. Ludwig Pfeiffer, 884–905. Frankfurt am Main: Suhrkamp.

Luhmann, Niklas, and Peter Fuchs. 1989. *Reden und Schweigen*. Frankfurt am Main: Suhrkamp.

Luhmann, Niklas. 1990. *Essays on Self-Reference*. New York, Oxford: Columbia University Press.

Luhmann, Niklas. 1990a. *Paradigm Lost. Über die ethische Reflexion der Moral*. Frankfurt am Main: Suhrkamp.

Luhmann, Niklas. 1992. *Die Wissenschaft der Gesellschaft*. Frankfurt am Main: Suhrkamp.

Luhmann, Niklas. 1996. *Social Systems*. Translated and edited by John Bednarz, Jr., and Dirk Baecker. Stanford, CA: Stanford University Press.

Luhmann, Niklas. 1997. *Gesellschaft der Gesellschaft. Vol. 1*. Frankfurt am Main: Suhrkamp.

Luhmann, Niklas. 1997a. *Gesellschaft der Gesellschaft. Vol. 2*. Frankfurt am Main: Suhrkamp.

Luhmann, Niklas. 2002. *Die Religion der Gesellschaft*. Frankfurt am Main: Suhrkamp.

Luhmann, Niklas. 2006. *Beobachtungen der Moderne*. Wiesbaden: Verlag für Sozialwissenschaften.

Luhmann, Niklas. 2008. *Die Moral der Gesellschaft*. Frankfurt am Main: Suhrkamp.

Luhmann, Niklas. 2010. *Love: A Sketch*. Cambridge, MA: Polity Press.

Marx, Karl. 2015. *Ökonomisch-philosophische Manuskripte*. Frankfurt am Main: Suhrkamp.

Pannenberg, Wolfhart. 1978. "Religion in der säkularen Gesellschaft. Niklas Luhmanns Religionssoziologie". *Evangelische Kommentare – Monatsschrift zum Zeitgeschehen in Kirche und Gesellschaft* 11: 99–103.

Pokorný, Petr. 2005. *Ježíš Nazaretský*. Praha: OIKOYMENH.

Rasch, William. 2000. *Niklas Luhmann's Modernity. The Paradoxes of Differentiation*. Stanford, CA: Stanford University Press.

Reder, Michael. 2018. "Niklas Luhmann (2000), Die Religion der Gesellschaft". In *Religionsphilosophie und Religionskritik. Ein Handbuch*, edited by Michael Kühnlein, 831–42. Frankfurt am Main: Suhrkamp.

Rilke, Rainer Maria. 1955. "Requiem für Wolf Graf von Kalckreuth". In *Sämtliche Werke*, edited by Rilke-Archiv, vol. 1, 656–64. Wiesbaden, Frankfurt am Main: Insel Verlag. Original edition, 1908.

Rousseau, Jean-Jacques. 2002. *The Social Contract and the First and Second Discourse*. Translated by Susann Dunn. New Haven, CT, London: Yale University Press. Original edition, 1762.

Roy, Olivier. 2008. *La sainte ignorance. Le temps de la religion sans culture*. Paris: Seuil.

Spencer-Brown, Georg. 1969. *Laws of Forms*, London: Allen & Unwin.

Spufford, Francis. 2013. *Unapologetic: Why, Despite Everything, Christianity Can Still Make Surprising Emotional Sense*. London: Faber & Faber.

Stichweh, Rudolf. 2003. "Niklas Luhmann". In *Klassiker der Soziologie. Vol. 2*, edited by Dirk Kaesler, 206–29. München: Verlag C. H. Beck.

Wittgenstein, Ludwig. 2001. *Tractatus Logico-philosophicus*. Translated by David F. Pears, and Brian F. McGuinness. London: Routledge. Original edition, 1921.

Historical Transformations of Christianity and Luhmann's Theory of Autopoietic Systems

Tomáš Halík

In this study I summarize in the form of twenty theses the main ideas of my forthcoming book, *The Afternoon of Christianity. Courage for Transformation* (Halík 2021). In it, I examine the historical transformations of Western Christianity, with an emphasis on the current situation and the possibilities for the further development of Christianity in a postmodern pluralist culture. My methodological approach to this topic draws on a variety of sources. Here I want to highlight a certain affinity of my approach with Luhmann's understanding of religion as an autopoietic system.

In my book, I argue that Western Christianity has undergone two different systems of religion in the course of its history – religion as *religio* (the integrating force of society) and religion as *confesio* (one of the world views). Both of these forms have lost their plausibility. At the present time, which is both the culmination and profound crisis of the process of globalization, various possibilities are opening up for the further transformation of religion. Will the Christian faith assume the form of either of these, or will it create a new system of religion?

1 Luhmann's Theory of Religion

Niklas Luhmann regards religion as one of the important social systems. Social systems are *autopoietic*. They must have boundaries that distinguish them from other systems, i.e. they must be relatively closed in respect of their environment. However, this carries the danger that a system may become so closed in on itself that its structures will not be able to resonate with the outside world and with other systems. The system will thus be marginalized until it eventually loses its ability to respond to environmental changes. Luhmann calls this the "loss of outside reality" (*Realitätsverlust*). One of the paradoxes of our time is that there is both greater autonomy and greater *interdependency* between systems.[1]

As society evolves towards ever greater complexity, religion is changing its forms and its social and psychological functions. For a long time, religion was indistinguishable from society as a whole. It was only in the process of modernity, with the increasing complexity of society, that religion became one of the subsystems of society. The function and form of religious phenomena change, along with the symbolism and modes of interpretation. What does not change is the inner content of religiosity: belief, concern and communication.

One of the important functions of religion is the management of contingency, both at the individual level and at the level of social systems. Religion is supposed to show what appears to be meaningless as meaningful. However, the level of this interpretation – the extent to which it is *compatible* with other sub-systems of society (e.g. science) – is crucial to the plausibility of religion.

Secularization is one of the consequences of the differentiation of society. Secularization does not mean that a religious worldview has become unsustainable. Any unifying view of society has become unsustainable. Secularization has ended the former function of religion: its ability to issue authoritative binding descriptions of the whole of society. According to Luhmann, secularization does not mean the diminishing influence of religion; on the contrary: in the new situation, the modern religious system can play a crucial role. Indeed, religion offers ways in which the opacity of both social and psychic systems can be communicated. Luhmann values a certain type of Christian theology and especially the mystical tradition, often quoting Nicholas of Cusa in this context. Mysticism has developed certain techniques to deal with paradoxes. Luhmann argues that modern society is a society of paradoxes that cannot be thought but must be lived.

According to Luhmann, religion and ecology are the two systems about which there has been the most communication in other subsystems since about the 1970s. Their importance lies in their ability to "irritate" other systems.

---

1   See Luhmann 2002; Luhmann 2015.

2 Twenty Theses on the Historical Transformations of Christianity

Thesis 1

In the course of history, both the meaning and words of *religion* and the socio-cultural phenomena and roles that can be identified as religious have changed. I distinguish, firstly, the original Roman understanding of religion as a *religio* – a system of symbols and rituals, which has above all the role of an all-encompassing integrating force in society and in the state, a common language; secondly, the modern conception of religion as one of the many sectors of life, one of the *worldviews*, represented by a religious institution; thirdly, the *post-secular* phase, in which religion takes on many different forms – it becomes individualized and privatized, becoming predominantly spiritual, but on the other hand it is politicized and becomes an instrument for the defense of group identity.[2]

Thesis 2

In my book I address the historical transformations of faith (Halík 2021). By faith I mean a certain attitude and orientation in life, rather than *religious convictions* and opinions; I am interested in *faith* rather than *beliefs*. People's faith is not determined by what views they hold about God's existence or what their church or religious affiliation is. Rather, it is about what role God plays in their lives, *how they believe (fides qua)*, how their faith lives (both in their inner world and in their relationships), how it is transformed over the course of their lives and how it transforms their lives – and whether, how and to what extent their faith also transforms the world in which they live. Therefore, only one's life experience can provide a kind of hermeneutical key that makes it possible to know what one *really* believes, not only what one verbally professes. Faith, as I understand it, is found not only in the lives of people who identify themselves as religious believers, but also in an implicit, *anonymous form* in the spiritual quest of men and women beyond the visible boundaries of religious doctrines and institutions. *Secular spirituality* is also part of the history of faith.

---

2   See Halík 2004.

Faith has its manifest and latent forms, it lives in human consciousness and unconsciousness. The manifest and the hidden, the conscious and the unconscious, the explicit and the implicit (*anonymous*) forms of belief (and unbelief) can sometimes be in tension; that is why in some cases we can also speak of the *belief of non-believers* and *the unbelief of believers*.

Thesis 3

We encounter the *concept* of faith (with the Hebrew verb *heemin*) among the Jewish prophets in the "Axial Age" (around the 5th century before Christ);[3] the *phenomenon* of faith itself, however, is older. I am focusing on that lineage of the history of faith that has its roots in Judaism and continues in Christianity; in a way it is also present in secular humanism, that *unwanted child* of traditional Christianity, and probably in various forms of contemporary non-traditional spiritualties, though here it again encounters and merges with the spiritual orientation that has been its competitor for centuries, gnosis.

On its journey through history, the Hebrew Bible imprinted two essential hallmarks on faith: the experience of the exodus, the journey from slavery to freedom (faith has a *pilgrim nature*), and the incarnation of faith in the practice of justice and solidarity: the manifestation of true faith, according to the prophets, is to "take in the orphan, take up the widow's cause". The archetype of the believer is Abraham, the "father of the faithful", of whom it is written that he set out on a journey without knowing where he was going (Heb. 11:8). Faith, especially the faith of the prophets, is thus in some tension not only with magic but also with the temple religion of priests and sacrificial rituals. This prophetic line is taken up by Jesus – at the center of his preaching is the call for transformation, for conversion (*metanoia*).

---

3   The term "Axial Age" was coined by Karl Jaspers; he was referring to the period of the 8th to 2nd century BC, when a number of religions that are still alive today emerge independently of each other and the older ones are transformed, and emphasis is placed on transcendence and ethics. See Jaspers 1996, 68.

Thesis 4

In the beginning, Christianity was not a religion in the sense of the "religio" of antiquity (Červenková 2012, 2); rather, it was the "way of following Christ", one of the Jewish sects, but one in which the claim to universality is already present. In the Hebrew Bible, we already encounter both the concept of the Lord as the God of the chosen people and – especially in the prophets – the Lord's claim to universality and uniqueness: He alone is the creator and Lord of heaven and earth and ruler of all nations; the other gods are insignificant fictions. In Jesus' preaching, too, a development can be discerned: first he considers himself sent primarily or exclusively "to the lost sheep of the house of Israel", then he sends his apostles out into the entire world to teach all nations (Matt. 28: 19–20).

Thesis 5

The apostle Paul in particular brought early Christianity out of the mold of one of the Jewish sects and presented it as the universal offering of the classical *oikumene* of those days. Paul first relieves Gentile Christians of the obligation of first becoming Jews (accepting circumcision and many other ritual regulations of the Law) and places faith, manifested in the practice of love of neighbor, at the center. In so doing, he provides "pious Gentiles" (Hellenistic sympathizers with Judaism, including adherents of philosophical monotheism) with a path into the Christian communities, and then enables these communities to enter the new world.

Christianity, in Paul's terms, transcends boundaries that had seemed insurmountable: boundaries between religions and cultures, boundaries of social stratification and clearly defined gender roles; in Christ, it is now immaterial whether one is Jewish or Greek, Gentile, free or slave, male or female – all are now "a new creation" in Christ (Gal. 3:28; 2 Cor. 5:17). By emancipating himself from the mission of Peter, James, and other early disciples of Jesus, by his emphasis on faith as a "new existence", and on the freedom of the Christian, Paul kept Christianity from assuming the form of a legal system. Paul brings his version of Christianity and Christian universalism to a world embodied by Hellenistic philosophy and Roman politics, at a time of crisis in the credibility of Greek mythology and Roman political religion. However, the idea of a "new Israel" without borders eventually runs up against the limits of the culture of antiquity; instead of an Israel without borders, the Church becomes a "second Israel" and a third "religion" alongside Judaism and Hellenistic paganism. It must also define itself against the Gnostic currents, the schools of wisdom and piety (*pietas*) of the time, as well as the many religious cults.

Thesis 6

The representatives of the Roman state religion see the curiously spreading Christianity as a competitor and subject it to persecution, thus reinforcing its status as a counterculture vis-a-vis the outside world. Religion as *religio* had a predominantly *political* significance in the ancient Roman Empire at that time, signifying a system of rituals and symbols expressing the identity of society; it was akin to what sociology today calls *civil religion*. Christians who refused to participate in Roman pagan rituals for religious reasons (considering them idolatry) were persecuted as disloyal and therefore politically dangerous citizens, as "atheists" depriving the empire of the protection of the gods (*pax deorum*). This was followed by several centuries of conflict between the Christian faith and the Roman *religio*.

Thesis 7

The testimony of the Christian martyrs, the efforts of the first theologians to incorporate the faith into the intellectual concepts of Hellenistic philosophy, and finally the political calculation of the emperors led to the "Constantine *volte face*": initially tolerated and soon privileged, Christianity takes over the political and cultural role of "religion". "Religio" in its Christian form brings together a number of previously separate spheres – ritual, philosophical, spiritual and political. With Constantine's legalization of Christianity and Justinian's declaration of this faith as the state religion, the way of following Christ becomes a *religion* in the sense of a Roman political *religio*, a "common language" and the main cultural pillar of a powerful civilization. Faith is thus given the protective (but also limiting) shell of religion, reminiscent of the role of the persona in Jung's concept of the human personality: a mask that allows communication externally while protecting the intimacy and integrity of the interior.

Thesis 8

As Christian faith becomes increasingly incorporated into philosophy, it takes the form of a metaphysical Christian theology in both Roman and Greek versions. Faith is increasingly understood as *doctrine*. Christianity in the Roman Empire also fulfils the role of spirituality, the systematic cultivation of the deep dimension of faith. This happens especially thanks to the Desert Fathers, that radical alternative version of Christianity, initially dissenting from mainstream *imperial Christianity*, which quickly became entrenched in power and privilege. This movement of hermits, both individuals and groups, is later integrated and institutionalized by the *greater church* in the form of religious life, monastic communities; it receives its legal form alongside other church structures.

Christianity as a combination of political *religio*, philosophically deliberated *fides* and schools of piety (*pietas*) is culturally fruitful and politically successful, building and consolidating one of the most powerful empires in the world for centuries. It is able to integrate many new impulses from different cultures and philosophies, to survive the fall of Rome and later the great schism between Rome and Byzantium, to resist even invasions from outside, and to expand gradually into newly discovered parts of the world. The Christian faith (especially in the form of doctrine and liturgy) became the common language of much of the world.[4]

Thesis 9

Medieval *Christianitas* would suffer a fatal blow in the form of the great schism in Western Christianity, with theological disputes spilling over from the intellectual into the political sphere and resulting in the devastating wars of the 17th century. But equally fatal is another schism: the break between traditional theology and the emancipating world of the natural sciences. Critical Christian intellectuals, disgusted with both warring camps of the church, attempt to create a kind of *third way of Christianity* – but when rejected by both camps, they become increasingly alienated from traditional Christianity until this current results in the Enlightenment (Halik 2004).

---

4   In the first millennium, in particular, there was considerable plurality in Christianity in terms of liturgy, spirituality, and theological emphases; only after the break with Byzantine Christianity did the Latin Church become significantly *Romanized*.

Thesis 10

On the threshold of modernity, which is a process of fragmentation, *Christianitas* disintegrates, while nation states and cultures grow, Latin loses its privileged position, and the elements of the former system in which theology dominated all culture are emancipated. As *Christian civilization* disintegrates, so does Christian religion in the sense of *religio*. A process of secularization takes place. But secularization, in the context of the modernization of European society, was neither the end of religion nor the end of Christian faith, but the transformation of the relationship between faith and religion: the dissolution of the age old *marriage* between Christian faith and religion in the sense of *religio*.

Thesis 11

The role of *religio*, religion as a common language and shared cultural basis of European civilization, starts to be played by other phenomena – the natural sciences, secular culture, especially art, but also nationalism and political religions such as communism, fascism and Nazism. We might identify the *religio* of today as the capitalist economy, the all-embracing global market and, since the mid-20th century, the media, which offers within this market today's most valuable commodity, information. The media is becoming the most influential interpreter of reality and arbiter of truthfulness, which were once important roles of religion.

Thesis 12

The concept of religion, as it developed during the process of secularization and became established especially after the Enlightenment, now has a completely different meaning and content. It is no longer an all-encompassing entity, a *language game* understood in the same way by everyone, whose rules are accepted by everyone, in which everyone participates and which brings everyone together. Modern religion is much poorer and narrower than mediaeval *religio* was.

In the Middle Ages the system of theology interacted actively with other systems of the time, not only in the field of knowledge, but also in the field of spiritual life (spirituality) and politics. Now all these fields have been transformed, gaining fresh self-confidence and renewed energy thanks to their emancipation from theology, whereas theology, which is, moreover, hampered by the censorship and control of an anxious and nervous church hierarchy, has gradually lost its ability to communicate. If we apply Luhmann's systems theory to this situation, then the system of *religio* on the threshold of the modern age could not cope with the "irritation" of modern culture, especially science, and ceased to be able to communicate creatively with it and to integrate its impulses. But the loss of a system's ability to interact with others is a sign of its decline.

Thesis 13

The biosphere of traditional pre-modern *religio*-type religiosity was a pre-modern, largely agrarian society where the rhythm of life was set by the organic combination of natural cycles with liturgy, especially the structuring of the liturgical year.

The Industrial Revolution gave birth to new strata who were already living outside the cultural and social biosphere of traditional pre-modern religiosity, and the Church was unable to provide them with sufficiently convincing spiritual and pastoral impulses for a style of Christian life and thought that would fit the new conditions. These were primarily the working classes, entrepreneurs and the intelligentsia.

Thesis 14

On the threshold of modernity, the word religion acquired a new connotation: it now denoted one sector of social life alongside others. Religion in the form in which it appeared on the threshold of the modern age – as a sector of life and a worldview – soon became the subject of study and criticism.

Christianity too acquired the status of one religion alongside others. Cambridge Enlightenment theologians in the 17th century would develop the now familiar model of thinking, reminiscent of Linnaeus' system of plant classification: there is a genus of religions that can be divided into different families – and Christianity is one of them.

Thesis 15

Christianity was now seen as a worldview, formally represented, asserted and defended by the institution of the Church. Christianity eventually adopted this role: It embodies what is meant by religion in the modern secular age: a worldview concerned primarily with the "other world" and, in this world, primarily with morality; it offers rituals that lend a solemn aura to specific moments in private, family, and, exceptionally, public and state life.

Thesis 16

Immediately after the cultural revolution of 1968, a new age, which we might term the internet or global era, or *planetarisation*, dawned. The key word for understanding the current state of society and the current state of religion is *plurality*.[5] The "modern world" and with it the modern understanding of religion are mired in postmodern plurality. The two distinctive forms of the Christian religion have been exhausted: *religio*, which was created by pagan Rome and merely transformed by Christianity, and the worldview, a form of religion as part of the modern (especially Enlightenment) understanding of the world.

Thesis 17

Since the period of secularization, when religion was transformed, two forms of religion have attracted the most attention; they are those which we usually consider as opposite poles of a wide range of religious phenomena. On the one hand there is the dramatic entry of religion into the public and political sphere (Keppel 1996), while on the other there is a growing interest in spirituality. Whereas the first of these forms – religion as an expression of the defense of a group (e.g. national or ethnic) identity – is primarily intended to reinforce group cohesion and is akin to a political ideology, the second, a spirituality separate from church

---

5 P. L. Berger, one of the leading theorists of secularization and later one of the most trenchant critics of theories of secularization, suggested replacing the term secularization with pluralization when characterizing our epoch.

and tradition, tends to offer some kind of integration of the personality and is closer to psychotherapy in terms of its role.

Thesis 18

Neither the gradual *soft* cultural secularization of mainly north-western Europe nor the hard secularization of countries under militantly atheistic communist regimes left behind a completely atheistic society. In recent decades, a growing number of people in countries of the Western civilization have either formally left the Church or do not participate in its activities, however, people do not usually become atheists by disassociating themselves from the Church. A growing number of people – especially in our Western civilization – give the answer "none" when asked about their religious affiliation. Sociologists have given this growing set of people the collective label of "*nones*". *Nones* form the third largest grouping on our planet today, after Christians and Muslims. However, even the community of *nones* does not consist primarily of atheists, but rather of people who, despite many differences, are united chiefly by their indifference, distrust, dislike and sometimes even hostility towards "organized religion" and religious institutions. Among the *nones* we can find atheists and agnostics, *apatheists* and followers of "alternative spiritualities".

Thesis 19

The modern form of Western Christianity seems to have exhausted itself, and any dreams of a return to premodernity are an illusion. This raises a number of questions; e.g. will the Christianity of tomorrow be non-religious? The idea that the Christian faith can and should live outside of religion, that it is even "anti-religious", was advanced by the dialectical theology associated with the Confessing Church in Germany (Karl Barth, Dietrich Bonhoeffer). But can the Christian faith live permanently without religion, or does every form of it necessarily sooner or later become incarnated in some type of religion? If Christianity becomes a religion after secularization, after the destruction of older forms of religion, then in what sense? Can the Christian faith create a new form of religion, different from the two previous and two current ones?

In the present crisis of the process of globalization, we stand at the cross-roads between the threat of a *clash of civilizations* and the hope of a *civitas oecumenica*. How far can Christianity develop its universality (*catholicity*) – without losing its identity?

Luhmann speaks of three subsystems of religion: the church (the system of spiritual communication), diakonia (the relationship to other subsystems), and theology (self-reflection, the relationship to one's own identity).

In my book, I argue that until now the Church has developed primarily three activities: pastoral care for its faithful and mission in the sense of the effort to expand its ranks. The third area since the beginning of Christianity has been charity (diakonia); it is primarily in this field that Christians have learned to serve all people in need, thus fulfilling Jesus' call to universal love, to mercy without frontiers or proselytizing intentions. Here they have borne and continue to bear witness in actions without words – in the form of love in solidarity, showing closeness.

In my opinion, the Church's ministry in the future should focus on one more area where its ministry is indispensable: the area of *spiritual accompaniment*, and not only the accompaniment of its faithful. A kind of vanguard of this ministry of the Church is so-called "categorial pastoring" – the ministry of chaplains in hospitals, prisons, the army and education, or in the area of spiritual accompaniment of people in various difficult life situations. Spiritual accompaniment is also needed for people in demanding professions where there is a risk of *burn-out syndrome* and moral breakdown. Unlike traditional mission and traditional therapy, this ministry of closeness is dialogical and reciprocal. It is not only a process of teaching others, but also a process of learning from others. *The spiritual* is about meaning; ministry nurtures a contemplative approach to life: it teaches how to make sense of one's own life story and of particular situations, especially crisis situations.

If the Church is to exercise this ministry, it must abandon its self-centeredness, and its fixation on its institutional interests. In a pluralist society, Christianity cannot fulfil the role of religion in the sense of *religio*, a political and cultural integrating force in society; it cannot be *religio* in the sense derived from the verb *religare*, to (re)unite. But there is another understanding of the word *religio*, derived from the verb *re-legere*, to read again. The Christianity of the future can be *religio*, a religion in the sense of an ecumenical communion of reading afresh, *re-lecture*, a new hermeneutic. There is a need to re-read together both the sacred texts of the world religions and to find in them inspiration for the application of the therapeutic role of faith, and to "read the signs of the times", to offer a spiritual diagnosis of society and culture. Efforts to deepen ecumenical cooperation between cultures and religions can help to transform the process of globalization into a process of communication, respect for diversity, and a culture of appreciation and understanding.

Translated by Gerald Turner.

References

Červenková, Denisa. 2012. *Jak se křesťanství stalo náboženstvím*. Praha: Karolinum.

Gabriel, Karl, and Hans R. Reuter. 2004. *Religion und Gesselschaft*. Paderborn: Schöningh.

Gauchet, Marcel. 2004. *Odkouzlení světa. Dějiny náboženství jako věci veřejné*. Translated by Pavla Doležalová. Brno: CDK.

Halík, Tomáš. 2004. *Vzýván i nevzýván. Evropské přednášky k filozofii a sociologii dějin křesťanství*. Praha: NLN.

Halík, Tomáš. 2021. *Odpoledne křesťanství. Odvaha k proměně*. Praha: NLN.

Hanyš, Milan, and Johann P. Arnason. 2016. *Mezi náboženstvím a politikou*. Praha: Togga.

Jaspers, Karl. 1996. *Úvod do filosofie*. Translated by Aleš Havlíček. Praha: OIKOYMENH.

Kepel, Gilles. 1996. *Boží pomsta*. Translated by Růžena Ostrá. Brno: Atlantis.

Luhmann, Niklas. 1982. *Funktion der Religion*. Frankfurt am Main: Suhrkamp.

Luhmann, Niklas. 1990. *Essays on Self-Reference*. New York, Oxford: Columbia University Press.

Luhmann, Niklas. 1997. *Gesellschaft der Gesellschaft. Vol. 1*. Frankfurt am Main: Suhrkamp.

Luhmann, Niklas. 1997a. *Gesellschaft der Gesellschaft. Vol. 2*. Frankfurt am Main: Suhrkamp.

Luhmann, Niklas. 2002. *Die Religion der Gesellschaft*. Frankfurt am Main: Suhrkamp.

Luhmann, Niklas. 2006. *Beobachtungen der Moderne*. Wiesbaden: Verlag für Sozialwissenschaften.

Luhmann, Niklas. 2015. *Náboženství společnosti*. Translated by Tomáš Chudý. Praha: Karolinum.

Petrusek, Milan. 2007. *Společnosti pozdní doby*. Praha: SLON.

On Universities and Contemporary Society: The Issue of Trust

Jakub Jirsa

1 Introduction

In the following paper I would like to reflect upon the roots of the contemporary situation of universities with a particular interest in Czech universities, where these national examples will serve merely as illustrations of more general claims. The universities can be understood as autopoietic, i.e. self-shaping social institutions (Hufford and Zelený 1991, Vanderstraeten 2002, Lenartowicz 2015). I will briefly describe how universities understood themselves and shape themselves at the time when they were established as the modern secular institutions of higher learning. Further, I will argue that it is exactly the heritage of this enclosed autopoietic aspect of the universities that it is hard for them to find a place in contemporary societies despite their undeniable growth and success.

The current situation of universities can be described as schizophrenic (Collini 2012, 3). The number of universities, students and teachers is unprecedented. Universities are highly successful research institutions and they now attract more funding (from public as well as private sources) than ever before. On the other hand, my paper is only one of many which observe growing uncertainty, pressure and fear at these institutions.[1] My aim will be to look into the concept of *university* in order to see whether

---

[1] See Burrows 2012 and recently Collini 2017. For a sceptical assessment of this rising number trend see Menand 2010, 143–9. Menand argues that there is a surplus of students and degrees, which results in lower standards and a decreased value of higher university degrees; according to him, this is one source of the contemporary problem of universities.

we can distinguish some features of traditional yet modern universities which might be problematic within contemporary society.

I will try to present the problem of this schizophrenic situation by arguing that modern universities are bodies that are foreign to contemporary popular democracies. This separation between a university and its social and political environment creates an atmosphere of distrust (Muller 2018, 39–42; Collini 2017, 239; Sztompka 1999, 43; Nash 2019, 183; Nichols 2019, 35). Therefore, the institutions controlling or regulating the operation of universities impose measures quite foreign to the universities' own workings, believing that these measures will help them to understand as well as manage these strange institutions. This results in the situation of schizophrenia and growing uncertainty mentioned earlier.

Universities are open systems which interact with the environment in which they are located, i.e. with the society around them. However, as Lenartowitz argues, on the one hand human institutions are open systems; on the other, "what they are open to is conditioned by the pattern of their own autopoiesis" (Lenartowicz 2015, 959). Generally, not only universities, but educational institutions *per se* can be called autopoietic (Vanderstraeten 2002): it is a dynamic system which in many respects renews itself via its own processes. It is important for my subsequent interpretation that universities are involved in "the process of discovering truth, which consists in continually adding the new to the already known" (Lenartowicz 2015, 956). Currently this function is not only disputed but some scholars claim that universities and experts nowadays are being disqualified because of this "truth production" process (Nichols 2019). The autopoietic understanding of universities avoids the pitfalls of both the essentialist as well as functionalist interpretation of university: it allows us to observe the life of university and to better understand its relation to the surrounding environment, namely the society.

There seem to be several ways to describe the dynamic process of self-creation; the most general account entails three phases of a circular autopoietic *in suo esse perseverare*: production – bonding – degradation – production (Hufford and Zelený 1991, 324–5; Zelený 2015, 187–8). This basic scheme seems suitable for describing the evolution of universities. The present paper thus describes an aspect of the degradation of universities and explains some possible causes.

Two more introductory remarks are in order. First, I will not deal with the managerial approach of university leadership, which is currently one of the main topics discussed.[2] There are two reasons for this, Czech universities (as well as universities in neighbouring countries) still enjoy considerable autonomy and academic self-government, the main legislative body is the academic senate and the dean or rector is elected from the academic body of the university itself. Further, capitalism has been around since the very beginning of the modern university and the contemporary situation cannot be explained easily by merely pointing to a hostile capitalist environment (Collini 2017, 15). Rather, I see the current business trends in universities' life and work as a result of the atmosphere of distrust and the application of measures foreign to universities introduced above.

Second, what do I mean by *university*? Let us have a look at the functions and roles of a university. A university has always considered knowledge to be an end in itself, which may not be subordinate to any other goal or outcome. Of course, many university research institutes conduct research that has an immediate or an expected use in the near future. But this use, this usefulness, is not what interests the university as a university. A university also recognizes the legitimacy of research where the usefulness is not apparent or, perhaps better, not yet apparent. Critical intellectual activity allows a university to ask questions about the questions themselves and the assumptions of the research that is being carried out within the university. Further, a university always combines research with teaching and teaching with research. No university is solely a research institution, meanwhile a university is not just a school, in the sense that it would specialize only in the transfer of skills and not in the dissemination of knowledge at the same time. It has been and still is true for universities that research is not a matter for an individual, but always for the collective. Knowledge is acquired at a university through dialogue within the academic community, i.e. between teachers and students. These are not only research teams, but also lectures, discussions and workshops where research results are presented, refined and criticized. Finally, a university has always included more disciplines from several areas of human knowledge. In addition to liberal arts, it initially required only theology, law and medicine, but these are still significantly different sciences that a university has been able to include under one roof. It should be added that, of course, there are other institutions that are active and successful in one

---

2   On this topic see Readings 1996; Menand 2010; Collini 2012, 132–67; Nussbaum 2016; Collini 2017, 91–154.

or more of the above criteria. They are often better than any university in the given field. However, I believe that only a university includes all the above criteria. To sum up, it is clear that the main purpose of a university is the pursuit and broadening of knowledge. It might have other goals and tasks, but this is its essential activity. From the argument of sufficient reason used by Fichte it follows that this activity constitutes the reason for a university's existence as well.

2 Origins of the Modern University

When reading the standard set of texts related to the history of universities one clearly sees the rapid process of transformation and change, which is nicely documented in Weber's account of European universities and Davis-Diamond's study of American institutions (Weber 2002; Graham and Diamond 1997). These changes happen not only because of external pressures but many times they are inherent in the autopoietic process described above. Concerning the velocity and scale of the change, one can only be reminded that there once was a time when professors and lecturers of philosophy and the classics sneered at the practical departments introduced to higher education, such as economy and agriculture. "He gets degrees in making jam / At Liverpool and Birmingham." This was the mocking verse spreading around the time when new institutions of higher learning, new universities were established in what once were provincial towns (Collini 2012, 58). In the following paragraphs I will treat universities as the products of (i) the spirit of enlightenment, (ii) nation building and (iii) an anti-utilitarian ethos.

First, a university is an explication of the idea that truth can be achieved in an institutionalized way and this achievement lies within the powers of human intellect. The truth is not a product of divine revelation; it is a result of intellectual work. Further, education is understood as a part of the liberation of mankind; on the basic level it is liberation from superstition, on a higher level it is liberation of the spirit within the process of history (Sobotka 2015, 134–6). The heritage of enlightenment includes the fact that for a university the conduct of research as a means to arrive at the truth is not a solitary endeavour, but it needs the proper institutional environment, which provides resources for the activity in question: space, time and money. As a result, the specialized branches of knowledge are considered *authoritative*. Knowledge results in authority, which differs from political authority. Science cannot substitute politics and it cannot be the sole source of social norms, but it has its own domain, its own authority over truth (Todorov 2009, 86–7).

Collini mentions an implicit contract between a university and society which acknowledges the value of higher learning in itself (Collini 2017, 18). Yet, this contract has a visible part as well, namely the contribution of the university to the magnificence and dignity of society. In modern history the societies which established universities were empires, but universities were seen as national institutions promoting the national cause in addition to the quest for knowledge for its own sake (Craig 1984). The establishment of modern universities took place during a time of growing national self-consciousness and self-constitution. This is particularly visible in the case of the building of American and German universities.

The second feature I want to call attention to is the relation between modern universities and nation building process. It might be astounding that this connection between a university and a nation carries over to now – and it did not stop even in the shadows of the Second World War. Consider the following quotes:

> People at the university came from the nation and continue to serve the nation with their research and teaching the truth. [...] University comes from the will of the nation to continuously search for truth in all things. [...] We want to say: we are coming from the nation which we serve. We hear the voice of the nation in us especially when we find ourselves in unanimity with peasants, artisans, workers, merchants and all those with whom life and conversation bring us together.

Which century, which political environment frames these sentences? It might come as a surprise, but the author of these lines is Karl Jaspers, in his 1947 article "Nation and University" (Jaspers 2016, 204–5). Perhaps Jaspers wrote with the perspective of defending the university after the post-war purges so that German society would accept new universities as its own.

The national ethos of the modern university is already evident in writings from the 19th century. Friedrich Schiller, in his essay "Was heißt und zu welchen Ende studiert man Universalgeschichte?" (1789) talks about "German woods" being enlightened by the presence of an institution of higher learning. Or one could observe how many times Friedrich Schleiermacher, in *Von den Sitten der Universität, und von der Aufsicht* (1809) refers to "we Germans" while presenting the university as an institution *of* the nation and *for* the nation. Finally, Wilhelm von Humboldt in the well-known text *Über die innere und äußere Organisation der höheren wissenschaftlichen Anstalten in Berlin* (1809) describes the establishing of a university as an event which happens directly for the sake of the moral culture of the nation ("für die moralische Kultur der Nation"). To sum up, the modern university is perceived as one of the institutions of the nation-state, as one of the institutions by which the nation progresses and in which it takes pride.

Finally, the third important characteristic inherently built into the concept or idea of the modern university is anti-utilitarianism. One could raise the question of how this anti-utilitarian character of the university goes together with its role during the nation-building process. What then is the *goal* of the university? Is it the progress of a nation or the pursuit of knowledge for its own sake? What emerges from the writings of the 19th century is that a university fulfils its national role exactly by the pursuit of knowledge for its own sake. In the understanding of Schleiermacher or Humboldt, it is an entity which is good both in the final and the instrumental sense of the world.

The most famous anti-utilitarian line of argument comes from Cardinal Newman's book *The Idea of a University Defined and Illustrated*, first published in 1852. Moreover, we can find the same, though in earlier, German writings as well. A particular anti-utilitarian tendency is apparent in Johan Benjamin Erhard's *Über die Einrichtung und den Zweck der höheren Lehranstalten* (1802) as well as in Johann Christian Reil (1759–1824) who writes:

> the apostles of utility must be ordered out of the universities to the technical schools, since they lack the sense for science, which they do not pursue for itself [...] yet they value it mainly because it is useful for building houses, cultivating fields and resuscitating the economy. (Weischedel 2019, xxi)

Similarly, Schiller in his inauguration speech "Was heißt und zu welchem Ende studiert man Universalgeschichte?" condemns those who consider science and knowledge as a mere tool for achieving other, external ends and do not realize that knowledge has value in itself: "Deplorable man who, with the noblest of tools, with science and art, wants and achieves nothing higher than the day labourer with the worst! Who carries a slave soul with him in the realm of the most perfect freedom!" (Schiller 1789, 109).

Cardinal Newman seems to acknowledge some relevant function of utilitarianism, which was a reformative ethical as well as social doctrine at that time,[3] yet he strictly resisted the idea that the principle of utility should be the only relevant criteria:

> hence it is that we have the principles of utility, of combination, of progress, of philanthropy, or, in material sciences, comparative anatomy, phrenology, electricity, exalted into leading ideas, and keys, if not of all knowledge, at least of many things more than belong to them, principles, all of them true to a certain point, yet all degenerating into error and quackery, because they are carried to excess [...] and because they are employed to do what is simply too much for them, inasmuch as a little science is not deep philosophy. (Newman 1996, 62)

There are at least two related objections Newman raises against a utilitarian way of thinking. First, happiness is not the only final end or ultimate value. Education and knowledge are valuable in themselves and not because of what they do or provide. Second, any monistic doctrine, i.e. a doctrine operating with one single principle, cannot do right to the diversity of our world. Any single principle of evaluation used for all cases necessarily suppresses their diversity and thus "degenerates into error" (Newman 1996, 62).

To conclude, I consider the modern university to be a result of the Enlightenment project that comes to be realized during the nation-building process (and the university understands itself as a part of this process) with strong anti-utilitarian tendencies. The university understands itself, shapes itself and thus reacts to the external demands for reform in accordance with the idea that it is an institution whose goal is pursuit of knowledge without necessarily utilitarian tendencies. In the following part of my paper I will show how several contemporary problems of universities arise from these aspects.

---

3   Jeremy Bentham published his *An Introduction to the Principles of Morals and Legislation* in 1789, James Mill published *Elements of Political Economy* in 1821 and his essays, including the essay titled "Education" in 1828. The first sentence of this essay is "the end of Education is to render the individual, as much as possible, an instrument of happiness, first to himself, and next to other beings." These thinkers considered education to be a means to an external end, namely happiness.

3 The Current Problem

The current situation of universities, which I characterized earlier as schizophrenic, is not a result of evil guys who intentionally destroy all that is good. I believe it is the result of confusion and a lack of confidence within academia itself.[4] As we have seen, a university might be described as a closed autopoietic system, therefore the self-understanding of such an institution is constitutive for its further development and functioning (Lenartowicz 2015, 958).

True, a liberal education seems to go hand in hand with liberal democracy. This relation is stressed by such different authors as Czesław Miłosz on the one hand and Martha C. Nussbaum on the other. Miłosz shows that undemocratic regimes might accommodate excellent mathematicians or engineers within their academic institutions, but there are hardly any official first-class scholars in humanities in undemocratic societies – or they are not there for long (Miłosz 1990, 3–24, 191–222). Nussbaum argues that liberal education, education in the humanities is a necessary condition for societies to flourish in accordance with democratic civic virtues such as critical thinking, responsibility, or autonomy (Nussbaum 2016). However, according to some critiques even this approach suggests that education and knowledge are *subordinate* to the idea of citizenship and civic virtues and thus violates the anti-utilitarian ethos of higher education. Hitz criticizes Nussbaum since, according to her Nussbaum

> appears not to understand that there are things beyond citizenship, more splendid and more fundamental – and that these very things, at the present moment more than ever, need to be secured – and need to be secured most especially from the infinite demands of citizenship. (Hitz 2016)

Despite a certain undeniable relation between the nature of higher education and democracy, universities are, due to their function a rather ambivalent element in modern popular democracies. As Collini writes:

> we should recognize that universities are in some senses inherently elitist in a restricted sense of that term. It's of course true that intellectual enquiry is in one sense irreducibly democratic – the best arguments and

---

4   Similarly see Hitz 2016.

the best evidence are decisive, no matter who puts them forward. But in another sense it is unavoidably selective – not everyone is going to be equally good at conducting the enquiry at the appropriate level. (Collini 2017, 27)

The relation of public as well as political representation towards universities mirrors this ambivalence. On the one hand, innovation and creative thinking are appreciated and freedom of research is rarely questioned as such. On the other hand, universities are charged with irresponsible and *useless* activities which are supposed to be eliminated by proper *accountability* related to the criteria upon which the finances are distributed. This is a conflict between how the university understands itself and the external requirements and expectations.[5]

One particular example of this ambivalence and emerging distrust may be the document governing the principles and orientation of research in the Czech Republic, namely the *National Research and Innovation Strategy for Smart Specialization of the Czech Republic (the National RIS3 Strategy)*. This document characterizes the humanities as a *threat* due to which there will not be enough workers in industry. The only use of the word "humanities" throughout the document is in this sentence:

Threat: The continuing decline in the quality of graduates and the growing proportion of graduates from humanities, along with the retirement of experienced workers, will lead to a shortage of labour demanded by industry. (Ministerstvo školství, mládeže a tělovýchovy 2014a, 78)

Perhaps one should not be too afraid, because the research and economic specialization of the Czech Republic recognizes the social sciences – even though it only speaks about them once. I prefer to quote the entire context:

At the same time, further research of usage of knowledge in these knowledge domains needs to focus on topics defined by both the public sector (especially with regard to social challenges) and by private business entities. Therefore, these genuinely technological knowledge domains were complemented by the knowledge of the social sciences necessary

---

5   See Hufford and Zelený 1991, 328–9 for conflict and degradation of social institution as auto-poietic entities.

for non-technical innovation (i.e. the knowledge needed to identify the changing needs of both public and private sectors, in particular social science knowledge, which is a prerequisite for marketing, organizational innovation, and governance in general innovation). (Ministerstvo školství, mládeže a tělovýchovy 2014a, 82)

The knowledge of social sciences thus has a single use: to complement and serve technological knowledge. It is rather astounding that despite the fact that the whole document repeats the phrase "social challenges" many times, the writers probably never thought that social sciences or humanities can not only help answer these "challenges" but above all, they are very familiar with the prior identification of social problems and the possible prevention thereof. This document is one particular example of certain misunderstanding between complex higher learning, which includes humanities as well as social sciences and the institutionalized political representation of contemporary society.

4 Trust: University as a Foreigner in a Populist, Market Democracy

Research – not only in the humanities or social sciences – is closely tied to conversation, *communication*. This communication takes place not only among scientists, but – and this is essential for universities – among all members of the group called the academic community. That is, between scholars and teachers, between these two groups and students, and, last but not least, among the students themselves.

Further, this conversation is not limited to academia. The university is the center of social life, educating future active citizens and communicating with society. However, this communication is presently flawed by distrust between the public, represented by its political elite, and universities (Muller 2018; Nichols 2019; Collini 2017, 239). Sztompka refers to the gradually decreasing trust in and social status of professors in Poland (Sztompka 1999, 43, 166). This distrust is not only mentioned in literature, it can be read from the available statistics as well.[6] Moreover, *The Strategy for Educational Politics 2020*, which is the most comprehensive

---

6   For example, Jones 2018, or Association of Governing Boards of Universities and Colleges 2018.

policy paper of the Czech Ministry of Education, directly identifies lack of trust as one of the problems of Czech higher education.[7]

One reason for this distrust is already clear, universities are foreign bodies within contemporary popular democracies. Most governments assume that *if* they should justify their care and spending on universities to their electorate, they must do it in terms of training future employees or of narrowly defined research with an immediate practical use (medicine, technology, economics).[8] Two results come from this assumption: (i) the governmental support will be orientated toward the fields and disciplines where spending is understandable to the government and the electorate and (ii) universities will try to adjust so that they do not decrease this support – and not only will they promote the profitable disciplines, they will try to model the remaining disciplines accordingly. This reshaping of disciplines can be illustrated by an example of colleague of mine who had to fill in an evaluation form asking about the short-term and long-term social impact of his new commentated translation of *Kalevala*.

The foreign character of universities is further strengthened by their selective behavior: "The surface egalitarianism of market democracies is uneasy with claims about the differential capacities of individuals and still more with ideas about intrinsic differences of worth between activities" (Collini 2012, 92–3). This adds to the problems of possible dialogue or understanding of universities by governments and public. The contemporary situation, Nichols claims, "is not a dialogue between experts and the larger community, but the use of established knowledge as an off-the-shelf convenience as needed and only so far as desired" (Nichols 2019, 14). Several years earlier, Stefan Collini indicated that contemporary discussion about universities is flawed by "growing distrust of reasoned argument", which is often perceived as "a form of elitist arrogance" (Collini 2012, 17).[9]

---

7   There is insufficient understanding of the basic values, principles and directions of long-term development of the education system. Key stakeholders in education do not share the baseline, which has major negative effects on action in promoting change at all levels [...] In the education system, uncertainty has increased in recent years, strengthened by the low predictability of the Ministry's and other key policy makers' actions [...] Mutual trust among individual actors in education is weakening, which can be considered as one of the prerequisites for successful development of the education system in the Czech Republic. (Ministerstvo školství, mládeže a tělovýchovy 2014b, 4–5)

8   For a general discussion of these trends, see Collini 2012, 35, 91.

9   On the other hand, trust in rationality and its processes is definitely one of academic virtues and virtues are in turn responsible for excellence, see Pelikan 1992, 50–1.

Nichols shows that distrust of expertise is another aspect of our era. If all opinions are equal, namely quality does not matter, the expert is no different from any layman. One thing is the lack of knowledge among the population concerning politics, history and science. That is an old problem apparently present in different forms throughout history. However, the contemporary situation is that *ignorance* is in many cases seen as a positive sign of *autonomy*. "To reject the advice of experts is to assert autonomy, a way for people to demonstrate their independence from elites – and insulate their increasingly fragile egos from ever being wrong" (Nichols 2019, x). Therefore, the problem is not only ignorance, it is ignorance being promoted among the values of contemporary society under the heading of *autonomy* or *authenticity*. According to Nichols, "we do not have a healthy skepticism about experts: instead, we actively resent them, with many people assuming that experts are wrong simply by virtue of being experts" (Nichols 2019, xiii).

The second worry or uncertainty within universities is tied to internationalization. This sounds *prima facie* extremely reactionary. I claimed above that the essential goal of the university is the enlargement and pursuit of knowledge. If that is the case, universities nowadays ought not to recognize any national or state barriers – unlike their modern ancestor, which originated as a part of a nation-building process. However, a university usually has another, minor goal as well. Especially in small language communities like Czech, Slovak, Hungarian and others, there is always the communitarian aspect of the university: its influence within the culture of a given community. This opens a tension between the primary aim of the university and its possible service to the language community. Internationalization, which is so badly needed in order to foster the primary goal of a university, changes the character of a university: it is no longer a national institution as was its modern ancestor, but an international institution of excellence and knowledge which is, so to speak, situated nowhere (or everywhere). This makes it different from most of contemporary society, which lives situated *somewhere*, i.e. it is rooted in a more or less local community (this terminology points to the analyses of contemporary society in Goodhart 2017).

5 Metrics: The Spectre of Accountability

The broadening gulf between experts, professionals within a certain area of human knowledge, is not only a source of possible misunderstandings. It is a seed of distrust when the public actually barely understands the goal and mission of institutions that are quite costly to maintain. From this distrust grows the need for *accountability*. The demand for accountability feeds upon the growing distrust of institutions and resentment of authority based on expertise (Muller 2018, 39–47).

This is the source of another worry frequently expressed in contemporary discussions about universities: namely, the application of the external audits of academic institutions based on metrics which are foreign to what universities actually do, yet fully comprehensible and fitting the market economy. As Muller argues, the metrics of accountability are particularly attractive in cultures marked by low social trust (Muller 2018, 37). As I have tried to show, this is precisely the situation of universities in contemporary society. Therefore, I understand the metrics of accountability to be a reply to the problem of trust generated by the foreignness or heterogeneity of a university in our contemporary world.

Science policy and measurement did not emerge as a way of controlling research and universities, but as a means of distributing research funding (Linková and Stöckelová 2012, 619). It was the system of peer review that was the main pillar of this accountability. At the beginning it actually strengthened the independence of research and universities, since the distribution of funding was no longer based on arbitrary decisions of the government (Linková and Stöckelová 2012, 619–20). As Lenartowicz puts it:

> on the autopoietic level, the traditional mission of public service did not call for any additional activities outside the process of self-production, remained an external narrative, an evaluation of the usefulness of the former two from the perspective of other social systems. (Lenartowicz 2015, 952)

This system within which university had its place as an autopoietic institution largely distinct from the rest of society, yet respected and believed to be a part of the common good, came to an end during the 1980s and 1990s. This was the time in which the idea became dominant that "the government was a problem and society did not exist" (Judt 2010, 97). Judt shows nicely that both the new left as well as the new conservative movement destroyed the notion of collective purpose and indeed, questioned the concept of society and authority (Judt 2010, 89, 96). The left disregarded both collective purpose (for the sake of individualism) and traditional authority, including the forms of authority occurring within universities. On the right, the paradigm was Margaret Thatcher's dictum that "there is no such thing as society, there are only individuals and families" (Judt 2010, 96). In a situation when the state is nothing but a facilitator of private interests, it is understandable that universities are put under pressure to be able to show how they promote these private interests.

Corresponding to this political change and its effect on self-understanding and self-reproduction of universities, metrics gradually changed their role. They started as a part of the auditing process based on peer review, which ensured the accountability demanded by the governments. Nowadays these metrics "function as a form a measure able to translate different forms of value" (Burrows 2012, 368) and this new processes is being called "qualified control". What happens is that we observe an endeavour to "translate informed judgements of quality into calculable measurements of quantity, and then to further reduce those quantitative proxies to a single ordinal ranking" (Collini 2017, 57). The *judgement* of quality is being substituted by the *measurement* of quantity (Collini 2017, 303).

The measurement of quantity covers many different values that were previously distinguished and acknowledged separately in the comprehensive judgement expressed in the peer review. As Grahame Lock and Herminio Martins express it:

> In the bygone world [...] different kinds of institutions embodied various, incommensurable kinds of value. Academic value was not to be identified with artistic value, nor artistic value with monetary value, and so on. But in our brave new world, it seems that a single final criterion of value is recognized: a quantitative, economic criterion. All else is no more than a means. And there is a single method for ensuring that this criterion is satisfied: quantified control. (Lock and Martins 2011)

The simplicity of metrics gives us the feeling of transparency and objectivity (Muller 2018, 40).[10] The reason that governments and manage-

---

10 See Collini 1999, 239.

ments like them so much is simple: they can serve well in justification since they seem to be intelligible to everybody and the general public can then feel that it is in control of even such complicated issues as research in astrophysics and ancient philology. The sociologist Nash even believes that "auditing is introduced because professionals cannot be trusted to do their jobs well" (Nash 2019, 6).

A further reason for strengthening the role of metrics may lie in the very heart of the meritocratic society with rather high social mobility. Muller claims that there is an elective affinity between measured accountability and a meritocratic society: "in meritocratic societies with more open and changing elites, those who reach positions of authority are less likely to feel secure in their judgments, and more likely to seek seemingly objective criteria by which to make decisions" (Muller 2018, 39–40).

The tendency for a simple or even simplistic measure has serious consequences, of course. Previously I spoke of the tendency of universities to promote disciplines that "pay off" and to model the remaining disciplines accordingly. After explaining the role of metrics, this tendency can be described with the help of "Campbell's Law", which observes the unwanted impact of metrics: The more any quantitative social indicator is used for social decision-making, the more subject it will be to corruption pressures and the more apt it will be to distort and corrupt the social processes it is intended to monitor. Institutions do not follow their original function, which is supposed to be measured, but they accommodate their functioning according to the metrics used.

Yet, there is even further effect of the accountability policy based on simple, seemingly easily understandable metrics: the disappearance of the importance of professionalism, which I will discuss in the next section.

6 Professionalism: The Trouble of Egalitarianism

The opening lines of Immanuel Kant's short treatise *Der Streit der Fakultäten* (1788) could be used as a programmatic slogan for professionalism and specialism:

> whoever it was that first hit on the notion of a university and proposed that a public institution of this kind be established, it was not a bad idea to handle the entire content of learning (really, the thinkers devoted to it) by mass production, so to speak – by a division of labour. (Kant 1979, 23)

Division of labour, professionalism has been an essential feature of a university since its modern beginnings (Lorenz 2015, 7). In this sense it is a part of modern society, which cannot operate without a division of labour and reliance on experts: "We prosper because we specialize, and because we develop both formal and informal mechanisms and practices that allow us to *trust* each other in those specializations" (Nichols 2019, 14).

However, the obsession with the metrics system based on a quantifiable approach basically destroys expertise and professionalism by making it obsolete. Professions need professional autonomy (Lorenz 2015, 7) and from a basic sociological point of view it is clear that each profession is defined by its own quality standards, its own hierarchy based on the reputation of the professionals. This reputation is based on nothing other than the assessment of the professional community concerning the contribution of the given individual to the body of knowledge or skill in question (Lorenz 2015, 7–8).[11]

Now, exchanging judgement for metrics, judged quality for measured quantity, makes professionalism obsolete exactly because of the seeming objectivity and transparency of quantifiable metrics. It does not matter when the external professional evaluators are former professionals: they do not behave as professionals of a given profession any more (Lorenz 2015, 9). There is different modus of talk and behaviour among the professionals of a given profession (i.e. communication among the colleagues – students and professors – of an academic community) and between evaluators and those being evaluated. Professionals then become interchangeable in so far as the change results in a positive effect upon the metrics.[12] The result is vague and empty talk about "excellence" in higher education. The term "excellence" was extensively criticized for its lack of reference by Bill Readings (Readings 1996, 21–43). Yet it is important to see what the emptiness of this notion allows: "since it is entirely devoid of content in itself, its presence can only be vouchsafed by some quantitative evidence recognized by outsiders" (Collini 2017, 43).

The absurdities of the ill-fated obsession with metrics can be illustrated in the case of the recent Czech methodology of evaluating quality in higher education and research. The Evaluation Methodology is

---

11 On the autopoietic aspects of this system see Lenartowicz 2015, 956.
12 See Lears 2000, 21.

colloquially referred to as a "coffee grinder": it grinds all diverse research results into one and the same scale of "points". The points are then the bases for institutional research funding. The Methodology thus serves for both evaluation and funding science and research (Good, Vermeulen, Tiefenthaler and Arnold 2015, 92). Actually, no analyses show a relationship between the introduction of the Evaluation Methodology and increasing performance in research, quite the contrary: the highest increase occurred before this Methodology was established, while it has been in progress there has been a certain slowdown (Good, Vermeulen, Tiefenthaler and Arnold 2015, 97).

According to Barbara Good and her research team (Good, Vermeulen, Tiefenthaler and Arnold 97–102), among the results of this Evaluation Methodology were (i) a statistically reported increase of opportunistic behaviour of research institutions, (ii) the fact that a large number of mediocre results can outweigh a single outstanding contribution and finally, (iii) the methodology caused large and erratic changes in institutional funding, so that planning and development strategies are nearly impossible (which is one of the results of "Campbell's Law" mentioned above). These unwanted results only increase the tension between academia and society, cause misunderstandings and undermine possible bonds of trust.

7 Conclusion

I have argued that universities are a foreign body within contemporary society formed around the central idea of a populist democracy. As soon as a university (and higher education in general) ceases to be seen as a public good, the public demands accountability of a university's activities and functions. Because of general distrust in expertise and professional knowledge, this accountability is based on seemingly objective and transparent metrics. This audit culture further deepens the distrust between a university and society.

The analysis so far has concerned rather the *unhappy aspects* of university life in contemporary society. I would like to finish with couple of remarks on what universities can do in order to rectify these unhappy aspects. First, universities will always be foreign institutions in popular democracies. As Collini puts it "universities are in this way doomed to be homes both to instrumentality on a large scale and to the critique of that instrumentality in a tension or conflict that cannot be wholly resolved"

(Collini 2017, 78). This means that there will always be critique of universities as well as defence of them.

Second, universities themselves should attempt to regain some trust in the eyes of the public. However, this should not follow the suggested route of objective metrics. Nichols, in his otherwise depressing book, suggests that mechanisms unique to each profession and expertise might be the correct way to regain trust:

> expert communities rely on peer-run institutions to maintain standards and to enhance social trust. Mechanisms like peer review, board certification, professional associations, and other organizations and professions help to protect quality and to assure society – that is, the expert's clients – that they're safe in accepting expert claims of competence. (Nichols 2019, 35)

A university must exercise its own intellectual virtues (Pelikan 1992, 49–50). Freedom of inquiry is closely related to freedom of speech,[13] trust in rationality and its processes, conveying the results of research to others, discipline of mind and finally, academic working ethics. Universities should be strict in keeping these professional standards under their internal control. I believe that this kind of care in and of itself can help universities not only in the eyes of the public, but it can help them to create a better academic life *per se*. It follows from my argument above that the university serves the society best if it is left to work as an autopoietic entity which it essentially is. The tendencies to disrupt its self-understanding, self-production and self-evaluation lead to malfunctioning of the university in its core function: pursuit of knowledge.

References

Association of Governing Boards of Universities and Colleges. 2018. *Public Confidence in Higher Education.* https://agb.org/sites/default/files/report_2018_guardians_public _confidence.pdf. Accessed 9 April 2021.

Burrows, Roger. 2012. "Living with the H-Index? Metric Assemblages in the Contemporary Academy". *The Sociological Review* 60 (2): 355–72.

Collini, Stefan. 1999. *English Pasts: Essays in History and Culture.* Oxford: Oxford University Press.

Collini, Stefan. 2012. *What Are Universities for?* London: Penguin Books.

---

13 Which does not mean arbitrariness (which conflicts with the intellectual virtue of rationality), gratuitousness or even malice; free speech is not hate speech; see Waldron 2012.

Collini, Stefan. 2017. *Speaking of Universities*. London: Verso.

Craig, John E. 1984. *Scholarship and Nation Building: The Universities of Strasbourg and Alsatian Society, 1870–1939*. Chicago, IL, London: University of Chicago Press.

Good, Barbara, Niki Vermeulen, Brigitte Tiefenthaler, and Erik Arnold. 2015. "Counting Quality? The Czech Performance-Based Research Funding System". *Research Evaluation* 24 (2): 91–105.

Goodhart, David. 2017. *The Road to Somewhere: The New Tribes Shaping British Politics*. London: Penguin Books.

Graham, Hugh Davis, and Nancy Diamond. 1997. *The Rise of American Research Universities: Elites and Challengers in the Postwar Era*. Baltimore, MD, London: Johns Hopkins University Press.

Hitz, Zena. 2016. "Freedom and Intellectual Life". First Things. 2016. https://www.firstthings.com/web-exclusives/2016/04/freedom-and-intellectual-life. Accessed 9 January 2021.

Hufford, Kevin D, and Milan Zelený. 1991. "All Autopoietic Systems Must Be Social Systems (Living Implies Autopoietic. But, Autopoietic Does Not Imply Living): An Application of Autopoietic Criteria in Systems Analysis". *Journal of Social and Biological Structures* 14 (3): 311–32.

Jaspers, Karl. 2016. "Volk und Universität". In *Schriften Zur Universitätsidee. Gesamtausgabe*, edited by Oliver Immel, 203–11. Basel: Schwabe Verlag.

Jones, Jeffrey. 2018. "Confidence in Higher Education Down Since 2015". *Gallup.Com*. 9 October 2018. https://news.gallup.com/opinion/gallup/242441/confidence-higher-education-down-2015.aspx. Accessed 4 February 2021.

Judt, Tony. 2010. *Ill Fares the Land*. New York: The Penguin Press.

Kant, Immanuel. 1979. *The Conflict of the Faculties*. Translated by Mary J. Gregor. New York: Abaris Books.

Lears, Jackson. 2000. "The Radicalism of Tradition: Teaching the Liberal Arts in a Managerial Age". *The Hedgehog Review* 2 (3): 7–23.

Lenartowicz, Marta. 2015. "The Nature of the University". *Higher Education* 69 (6): 947–61.

Linková, Marcela, and Tereza Stöckelová. 2012. "Public Accountability and the Politicization of Science: The Peculiar Journey of Czech Research Assessment". *Science and Public Policy* 39 (5): 618–29.

Lock, Grahame, and Herminio Martins. 2011. "Quantified Control and the Mass Production of 'Psychotic Citizens'". *EspacesTemps.net Revue électronique des sciences humaines et sociales.*, January. https://www.espacestemps.net/articles/quantified-control-and-the-mass-production-of-ldquopsychotic-citizensrdquo/. Accessed 5 April 2021.

Lorenz, Chris. 2015. "The Metrification of 'Quality' and the Fall of the Academic Profession". *Oxford Magazine* Hilary Week, Trinity Term: 7–12.

Menand, Louis. 2010. *The Marketplace of Ideas. Issues of Our Time*. New York, London: W. W. Norton & Company.

Miłosz, Czesław. 1990. *The Captive Mind*. New York: Vintage International.

Ministerstvo školství, mládeže a tělovýchovy. 2014a. *Národní výzkumná a inovační strategie pro inteligentní specializaci České Republiky* (National Research and Innovation Strategy for Intelligent Specialization of the Czech Republic). https://www.msmt.cz/strukturalni-fondy-1/ris3-strategie-cr. Accessed 7 April 2021.

Ministerstvo školství, mládeže a tělovýchovy. 2014b. *Strategie vzdělávací politiky 2020* (Strategy of educational policy 2020). https://www.msmt.cz/uploads/Strategie_2020_web.pdf. Accessed 7 April 2021.

Muller, Jerry Z. 2018. *The Tyranny of Metrics*. Princeton, NJ: Princeton University Press.

Nash, Kate. 2019. "Neo-Liberalisation, Universities and the Values of Bureaucracy". *The Sociological Review* 67 (1): 178–93.

Newman, John Henry. 1996. *The Idea of a University*. New Haven, CT, London: Yale University Press.

Nichols, Thomas M. 2019. *The Death of Expertise: The Campaign against Established Knowledge and Why It Matters*. New York: Oxford University Press.

Nussbaum, Martha C. 2016. *Not for Profit: Why Democracy Needs the Humanities. Updated edition*. Princeton, NJ: Princeton University Press.

Pelikan, Jaroslav. 1992. *The Idea of the University: A Reexamination*. New Haven, CT, London: Yale University Press.

Readings, Bill. 1996. *The University in Ruins*. Cambridge, MA, London: Harvard University Press.

Schiller, Friedrich. 1789. "Was heißt und zu welchem Ende studiert Man Universalgeschichte?" In *Der Teutsche Merkur. 1773–1789*, edited by Christoph Martin Wieland, 105–35. Weimar: Hofmann.

Sobotka, Milan. 2015. "Vzdělávání lidstva v dějinách. K širšímu pojetí pojmu vzdělání v německé klasické filosofii". In *Moderní Univerzita. Ideál a realita*, edited by Jiří Chotaš, Aleš Prázný, and Tomáš Hejduk, 115–38. Praha: Filosofia.

Sztompka, Piotr. 1999. *Trust: A Sociological Theory*. Cambridge, MA: University Press.

Todorov, Tzvetan. 2009. *In Defence of the Enlightenment*. Translated by Gila Walker. London: Atlantic Books.

Vanderstraeten, Raf. 2002. "The Autopoiesis of Educational Organizations: The Impact of the Organizational Setting on Educational Interaction". *Systems Research and Behavioral Science* 19 (3): 243–53.

Waldron, Jeremy. 2012. *The Harm in Hate Speech. Oliver Wendell Holmes Lectures 2009*. Cambridge, MA, London: Harvard University Press.

Weber, Wolfgang. 2002. *Geschichte der europäischen Universität*. Stuttgart: Kohlhammer.

Weischedel, Wilhelm. 2019. "Einleitung". In *Idee Und Wirklichkeit Einer Universität*, edited by Wilhelm Weischedel, Wolfgang Müller-Lauter, and Michael Theunissen, xi–xxxiv. Berlin: De Gruyter.

Zeleny, Milan. 2015. "Autopoiesis Applies to Social Systems Only". *Constructivist Foundations* 10 (2): 186–9.

Part 4
Society in an Autopoietic Perspective

An Autopoieticist Vision of Society: Luhmann's Social System Theory and the Understanding of Medieval Transformation

Tomáš Klír

1 Introduction

In terms of historical research, the Middle Ages is a rich and extremely attractive period. It is the last epoch to be largely archaeologized, and we know it to a large extent thanks to the silent material remains. It is thus difficult to find the causal connections underlying the documented social, economic and cultural changes and we use analogies and a traditional systems approach. These promise comprehensive and integrated knowledge even on the basis of small fragments and also offer an explanation/prediction of the trajectory of historical development. The initial mechanical idea of balanced and stable systems was soon replaced by the vision of society/culture as an open and adaptive complex system, which consists of an extensive and variable network of actors (persons, things) and the relationships between them. The attractiveness of system approaches increased especially after the incorporation of the theory of resilience, which describes the ability of systems to absorb stress and the degree of resistance of the links between its elements (Olsson et al. 2015, 2; Trigger 2006, 355–7, 419–24, 439–40; Johnson 2010, 70–4). These system approaches describe reality quite successfully, on the other hand, they are not suitable in many respects, they arouse disappointment and doubt. This concerns in particular (i) an overemphasis of the role of the environment and exogenous factors in explaining change within the system, (ii) failure to explain social variability, (iii) inconclusive results in finding causal connections of historical change, and (iv) defining what belongs to the system and what does not (Guptill and Peine 2021, 2–3; Van der Ploeg 2012; Mingers 2002, 279–80).

An alternative to traditional systems theory is offered by the concept of autopoietic systems (Varela and Maturana 1980), which was consistently brought into social theory by the German sociologist Niklas Luhmann.[1] His radical vision makes it possible to formulate questions in new ways, frees us from the imperative of seeking direct causal connections, and deprives us of the idea of determining systems change by the environment. Instead, it opens up a perspective for a series of entirely new types of research that explain the immeasurable variability of social reality, today and in the past, and opens our perception to the role of contingency. Therefore, it is important to invest in Luhmann's challenging theory, even in the field of the historical sciences.

We devote the following second section to the theory of autopoietic social systems and at the same time focus on the parts relevant for historical research. We consider relatively extensive description to be useful here, as Luhmann's ideas are not well-known among medievalists and especially archaeologists, and moreover Luhmann operated with a specific vocabulary. In the third section, we introduce the concept of medieval transformation and show its striking similarities to Luhmann's theory, especially in terms of perceptions of social evolution, differentiation, indeterminism, and social variability. In the last section, we turn our attention to the issue of materiality and spatiality, which is central to disciplines such as archaeology, but Luhmann paid minimal attention to them. We will use specific examples from the field of rural sociology, peasantology and agrarian history.

2 The Theory of Autopoietic Social Systems

The starting point of Niklas Luhmann's theory of social systems is considered to be a combination of social constructivism and communication theory,[2] but the biological concept of autopoietic systems was decisive for

---

1   See Baecker 2001.

2   Niklas Luhmann was one of the extremely productive social theorists with a bibliography comprising around 60 monographs and 400 studies. His theory of social systems is accepted to this day significantly unevenly, although the essential studies were relatively quickly translated or directly published in English (Luhmann 1989; 1990; 1995; 2012; 2013. See also Stichweh et al 1999; Stichweh 2011). An effective introduction into his world of thought is mediated not only by a number of differently conceived monographs (Krause 2001; Jahraus et al. 2012; La Cour and Philippopoulos-Mihalopoulos et al. 2013), but also a number of discipline-focused, condensed and often discussion-provoking summaries on which we also rely to a great extent (Lee 2000; Mingers 1995; 2002; Gren and Zierhofer 2003; Seidl 2005; Kessler and Helmig 2007;

its grand finalization (Mingers 2002, 279–81; Gren and Zierhofer 2003, 616; Seidl 2005, 21–4; Kessler and Helmig 2007, 243–4; Von Schlippe and Hermann 2013, 391; Tyrell 2015). Following this concept, the system is able to reproduce itself by observing itself (*self-referential*) and only elements that it produces itself are its own components (*self-producing/constructing*). The systems (for instance, cells) are open for the flow of matter and energy but all of the operations that comprise it are only its internal affair. Or, each system has on the one hand *operative/organizational closure* and on the other hand has *interactional/structural openness*. This openness means that the system can perceive its environment and react to it, but in a way that is determined only by its internal structure and not by the environment. An example is the objectively identical injection of a syringe that someone feels, another does not, which we dodge if it comes unexpectedly, but which we do not resist at the hands of a doctor. Autopoietic systems cannot be affected in terms of direct causality. At the same time, each system creates its own structure according to its organizational principles and it only depends on it how permeable its boundaries are. The system can coordinate with other systems in its environment and be sensitive to their irritations (which is covered by the concept of *structural coupling*) but it cannot be directly connected to them. The structural coupling cannot be considered to be adaptation but rather bilateral coevolution. It is possible to see it as a bridging between the system and the environment (Lee 2000, 325). The question of the differentiation of the system from its environment is related to this. Every system creates and determines its boundaries itself with its self-observation and according to its own code. Autopoietic systems are autonomous, create everything necessary for their own reproduction, which when it ceases, the system disappears.

Niklas Luhmann abstracted the basic assumptions of this concept and, in general, distinguished between three types of autopoietic systems – living/biological systems, psychic/mental systems (systems of consciousness) and social systems (Luhmann 1995; Seidl 2005, 25–7; Gren and Zierhofer 2003, 616–17). These three types are distinguished between according to the basis on which the system is reproduced. For living systems, it is life; for the psychic it is thought/consciousness/experience and for social systems it is communication. Social systems are

Von Schlippe and Hermann 2013). See also *Niklas Luhmann-Archiv*, https://niklas-luhmann-archiv.de/.

therefore communication systems. Although the individual systems are autonomous, they are also dependent on each other. The existence of psychic and social systems cannot do without living systems and allopoietic material systems. Niklas Luhmann thus divorced all previous concepts of social systems, because according to him the system exists only as a continuous production of the elements that comprise it (Von Schlippe and Hermann 2013, 389).

Luhmann's theory of social systems anticipates three basic interpretive components – communications, evolution and differentiation (Luhmann 2012; 2013; Lee 2000, 324–5). [Fig. 1] Each of these components is also related to one of three dimensions, in which the autopoiesis of social systems takes place. Communications are purely social phenomena and distinguish between psychic systems (Alter versus Ego). Evolution is connected with the temporal dimension in which the past and the future are distinguished between. Differentiation is related to the functional dimension in which the difference between the system and its environment is created.

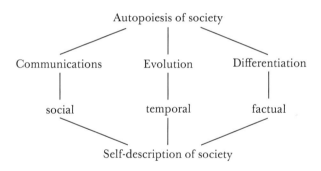

Fig. 1: Autopiesis and Self-Description of society (Luhmann 2013, 341).

According to Luhmann, social systems are created by neither people nor relations nor acts but by *communications* or point communicative events as the only real forms of social reality (Von Schlippe and Hermann 2013, 389–90; Seidl 2005, 28–30; Gren and Zierhofer 2003, 616–17; Mingers 2002, 286–8). It should be emphasized that Luhmann's conception of communications is specific and does not correspond to the general meaning of the word. Luhmann's communication is comprised of three components – information (what is communicated), utterance (how and why it is communicated) and understanding (distinguishing between information and utterance). Without understanding there is no communication, it is only understanding that makes communication meaningful. All of the components of communication form an insoluble unit (a communication event) and emerge as a triple selection from a set of possible information, utterances and understandings, first on the sender's part and then on the recipient's part. A person (psychic system) purposefully sends information and selects the form of utterance (medium), but it is not yet communication in Luhmann's conception. Understanding by the other person and resonance in the form of new communication is essential (Lee 2000, 325). Therefore, communication cannot be attributed to persons, because communications are social events standing between psychic systems. And in Luhmann's conception, it is not the addressee who caps the communication act with understanding and gives it meaning, but it is a subsequent communication event that actually begins as the fourth selection (acceptance/rejection of the meaning of the communication). It is similar to the word being given meaning only by the next word. Understanding is therefore not tied to psychic systems. People come and go, their individual motivation disappears, but the communication dynamics remain. The social system can thus be imagined as a network, including communications that create communications and nothing but communications. Each communication in that refers to the previous communication. Without relation to other communications, communication cannot exist.

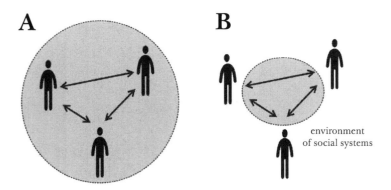

Fig. 2: A. Traditional conception of social systems, including actors and the relationships between them. B. Social systems according to Niklas Luhmann, including communications only (Tiffert 2013, 389, modified).

In Luhmann's conception, society fills the space between human beings, mediates contact between them, but human beings are not part of it. [Fig. 2] Luhmann did not push human beings out of his considerations, but merely moved them into the environment of society (Lee 2000, 322, 325; Kessler and Helmig 2007, 244).

The content of communication is determined by the structure of the relevant social system (Von Schlippe and Hermann 2013, 390–1; Seidl 2005, 31). Luhmann understands the structure of the system as an expectation of which communication event will follow the previous communication event. This expectation partly limits the possibilities of what the event chain communicates about. If everything matches, the structure of the system does not change, if not, the structure may change. The current structure determines the system's response to the environments; it is also the result of a learning process, which means that social systems are dependent on their own history.

The sense of the communication is generated according to the context, that is, by framing the communication. Psychic and social systems respond differently to the same stimulus, depending on the environment. Sometimes we speak of a context marker that tells the system how it is to communicate (Von Schlippe and Hermann 2013, 390–1). This marker can also have a material substance in the background (an office versus a private flat).

Luhmann does not perceive human beings as a unity, but as a structurally coupled psychic and living system (Luhmann 1995, 6–7; 2012, 59–61; Von Schlippe and Hermann 2013, 391; Seidl 2005, 31–4; Gren and Zierhofer 2003, 617, 621; Mingers 2002, 288). Although both systems are operationally closed, they are structurally adjusted by long-term coevolution during childhood and growth. For the social system, however, the conglomerate of the psychic and living system acts as one person, perceived as a complex of expectations. Psychic and social systems are operationally closed and create an environment for each other, at the same time they have created channels through which stimuli are perceived and transmitted. At the same time, it is the case that the reproduction of social and psychic systems is based on each other. Communication is not without experience/memory, which is carried by psychic systems. Each communication presupposes a parallel response in thought. Communication processes in social systems shake psychic systems, encourage the reproduction of thoughts, which in turn encourage the production of subsequent communications (resonance). We can imagine contact as a continuous impact of rattles, which are closed, but coordinate and irritate each other. Language is a distinct way of structural coupling of psychic and social systems.

The considerations of *evolution* as a temporal dimension of social systems are remarkable (Luhmann 2012, 251–359; Lee 2000, 323, 327–8; Mathias 2019). The evolution of social systems is not a story about the adaptation of systems to the environment, but about the adaptation of social systems to themselves, that is, to their own internal structures. Although social systems depend on their environment, which satisfies their basic needs, this environment does not determine the evolution of society. The evolutionary trajectory follows only from the operational history of each social system. Social evolution takes place in three steps – first new communications bringing variations into the system, then selection of these variations and finally a new state is created as a re-stabilization. In time, one communication is chained after another, structure after structure, without anything predetermining the exact direction of evolution. The long-term joint evolution of social systems can lead to the creation of structures that are sensitive to mutual irritations and are able to process them according to their own logic. This manifests itself as structural coupling (structural correspondence, structure of expectations), which can take a variety of forms, for example, a functional subsystem or an organizational system. Over time, we can observe a growing complexity of society, which is reflected in an ever deeper and sharper differentiation, and thus in a higher need for structural coupling. Luhmann's social evolution is the evolution of the ways in which communications are interconnected, which has nothing to do with natural evolution. Therefore, there is talk of a non-Darwinian form of coevolution (Gren and Zierhofer 2003, 621).

Luhmann assumes that society faces an environment (everything outside it) that is always more complex than itself. The result is a growing complexity of society in the form of ever deeper internal *differentiation*. In principle, three or four principles of internal differentiation are offered – segmental, stratified, by logic a center and periphery, and functional. The type of differentiation tells us how the society distributes and solves problems that occur in its environment. That is to which system it will first include/exclude. Niklas Luhmann initially anticipated three ways (Luhmann 1977), he later added the differentiation of center and periphery (Luhmann 2013, 10–166; Lee 2000, 327–8; Mingers 2002, 285; Seidl 2005, 35–6; Kessler and Helmig 2007, 245; Stichweh 2011; Roth and Schütz 2015, 15–17). All methods of differentiation can be combined with each other; however, the decisive factor is which is the primary one – that is, according to which the communications are first selected (Roth 2014, 41–3). It is from this point of view that Luhmann identified four structural stages. Society (hunters and gatherers) was first divided into many internally equally structured and socially equal subsystems such as tribes, clans, or family (*segmentation*). Then, hierarchical differentiation or *stratification* prevailed in the primary position, dividing society into unequal parts such as classes or castes, which determined the lives of its members. The origin of a person gave it social significance in various social systems. The social systems were not equal, but some dominated (for instance, religion). The unequal relationship of stratified and segmented societies led to another type of differentiation, namely to the superior, stratified center and segmental periphery (*center and periphery*), between which there was a key and institutionalized differentiation in the control of economic resources and information. This division has lost its significance due to assimilation and globalization. The hierarchical arrangement has changed to a heterarchical one. Modern society is characterized by the development of a primarily functional differentiation into socially equivalent and operationally closed subsystems (*functional differentiation*). In recent years, consensus has been promoted on ten basic functional subsystems – political system, economy, science, art, religion, legal system, sport, health system, education and mass media (Roth 2014, 41–3; Roth and Schütz 2015; Plaza-Úbeda et al. 2019).

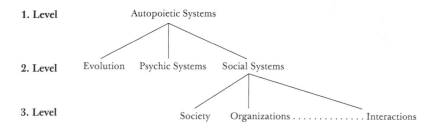

Fig. 3: Three levels and typologies of social systems (Luhmann 1996, 2; Kühl 2020, 391, modified).

On a more detailed level, Luhmann distinguishes between three types of social systems – (i) *society*, (ii) *interactions* and (iii) *organizations*, which reproduce in different ways by communication. [Fig. 3] The society includes all communications and automatically with them the other two types of social systems. Communication creates the boundaries of society, there are no communications outside society.

Niklas Luhmann understands his theory as a tool for the study of modern *society* in particular, which is characterized by a process of increasingly sharp differentiation of functional subsystems (Luhmann 2012, 113–250; Seidl 2005, 36–8; Gren and Zierhofer 2003, 618–21; Mingers 2002, 288–9). Each subsystem, understood as a closed communication network, has its own unique binary code, symbolic medium, program and function or agenda. The *binary code* determines what is good/bad, negative/positive, or acceptable/unacceptable to the system. According to this code, the subsystem communicates with its environment and determines what and to what extent is relevant to it and what is not. It is precisely in this way that it sets its boundaries. For example, for the economic subsystem, it is to pay/not pay or to have/not to have, for the legal subsystem, legal/illegal, for the scientific, truth/lie, for the political, to have power/not to have power or power superior/subordinate, and so on. Only communications that carry a specific binary code can participate in the reproduction and operations of the relevant subsystem (all binary codes express belongs/does not belong to the system). Each subsystem has specific rules for code interpretation (*program*), according to which it sorts communication events and determines their relevance. The binary code is stable and characterizes the system, while the program can change, such as the paradigm in science, law in the legal system, or the monetary system in the economic system. This distinction between stable code and variable program allows for internal changes to subsystems. Each subsystem has its own *symbolically generalised media*, which mediate meaning within the subsystem and are also a measure of success (therefore also success media; Lee 2000, 326). For instance, for the economic system, it is money (with income/without income), for a political system, power (winner/loser), for an education system, marks (passed/fail), for a legal system, the existing law. In an ideal modern society, all functional subsystems are equal, none of them is dominant. They are autonomous, everyone follows their binary code and program, they are not directly connected and they create an environment with each other. At the same time, they are perceived and their irritations can lead to resonance in the second system. Specific forms of structural coupling are created, where one operation can have the nature of two/more communications in two/more subsystems. For example, the economic and legal subsystem are coupled by means of property law and the relevant contracts, the political and legal subsystem by constitutional law, the economic and political subsystem by taxes, and so on.

The second distinct type of social systems are direct *interactions*, in which communication is based on direct physical perception of the participants (face-to-face copresence), that is, senders and addressees (Chettiparamb 2020, 434–5; Seidl 2005, 38–9; Gren and Zierhofer 2003, 618, 625–6). It can be said that in this case the distinguishing binary code is presence/absence. Only those persons who are present (more precisely, considered present) influence communication in the interactive social system. During a pair's conversation on the street, only this couple is present, passers-by are considered absent. Interaction systems can be seen as a substrate for functional systems. Metaphorically, it is conceivable that functional subsystems float in a sea of ever-evolving and declining interaction systems.

Great attention is paid by research to the third main type of social systems – *organizations* (organizational systems), which reproduce themselves based on *decisions* (Seidl 2005, 39–46; Gren and Zierhofer 2003, 626). The decision is defined as a specific type of communication and is again attributed not to human beings, but to the social system – the organization. While normal communication communicates some content selected from the possible ("I love you"), decisions implicitly or explicitly state that other options may have been selected ("We will buy electronic publications [not printed books]"). The organization has specific initial assumptions for making decisions based on previous decisions, as well as programs or a plan. Each organizational system is connected to at least one functional subsystem, whose binary code and symbolic medium it uses. Organizational systems can therefore be considered to be a network of specialized communications and a structure of functionally specific decisions. Monophonic organizational systems are primarily tied to just one subsystem, and therefore have only one primary medium and coding for creating their program. However, this does not preclude them from being secondarily linked to other functional subsystems. Heterophonic organizational systems are equally tied to multiple functional subsystems and can use more media. This leads to conflicts of incomparable values and programs (Andersen and Born 2007, 176–7).

Luhmann's theory is based primarily on the description of developmental tendencies within modern society, which is characterized by a sharp differentiation of social systems at the level of society, interaction and organization, as well as functional subsystems within society (Kühl

2020, 496; Drepper 2005). A characteristic of functional subsystems in modern society is open participation, because anyone can participate in their communication, the decisive factor is whether the communication corresponds to the binary code and program of the functional subsystem. The organization differs in that only communication concerning its members is relevant to them. Organizations are therefore defined not only by the type of communication (decision), but also by the people (membership). The modern organization itself decides on non-/membership and all persons are equal on entry (Kühl 2020, 499–500).

An essential element of Luhmann's concept is the fact that social systems – unlike physical things in space – are not mutually exclusive. This is because one and the same communication can be integrated into multiple social systems at the same time. It can belong to the interactive social system as well as the organization and the functional subsystem at the same time. Social systems of different types are thus nested or equally combine (Kühl 2020, 508–9; Luhmann 1982, 86). In terms of the relationship to people, it is conceivable that psychic systems run through a sea of different systems, each with its own meaning, that is, the program and binary codes (Von Schlippe and Hermann 2013, 389).

Luhmann's classification of social systems seems to be open already at the level of the originally tripartite distinction of society, interaction and organizational systems. Many social phenomena of modern society are – at least on the analytical level – candidates for the expansion of social systems in the broad interval between society and interaction systems. [Fig. 3] A model example of the benefits of this approach is a recent study by Stefan Kühl, which defined the common and different features of organizations, movements, groups (of friends) and mono-functional families (Kühl 2020). From his point of view, all these social systems are connected by membership, but it is treated differently in each of them. There are also different forms of communication. Communication leading to taking a decision is typical for organizations, communication about values for a movement, personal communication for groups and intimate communication for monofunctional families. In the case of the family, it is possible to add that anything can be communicated, the content is not important, the communication itself is essential, as it deepens the affiliation and identity.[3] All these social systems separated from society and at the same time from each other only with the crystallization of

---

3   See also Von Schlippe and Hermann 2013, 394–5.

a functionally differentiated society. Similarly, it would be possible to deal with, for example, states, professional groups or religious communities.

The abstract passages above can be concretized by at least one example, namely modern agriculture as a social system (Casanova-Pérez et al. 2015). Agriculture can be perceived as a partial system of a functional subsystem of the economy. Agriculture itself is not homogeneous, but consists of a subsistence and market production. The programme of agriculture is to satisfy the food and other material demands of human beings (Guptill and Peine 2021). Communication operations take place through language and include information contained in various documents relating to law, regulations, agreements, rules, instructions, and so on; its important part is also the collective memory and tradition. The social agricultural system is based on a continuum of physical reality, which is conceptualized as an allopoietic agro-ecological system (Langthaler 2006). The link between agriculture and physical reality are psychic systems that are structurally coupled with them and at the same time are the drivers and controllers of changes in the physical agro-ecological system. [Fig. 4] The coevolution of the psychic systems and agriculture has resulted in specific structural adjustments. Both systems irritate each other. If irritation leads to a change in structure, we speak of resonance. Through the psychic systems, agriculture perceives the information from other communication systems that is compatible with its structure and vice versa. Selected information penetrates agriculture and participates in their autopoiesis (for example, information on prices, interest rates, punishments for illegal production, ecological conditions). Some resonances can stop autopoiesis. The system also knows self-irritation, that is, an internal conflict created by itself. An example is the traditional seasonal prophecies of weather (Mexican *cabañuelas*), which are part of the collective memory of psychic systems and, through structural coupling, enter the agricultural system, especially its subsistence branch. Every family household, farm and peasant community (that is, the organizational systems that comprise the infrastructure of agriculture) evaluates the irritation and self-irritation through its own communication operations, program and functional logic (each has a different farming style). Their resonances are therefore different. Thus, the stoppage of the autopoiesis of the organizational systems, recorded as the abandonment of some farms and land, has no determined, predictable and objectively explainable causes (Casanova-Pérez et al. 2015, 856–60, 862).

The set of individual memories and expectations of the psychic systems is referred to as collective memory. It is a selected set of positive and negative information within all the parts of the agricultural system. Each of them has a different memory. Through structural coupling, this information comes to the consciousness of the psychic systems and influences the ideas that lead to decisions about farming practices within the physical agroecological system. It is therefore perceived as a model representing the physical effect of the autopoiesis of the psychic and indirectly the agricultural systems. What is important is that each part of the agricultural system as well as its organizational infrastructure in the form of farms is influenced by the current assessment of the self-/irritation and its own collective memory. Such a conception allows us to understand the seemingly contingent, irrational, complex and especially extremely variable behavior of agricultural producers in the past and today (Casanova-Pérez et al. 2015, 860–2).

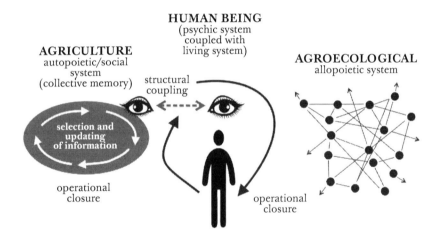

Fig. 4: Links between the agricultural system/collective memory, human beings and the agroecological system (Casanova-Pérez et al. 2015, 861, modified).

Luhmann's theory of social systems is one of the important paradigmatic approaches in a number of scientific areas, at the theoretical, methodological and analytical levels. It significantly shapes the contemporary sociology of law, economics, art, religion or education (summarized, for instance, by Berg and Schmidt 2000; Cadenas and Arnold 2015, 171–2). Its reception can also be observed in the historical sciences, although to a considerably uneven extent. What is significant is that Luhmann's theory offers a framework for grasping and explaining historical processes in a way that allows for broad interdisciplinary interaction within the social sciences. In medieval studies, it seems attractive to follow the medieval beginnings of the functional differentiation of social systems (e.g. Pollack 2013; 2013a; 2015; Steckel 2013; Althoff 2013). There is also an attempt frequently to capture the formation of individual functional subsystems or the identification, description and explanation of the organizational systems (Hirschbiegel 2004; Becker et al. 2004; Dvořáčková-Malá 2009; D'Avray 2017; Arlinghaus 2018; Popić 2019). Many of these studies are partly experimental in their character. The present study belongs to this current in order to show the compatibility of Luhmann's theory of autopoietic social systems with one of the main concepts of European historiography – the medieval transformation.

3 The Medieval Transformation on the Background of Luhmann's Social Theory

Historians and archaeologists point to a fundamental transformation that affected all the spheres of medieval society. It was not a singular but a long-term process gradually connecting social, economic and cultural changes, the sequence of which is an important subject of research. This transformation was not limited regionally but took place in all of the Latin parts of Europe, and it is even possible to say that it defined its boundaries (Bartlett 1993; Alfonso et al. 2007; Graham-Campbell and Valor et al. 2007; Kitsikopoulos 2010; Berend 2012). The development in the Czech lands was placed in the European-wide context particularly by Jan Klápště (1994; 2012; 2016), Josef Žemlička (1997; 2002) and others (Gringmuth-Dallmer and Klápšte et al. 2014). The broader social-theoretical starting points was only reflected on by J. Klápště, who had been inspired i.a. by the concept of the "mutation féodale / de l'an mil' of French social history" (Barthélemy 1997; 2012).

In the first cognitive step, we simplify the complex and chronologically diverse reality into the form of two contrasting images, of which one represents Czech society and the landscape around the year 1000 (Early Middle Ages) and the second circa 1300 (High Middle Ages) (Klápště 1994; 1994a; 2012). The Early Middle Ages was characterized by a unity of the power, religious and production spheres; the market and monetarized economy was almost non-existent on the local or regional level. Both agricultural and non-agricultural production had a more or less subsistence character, while the surplus was exploited by the state power, which organized specialized production and services and also controlled long-distance trade (redistribution mechanism). There were no institutional towns in the Early Middle Ages. We only encounter settlement agglomerations, usually near administrative castles. Agrarian and non-agrarian production was not strictly separated, both of which can be found in approximately the same quality both in the countryside (scattered here) and in agglomerations near castles (concentrated here). Rural settlements were qualitatively similar to each other and it is not possible to observe a more significant hierarchy, which was also reflected in the fact that we assume own burial site for each settlement community. There was no network of parish churches in the rural areas, which were located in administrative castles and in the places of the residence of the duke. The social elites had not yet been separated from state power, which was materially reflected also in the fact that we find their divided residences only in agglomerations near administrative castles. The law was differentiated and tied to the individual social groups into which the individual entered by birth.

In the High Middle Ages, we still find the power and production spheres together, but to some extent the market and monetized economies were already differentiated. Agricultural production was therefore dual in nature, that is, subsistence and market. Market non-agricultural production was tied to towns, only some necessary services remained in the countryside. It is therefore possible to speak of a sharp separation of urban and rural areas, which, however, were also linked by market mechanisms. The countryside was permeated by a hierarchical network of settlements: hamlets – villages – parish villages – market villages. The class of direct landowners was separated from the state power, who leased most of the land in various legal frameworks, most often hereditary to the peasants. The residences of the landlords lay for the most part directly in the countryside. The network of available parish churches enabled the real Christianization of the country. Law took on partly a territorial aspect and the individual acquired it on the basis of a subject relationship – the peasant by taking over the land (*subject* tenants) and the burgher by acquiring real estate in the town.

It is possible to model very well the striking contrasts between the early and high medieval societies. However, controversies arise in the interpretation of the causalities of the medieval transformation. Older interpretations were based primarily on the testimony of the written sources, which evoked the appearance of a sharp turn. As early as the

19th century, therefore, the idea appeared of wide areas of Central and Eastern Europe, which were only sparsely populated, with low economic productivity and outside the influence of first Ancient and later Franconian, or Byzantine world. In the course of the Early Middle Ages, state formations arose here, Christianity spread and the social elites were in close contact with the surrounding world, but this did not change the traditional social and economic structure, sometimes referred to as archaic or pre-feudal. The change, meaning developmental discontinuity, was only brought about by the migration of persons and the transfer of technological and organizational innovations from the second half of the 12th century. This straightforward and flat narrative, which envisages a revolutionary innovative package, is still accepted to this day especially in Anglo-Saxon literature (Melton 2015, 429–37; Berend, Urbanczyk and Wiszewski 2013, 408–9). In the case of the Czech lands, this idea was embodied in the concept of so-called German colonization and formulated in a politically engaged form as part of the so-called Sudeten German historical paradigm.[4]

Alternative views, to some extent inspired by Marxism, questioned the causal role of the mere transfer of people, capital and innovative technologies, and instead sought an answer in the inevitable laws and determined trajectory of historical development. The emphasis was placed on changes in economic production and the subsequent changes in the social sphere. In this context, researchers orientated on a systems approach have highlighted the impact of climate change, demographic growth and advanced agrarian technologies (Klápště 1994, 9–28; Hatcher and Bailey 2001; Kitsikopoulos 2010).

Archaeology has brought a significant shift in understanding the causal connections of the medieval transformation, documenting the ongoing structural changes and at the same time finding innovations across Europe. All European regions have experienced, in principle, a similar but in specific form a different social and economic transformation, where for a certain time they became an active zone of innovation. The driving force of the changes was not the contact of some center and the periphery, as neighbouring areas could develop side by side for a long time without deeper influence, but the internal structural transformation that at a certain time allowed the reception of innovations and their further development. For instance, in the Czech lands (i) the early landed

4   On the historiography, see Leśniewska 2004; Žemlička 2003; 2012; Konrád 2011.

nobility built their separated residences, but these residences did not yet take the form of fortified manors and castles, as we know them from the High Middle Ages; (ii) *subject* peasant holdings and peasant communities were constituted in the countryside, but without formalized (so-called *emphyteutic*) law; and (iii) market mechanisms developed without the existence of institutional towns. According to the current historical concept, there was first a shift in the field of social relations (the emergence of a landed nobility), then crystallization of peasant communities and the development of the preconditions for market agrarian and non-agrarian production. Only in this way could the demand for technological and organizational innovations be formed, which – at the moment – could enter the Czech lands in the form of municipal law, *emphyteutic* law and agrarian technologies (Klápště 1994; 1994a; 2012; 2016).

The reception of this distinctive Czech view, moreover supported by a uniquely combined record of archaeological, written and architectonical sources, still remains relatively limited in contemporary European medieval studies. We believe that one of the causes of this situation is, among other things, the absence of an explicit link to a comprehensive social theory. Such a link, although hardly permanent, will make historical interpretations generally comprehensible and attractive to the social sciences, allow hypotheses to be formulated precisely, identify weaknesses in existing knowledge, and open up new and exciting research perspectives. I believe that the main thought premises of Czech research on the medieval transformation can be very well coordinated with Luhmann's theory of autopoietic social systems. On the part of the historical concept, I consider as connecting links (i) the emphasis on multicausal interpretation and internal structural changes, which take place over a long period of time and gradually in various spheres; (ii) the rejection of any form of determinism, and also a mechanical systems approach; (iii) the secondary importance attributed to migration and innovation; the infinite variability of historical development and differences at the local and regional levels (Klápště 1994).

There is no need to go into details at this point. What is important is that the theory of autopoietic social systems makes it possible to understand the principles of social evolution and differentiation, which, however, has nothing to do with Darwinism. The driving force of evolution is the reduction of complexity. Change and movement are a natural feature of all systems, as structures and processes are not permanently given, but are constantly reproduced as a result of contingent and undetermined selection from infinite possibilities. The structure of systems changes from within and is not determined by the environment, that is, by external factors. Social systems evolve side by side, and a change in one may not cause a change in the other. This is the difference from the traditional system theory, according to which a change of a part leads to a change of the whole. How (and if at all) social systems respond to change in their environment depends on the compatibility of their structures. Systems evolve and interact bilaterally. The theory of social systems thus provides historical research with an analytical tool for studying change and variability, without the need to look for a single primary driving force.

The concept of the medieval transformation aligns surprisingly well with Luhmann's ideal conception of the trajectory of social differentiation in the sense that the primary emphasis on segmental and stratified differentiation, typical of the Early Middle Ages, had receded in favor of territorial center and periphery differentiation and functional differentiation. The hierarchical division permeated the countryside, distinguishing the town and the countryside, as well as the urban centers from one another. The power subsystem was functionally differentiated, from which the sub-systems representing the state, the landlords and the church were divided. The power and production subsystems remained interconnected, but the market economy subsystem began to become divided. In this respect, our attention is drawn to, for example, organizational systems and functional subsystems, which enabled the structural coupling of the power/production and economic subsystems. Thus, the peasantry and peasant holdings (Klír 2020, 36–56; Rösener 1987; Shanin et al. 1990; Shanin et al. 1990a; Ellis 2003, 4–16).

In the Early Middle Ages, we record family households, which constantly emerged and disappeared because they were tied to the demographic family cycle. The medieval transformation brought about a change in that family households were coupled with newly emerged organizational systems – peasant holdings as firmly-set socio-economic units with certain rights and obligations. Family households came and went, but peasant holdings remained. According to social theory – and only hypothetically so far – we perceive the peasant holding as an organizational system constantly reproduced by a chain of specific communications, in which the landlords participated. A peasant holding defined in this way, created as a component of the infrastructure of the power and also production systems, structurally coupled not only with the family household (which itself adjusted to the peasant holding through its structure of expectations in a specific way), but also with the market economic subsystem, other organizational systems as well as the allopoietic material system (farmstead and fields, agroecosystem), but was not existentially dependent on them. It was precisely the communication of the landlords that was decisive, as the peasant holding as a social system existed and developed even without a farming family and a farmstead, as the phenomenon of abandoned peasant holdings shows.

By first looking at family households and peasant holdings as at coupled organization systems, and, second, focusing on communication instead of people, we acquire an important analytical tool to stimulate further empirical research (Von Schlippe and Hermann 2013, 393–5). [Fig. 5] Individual systems differed in communication types, expectations, and context markers; each had its own functional logic (Ellis 2003; Van der Ploeg 2013). This could, on the one hand, cause internal misunderstandings or conflicts, and, on the other hand, lead to structural adjustment and coevolution. We would like to identify the communication patterns, rules of the game and also the patterns of structural coupling in each system. We could further raise questions and ask how the peasant holdings were constituted against the background of the formation of the class of landowners (we mean the bilateral relationship in the form of coevolution) and how they contributed to the distinction of the economic subsystem, separation of agricultural and non-agricultural production and the constitution of towns. We would also aim to understand the monetization and commercialization of internal family relationships in the late Middle Ages and on the threshold of the Early Modern Period (Klír 2020a). At this point, nevertheless, let us continue to consider the material and spatial aspects of the medieval transformation.

We can remain at the example of the rural areas and the peasantry. Early medieval settlements were characterized by a continuity of

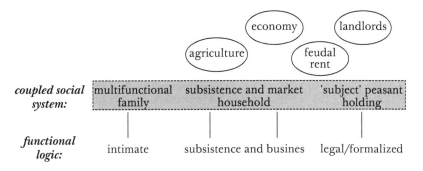

Fig. 5: A family household and a peasant holding as coupled social systems (author).

settlement communities, which have long been associated with certain settlement areas. The communities consisted of temporary family households. Living buildings and outbuildings were therefore not built with the requirement for long durability, their structures were firmly connected to the soil ground, and therefore lasted for a maximum of two to three decades, that is, for about one generation, then rebuilt, which could be associated with various sizes of topographic shift. We are therefore talking about the fact that the settlement was not yet stabilized in the Early Middle Ages. The villages of the High Middle Ages were characterized by relatively well-defined peasant holdings, independent of the fluctuating families. This was related to the stable parceling of the agricultural hinterland and the built-up area of villages, with the land (re)distributed among the individual peasant holdings. It was not until the High Middle Ages that the need for building structures with a claim to duration and also a *stable*, albeit *pulsating* subdivision of the built-up areas arose. The historic village as we imagine it emerged. In this way, we could continue and emphasize the explosion of the material demarcation of boundaries, which at the same time defined different legal systems in the High Middle Ages. Sharp boundaries separated the built-up areas of villages with individual rights from the fields with communal rights (Klír 2020, 433–6; Hopcroft 1999, 1–57; Rösener 1987, 67, 87, 167). The residences of the landlords were symbolically separated from the built-up area. The walls or even simpler ways of physical distinction clearly defined the areas of municipal law. We see in a very concrete way that changes in social systems have had a major impact on spatial behavior and the formation of the physical world. In the following section, we therefore ask what possibilities the theory of autopoietic social systems offers in this regard. To what extent can the form and development of social systems be recognized from the transformations in the physical world recorded by archaeology and geography?

4 Space, Materiality and the Theory of Social Systems

Niklas Luhmann considered the material world and psychic and living systems to be the basic preconditions for the existence of social systems, but they did not have a direct influence on them. Therefore, he put them into the environment of social systems and did not pay deeper attention to them in the elaboration of his social theory (Jacobs and Van Assche

2014, 183–4). One of the ways to systematically integrate space into the theory of social systems was discussed by social geographers Martin Gren and Wolfgang Zierhofer. They drew particular attention to the contrast between Luhmann's reluctance to discuss spatial aspects and, conversely, the detailed elaboration of the concept of time. Nevertheless, in Luhmann's conception, space may not only be a topic of communication, but it may represent a dimension of operations in the sense of a framework of references that allow the observer (that is, the system) a special way of producing distinctions. Gren and Zierhofer further proposed to conceptualize space, along with corporeality, as a prerequisite for accessibility, which is important for the chaining of communications, and thus the evolution and organization of the structures of social systems. Living, psychic and social systems must be accessible to one another so that they can observe each other and that communication between them be possible at all. Space, like some other systems in the environment, regulates/coordinates the selection sequence of operations within social systems. In functionally specialized subsystems, their coordination role is primarily played by their programs (Gren and Zierhofer 2003, 621–5; Kessler and Helmig 2007, 245–6).

Gren and Zierhofer further suggested expanding the definition of interaction systems to include other forms of the presence or accessibility of living, psychic and social systems than just physical presence. It therefore speaks of *accessibility systems*, in the formation of which both living and psychic systems also participate. For this reason, accessibility systems are not seen as social systems, but as the systems by which social systems are coordinated. In a similar way, they also approach organizational systems, which they perceive as an infrastructure of functional subsystems. Organizational systems necessarily involve specific coordination of social, living, psychic and also material (allopoietic) systems (Gren and Zierhofer 2003, 625–6).

In a modern, globalized and functionally differentiated society, territorial and regional boundaries are important for internal differentiation. That is, they do not have such an operational quality to distinguish what belongs to a functional system and what does not (Kessler and Helmig 2007). However, they represent a way of distinction within functional systems, which is realized through organizational systems, or accessibility systems. Material and/or geographic delimitation thus determines the adequate functional logic of the organizational systems. An example is a family business, in which the meaning of communication depends on whether it takes place in the office or at home. Failure to respect the spatial context leads to misunderstanding, misinterpretation of information and conflicts.[5] It can be said that a large part of social systems, and especially organizations, depend on the coordination of psychic, living and material systems, which the theory of social systems should also take into account (Gren and Zierhofer 2003, 626–9).

However, there are many ways to treat space in accordance with the theory of autopoietic social systems (Kessler and Helmig 2007, 242, 245–9; Egner and Von Elverfeldt 2009; Lippuner 2007; 2010; Kühl 2020). An extremely exciting solution was offered by the German social geographer Alexander Koch (2005).[6] According to his arguments, spatial systems can be understood as autopoietic, self-referential systems, which themselves are formed by differentiation from the environment (Koch 2005, 11). He thus rejected other possible conceptualizations such as (i) the identity of spatial and social systems, (ii) the identity of spatial systems and the environment of social systems, (iii) considering space as the fourth dimension in which social systems operate, (iv) considering space as a topic of communication within social systems, and (v) considering space as the limits of the social system (Koch 2005, 11; Kessler and Helmig 2007, 246; Gren and Zierhofer 2003).

The concept of spatial systems and their relation to social systems are not trivial and require a whole sequence of statements (Koch 2005, 5–11; Vis 2009, 111–20). First, Alexander Koch believes that the theory of autopoietic social systems implies reciprocal relationships between social and spatial characteristics. Therefore, it is necessary to admit a symmetry between the social construction of space and the spatial construction of society. Second, he suggests considering space as one of the specific representations of the real physical world that is otherwise inaccessible to us. One of the ways to approach the spatial representation of the real world is offered by the concept of multi-stage translation of the philosopher Vilém Flusser, which says that we perceive the real world based on a combination of several different representations and reductions. Third, Flusser's concept of translation is in some aspects close to actor-network theory, which assumes more ways of translation by which objects and spaces are mobilized in networks. Specifically, for the translations of objects and spaces, a circle of references is assumed including the *semiotics of materiality* (an object or space is formed by relations to other objects

---

5   See context marker, Von Schlippe and Hermann 2013, 390, 393, 395
6   See also Vis 2009, 111–26

and spaces), *material heterogeneity* (nothing has only one, for instance, social dimension), *topology* (variable relations between objects and/or spaces) and *performativity* (objects and spaces mutually limit one another). This circle of references makes it possible to conceptualize space as a product, where spatial characteristics influence objects as well as social relations and characteristics. Fourth, with the help of actor-network theory, it is possible to connect spatiality and sociality with the concept of framed interaction. It says that every social interaction of human beings is realistically or virtually framed, or localized. It thus follows that social interactions are reduced to those that are possible in a given context. Or, the number of potential social interactions is reduced by space. A. Koch presents the example of a building with the function of a post office, in which we will not deal with intimate problems with the post official.

Based on this series of explanations and justifications, Koch gives the characteristics of spatial systems and suggests a way to understand their relationship to social systems (Koch 2005, 6–12; Vis 2009, 120–1). Koch considers the spatial system to be an autopoietic, self-referential system that creates itself by distinction itself from its environments. Whereas social systems are created based on *meaning* in social, temporal and functional dimensions, the spatial systems are based on the *congruency* of the geometric and topological dimensions and also fuzziness in a geocomputational sense. [Fig. 6] Communication in spatial systems is specific and consists of networks, places and locations. Or, a spatial system is created as a selection of a number of networks, places, and locations, where, in this sense, the network includes the fullness of relations that exist during the communication process. Social systems create an environment for spatial systems and vice versa. Both systems are structurally coupled and observe and irritate one another. Koch also elaborated a model of translation that describes the way in which autopoietic social and spatial systems can understand each other.

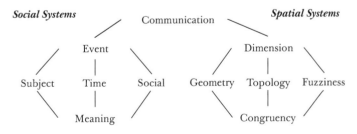

Fig. 6: Communication in social and spatial systems (Koch 2005, 7, modified).

Koch (2005, 7, 12) presents the example of the family as a social system and the home as a coupling spatial system. For the emergence and existence of the social system of the family, it is necessary that it be coupled both with psychic systems and a spatial system. The spatial system of the home is further coupled with the physical house (an allopoietic architectonic system). The elements of the autopoietic spatial system are not the rooms or the garden, but the congruent interplay of their shapes (*geometry*), spatial relations (*topology*) and *fuzziness*. We imagine that many places in a network of rooms can accommodate social interaction, but only when this interaction takes place does location occur. And it is precisely the chaining of locations through networks and a number of places that generates the spatial system of the home.

The concept of structurally coupled social and spatial systems says that there is no direct and predictable relationship between them. There is no determined relationship between spatial and allopoietic (physical, architectonic) systems. Space has the role of a reference framework for the social system. It is also true that social and spatial systems can be materially consolidated by the transformation of nature (Vis 2009, 125–6). Some of the paths thus close for archaeology others open. We cannot reconstruct society from the physical world (more precisely from its translation), but the empirical research of their coevolution and structural coupling is all the more exciting for that.

Another promising way to approach space, materiality and corporeality was suggested by the Danish rural sociologists Egon Noe and Hugo F. Alrøe (2006; 2012). According to them, Luhmann's set of autopoietic systems can be supplemented by a fourth type – heterogeneous systems, represented by a complex network of social, biological and technical relationships. Examples of autopoietic heterogeneous systems are farming systems. In the first step, it is once again necessary to start from the actor-network theory, according to which the system does not create the elements of the physical world (persons, things, buildings, land), but the way of their translation in the actor's project. In the network, only some characteristics of mobilized physical entities are emphasized and developed. In other words, in the creation of a farming system, it is possible to choose from a large number of persons, things, pieces of the landscape, organizations or institutions, and from the infinite possibilities of their translations, that is, the ways of their engagement in the system. The entities integrated into the farming system acquire their form and role through their relationships and interactions, so they are not directly determined by the characteristics of the real physical and dynamic objects. An example is a cow that each actor imagines differently (for instance, a highly productive dairy cow in the concept of a farmer and a banking consultant, a clean cow in the concept of a milker, a beautiful cow in the concept of a farmer's wife, a happy organic cow in the concept of a consumer, a healthy cow in the concept of a veterinarian and so on). However, the actor-network theory does not solve the question of the system or network boundary, that is, what still belongs to it and what does not. It is precisely the theory of autopoietic systems that answers this question. The life and functioning of the system presuppose differentiation from the environment, that is, a reduction of complexity. Determining the meaning, that is, the code of selection, in the case of a farming system a coherent production strategy (specialization) serves this purpose. Accordingly, entities from the physical world are integrated into the system and the method of their translation (mobilization) is determined. For the system not to collapse from an excess of possibilities, it must set the boundaries of what still makes sense to perceive. Therefore, each farming system builds its own subjective world, the central theme of communication, internal logic, and rationality. It determines its structure of expectations, the way it responds to external irritations and also the potential for structural coupling. The concept of heterogeneous autopoietic systems offers an alternative for empirical research and understanding of complex bodies composed of social, economic, technical and natural elements and interactions. In our case discussed above, the medieval family households and peasant holdings. In practice, we would prefer it to a relatively complex concept of coupled social and spatial systems.

5 Conclusion

The theory of autopoietic social systems has the potential to connect historical sciences with the dynamic world of social sciences. The intersectional node is the desire to understand the principles of social change and the opportunity to influence its course in the future. Historians and archaeologists appreciate that it allows a liberation from deterministic views, the questioning of the predictable role of exogenous factors and the existence of one optimal solution. Belief in a one-sided chain of causalities, triggered by external forces, appears to be a naive delusion. Instead, the theory of autopoietic social systems offers us a number of diverse perspectives explaining social diversity and the apparent contingency of the trajectory of historical development. The concept that social systems persist even if their internal structure as well as the environment change radically is also attractive. Luhmann's social systems can perceive one another, develop together, but the links between them are never direct. Each social system creates a specific arena, where its own rules and values apply, which determine what enters it and what on the contrary does not. On an empirical level, therefore, we are tempted to observe the logic around which individual social systems, as autonomous entities, are constituted and reconstituted.

Niklas Luhmann's universal social theory remains open, is the subject of controversies, criticism and modification (e.g. Cadenas and Arnold 2015). So far, it is used primarily for synchronic social research, so in the form of an experiment we turned our attention to the deep past and tried to unravel the series convergent changes that European society and the Czech lands experienced in the medieval period. Significant changes have identified here in the ways of social differentiation, the distinction of new functional subsystems and profiling of the relevant organizational infrastructure, that is, the phenomena and processes characteristic of the entire Latin part of medieval Europe. Of course, development did not stop and we could continue with the social transformation on the threshold of the Early Modern Period, which, however, was of a markedly divergent nature and divided Europe in the way we still experience today.

Great potential can be seen for a complex historical interpretation in the integration of materiality, spatiality and corporeality into the theory of autopoietic systems. We can be inspired, among other things, in social geography and rural sociology, where some researchers have combined the theory of autopoietic social systems with a well-established but seemingly opposite actor-network theory.

Translated by Sean M. Miller.

References

Alfonso, Antón María Isabel et al. 2007. *The Rural History of Medieval European Societies: Trends and Perspectives*. Turnhout: Brepols.

Althoff, Gerd. 2013. "Differenzierung zwischen Kirche und Königtum im Mittelalter. Ein Kommentar zum Beitrag Detlef Pollacks". *Frühmittelalterliche Studien* 47: 353–67.

Andersen, Niels Åkerstrøm, and Asmund W. Born. 2007. "Heterophony and the Postponed Organization Organizing Autopoietic Systems". *TAMARA: Journal of Critical Postmodern Organization Science* 6 (1/2): 176–87.

Arlinghaus, Franz-Josef. 2018. *Inklusion – Exklusion: Funktion und Formen des Rechts in der spätmittelalterlichen Stadt. Das Beispiel Köln*. Köln: Böhlau Verlag.

Baecker, Dirk. 2001. "Why Systems?" *Theory, Culture & Society* 18 (1): 59–74.

Barthélemy, Dominique. 1997. *La mutation de l'an mil a-t-elle eu lieu?: servage et chevalerie dans la France des Xe et XIe siècles*. Paris: Fayard.

Barthélemy, Dominique. 2012. *Nouvelle histoire des Capétiens. 987–1214*. Paris: Seuil.

Bartlett, Robert. 1993. *The Making of Europe: Conquest, Colonization, and Cultural Change, 950–1350*. London: Penguin.

Becker, Frank et al. 2004. *Geschichte und Systemtheorie: Exemplarische Fallstudien*. Frankfurt am Main: Campus.

Berend, Nora, Przemyslaw Urbanczyk, and Przemyslaw Wiszewski. 2013. *Central Europe in the High Middle Ages: Bohemia, Hungary and Poland, c. 900–c. 1300*. Cambridge: Cambridge University Press.

Berend, Nora. 2012. *The Expansion of Central Europe in the Middle Ages*. Farnham: Routledge.

Berg, Henk de, and Johannes Schmidt. 2000. *Rezeption und Reflexion. Zur Resonanz der Systemtheorie Niklas Luhmanns ausserhalb der Soziologie*. Frankfurt am Main: Suhrkamp.

Cadenas, Hugo, and Marcelo Arnold. 2015. "The Autopoiesis of Social Systems and its Criticisms". *Constructivist Foundations* 10 (2): 169–76.

Casanova-Pérez, Lorena et al. 2015. "El agroecosistema comprendido desde la teoría de sistemas sociales autopoiéticos – The Agroecosystem Understood from the Theory of Autopoietic Social Systems". *Revista mexicana de ciencias agrícolas* 6 (4): 855–65.

Chettiparamb, Angelique. 2020. "Autopoietic Interaction Systems: Micro-dynamics of Participation and its Limits". *International Planning Studies* 25 (4): 427–40.

D'Avray, David L. 2017. "The Origins and Aftermath of the Eleventh Century Reform in the Light of Niklas Luhmann's Systems Theory". In *"Vicarius Petri," "Vicarius Christi". La titolatura del Papa nell'XI secolo. Dibattiti e prospettive*, edited by Fabrizio Amerini, and Riccardo Saccenti, 211–28. Pisa: ETS.

Drepper, Thomas. 2005. "Organization and Society – On the Desideratum of a Society Theory of Organizations in the Work of Niklas Luhmann". In *Niklas Luhmann and Organization Studies*, edited by David Seidl, and Kai Helge Becker, 171–90. Herndon, VA: Copenhagen Business School Press.

Dvořáčková-Malá, Dana. 2009. "K modelu středověkého panovnického dvora jako sociálního systému". *Český časopis historický* 107 (2): 309–35.

Egner, Heike, and Kirsten Von Elverfeldt. 2009. "A Bridge Over Troubled Waters? Systems Theory and Dialogue in Geography". *Area* 41 (3): 319–28.

Ellis, Frank. 2003. *Peasant Economics: Farm Households and Agrarian Development*. Cambridge: Cambridge University Press.

Gerrard, Christopher M. 2018. "Overview. People and Projects". In *The Oxford Handbook of Later Medieval Archaeology in Britain*, edited by Christopher M. Gerrard, and Alejandra Gutiérrez, 3–19. Oxford: Oxford University Press.

Graham-Campbell, James, and Magdalena Valor et al. 2007. *The Archaeology of Medieval Europe 1: The Eighth to Twelfth Centuries AD*. Aarhus: Aarhus University Press.

Gren, Martin, and Wolfgang Zierhofer. 2003. "The Unity of Difference: A Critical Appraisal of Niklas Luhmann's Theory of Social Systems in the Context of Corporeality and Spatiality". *Environment and Planning* 35 (4): 615–30.

Gringmuth-Dallmer, Eike, and Jan Klápště et al. 2014. *Tradition – Umgestaltung – Innovation: Transformationsprozesse im hohen Mittelalter*. Praha: Karolinum.

Guptill, Amy, and Emelie Peine. 2021. "Feeding Relations: Applying Luhmann's Operational Theory to the Food System". *Agriculture and Human Values*. https://link.springer.com/content/pdf/10.1007/s10460-020-10185-8.pdf. Accessed 21 June 2021.

Hatcher, John, and Mark Bailey. 2001. *Modelling the Middle Ages*. Oxford: Oxford University Press.

Hirschbiegel, Jan. 2004. "Hof als soziales System: Der Beitrag der Systemtheorie nach Niklas Luhmann für eine Theorie des Hofes". In *Hof und Theorie. Annäherungen an ein historisches Phänomen*, edited by Reinhardt Butz, Jan Hirschbiegel, and Dietmar Willoweit, 43–54. Köln: Böhlau Verlag.

Hopcroft, Rosemary L. 1999. *Regions, Institutions, and Agrarian Change in European History*. Ann Arbor: Michigan Publishing.

Jacobs, Joren, and Kristof Van Assche. 2014. "Understanding Empirical Boundaries: A Systems-theoretical Avenue in Border Studies". *Geopolitics* 19 (1): 182–205.

Jahraus, Oliver et al. 2012. *Luhmann-Handbuch: Leben-Werk-Wirkung*. Stuttgart: J.B. Metzler.

Johnson, Matthew. 2010. *Archaeological Theory: An Introduction*. New York: Wiley-Blackwell.

Kessler, Oliver, and Jan Helmig. 2007. "Of Systems, Boundaries, and Regionalisation". *Geopolitics* 12 (4): 570–85.

Kitsikopoulos, Harry. 2010 "Social and Economic Theory in Medieval Studies". In: *Handbook of Medieval Studies: Terms, Methods, Trends*, edited by Albrecht Classen, 1270–92. Berlin, New York: De Gruyter.

Klápště, Jan. 1994. "Změna – středověká transformace a její předpoklady: transformation – la transformation médievale et ses conditions préalables". *Památky archeologické* 85 (2): 9–59.

Klápště, Jan. 1994a. *Paměť krajiny středověkého Mostecka*. Praha: Státní galerie výtvarného umění.

Klápště, Jan. 2012. *The Czech Lands in Medieval Transformation*. Leiden, Boston, MA: Brill.

Klápště, Jan. 2016. *The Archaeology of Prague and the Medieval Czech lands, 1100–1600*. Sheffield: Equinox.

Klír, Tomáš. 2020. *Rolnictvo na pozdně středověkém Chebsku. Sociální mobiluta, migrace a procesy pustnutí*. Praha: Karolinum.

Klír, Tomáš. 2020a. "Rural Credit and Monetarisation of the Peasantry in the Late Middle Ages: The Eger City State c. 1450". In *A History of the Credit Market in Central Europe*, edited by Petra Slavíčková, 113–30. London, New York: Routledge.

Koch, Andreas. 2005. "Autopoietic Spatial Systems: The Significance of Actor Network Theory and System Theory for the Development of a System Theoretical Approach of Space". *Social Geography* 1 (1): 5–14.

Konrád, Ota. 2011. *Dějepisectví, germanistika a slavistika na Německé univerzitě v Praze 1918–1945*. Praha: Karolinum.

Krause, Detlef. 2001. *Luhmann-Lexikon. Eine Einführung in das Gesamtwerk von Niklas Luhmann 3*. Stuttgart: Lucius & Lucius.

Kühl, Stefan. 2020. "Groups, Organizations, Families and Movements: The Sociology of Social Systems between Interaction and Society". *Systems Research and Behavioral Science* 37 (3): 496–515.

Kühne, Olaf. 2019. "Autopoietische Systemtheorie und Landschaft". In *Handbuch Landschaft. Raumfragen: Stadt – Region – Landschaft*, edited by Olaf Kühne et al., 91–103. Wiesbaden: Springer.

La Cour, Anders, and Andreas Philippopoulos-Mihalopoulos et al. 2013. *Luhmann Observed: Radical Theoretical Encounters*. Houndmills, Basingstoke, Hampshire: Palgrave Macmillan.

Langthaler, Ernst. 2006. "Agrarsysteme ohne Akteure?" *Jahrbuch für Geschichte des ländlichen Raumes* 3: 216–38.

Lee, Daniel. 2000. "The Society of Society: The Grand Finale of Niklas Luhmann". *Sociological Theory* 18 (2): 320–30.

Leśniewska, Dorota. 2004. *Kolonizacja niemiecka i na prawie niemieckim w średniowiecznych Cze-chach i na Morawach w świetle historiografii.* Poznań, Marburg: Poznańskie Towarzystwo Przyjaciół Nauk – Herder Institut.

Lippuner, Roland. 2007. "Kopplung, Steuerung, Differenzierung zur Geographie Sozialer Systeme". *Erdkunde* 61 (2): 174–85.

Lippuner, Roland. 2010. "Operative Geschlossenheit und strukturelle Kopplung. Zum Verhältnis von Gesellschaft und Umwelt aus systemtheoretischer Sicht". *Geographische Zeitschrift* 98 (4): 194–212.

Luhmann, Niklas. 1977. "Differentiation of Society". *The Canadian Journal of Sociology/ Cahiers canadiens de sociologie* 2 (1): 29–53.

Luhmann, Niklas. 1982 "Interaction, Organization, and Society". In *The Differentiation of Society*, 69–89. New York: Columbia University Press.

Luhmann, Niklas. 1989. *Ecological Communication.* Translated by John Bednarz, Jr. Chicago, IL: University of Chicago Press.

Luhmann, Niklas. 1990. *Essays on Self-Reference.* New York: Columbia University Press.

Luhmann, Niklas. 1995. *Social Systems.* Translated and edited by John Bednarz, Jr., and Dirk Baecker. Stanford, CA: Stanford University Press.

Luhmann, Niklas. 2000. *Organisation und Entscheidung.* Opladen: Westdeutscher Verlag.

Luhmann, Niklas. 2012. *Theory of Society. Vol. 1.* Stanford, CA: Stanford University Press.

Luhmann, Niklas. 2013. *Theory of Society. Vol. 2.* Stanford, CA: Stanford University Press.

Mathias, Albert. 2019. "Luhmann and Systems Theory". *Oxford Research Encyclopedia of Politics*, https://oxfordre.com/politics/view/10.1093/acrefore/9780190228637.001.0001/acrefore-9780190228637-e-7. Accessed 30 May 2021.

Melton, Edgar. 2015. "The Agrarian East". In *The Oxford Handbook of Early Modern European History, 1350–1750: Volume I: Peoples and Place*, edited by Hamish Scott, 428–54. Oxford: Oxford University Press.

Mingers, John. 1995. *Self-Producing Systems: Implications and Applications of Autopoiesis.* New York: Plenum Press.

Mingers, John. 2002. "Can Social Systems be Autopoietic? Assessing Luhmann's Social Theory". *The Sociological Review* 50 (2): 278–99.

Noe, Egon, and Hugo F. Alrøe. 2006. "Combining Luhmann and Actor-network Theory to See Farm Enterprises as Self-Organizing Systems". *Cybernetics and Human Knowing* 13: 34–48.

Noe, Egon, and Hugo F. Alrøe. 2012. "Observing Farming Systems: Insights from Social Systems Theory". In *Farming Systems Research into the 21st Century: The New Dynamic*, edited by Ika Darnhofer, David Gibbon, and Benoît Dedieu, 387–403. Dordrecht: Springer.

Olsson, Lennart et al. 2015. "Why Resilience is Unappealing to Social Science: Theoretical and Empirical Investigations of the Scientific Use of Resilience". *Science advances* 1 (4), https://advances.sciencemag.org/content/1/4/e1400217. Accessed 22 June 2021.

Plaza-Úbeda, José Antonio et al. 2019. "The Contribution of Systems Theory to Sustainability in Degrowth Contexts: The Role of Subsystems". *Systems Research and Behavioral Science* 37 (1): 68–81.

Pollack, Detlef. 2013. "Die Genese der westlichen Moderne. Religiöse Bedingungen der Emergenz funktionaler Differenzierung im Mittelalter". *Frühmittelalterliche Studien* 47: 273–305.

Pollack, Detlef. 2013a. "Replik auf die Beiträge von Sita Steckel und Gerd Althoff". *Frühmittelalterliche Studien* 47: 369–77.

Pollack, Detlef. 2015. "Die Genese der westlichen Moderne: religiöse Bedingungen der Emergenz funktionaler Differenzierung im Mittelalter". In *Postsäkularismus. Zur Diskussion eines umstrittenen Begriffs*, edited by Matthias Lutz-Bachmann, 289–333. Frankfurt am Main: Campus Verlag.

Popić, Tomislav. 2019. "Traces of the Past and Social Realities: Late Medieval Court Records from Dalmatian Cities". *Open Library of Humanities* 5 (1), https://olh.openlibhums.org/article /id/4570/. Accessed 22 June 2021.

Rösener, Werner. 1987. *Bauern im Mittelalter*. München: Verlag C.H. Beck.

Roth, Steffen, and Anton Schütz. 2015. "Ten Systems: Toward a Canon of Function Systems". *Cybernetics and Human Knowing* 22 (4): 11–31.

Roth, Steffen. 2014. "The Multifunctional Organization. Two Cases for a Critical Update for Research Programs in Organization". *TAMARA: Journal for Critical Organization Inquiry* 12 (3): 37–54.

Seidl, David. 2005. "The Basic Concepts of Luhmann's Theory of Social Systems". In *Niklas Luhmann and Organization* Studies, edited by David Seidl, and Kai Helge Becker, 21–53. Herndon, VA: Copenhagen Business School Press.

Shanin, Theodor et al. 1990. *Defining Peasants: Essays Concerning Rural Societies, Expolary Economies, and Learning from Them in the Contemporary World*. Oxford, Cambridge, MA: Blackwell Publishing.

Shanin, Theodor et al. 1990a. *Peasants and Peasant Societies*. Oxford: Oxford University Press.

Steckel, Sita. 2013. "Differenzierung jenseits der Moderne. Eine Debatte zu mittelalterlicher Religion und moderner Differenzierungstheorie". *Frühmittelalterliche Studien* 47: 307–51.

Stichweh, Rudolf et al. 1999. *Niklas Luhmann. Wirkungen eines Theoretikers*. Bielefeld: Verlag Bielefeld.

Stichweh, Rudolf. 2011. "Niklas Luhmann". In *The Wiley-Blackwell Companion to Major Social Theorists*, edited by George Ritzer, and Jeffrey Stepnisky, 287–309. New York: Wiley-Blackwell.

Tiffert, Alexander. 2013. "Everything Changes – systemische Ansätze für das Change Management." In *Führung von Vertriebsorganisationen*, edited by Lars Binckebanck, Ann-Kristin Hölter, and Alexander Tiffert, 381–401. Wiesbaden: Springer Gabler.

Trigger, Bruce G. 2006. *A History of Archaeological Thought*. Cambridge: Cambridge University Press.

Tyrell, Hartmann. 2015. "Interaktion, Organisation, Gesellschaft – Niklas Luhmann und die Soziologie der Nachkriegszeit". *Soziale Systeme* 20 (2): 337–86.

Van der Ploeg, Jan Douwe. 2012. "The Genesis and Further Unfolding of Farming Styles Research". *Historische Anthropologie* 20 (3): 427–39.

Van der Ploeg, Jan Douwe. 2013. *Peasants and the Art of Farming: A Chayanovian Manifesto*. Halifax, Winnipeg: Fernwood.

Varela, Francisco, and Humberto Maturana. 1980. *Autopoiesis and Cognition: The Realization of the Living*. Dordrecht: Reidel.

Vis, Benjamin N. 2009. *Built Environments, Constructed Societies: Inverting Spatial Analysis*. Leiden: Sidestone Press.

Von Schlippe, Arist, and Frank Hermann. 2013. "The Theory of Social Systems as a Framework for Understanding Family Businesses". *Family Relations* 62 (3): 384–98.

Žemlička, Josef. 1997. *Čechy v době knížecí: (1034–1198)*. Praha: NLN.

Žemlička, Josef. 2002. *Počátky Čech královských: 1198–1253: proměna státu a společnosti*. Praha: NLN.

Žemlička, Josef. 2003. "Němci, německé právo a transformační změny 13. století: (několik úvah a jeden závěr)". *Archaeologia historica* 34: 33–46.

Žemlička, Josef. 2012. "The Germans and the Implantation of German Law among the Bohemians and Moravians in the Middle Ages". In *The Expansion of Central Europe in the Middle Ages*, edited by Nora Berend, 237–70. Farnham: Routledge.

Participatory Sense-Making through Bodies: Self-Organizing Principles in the Continuity of Life and Mind

Eva Lehečková and Jakub Jehlička

> He raised shape, the ordinary word, from everyday language use.
> Jiří Cieslar: *Hlas deníku*.[1]

> *Everything we do is a structural dance in the choreography of coexistence.*
> Humberto R. Maturana and Francisco J. Varela: *The Tree of Knowledge: The Biological Roots of Human Understanding*

1 Introduction

In his attempt to mediate the essence of the oeuvre created by Vladimír Boudník (the Czech graphic artist immortalized in Bohumil Hrabal's works), film and literary critic Jiří Cieslar assumes that it was the *shape* that Boudník had placed at the center of his universe, profiling it as prominent not only to himself but also, with equal importance, to others in the world. For Boudník the shape is not a static, pleasing composition of lines. Rather it is a product of physically challenging creative action, where the outcome exhales the energy put into its creation. Under the rubric of *Explosionism*, Boudník conceived his action graphics as a participatory sense-making, enactive process, supported by his belief in

---

1 "Tvar, to obyčejné slovo, zdvihl z běžného jazykového užívání." Jiří Cieslar's reference from his *Journal Pages* on Czech graphic artist Vladimír Boudník.

the creative force in every human being. The ultimate potential of such an enactive art form was the "positive reshaping of human society",[2] manifested through situated, individual explosive moments of awe *vis à vis* art. Cieslar's phrasing is congenial in that it relates shape to the world-changing action of raising it from everyday life to an extraordinary and unique experience, showing that language and action are two facets of one and the same reality. With respect to Boudník, it is particularly useful to observe how his artistic and personal uniqueness ossifies over time through a sort of cult-building in the memories shared by his peers and Hrabal's novels, alongside critical reflections of his work. It is in this context that Cieslar longs for the sedimented patina to be stripped away, that we might touch upon the authentic self of the artist.

It this study, we address the "structural dance in the choreography of coexistence" (Maturana and Varela 1992, 248). While not taking this quote as purely metaphorical, we examine the enactive potential of hands in literal motion in two contexts: in contemporary performances of the noted romantic ballet d'action *Giselle*, and in the way that co-speech gestures are manifested in spontaneous everyday interactions. We elaborate on the tension between the conventional and the extraordinary in these situations, and how the perceiver of the action contributes to their assessment as such through the loop of participatory sense-making by bodies.

2 From Embodied Mind to Intercorporeality

The kinship of body and language in the context of social semiotic processes has long been recognized. This is manifested, *inter alia*, by a tendency to subsume both under a common denominator. However, this recognition can mean two different things: either we appreciate the gestural potential in any communicative behavior (Merleau-Ponty 1945; Goodwin 2000), or we adhere to the inverse position:

> Language itself, that infinitely unstable entity which expands and contracts under our very eyes as we attempt to pin it down, now causing us to conclude that there is nothing – gestures, commodities, sex, eating – which is not essentially language to its very core.[3] (Jameson 1974, 536)

---

2   For the basic information about Boudník's work see e.g. https://www.artlist.cz/en/vladimir-boudnik-101681/.

3   Cited by Di Paolo, Cuffari, and De Jaegher 2018, 107.

However, the genuine curiosity about the specifics of the relationship between language and body is permeating the pluralized field of linguistics rather slowly. This curiosity is driven by (i) *cognitive linguistics*, which, in its pursuit of the general cognitive principles underlying the knowledge of language, raises awareness about the effect of embodiment on the construal of linguistic structures,[4] accentuating the fact that knowledge is experiential; (ii) *interactional linguistics*, led by an interest in situated communicative events, in which the enactive contribution of the living body cannot be excluded (Goffman 1966; Streeck, Goodwin and LeBaron 2011). Although both of these streams of thought are contributing substantially to the current rise of linguistic research into multimodality, the significantly distinct reasons why these approaches originally took an interest in the body result from a certain restraint with regard to attempts to integrate cognitive and interactional perspectives on multimodality into more robust socio-cognitive accounts. And yet, the intricate body-language relationship represents one of the crucial questions in contemporary linguistics, and solid answers have yet to be found, as aptly addressed by Jordan Zlatev:

> Is linguistic meaning grounded in bodily experiences or in language use? Many would probably wish to say "in both", but how such a synthesis would be worked through is far from obvious, as there is an inherent tension between the "embodiment-based" and "usage-based" ideologies of language. (Zlatev 2016, 563)

The original schism between these approaches results from the difference in their primary focus: for cognitivists, it was the study of the knowledge of language as shaped by mind and represented in the mind of an idealized speaker (*functionalist epistemic frame*); for interactionists, it is the study of the language in use and relevant social practices, including language behavior, that have to be addressed, typically leaving the cognitive underpinnings of these practices aside. Fortunately, recent developments in the respective subfields seem to have broadened the original perspectives and created a shared space where a more elaborate answer to the grounding of linguistic meaning could emerge.

The functionalist approach to mind and mental representation has been challenged by cognitive linguistics itself. Addressing the

---

4   See Johnson 2018 for a recent overview.

predominantly mentalist approach as too reductionist to adequately account for the linguistic reality of everyday language use, cognitive linguists stress either the need to incorporate studies of the speaker, genre and other types of variance with the help of variationist sociolinguistics (Geeraerts 2016), or, under the label of social/interactional cognitive linguistics (Harder 2010; Divjak, Levshina, and Klavan 2016; Wide 2009), they delve into the complexity of speakers' interactional experience, embracing ever-changing situational traits alongside socially and culturally-based conditions on multimodal communication as well as its cognitive and biological underpinnings. Such a divergence from the historically original conception of cognitive linguistics as a purely mentalist enterprise, not only in theory, but in analytical practice, brings cognitive linguistics closer to interactional approaches, including participatory sense-making models, but also raises a crucial question for cognitive approaches: how to embrace both individual and social perspective at the same time within an approach that sets the goal of describing the abstract knowledge of language of an idealized speaker as the strongest driving force of its theoretical and methodological development. Zlatev (2016) suggests that this, in fact, represents a false dilemma, as these two perspectives coexist inseparably in natural experience if observed from the point of view of phenomenology. Cognitive linguistics is particularly susceptible to embracing phenomenology, given its core assumption of knowledge emerging from experience via repetition and conventionalization, and, in the case of novel experience, via re-contextualization and adaptation of familiar linguistic means to new situations and contexts.

Within the approaches to embodied cognition (Johnson 1987; Varela, Thompson, and Rosch 1991), the originally prominent question of assessing to what extent conceptual representation is grounded in sensorimotor schemata or processes has been broadened to embrace the manifestation of embodiment in interaction "in the wild". In other words, the focus now is on *bodily action* not only as (i) the *ground* for cognition (conceptual metaphor, embodied schemata) but as (ii) the *carrier* of cognition. Such a perspective is distinguished by a number of paradigmatic shifts:

A shift from *cognition* as an individual property to *distributed cognition*. In the distributed cognition theories (Hutchins 2006), cognition is understood in terms of the so-called *cognitive ecology*, constituted by interaction and organization of human agents and their situatedness, including the tools, artefacts, and physical space they occupy.

A shift from Cartesian duality towards the idea of *continuity between the mind and the body*. The "mental" can no longer be dissociated from the "corporeal", as cognition is identified with *embodied enaction* (Di Paolo, Cuffari, and De Jaegher 2018). By dissolving this boundary, other dualisms can be discarded, replaced by the continuity between *meaning* and *enacting*.

A shift towards a dynamic and interactional concept of inter-bodily enaction, rather than a generalized and static (in fact, "disembodied") concept of the *body* (Cuffari and Jensen 2013). This shift is marked by the studies of so-called *bodily relativity* (different bodies lead to different conceptualization) that pertains to even the most fundamental concepts such as RIGHT IS GOOD and LEFT IS BAD (Casasanto 2009).

A shift from intersubjectivity ("sharing of affective, perceptual and reflective experiences between two or more subjects"; Zlatev 2008, 215) towards embodied intersubjectivity, or *intercorporeality*, first introduced by Maurice Merleau-Ponty (1945), understood as experiential sharing among (extended) living bodies.

One of the leading proponents of the intercorporeal approach to the study of interaction is Jürgen Streeck, whose particular focus is on gestural practices. He labels his approach as "praxeological", recalling the Marxist use of the term *praxis* to emphasize that communicative (inter-)actions are profoundly social acts, inseparable from the ecology in which they emerge. Streeck turns to the "real-world practice communities, from grocery stores to butcher shops and the workshops of tailors and blacksmiths" (Streeck 2017, 30), ultimately responding to William Labov's early call for the study of *mundane* language production (Labov 1964). A clear example of the praxeological approach is Streeck's case study – a close, ethnographic description of a day in the life of a car mechanic (Streeck 2017). Following his everyday actions, Streeck notices that

> [his] repertoire of gestural sense-making habits […] is the result of ongoing self-making. But by habitually gesturing in certain ways, [he] is also continuously making and remaking the person that he is, and, given that making gestures is a kinesthetic experience, the man who *feels* a certain way. (Streeck 2017, 287)

When approached from the perspective of intercorporeality, the mutual closeness of embodiment and intersubjectivity reveals itself; it is acknowledged that it is in fact phenomenology that allows us to maintain the distinction between individual and social experience, "but without relegating these to different 'worlds'" (Zlatev 2016, 5). Consequently, the shared space of body, language and mind resides in enactive situations of participatory sense-making, where humans engage in joint actions, emanating from shared background experience and situated adherence to joint tasks, which can be fulfilled through communication. By adopting the frame of situated enactive actions involving both bodies in action and minds, all kinds of once unbridgeable reductionisms can be eliminated:[5]

> the enactive perspective takes the life-mind continuity seriously as a way to conceive of mental and biological phenomena not merely as causally connected, but as constitutively linked, without this implying a reduction of psychology to biology. A dialectical understanding of these relations therefore implies that as we move from active matter to life and to the realm of agency and sense-making, we simultaneously move into a sharper understanding of materiality, and also into an understanding of how active matter becomes transformed by mental phenomena. Accommodations occur at all scales. Not only do we have minds that are material and biological, but with minds, biology and materiality become minded, or partake of the complexities of the mind. (Di Paolo, Cuffari and de Jaegher 2018, 110)

Crucially, such an approach allows us to embrace the observed duality in linguistic bodies in action:

> Linguistic bodies are defined by the tendency to make up a coherent identity out of materials that bring into play the influence of other identities. Because of this influence, linguistic bodies are also defined by a countertendency toward decoherence. [...] Linguistic bodies, in other words, are inherently self-contradictory. (Di Paolo, Cuffari and de Jaegher 2018, 194)

Sense-making actions are an *effect* (and, at the same time, *a cause*) of self-making, or *autopoiesis* (Maturana and Varela 1980). This applies not only to an individual's actions but also to the interaction between two

---

5   Another consequence of adopting this perspective is the possibility to eliminate the prediction of the intermediate level of mental representation, dealing with the dynamic processes of self-organizing construal operations instead (see Zlatev 2016; Streeck 2017; Di Paolo, Cuffari and de Jaegher 2018). However substantial for linguistic models this aspect of the enactive theory is, it is not prominent for the focus of this study, and we therefore leave it aside for the time being.

or several living bodies. In this study, we acknowledge the hierarchical nature of the autopoietic organization. A single participant of interaction is understood as an autonomous system interacting with its *Umwelt* (Uexküll [1934] 1992) where the presence of others is always presumed. Two participants interacting with each other represent an autonomous system of a higher level, and so on. The currently embraced co-presence of individual and social experience in linguistic bodies allows us to address the question of how, in a shared space between engaging participants, coherent individual elaboration of one's experience relates to the conventional, shared experience upon which it is built.

3 Self-Organization in Gestural Movements: Alignment and Elaboration

The enactive perspective enables us to perceive the seemingly empty space between the actors (a no man's land of social interaction) as a kind of a three-dimensional projection plane where the inter-corporeally created meaning comes to life, where it is maintained and elaborated, where it vanishes – often only to be revived unexpectedly a few moments later. *Hands* are amongst the most salient sense-making devices that come into play in the physical space between the participants of an interaction.[6]

In gesture studies, the term *shared space* (Özyürek 2000) refers to coordination between two or more gesture spaces (i.e. articulatory spaces delimited by the extent of a speaker's limbs). Shared space should not be understood as a mere juxtaposition of gesture spaces, as it transcends the physical gesture spaces of the speakers involved. It also includes the aforementioned "empty" space between them, which is not empty after all. On the contrary, it is filled with shared conceptual objects, represented gesturally by the speakers and referred to by pointing. For shared space to emerge, the speakers are not required to be in particularly close proximity: they can be established in the situations of monologic public speaking, during remote video calls as well as in live art performances (Garner 2018).

In the qualitative analyses presented in this study, two notions pertaining to the sense-making processes in the shared space are central: *alignment* of gesture and bodily configuration, and multimodal *elaboration*.

---

6   As will be clear from the further discussion, *interaction* is not understood simply as a one-to-one situation with participants facing themselves at close range.

Alignment in this context refers to the situation in which an embodied representation (e.g. an iconic gesture) produced by one participant is adopted or referred to by another participant. In everyday language interaction, alignment is ubiquitous: it helps the participants to navigate discourse or in stance-taking (Haddington 2007). It is not only that the participants represent conceptual entities (both concrete and abstract) through gestures and place them in physical space, point to them and re-create them. Speakers were reported to elaborate on each other's gestural representations, often together with some kind of a participatory sense-making process (Furuyama 2002; Lehečková and Jehlička 2019).

A sequence of multimodal elaboration, generally defined as "augmentation, adaptation, or further processing [of an already established baseline (B)] produc[ing] a structure that may itself function as B at another stage or level of organization" (Langacker 2017, 239) is, in itself, a type of *autopoietic* process. Collaborative shaping of a conceptual object in a shared space may be viewed as a *structural coupling* (Maturana and Varela 1980) between several autonomous systems – the gesturing speakers, who alter certain parameters of their gestures until they reach *structural congruence* (or allow the conceptual entity to vanish). In compliance with the intercorporeal view, we do not view the multimodal representation itself as an autonomous system undergoing a series of perturbations, but as an integral part of the speaker as an extended *lived body* (Husserl 1952) related to the world inhabited by others. Clear-cut cases of *alignment*, such as repetition of the same gestural form, stem from conventionality. *Elaboration*, on the other hand, is induced by creative divergence from conventions. In the following two sections, we will focus on the dynamic relationship between these two tendencies in performative art and in everyday language interaction.

4 "You'd think there'd be nothing left to say"[7]

Premiered in 1841 in Paris, the two-act *Giselle* represents a remarkable example of a romantic ballet d'action,[8] which, in a moving story about a peasant devoted to her lover Albrecht, a count in disguise, introduces

---

7   Winship 2014.
8   It is a hybrid ballet genre that helped to free ballet from the servient function to vocal music during the second half of the 18th century; it combines expressive, i.e. dancing, and symbolic, i.e. codified mime, means to deliver a complex narrative structure.

a plethora of quintessential romantic motives – frank villagers confronted with cultured, yet heartless aristocracy, living bodies succumbing to supernatural creatures, betrayal, madness and death and, above all, love so deep that it gives the power to save life and overcome a deadly curse.

Like other French ballets of this period, including *Le Corsaire* and *La fille mal gardée*, the final version of the dance script for Giselle, dating back to 1884, comes from the ballet icon of the second half of the 19th century, Marius Petipa. Petipa, although of French origin, built a decades-long career as ballet master and choreographer for Imperial Ballet Theatres in Russia. In order to enrich the local ballet repertoire, he introduced new versions of French romantic ballets, which, premiered in Opéra de Paris in the 1830s and 1840s, experienced a subsequent gap in staging not only in Paris but throughout Europe. Thus, by staging them in Russia, Petipa contributed significantly to keeping these pieces in cognizance across generations and stimulating their reintroduction to Europe at the beginning of the 20th century. Petipa's creditable agenda nevertheless has its problematic side as well, sometimes called *Petipa's problem* (Smith 2010).[9] His versions represent the dominant interpretation of these masterworks of romanticism, without explicitly addressing the extent and nature of modifications to the original dance script undertaken in order to better suit the ballets to Petipa's contemporaries adhering to the more classical ballet style of the end of the 19th century. Consequently, the blasting influence of Petipa's choreographic stardom might obscure insight into the staging developments of romantic ballets throughout the 19th century as well as a proper assessment of Petipa's contribution.

In the case of Giselle, the influence of Petipa on the choreography was until recently unanimously believed to be substantial (Krasovskaya 1998). However, a newly discovered manuscript of the dance script of Giselle from the 1860s, created by the choreographer Henri Justamant and published in 2008, allowed us to trace the changes in the script from the original 1841 version as well as in the subsequent Petipa version. Surprisingly, many aspects of the so-called definitive version by Petipa believed to be his inventions (for instance, numerous dance formations of circles, half-circles and crosses) occur in Justamant's manuscript as well. The overall shift from Justamant to Petipa, on the other hand, consists of a reduction in the dramatic scenes without dance, i.e. those employing pantomime (e.g. the original intro of the second act consisting of

---

9   Smith refers to Collins 2009.

non-dancing interactions between hunters from Albrecht's suite) to narrate through dance scenes. This finding puts the alleged radicality of Petipa's modifications into perspective and allows a subtler assessment of the development of the script between the original, the 1860s and Petipa's productions.

Whatever the true nature of Petipa's contribution to the dance script of Giselle, it still constitutes an obligatory starting point for all contemporary classical ballet productions, a long-preserved and repeatedly confirmed canon. The sedimented experience of generations of both the producers and performers on one side and the audience on the other leads to a mutual consent on Giselle as an artefact and sets up an expectation underlying every subsequent production of the ballet. The strong foundation of Petipa's version for Giselle's production offers a convenient opportunity to ask a focal question of this chapter: under the given circumstances, how can a novel experience be evoked? What possibility for innovation and creativity lies within the canon, and how can it be ignited? To address these questions, we will take into consideration the ways of interpreting the first part of the second act from two productions of Giselle. Namely, we will compare two productions of the Royal Ballet in London, the first from 2006, starring the phenomenal ballet couple Alina Cojocaru and Johann Kobborg, the second from 2014, introducing the Russian ballerina Natalia Osipova in her debut at the Royal Ballet paired with principal dancer Carlos Acosta, who retired two years later. Although both were based on Peter Wright's renowned 1960s production, the two performances differ remarkably in how Giselle is portrayed.

Giselle is a ballet of a heroine's transformation, signified by the shift in scenery and atmosphere between the two acts: the first act, set in Giselle's native village, tells the story of a naïve girl who falls for the pleasure-seeking count Albrecht, the subsequent revelation of Albrecht's origin, and an aristocratic wedding announcement leading to Giselle's madness followed by a fatal failure of her fragile heart. Petipa's beginning of the second act introduces the supernatural forest beings – the *Wilis* – with Myrtha as their leader, whose unearthly beauty lures young men into a dance trance where they either find death from exhaustion or, if still alive, are drowned by the Wilis in a lake. Myrtha raises Giselle's corpse from her grave at the edge of the forest to turn her into a Wili.[10]

---

10 The atypical location of Giselle's grave (outside the village graveyard) alongside the particularly cruel demeanour of the Wilis are often interpreted as implicit signs of the fact that only fallen girls betrayed by their lovers could be turned into Wilis.

Contrary to the rules of the supernatural world, Giselle, who is forced to dance with Albrecht, mourning on her grave, fiercely fights her tragic malediction by rejecting a vindictive manner, reviving her human love for Albrecht in her undead corpse and thus breaking the curse of the Wilis at the break of dawn, saving his life and earning herself a return to a peaceful rest in her grave. Dancing Giselle, hence, necessitates depiction of the heroine at all three stages of her life (from loving a peasant to a lover driven mad by betrayal and then to a Wili fighting her tragic destiny in the name of love) and making the transitions believable. It is the second transition that we focus on in the comparison of the two productions from the Royal Ballet.

Alina Cojocaru as Giselle turned into a Wili accentuates the ethereal quality of the heroine through superb execution of limb movements precise both in timing and extension. It is controlled and effortless at the same time. Lines are soft and transitions smooth. This is a Wili that a young hunter can fall madly in love with at first sight because he has never seen anything of such fineness in the world of the living. This, in fact, is a Wili that the classical ballet audience is used to seeing across different staging, as confirmed by the performance DVD review by Margarida Bota Bull: "There is nothing new or revolutionary about this Giselle", but it is "a beautiful production, superbly danced".[11] What we are allowed to be beguiled by is the beauty and technical superiority of the execution.

As mentioned above, the step sequences in both performances, based on Petipa and Peter Wright, are the same. And still, Osipova succeeds in deconstructing the conventional image of Giselle. As if she had dismantled the dance flow into individual components and put them back together in the proper order, but with a different impact on the audience. The audience perceives her Giselle, seen a thousand times before, as if for the first time. An experienced ballet-goer would expect that "there'd be nothing left to say" in Giselle, and yet, what he/she gets is "the most radical [Giselle] I've ever seen" (Anderson 2014). And like the small child in Hans Christian Andersen's tale about the emperor's new clothes, they find themselves pointing at the heroine in bewilderment and shouting: "Look, she is undead!"

Where does the opportunity for Osipova to divert her interpretation from common expectations come from, and to what effect? As the bodily

---

11 http://www.musicweb-international.com/classrev/2008/Nov08/Adam_Giselle_oa0993d.htm. Accessed 15 May 2021.

and, more specifically, limb movements are given, the few things available for modification are timing, range of motion and head and limb orientation. Although the precise differences in the timing of the ballerina's dancing in the second act, for instance in the second-act *pas-de-deux*, is yet to be measured, what matters here is the effect that Osipova evokes through her dancing – and she looks as if she is dancing according to

Fig. 1a: Osipova and Acosta in Act II of Giselle (still from a performance record, modified).

Fig. 1b: Osipova and Acosta in Act II of Giselle (still from a performance record, modified).

some otherworldly tempo unfamiliar to humans. She uses her extraordinary strength and range of motion, in jumps as well as extensions, alongside her typical Russian style of arm work, to embrace the eeriness of the Wili she has been turned into. In so doing, she makes the macabreness of the transitional phase of a peasant into a Wili stand out. By delivering slow jumps of extreme height and by extending her limbs and head at cadaverous angles (both in her solos and in duets with Acosta), Osipova suppresses the superficial prettiness of the Wilis so as to profile their true, nightmarish nature. [Fig. 1a and 1b] In these moments, Osipova dances as if the inner feeling of having become a Wili is almost unbearable to herself, captivatingly translating this emotion to the audience.

In this execution, Giselle is a genuine post-mortem suffering creature. In her dancing, she exhales the dolorous journey she was forced to take. She creates the impression that she is facing an inevitable tragic end: hunting down men for all eternity after dancing Albrecht to death. And it is only in contrast with the materialized destiny of Giselle through Osipova's dancing that we can appreciate the positive effect of forgiveness and sacrifice for love that follows as a heart-breaking outcome of the narration. By showing us a Giselle who is ugly and macabre, Osipova has made us understand what evil disguised in ethereal glory her Giselle had to fight in order to win Albrecht's life and her yearned-for *requiescat in pace*. It is only this perspective, invoked by Osipova's intercorporeal relating to the destiny of her heroine as well as to the audience, which can show that by standing for Albrecht, in spite of his betrayal, she becomes a true heroine, active and game-changing.

Yet the radicality of Osipova's interpretation is not absolute, but relative, tightly bound both to the storyline and the sedimented experience of past productions. As for the former, she builds the development of her heroine on purely logical relations: Giselle's fragile heart in her human life symbolizes an extraordinary, almost supernatural strength of the heart on the abstract, emotional level. Sweet and cordial in her earthly life, she was not naturally inclined to embrace the prospects of the ghostly afterlife. Osipova's Giselle-Willi is born of the same source as one of the numerous incarnations of Ophelia from Hamlet, namely, the one performed by Hana Kvapilová and eloquently praised by the Czech decadent poet and critic Jiří Karásek ze Lvovic:

Rather than the fragrance of freshly picked violets, she radiated the paleness of the cemetery roses. Her madness did not lie in the confusion of the betrayed young heart, but in the experience of seeing through the vanity of life and love. The most tragic Ophelia I have ever seen, she was not only let down by Hamlet, she was betrayed by everything, she was not only mad with herself, but with being in general. For "we know what we are but know not what we may be…".[12] (Karásek ze Lvovic 1927, 173)

As for the latter, Osipova profiles her novel interpretation of Giselle-Wili in relation to the conventional depiction to which she, naturally, owes much. Only through mixing well-known pieces of the choreography with innovative bodily movement execution here and there are the shared expectations of the audience challenged, and the extraordinary can be raised from everyday life:

> We notice that the mechanicality present in the formation of habit by repetition is not only regressive in nature, like "dead leaves floating on the surface of the human soul" (Bergson, 1994, *Laughter*), it is also progressive, enabling motion relative to what is and has to be static [...]. The withering is never meaningful by itself, it becomes meaningful through its reviving function.[13] (Kolman 2020, 164)

Osipova's interpretation of Giselle is more on the gothic side of romanticism, sending unsettling shivers down the audience's spine. While it may constitute a relatable aesthetic to the present-day audience, it is by no means a new facet in Giselle. In fact, the gothic aspects were acknowledged as early as in the original 1840s productions, inhibited only later, for instance among 1940s and 1950s British critics, in order to promote the ballet as romantic, i.e. devoid of the traces of popular culture (Morris 2017).[14] On the whole, what we encounter in Osipova's interpretation is a sophisticated balance between conventionality and creative innovation, the latter stemming from close examination of the inner logic of

---

12   Vyzařovala více bledosti hřbitovních růží než vonnou vlhkostí právě utržených fialek. Její šílení nebylo zmateností oklamaného mladého srdce, ale vědomím zkušeně prohlédnuté marnosti všeho, života i lásky. Nejtragičtější Ofelie, již jsem kdy viděl: nebyla zklamána jen Hamletem, ale byla podvedena vším, nešílila jen nad sebou, ale nad bytím vůbec. Neboť "víme, co jsme, ale nevíme, co z nás bude…"

13   Zároveň si všímáme, že mechaničnost něčeho, jak je přítomna v utváření zvyku skrze opakování, nemá jen regresivní povahu, jako "suché listí na hladině lidské duše" (Bergson, 1994, *Smích*), ale i povahu progresivní, jež umožňuje pohyb jako relativní vůči tomu, co je a musí být nehybné. [...] dané umrtvení nemá svůj smysl nikdy o sobě, ale právě v oné oživující funkci.

14   The fruitful interaction between the gothic aesthetic and the world of romantic ballet can be further supported by E. T. A. Hoffmann's influence on the librettos of the ballets such as Nutcracker and Coppélia.

the story and new ways of conveying the macabre perspective through dance moves. By shifting the most common perspective to profile the latent gothic elements, she promotes some of the original features of the piece, creating an extraordinary relation of Giselle performances across centuries in a head-turning autopoietic loop. In fact, what she applies in "[p]ulling against the choreography's thistledown prettiness" (Mackrell 2014), is Adorno's "objective freedom", when she willingly invites the audience to participate in the enactive process as "[t]he capacities for experience and for positive reaction to something new are identical" (Adorno [1962] 1976, 179).

5 Layers, Dimensions and Units: Participatory Sense-making with Gestures

Over the last two decades, research in the area of gesture studies has proved that gestures accompanying spoken utterances (*co-speech gestures*) are far from being the idiosyncratic and random epiphenomenon of language production that they were previously believed to be. The more we explore co-speech gestures, the more they reveal their underlying systematicity and intersubjective basis.

In spoken interactions, collaborative elaboration of a representation of conceptual entities, co-expressed with co-speech gestures, is a commonplace phenomenon. We illustrate this process with the help of an extract of a conversation from a multimodal corpus of Czech interactions.[15] The segment in focus captures a part of a meeting between five faculty members, two women and three men, discussing methodological issues related to language corpora. It features a multi-party interaction between all speakers present, with a major role of the two female participants (*f01* and *f02*). The main topic concerns the differences between two language corpora. First, the two female speakers establish an understanding that they are in fact talking about two different corpus projects, rather than one as initially assumed, then they take turns in describing the relevant features of the corpora. The male speakers (*m01–03*) play supporting roles, only adding minor comments occasionally.

The first segment of interest commences with the first female participant (*f01*) talking about a language corpus and enquiring of the

---

15   See https://epocc.ff.cuni.cz/czico/.

other participants whether they have had experience of it. Participant *f02* follows up asking if *f01* was talking about the corpus that has an orthographic *transcription*, accompanying the word (*přepsaný*, "transcribed") with an iconic gesture with extended thumb and index finger and a one-time arced wrist movement towards the shared space.[16] [Fig. 2]

Fig. 2: The "transcription" gesture (Kawulok, Kawulok, Nalepa and Smolka 2014, modified).

In the subsequent turn, one of the male speakers (*m01*) replies that the corpus in question has a different kind of transcription, namely conversation-analytic, producing a gesture together with the word *konverzačněanalyticky* ("conversation-analytic"). The gesture mirrors the one produced by *f02* in terms of handshape, position and hand orientation, but differs in movement quality, as *m01* repeats the wrist movement several times rapidly.

The segment continues with a 2-minute passage in which *f02* describes the corpus she has in mind, unable to recall its name. She highlights its characteristic features related to the layers of annotation, again using the same gesture to accompany TRANSCRIPTION concepts. *F01* follows up by describing the different layers of annotation in the corpus she wanted to talk about in the first place. At one moment, she produces the "transcription" gesture twice, but this time not only to represent TRANSCRIPTION. In the first instance she uses it together with an utterance *můžeš si pustit*

---

16   Figures 2–6 have been derived from a free photograph database for hand gesture recognition created by Michal and Jolanta Kawulok with Jakub Nalepa and Bogdan Smolka in 2014. Figures in this study have been modified by the authors.

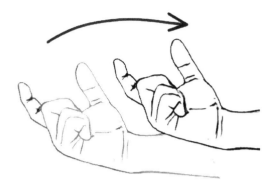

Fig. 3: "You can play the video and take a look at the transcription" (Kawulok, Kawulok, Nalepa and Smolka 2014, modified).

to video – ("you can play the video –"), then she uses it again with the following utterance – *a podívat se na ten přepis* ("– and take a look at the transcription"). [Fig. 3]

The conversation goes on for a moment until speaker *f02* again uses the "transcription" gesture. Now she produces it several times with a straight top-down movement in a cutting-like manner, accompanying *ale jako že to není rozsekaný do replik, že tam nejsou repliky ňák značený* ("it's not cut up into turns, there is no marking of the turns"). [Fig. 4] The gesture is now aligned with *rozsekaný* ("cut-up") and *repliky* ("[conversational] turns").

Hence, the general shape of the "transcription" gesture, introduced as captured in Fig. 2, runs through the segment as a scarlet thread, becoming

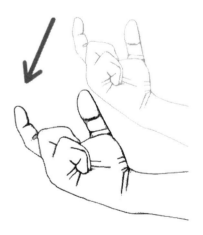

Fig. 4: "It's not cut up into turns" (Kawulok, Kawulok, Nalepa and Smolka 2014, modified).

a key instrument in the process of gradually making sense of the whole situation with the conflicting concepts (first, the two distinct corpora that the speakers talk about, and second, various properties of the corpora in question).

Initially, the shape is an iconic/metaphorical representation of transcription (as a physical act of transposition of two entities following the general metaphorical image schema IDEAS ARE OBJECTS; Lakoff and Johnson 1980). Through the follow-up turns, the gesture becomes a metonymic representation of any structural unit of a corpus referred to (either a video or a conversational turn, or a transcript or a segment of annotation). What we witness here is a process of iconic transparency loss, similar to the "grammaticalization of gestures" in the evolution of sign languages (Pfau and Steinbach 2006). Spontaneous interaction is full of such moments, when traces of *diachronic* processes flash through *enchrony*, a conversational timescale, which enables social actions to take place and to affect one another in linear ordering (Enfield 2014). First establishing the mutual knowledge of situated speakers to the concept of transcription by using the said clearly articulated "transcription" co-speech gesture, the potential for its follow-up alignment as well as elaboration is activated.

The baseline gesture [Fig. 2] has a convenient affordance to be elaborated in several ways. While retaining the general handshape, the movement and hand orientation parameters mutate, generating a wide range of new ways of representation. For instance, the movement variation serves to profile the relationship between the units (transversal axis) or the layers of annotation (sagittal axis). Apart from the elaboration of the "transcription" gesture, another noteworthy phenomenon occurs in

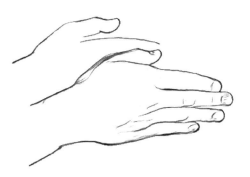

Fig. 5: Palm lateral – open hand gesture moving along the transversal axis (Kawulok, Kawulok, Nalepa and Smolka 2014, modified).

the very same segment of interaction. Immediately after saying "you can play the video and take a look at the transcription" (described above), speaker *f01* changes the configuration of both her hands, articulating a flat hand gesture with the two palms laterally positioned next to each other. [Fig. 5]

Having articulated a new gesture, she says *ale* – ("but"), but before she finishes the sentence, speaker *m01* interrupts her saying *není tam časová o[sa]– není tam časová značka* ("there is no temporal ax[is]– there is no timestamp"). He is apparently prompted by *f01*'s gesture, as he, in his gesture, first represents a span of a temporal axis with a transversal movement of two flat hands, then, with a single hand, represents a certain point on the axis (*časová značka*, "timestamp").

In Western culture and beyond, it is conventional to conceptualize time as a physical entity proceeding along a line in the left-right direction.[17] This spatiotemporal metaphor (Lakoff and Johnson 1980) is embodied in co-speech gestures: temporal expressions are often accompanied by gestural movement across the speaker's transversal axis (Walker and Cooperrider 2016) led from the left, representing past or anterior time points, to the right, representing future as well as posterior moments. This gestural pattern is clearly a part of the shared general knowledge of the speakers involved in the conversation relevant for fulfilling the joint goal they have committed to, namely that of reaching a mutual understanding of the properties of the two corpora in question).[18] Like the "transcription" gesture, the transversal temporal gesture is also adopted by the participants and is further elaborated in the discourse. Profiling a certain point on the temporal axis with a "cutting" gesture is a case of elaboration of the basic image schema prominent in the context of discussing language corpora defined by linear annotation and segmentation.[19]

However, participant *f01* shortly introduces another dimension to the gestural representation of the corpus structure. [Fig. 6] She supplements the transversal movement with movement across the sagittal axis (i.e. along the horizontal line leading off the subject forward) to distinguish between the linear organization of the corpus annotation

17 Depends on the writing system and handedness (Casasanto 2014).
18 On the nature of commitment to a joint task in joint actions, see e.g. Clark 1996, or Matiaso-vitsová and Lehečková 2020.
19 As this type of gestural elaboration of temporal axis representation is not rare, it has been already addressed in the literature, e.g. Calbris 2003.

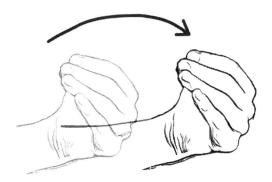

Fig. 6: Movement along the sagittal axis (Kawulok, Kawulok, Nalepa and Smolka 2014, modified).

(transversal) and the relationship between the separate layers of annotation or corpus material. This may be described as a *diagrammatically* iconic representation (Peirce 1931).

Thus, from a conventional metaphor, a new embodied representational pattern emerges. The novel pattern is readily understood by the participants, as it is built upon the shared knowledge of the multidimensionality of language corpus structure. In order to build up such a situated novel conceptualization through intercorporeal enactive action, both the long- and short-term layers of mutual knowledge come into play; without their contribution, the joint task of distinguishing between the two corpora and their shared and distinct properties would be hard to achieve, and the communicative success would be jeopardized. Therefore, the intentional striving for communicative success might play a crucial role as an intrinsic driving force for the emergence of novel semiotic devices through meaning extension and re-contextualization, as predicted for instance by models of language evolution (Steels 2012).

6 Discussion: Intercorporeal Creativity and Illusive Innovation

The two case studies represent two rather distinct communicative situations: performative arts and spontaneous interaction. Disparate as they are, they still involve the very same mechanisms of the creation of the *new* from the *old* on the one hand and sedimentation of the *new* on the other. The fact that this perpetual innovation stems from the autopoietic nature of *performance* (be it *artistic* or *linguistic*) is of course by no means an original observation. It is inherent in the behavior of living things, as "their organization is such that their only product is themselves, with no separation between producer and product" (Maturana and Varela 1992, 48–9).

What we intended to illustrate here was that if we focus on the principles of self-organization, both the emergence of original forms in artistic performance and mundane social interaction can be analyzed in terms of *participatory sense-making*, allowing for a more general approach to human interaction. Taking this stance also ultimately opens up a path to resolving the conceptual tension between *individual cognition* and *intersubjectivity* in contemporary linguistics.

The *body* and its creative affordances were in focus in this study. In the fourth chapter, we examine the modification of a canonical execution of dance movements in ballet. We show that, on the level of the particular performance, what can be seen as radical innovation is, in fact, at the same time contingent on the unearthing of sedimented layers of an old convention. In the fifth chapter, we focused on the role of hand movements in participatory sense-making. We demonstrated how experience is intercorporeally shared and elaborated over an enchronic timescale. Novel forms emerge from various sources: in our microanalysis, we have recognized two different strategies. First, a representation directly construed as iconic becomes an arbitrary symbolic representation, recapitulating a common evolutionary pathway. Second, a conventional multimodal metaphor serves as a baseline for elaboration.

The success of the particular instantiations of the two strategies described above lies in the interplay of many specific factors beyond the scope of this study. To generalize, the crucial prerequisite is that the moments of *incongruence* (produced by structural perturbations to a self-organizing system) cannot happen accidentally. Only the moments when the incongruences are *situated* (Kolman 2020) have the potential to give rise to an intersubjectively shared change. Situatedness is constituted at various levels: to assess something as incongruent, we need to measure it against socially shared conventions as well as the common-ground expectations that emerge during the particular interaction.

Haphazard innovations are predestined to go awry. In the context of spontaneous interactions, such cases are either not elaborated further, or, if they capture the participants' attention, they may prompt a *repair sequence* (Sacks, Schegloff and Jefferson 1974). Subjected to repair, a "faulty innovation" can be provided with additional situatedness. The same applies to the case of Giselle: the triumph of the gothic reimagining of the story connects to the latent roots of the canonical rendition of the piece as well as to other pieces of experience successfully predicted to be available to the audience.

Although we did not focus on *linguistic expression*, we argue that the self-organizing mechanisms observed in the expressive bodily movements do not differ from other semiotic channels, including speech. The only differences are the modality-specific constraints on creativity based on the affordances of the visual-motoric and aural-oral modalities of communication. Therefore, our small-scale analyses support the prediction that participatory sense-making of linguistic bodies is a promising path towards the reconciliation of the individual and social in an adequate theory of semiotically endowed actions: a path where we as individuals engage in creating something unique from what is comfortingly familiar.

References

Adorno, Theodor W. 1976. *Introduction to the Sociology of Music*. New York: Seabury Press. Original edition, 1962.

Anderson, Zo. 2014. "Giselle, ballet review: Carlos Acosta partners Natalia Osipova with devoted care". *Independent* 20 January, https://www.independent.co.uk/arts-entertainment /classical/reviews/giselle-ballet-review-carlos-acosta-partners-natalia-osipova-with-devoted -care-9072989.html. Accessed 15 May 2021.

Calbris, Geneviève. 2003. "From Cutting an Object to a Clear Cut Analysis: Gesture as the Representation of a Preconceptual Schema Linking Concrete Actions to Abstract Notions". *Gesture* 3 (1): 19–46.

Casasanto, Daniel. 2009. "Embodiment of Abstract Concepts: Good and Bad in Right- and Left-Handers". *Journal of Experimental Psychology: General* 138 (3): 351–67.

Casasanto, Daniel. 2014. "Bodily Relativity". In *Routledge Handbook of Embodied Cognition*, edited by Lawrence Shapiro, 108–17. New York: Routledge.

Cieslar, Jiří. 2002. *Hlas deníku*. Praha: Torst.

Clark, Herbert H. 1996. *Using Language*. Cambridge: Cambridge University Press.

Collins, Willa. 2009. "The Petipa Problem". In *Proceedings of the Society of Dance History Scholars Annual Conference*, edited by Marion Kant, and Sarah Davies Cordova, 66–70. Stanford, CA: Stanford University Press.

Cuffari, Elena Clare, and Thomas Wiben Jensen. 2013. "Living Bodies: Co-Enacting Experience". In *Body – Language – Communication. An International Handbook on Multimodality in Human Interaction*, edited by Cornelia Müller, Alan J. Cienki, Ellen Fricke, Silva H. Ladewig, David McNeill, and Sedinha Tessendorf, 2016–25. Berlin: De Gruyter.

Di Paolo, Ezequiel A., Elena Clare Cuffari, and Hanne De Jaegher. 2018. *Linguistic Bodies: The Continuity between Life and Language*. Cambridge, MA: The MIT Press.

Divjak, Dagmar, Natalia Levshina, and Jane Klavan. 2016. "Cognitive Linguistics: Looking Back, Looking Forward". *Cognitive Linguistics* 27 (4): 447–63.

Enfield, N. J. 2014. *Natural Causes of Language: Frames, Biases, and Cultural Transmission*. Berlin: Language Science Press.

Furuyama, Nobuhiro. 2002. "Prolegomena of a Theory of Between-Person Coordination of Speech and Gesture". *International Journal of Human-Computer Studies* 57 (4): 347–74.

Garner, Stanton B. 2018. *Kinesthetic Spectatorship in the Theatre: Phenomenology, Cognition, Movement*. Cham: Springer International Publishing.

Geeraerts, Dirk. 2016. "The Sociosemiotic Commitment". *Cognitive Linguistics* 27 (4): 527–42.

Goffman, Erving. 1966. *Behavior in Public Places: Notes on the Social Organization of Gatherings*. New York: The Free Press.

Goodwin, Charles. 2000. "Action and Embodiment within Situated Human Interaction". *Journal of Pragmatics* 32 (10): 1489–522.

Haddington, Pentti. 2007. "Positioning and Alignment as Activities of Stancetaking in News Interviews". In *Pragmatics & Beyond*, edited by Robert Englebretson, 283–317. Amsterdam: John Benjamins Publishing Company.

Harder, Peter. 2010. *Meaning in Mind and Society*. Berlin: De Gruyter.

Husserl, Edmund. 1952. *Ideen zu einer reinen Phänomenologie und phänomenologischen Philosophie. Zweites Buch: Phänomenologische Untersuchungen zur Konstitution*. Den Haag: Martinus Nijhoff.

Hutchins, Edwin. 2006. "The Distributed Cognition Perspective on Human Interaction". In *Roots of Human Sociality: Culture, Cognition and Interaction*, edited by Stephen C. Levinson, and Nicholas J. Enfield, 375–98. London: Berg.

Jameson, Fredric. 1974. "Review of Marxism and the Philosophy of Language". *Style* 8 (3): 535–43.

Johnson, Mark. 1987. *The Body in the Mind: The Bodily Basis of Meaning, Imagination, and Reason*. Chicago, IL: University of Chicago Press.

Johnson, Mark. 2018. "The Embodiment of Language". In *The Oxford Handbook of 4E Cognition*, edited by Albert Newen, Leon De Bruin, and Shaun Gallagher, 622–40. Oxford: Oxford University Press.

Karásek ze Lvovic, Jiří. 1927. *Tvůrcové a epigoni. Kritické studie*. Praha: Aventinum.

Kawulok, Michal, Jolanta Kawulok, Jakub Nalepa, and Bogdan Smolka. 2014. "Self-Adaptive Algorithm for Segmenting Skin Regions". *EURASIP Journal on Advances in Signal Processing* 2014 (1): 170.

Kolman, Vojtěch. 2020. *Noc, v níž se pořádají medvědí hony na zajíce: filosofický původ jazykové komiky*. Praha: Argo.

Krasovskaya, Vera M. 1998. "Petipa, Marius". In *International Encyclopedia of Dance*, edited by Selma Jean Cohen, 150. Oxford: Oxford University Press.

Labov, William. 1964. "Phonological Correlates of Social Stratification". *American Anthropologist* 66 (6): 164–76.

Lakoff, George, and Mark Johnson. 1980. *Metaphors We Live by*. Chicago, IL: University of Chicago Press.

Langacker, Ronald W. 2017. *Ten Lectures on the Elaboration of Cognitive Grammar*. Leiden: Brill.

Lehečková, Eva, and Jakub Jehlička. 2019. "Gestikulace ve sdíleném prostoru jako kooperativní utváření významu". *Časopis pro moderní filologii* 101 (2): 150–69.

Mackrell, Judith. 2014. "Royal Ballet: Giselle – review". *Guardian* 19 January, https://www.theguardian.com/stage/2014/jan/19/royal-ballet-giselle-review. Accessed 15 May 2021.

Matiasovitsová, Klára, and Eva Lehečková. 2020. "Intersubjektivita ve hře rodiče s dítětem". *Studie z aplikované lingvistiky – Studies in Applied Linguistics* 11 (1): 54–78.

Maturana, Humberto R., and Francisco J. Varela. 1980. *Autopoiesis and Cognition: The Realization of the Living*. Dordrecht, Boston, MA: D. Reidel Pub. Co.

Maturana, Humberto R., and Francisco J. Varela. 1992. *The Tree of Knowledge: The Biological Roots of Human Understanding*. Boston, MA, New York: Shambhala.

Merleau-Ponty, Maurice. 1945. *Phénoménologie de la perception*. Paris: Gallimard.

Morris, Geraldine. 2017. "Giselle and the Gothic: Contesting the Romantic Idealisation of the Woman". In *Rethinking Dance History*, edited by Geraldine Morris, and Larraine Nicholas, 235–47. London: Routledge.

Özyürek, Aslı. 2000. "The Influence of Addressee Location Speaker's Spatial Language and Representational Gestures of Direction". In *Language and Gesture*, edited by David McNeill, 64–83. Cambridge: Cambridge University Press.

Peirce, Charles Sanders. 1931. *Collected Papers of Charles Sanders Peirce*. Cambridge, MA: Harvard University Press.

Pfau, Roland, and Markus Steinbach. 2006. *Modality-Independent and Modality-Specific Aspects of Grammaticalization in Sign Languages*. Potsdam: Universitätsverlag Potsdam.

Sacks, Harvey, Emanuel A. Schegloff, and Gail Jefferson. 1974. "A Simplest Systematics for the Organization of Turn-Taking for Conversation". *Language* 50 (4): 696–735.

Smith, Marian. 2010. "Beyond the Veil: Giselle Revealed". *Dance Chronicle* 33 (3): 460–4.

Steels, Luc. 2012. *Experiments in Cultural Language Evolution*. Amsterdam: John Benjamins.

Streeck, Jürgen, Charles Goodwin, and Curtis D. LeBaron. 2011. *Embodied Interaction: Language and Body in the Material World*. New York: Cambridge University Press.

Streeck, Jürgen. 2017. *Self-Making Man: A Day of Action, Life, and Language*. Cambridge: Cambridge University Press.

Uexküll, Jakob von. 1992. "A Stroll through the Worlds of Animals and Men: A Picture Book of Invisible Worlds". *Semiotica* 89 (4): 319–91. Original edition, 1934.

Varela, Francisco J., Evan Thompson, and Eleanor Rosch. 1991. *The Embodied Mind: Cognitive Science and Human Experience*. Cambridge, MA: MIT Press.

Walker, Esther, and Kensy Cooperrider. 2016. "The Continuity of Metaphor: Evidence from Temporal Gestures". *Cognitive Science* 40 (2): 481–95.

Wide, Camilla. 2009. "Interactional Construction Grammar: Contextual Features of Determination in Dialectal Swedish". In *Contexts and Constructions*, edited by Alex Bergs, and Gabriele Diewald, 111–42. Amsterdam: John Benjamins.

Winship, Lindsey. 2014. "Royal Ballet: Giselle, Royal Opera House: Natalia Osipova excels". *Evening Standart* 6 September, https://www.standard.co.uk/culture/theatre/royal-ballet -giselle-royal-opera-house-natalia-osipova-excels-9071313.html. Accessed 26 July 2021.

Zlatev, Jordan. 2008. "The Co-Evolution of Intersubjectivity and Bodily Mimesis". In *Converging Evidence in Language and Communication Research*, edited by Jordan Zlatev, Timothy P. Racine, Chris Sinha, and Esa Itkonen, 215–44. Amsterdam: John Benjamins.

Zlatev, Jordan. 2016. "Turning Back to Experience in Cognitive Linguistics via Phenomenology". *Cognitive Linguistics* 27 (4), 559–72.

Conspiracy Theories and Disinformation as Viruses in Social Media

Josef Šlerka

The attack on the United States Capitol after the January 2021 presidential elections was one of many events that threw a spotlight on the dangers of the radicalization of a section of society through conspiracy theories (CTs), disinformation and lies. Some of Donald Trump's supporters, inflamed by his tweets and his speeches, laid siege to the Capitol Building. Several people lost their lives during the attack. All the evidence points to many of the rioters being supporters of the informal QAnon movement, which, among other things, believes in the existence of a secret cabal of Satanists operating an international pedophile network that was seeking to unseat the then incumbent President Donald Trump.[1]

In response to this unprecedented violence against US lawmakers, all the major social networks decided enough was enough and blocked Trump's accounts. One week later, the media reported on research conducted by Zygnal Labs,[2] which showed that disinformation and conspiracy theories regarding the stolen elections had fallen by 73%.

However, physical attacks linked to the spread of CTs are nothing new in the USA. For instance, a predecessor to QAnon was Pizzagate, according to which Hillary Clinton was one of the leaders of a pedophile conspiracy that had chosen the Comet Ping Pong pizzeria as its

---

1   According to the Public Religion Research Institute (PRRI): "A nontrivial 15% of Americans agree with the sweeping QAnon allegation that the government, media, and financial worlds in the U.S. are controlled by a group of Satan-worshipping pedophiles who run a global child sex trafficking operation". See https://www.prri.org/research/qanon-conspiracy-american-politics -report/. Accessed 9 August 2021.
2   See https://www.washingtonpost.com/technology/2021/01/16/misinformation-trump-twitter/. Accessed 9 August 2021.

center, in the basement of which the conspirators maintained a prison for young and sexually abused children. This CT was spread on a massive scale by people such as Alex Jones, and eventually led 29-year-old Edgar M. Welch to walk into the pizzeria armed with an assault rifle in an attempt to free the non-existent prisoners. We in the Czech Republic are not immune to such goings-on. In 2017, Jaromír Balda, a pensioner, attempted to derail a train in the region of Mladá Boleslav and put the blame for the attack on Islamists.

These and other such events have seen the terms of the debate on how best to deal with conspiracy theories and disinformation in the online space shift from the issue of free speech versus the right to dispose of one's property as one sees fit, to a consideration of the conflict between freedom of speech and the right to life. Initially, the question was whether the harm that CTs and disinformation could cause was such that it could justify intervening in people's right to search for, receive and disseminate information and ideas.

However, the game has changed and the overall situation exacerbated by the Covid-19 pandemic and the mass vaccination program. Entire countries are at risk, and now face the question not only of how to convince their populations of the need to be vaccinated, but also how to defend against the wide range of CTs, disinformation and lies that are impacting on people's willingness to be vaccinated, thus helping to prevent the collapse of hospitals and other infrastructure.

The strongly formulated thesis of advocates of restrictions on free speech now reads as follows: if freedom of speech leads to people dying, then it should be restricted. However, the counter-argument is that free speech is not simply about the physical expulsion of information from the body in the way that, for instance, perspiration is, but is above all a necessary condition for the search for truth. The debate is further complicated by the question of truthfulness and the "right to one's own truth". The slogan now is that everyone has a right to their own truth, as though some ghastly caricature of postmodernism has emerged victorious.

However, is such an approach, which relies heavily, albeit unconsciously, on the correspondence theory of truth and conceives of CTs and disinformation primarily as false statements, really going to help us fine a pragmatic solution to the current situation? I don't believe so. On the contrary, I believe that if we abandon the correspondence approach and replace it with strategy based on pragmatism, we will attain a far better starting position.

1 Conspiracy Theories and Disinformation without the Need for Truth

However, in my opinion our first step should be away from truth theory, i.e. the correspondence approach and theories of conspiracies and disinformation, in the direction of pragmatic theories that emphasize the very function of information and are more interested in networks of beliefs than truth (Rorty, Davidson, Goodman). We are not obliged to base a successful operational definition of CTs and disinformation on whether the information being transmitted is true or not.

Disinformation can be defined as a type of information designed to persuade its recipient or victim into reaching a decision that is in accordance with the attacker's objectives in such a way that the goals and identity of the attacker remain concealed from the recipient. The first thing to observe is that this definition does not relate communication only to action, but assumes that information is part of a decision-making process, in which case it is also related to a specific conflict situation in which we can speak of adversaries whose interests are in conflict with each other. It would make no sense to speak of disinformation without bad intentions. The second point to make is that we are not concerned as to whether the information is true or not. A party may use true information in order to achieve their goal, while nonetheless keeping their identity concealed. Nevertheless, there exist situations in which a party attempts to provide information under their own identity on a mass scale in order to influence an adversary. Such cases are best described as propaganda.

Both disinformation and propaganda seek to persuade the message recipient to act in a way that furthers the interests of the sender rather than their own. Though the message makes every effort to suggest that referential function of language is predominant, in reality the main function is connotative. The transparency of the message sender is important if we are to distinguish disinformation from propaganda. The disseminator of disinformation will make strenuous efforts to conceal their identity: this is not so in the case of propaganda. However, the concept of truth is not required when defining either disinformation or propaganda. Instead, we place an emphasis on the situation, attitudes and intentions of the participants.

Similarly, we do not need to include a concept of truth in the basic definition of conspiracy theories. According to Michael Barkun, CTs are organized in accordance with three basic principles:

1. Nothing happens by accident. Conspiracy implies a world based on intentionality, from which accident and coincidence have been removed. Anything that happens occurs because it has been willed. At its most extreme, the result is a "fantasy" [world] [...] far more coherent than the real world.

2. Nothing is as it seems. Appearances are deceptive, because conspirators wish to deceive in order to disguise their identities or their activities. Thus the appearance of innocence is deemed to be no guarantee that an individual or group is benign.

3. Everything is connected. Because the conspiracists' world has no room for accident, pattern is believed to be everywhere, albeit hidden from plain view. Hence the conspiracy theorist must engage in a constant process of linkage and correlation in order to map the hidden connections. (Barkun 2003, 3–4)

As Bergmann's analyses have shown, in reality the world of CTs has a relatively stable list of higher thematic aggregates, which he divides into the following categories: assassinations, unresolved deaths and historical figures; deceptions, disasters, diseases and medicine; the New World Order; extraterrestrials and esotericism; false flag operations; a "state within a state" and political affairs; anti-Islam CTs; anti-Catholic CTs and White and Black genocide.

It is interesting in this context that individual CTs falling into one of these categories have no respect for geographical borders, as demonstrated by the Atlas of Conspiracies project run by the New Media Studio,[3] which identified a large number of CTs in the Czech information space.

So far we have examined the first part of the grammar of CTs. The second part is defined by the basic narrative structure, a good example of which is the report "Mapping the Narrative Ecosystem of Conspiracy Theories in Online Anti-vaccination Discussions". The report's authors proceeded on the assumption that

a conspiracy theory is a narrative explaining an event or series of events that involve deceptive, coordinated actors working together to achieve a goal through an action or series of actions that have consequences that intentionally disenfranchise or harm an individual or population. (Introne, Korsunska, Krsova and Zhang 2020, 186)

---

3   See https://atlaskonspiraci.cz. Accessed 9 August 2021.

During the course of their research, the authors were able to identify basic sets of actors, from which new worlds of conspiracy gradually arose, thus confirming the theories of the analytical philosopher Nelson Goodman, who argues that our worlds are not formed from anything, but simply from other worlds (Goodman 1978).

An important point is that, in order to identify CTs it was not necessary to address the question of whether such theories were true or not, but rather to operate on a pragmatic level and examine how these theories reduce the complexity of the world to a typical, repetitive pattern. This pragmatic theory distinguishes between CTs that create a world in which nothing is merely coincidence and everything is part of a plan, and disinformation, i.e. information intended to encourage its recipient to behave in accordance with the sender's interests. CTs and disinformation thus become ways of naming a certain species of information with specific parameters.

2 Meme Theory, Information Contagion and Epidemiology

Abandoning the need to address the truth or falsity of CTs and disinformation as a necessary condition for their definition allows us to take another step forward and avail ourselves of the theory of memes by the evolutionary biologist Richard Dawkins developed by Aaron Lynch and Richard Brodie among others: "a meme is a unit of information in a mind whose existence influences events such that more copies of itself get created in other minds" (Brodie 2009, 11).

Like genes, memes have the ability to cluster into larger vehicles often known as *memeplexes*. According to the proponents of this theory, this includes both ideology and organizational structures such as the church, as well as various rituals. In short, a *memeplex* is a grouping of memes that have evolved into a higher unit that enables to them replicate more effectively. The evolution of memes, like that of genes, is determined by three principles:

1. variation: a continuing abundance of different elements
2. heredity or replication: the elements have the capacity to create copies or replicas of themselves
3. differential "fitness": the number of copies of an element that are created in a given time varies, depending on interactions between the features

of that element (whatever it is that makes it different from other elements) and features of the environment in which it persists. (Dennet 1991, 200)

Though we lack a rigorous definition of memes, it is still possible to work relatively successfully with the concept. If we then examine the entirety of culture and CTs and disinformation with this in mind, we can find much deeper inspiration in the natural sciences and choose between two different approaches to memes. I should add that these two ways of modelling memes are not mutually exclusive.

Firstly, we can think of them as specific organisms that live in a certain environment and in competition with other organisms. We may thus find inspiration in ecological considerations of memes. Secondly, we can think about them from the point of view of viruses and epidemiology and ask ourselves the questions we usually ask when modelling an epidemic.

The ecological conceptual standpoint will include questions devoted to the kind of environment in which the organisms of CTs and disinformation live, the specific conditions that allow them to live and reproduce, and the other organisms with which they exist within a mutual relationship. We can use other terms and distinguish, for example, between cosmopolitan and endemic CTs, or speak of adaptation and selection. In this respect CTs and disinformation will take their place within an ecological theory of culture that regards the boundary between nature and culture to be ambivalent, to say the least.

However, for the moment we will be more interested in the epidemiological model and approach. In this context, we will regard CTs and disinformation as viruses, whose only purpose is to replicate well but which, by spreading, can under certain circumstances lead to actions that have fatal consequences for the functioning and well-being of society.

3 The Epidemiology of Memes

Epidemiology as a scientific discipline is usually defined as follows:

the study (scientific, systematic, data-driven) of the distribution (frequency, pattern) and determinants (causes, risk factors) of health-related states and events (not just diseases) in specified populations (the patient is the community, individuals are viewed collectively), and the application (since epidemiology is a discipline within public health) of this study to the control of health problems.[4]

The origins of modern epidemiology go back to the application of mathematic models to the spread of disease. Ronald Ross, one of the discipline's founders, not only received the Nobel Prize for his help in understanding the mechanics of malaria transmission, but also applied mathematical models to epidemics and proved them to be an essential part of epidemiological practice.

Most of these models reduce the dynamics of spread to movement between the three basic states in which an individual can find themselves in a population: susceptible, infectious and/or recovered (the SIR model). The rate of spread in a population is then governed by the infection rate and cure rate. The infection rate basically refers to the probability of moving from S to I and is influenced by the parameters of the disease as well as by preventive and repressive measures. The recovery rate expresses the speed and completeness of the transition from I to R.

The SIR model represents a relatively simple way to model the dynamics of spread of not only infectious diseases, but any information for which we can identify the same basic parameters. It is therefore not surprising that it has for some time been applied to the dissemination of information within and across social media.

For instance, the authors of "An Epidemic Model for News Spreading on Twitter" transpose the SIR as follows:

Each news topic on Twitter spreads like "a contagious disease", where the **infectious** are the twitterers who have participated in news spreading by tweeting about that topic.

The **susceptible** are the set of twitterers who follow the infected twitterers as they receive those tweets (infectious contacts) on their stream and as a result they too can tweet about that topic (risk of being infected).

As **recency** is an important issue in news spreading, to penalize older contents, we assume that infectious individuals lose their ability to spread news after a certain amount of time – becoming the recovered in epidemiological terms. (Abdullah and Wu 2011, 165)

---

4   See https://www.cdc.gov/csels/dsepd/ss1978/Lesson1/Section1.html. Accessed 9 August 2021.

This represents the modelling of communication in the social media environment, where we are able to observe information spread in real time.

If we return to the attack on Capitol Hill we are now in a position to assert that we were witnesses to a QAnon CT epidemic finding itself in an environment inflamed by the populist appeals of a defeated presidential candidate,[5] which led to life-threatening action being taken. There is already a wide range of analyses available that show in retrospect how this CT epidemic spread and what accompanied it, including diverse kinds of mutually beneficial co-existence with other theories and *memeplexes*, such as anti-Semitism, etc.[6]

Just as epidemiology offers inspiration on how to model the spread of memes as viruses in social networks, it can also help us decide how to approach these situations practically: not only preventively, but also, if necessary, repressively.

4 Anti-Epidemic Measures as a Model Course of Action Against the Spread of Disinformation

If we take epidemiology as a metaphor seriously, it offers us a wide range of options for dealing with disinformation. However, we should never lose sight of the fact that none of these solutions represents the only one possible, and all come at a cost. Just as we have preventive and repressive measures in the case of an epidemic, so we should weigh up these same options in our reaction to the spread of CTs and disinformation.

As regards preventive measures we should have the equivalent of vaccination and health education, preventive screening and collective protection against infection. In the case of medical education, the teaching of media literacy offers itself automatically as an analogy.

As regards identifying the risk environment in which these infections thrive, this requires ongoing research into what determinants help keep these viruses in circulation, what other memes they are clustered with, and what environment would limit their ability to replicate. We should

---

5   It should be added that not all epidemics are caused by infectious diseases. An epidemic is a condition in which there is a massive spread of a disease (the figure given is usually 2% per 100,000 of the population). However, an epidemic can be caused by a determinant other than infectious organisms. For example, a toxic waste landfill site may cause a cancer epidemic in the vicinity.

6   See https://www.media-diversity.org/how-does-qanon-spread-online/. Accessed 9 August 2021.

examine how conspiracies cluster within the individual until they culminate in cases such as that of the pensioner Balda referred to above. This means drawing on research being conducted by sociologists and behavioral economists, among others.

Another important factor is the continuous strengthening of immunity. It is naive to believe that media literacy in schools will save us. If we did not write on a regular basis, our literacy would soon wither and die. Conversely, if someone becomes infected with jaundice, washing their hands will not harm them, though it will do nothing to solve the problem of the disease itself.

Finally, we need to focus on an ongoing measurement of the occurrence of CTs in society and on social media. Regular screening, which would complement research into conspiracists and their supporters, would allow for better protection of vulnerable groups. Which brings us back to the start. We have no detailed idea of the extent to which CTs and disinformation have spread in society.

While preventive measures should be ongoing and a *de facto* part of societal hygiene in the sense of public healthcare, in the case of CTs an extremely sensitive question is the extent to which these theories are dangerous to the functioning of a democratic society. When we have answered that question, we should select repressive measures accordingly. In epidemiology this mainly refers to measures that lead to the exclusion of the source of the infection, the interruption of transmission, and immunization. These measures also have their equivalent in the online environment.

In the event of an epidemic of CTs breaking out that could lead to civil unrest, looting, etc., there exist equivalent measures ranging from tracking and isolating the infection sources to electronic lockdown. This would include an active search for the infection locations, intensive monitoring of its spread, a temporary blackout of posts on social media, and a temporary closure of accounts.

It is important that these measures are deemed extraordinary. In the introduction to this essay, I spoke of the controversy surrounding the cancellation of social media accounts, the deletion of unsuitable content, etc. When considering the measures being proposed here we should bear in mind that they are extraordinary and not standard.

The ban on Holocaust denial, for example, is a useful hygienic measure that radically reduces the source of an outbreak of a meme that tends to merge with neo-Nazi *memeplexes*. Given the outcomes this cluster of memes has had in human history, it can be deemed a highly dangerous idea and a ban on Holocaust denial may therefore be deemed proportionate.

In contrast, the CT that states that the Americans never landed on the moon, though it has millions of fans, cannot be deemed dangerous in terms of endangering human lives or rights and freedoms. It is for this reason that we must always proceed in a manner proportionate to the seriousness of the threat. The mere fact of something being an example of a conspiracy theory or disinformation may not be reason for radical action to be taken.

5 Conclusion

With all of this in mind, if we return to the attack on the Capitol and the subsequent blocking of Donald Trump's accounts, we can now interpret this as a very late intervention, the aim of which was to prevent the spread of certain types of CTs threatening democracy in the United States. At the same time, I suspect that such a radical measure was taken because over previous years an environment had been created in which such viruses thrived, and isolation alone does not resolve this problem, just as more frequent hand washing will not help with jaundice.

We suggest ways in which such outbreaks can be prevented so as to avoid the need to apply radical measures, which often involve problematic interventions in civil rights and freedoms.

The utilization of meme theory allows us not only to better model mathematically the spread of information on social media, but also to influence the dissemination of information throughout the environment.

However, this change of perspective also includes a departure from the idea of humankind as the confident center of events. Within this new model, humankind is merely one environment among many, in which a wide range of processes take place over which the individual does not have anything like the influence they often imagine they have.

Perhaps we are one step closer to a notion of the world in which humankind is not a sovereign being who has everything under control. Instead, we now see an image of humankind beneath which there is an inscription: *We are merely vehicles created by our genes in order that they might replicate. We are driven by impersonal memes that have no interest in anything but their own reproduction.*

Translated by Phil Jones.

References

Abdullah, Saeed, and Xidong Wu. 2011. "An Epidemic Model for News Spreading on Twitter". *IEEE 23rd International Conference on Tools with Artificial Intelligence*, 163–9.

Barkun, Michael. 2003. *A Culture of Conspiracy: Apocalyptic Visions in Contemporary America*. Berkeley: University of California Press.

Bergmann, Erikur. 2018. *Conspiracy and Populism. The Politics of Misinformation*. Cham: Palgrave Macmillan.

Brodie, Richard. 2009. *Virus of the Mind: The New Science of the Meme*. Carlsbad, CA: Hay House.

Dennet, Daniel C. 1991. *Consciousness Explained*, Boston, MA: Little, Brown and Co.

Goodman, Nelson. 1978. *Ways of Worldmaking*. Hassoks: Harvester Press.

Introne, Joshua, Ania Korsunska, Leni Krsova, and Zefeng Zhang. 2020. "Mapping the Narrative Ecosystem of Conspiracy Theories in Online Anti-vaccination Discussions". *International Conference on Social Media and Society* 20: 184–92.

Aspiring Autopoiesis and Its Troubles: What Else Is Produced When the Nation Is Reproduced

Ondřej Slačálek

1 Introduction

From the most common point of view, the nation is as close to an autopoietic system as is possible in the social world. It is, of course, precisely this point of view, often ironized with the opposite view, that underlines the constructed nature of the nation. The vision of the nation as something that constitutes, creates, and re-creates itself conflicts with the vision of the nation as a construct of a group of intellectuals who transmit their ideas to the indifferent masses by various means of cultural transfer.

In this study, I do not want to judge these two positions. Instead, I want to take both of them beyond their limits. I want to take both positions seriously but critically: to understand the nation as a construct that reconstructs itself and thus to understand how elements of spontaneity and elements of construction are present. Above all, however, my focus is on *what is produced when a nation is (re)produced*. I will focus on the surplus energy produced during the re-constitution of a nation.

The thinkers who can be understood as political theoreticians of the nation (in my view Rousseau and Fichte above all) evoke nations as something closed and defensive – as if nation-building produced no surplus energy. To describe this energy, I will start after discussion of Rousseau instead of Fichte with his contemporary and sympathetic opponent, Carl von Clausewitz, who described a new form of war infused by national solidarity to which both he and Fichte tried to actively contribute. Then I will focus on the insights of three authors who critically observed their effects and working: István Bibó for "small nations" with existential fears, Julien Benda for analysis of "political passions" in the modern French nation, and Hannah Arendt for her analysis of the inversion of (not only great) nations into empires. What we see in all these cases is that nations produce much more than they promised; to some extent they even produced their own negation.

2 Construct without Constructors?

No more arresting emblems of the modern culture of nationalism exist than cenotaphs and tombs of Unknown Soldiers. The public ceremonial reverence accorded these monuments precisely because they are either deliberately empty or no one knows who lies inside them. [...] The cultural significance of such monuments becomes even clearer if one tries to imagine, say, a Tomb of the Unknown Marxist or a cenotaph for fallen Liberals. Is a sense of absurdity avoidable? The reason is that neither Marxism nor Liberalism is much concerned with death and Immortality. (Anderson 2006, 10)

Anderson's *Imagined Communities* are often quoted and sometimes misrepresented. The word *imagined* in the name provokes: it contributes to the impression that nations are simply "constructs", products of our imagination which we can overcome if we imagine differently. This is not, however, what Anderson wanted to say. For him, the nation is different from other ideologies (and closer to religions) because it addresses topics of death and eternity. But it is definitely not an arbitrary construct. On the contrary, it is a logical result of historical development and cannot be easily escaped or overcome.

As one of the most important paradoxes of nationalism, Benedict Anderson identifies the difference between a nation's "political power" and "philosophical poverty and even incoherence [...] unlike most other isms, nationalism has never produced its own grand thinkers: no Hobbeses, Tocquevilles, Marxes, or Webers" (Anderson 2006, 5). This is something with which we might take issue. After all, are not Rousseau, Herder, or Fichte grand thinkers of nationalism? Yes, there is a paradox in nationalism, as its declared particularism ought to prevent its theoreticians from the formulation of grand abstractions. But even this limitation is very doubtful – with nations being a general condition, to theorize one often means to theorize all others, at least partially.

In the famous words of Ernst Renan, the nation is an everyday plebiscite (Renan 2018, 261–2). In this combination of words, we can find a peculiar combination of spontaneity and intention. Indeed, Renan believes that by many of our spontaneous and often even automatized actions we confirm our membership of the nation, and through it also the existence and continuity of the nation. Thus, we are all constructors of the nation. We can vote *no* in this plebiscite, after all. (No, we cannot, and it is exactly one of the reasons of very limited validity of the metaphor.)

In this study, I want to challenge this idea of spontaneity and the a-theoretical nature of the nation. I will present the nation as an object of theoretical contemplation and the possibility of its (re)creation in the mind of political theorists (I will discuss Rousseau as a privileged case, and also Clausewitz as a more practical theoretician). But I do not want to end here. I will show that further deep theoretical insights can be produced by authors who were more critical of the nation's effect.

3 Public Space as Panoptical Manufacture of Civic Virtue (Rousseau on Poland)

Jean-Jacques Rousseau is considered the founding father of modern nationalism. The paradigmatic conflict between the *mondialist*, enlightened elitist Voltaire and the *sensitivist*, preromantic Rousseau also had a political dimension. Voltaire, wishing to subject the world to universal rules of reason, has a great sympathy for the imperial politics of the Russian empire, its former westernizer Peter the Great, and its contemporary empress Catherine the Great. In contrast, Rousseau despised the Russian empire as well as the French empire, and expressed sympathy with the smaller nations, especially with Poles (Wolff 1994, 235–83; Mishra 2017, 82–113). In his romantically orientalist view, Poles embodied the negation of what he hated in the West. Thus, their position (which was in fact hopeless) paradoxically represented his hope.

> I see all the States of Europe rushing to their ruin. Monarchies, Republics, all these nations so magnificently instituted, all these fine governments so wisely balanced, fallen into decrepitude, menaced by an impending death; and Poland, that region depopulated, devastated, oppressed, open to its aggressors, at the height of its misfortunes and its anarchy, still

shows all the fire of youth. [...] Brave Poles, beware; beware that for wanting to be too well, you might make your situation worse. In considering what you want to acquire, do not forget what you can lose. Correct, if possible, the abuses of your constitution; but do not despise the one that has made you what you are. (Rousseau 2005, 170)

Some insight into Rousseau's vision of the nation can be found in his advice to Polish rebels on how to change the Polish constitution. The text, which was not intended for publication, was meant to inspire the rebellious movement which was defeated while the text was being finalized. Nevertheless, it was published afterwards and inspired many debates in Poland. We can read it as a contribution towards national development from a sympathetic stranger, and thus a national *ideologist par excellence* (as his distant sympathy had to be mediated via ideas).

The nation for Rousseau was not an objective fact which simply exists. It needed to be perpetually re-produced. By ceremonies, by customs, by special clothes as well as by values – there were many ways in which the difference can be cultivated. These old practices needed to be maintained or re-established, and suitable new ones introduced, specific to the Poles:

These practices, even if they are indifferent, even if they are bad in certain respects, as long as they are not essentially so, will always have the advantage of winning the affection of the Poles for their country and of giving them a natural repugnance for mingling with foreigners. I regard it as a piece of good fortune that they have a distinctive form of dress. Preserve this advantage carefully [...]. (Rousseau 2005, 176)

Rousseau was advising a nation in serious crisis which would soon cease to exist for more than a century as a political unit. The only way to sustain Polishness became to save the national identity in the culture and make this culture so distinctive, xenophobic, and closed that it was impossible for it to be assimilated. "If you make it so that a Pole can never become a Russian, I answer to you for it that Russia will never subjugate Poland" (Rousseau 2005, 174).

Distinction is key to everything. For the Polish nation the critical thing was "to be always itself and not someone else" (Rousseau 2005, 217). These words are quoted from the chapter on the army. While variations on them may be found elsewhere, essentialism is even more acutely necessary in the case of an armed struggle than in other cases. For example, fortified places "do not suit the Polish genius at all" (Rousseau 2005, 221). Rousseau advised replacing the regular army (a tool of expansion) with a Swiss-type militia, to be used for defense only.

There was only one trait of Poland which Rousseau did not like: its size. Ideally, he would replace it with a confederation of 33 lesser territorial units. He was pretty aware that Poland, even in its early 1770s version, was something between nation and empire that made his national project harder to realize. Nevertheless, there was also another reason why Rousseau preferred smallness. This was visibility in the public sphere, which, as in the classical tradition, was meant to serve the cultivation and production of virtues.

Rousseau wrote that "a single thing is enough to make it impossible to subjugate; love of the fatherland and of freedom animated by the virtues that are inseparable from it" (Rousseau 2005, 222). But he was not naïve. He knew that the love and virtues that are spontaneously present in men's souls are not a strong enough foundation on which to base his sort of political building. To "carry patriotism to the highest degree in all Polish hearts" (Rousseau 2005, 222) he employed tools that we would not expect from him: ambition and maybe even *amour-propre*. Virtues had to be cultivated in the public sphere and in the public view, with a connected chain of sanctions and benefits in order to enable the performance, exhibition, imitation, and reproduction of civic virtues. Needed was to

> make it so that all Citizens feel themselves incessantly under the public's eyes, that no one advance and succeed except by public favor, that no position, no employment be filled except by the wish of the nation, and finally that everyone from the lowest noble, from even the lowest peasant up to the King if possible, depend so much on public esteem, that no one can do anything, acquire anything, succeed in anything without it. From the effervescence excited by this common emulation will be born that patriotic intoxication which alone can raise men up above themselves, and without which freedom is only a vain name and legislation only an illusion. (Rousseau 2005, 222)

Virtues would be rewarded – not only by "patriotic intoxication", but also by honors and positions, including the top position of (non-hereditary) king. Nevertheless, virtues would also be controlled. The public sphere evoked by Rousseau is reminiscent of the image of a panopticon, especially for anybody who wants to serve the state.

Each is free not to present himself; but as soon as someone enters, he must either – barring a voluntary retirement – advance or be rebuffed with disapproval. Seen and judged by his fellow citizens in all his behavior, he must know that all his steps are being followed, that all his actions are being weighed, and that a faithful account of good and evil is being kept whose influence will extend over all the rest of his life. (Rousseau 2005, 222)

The passing of judgment by citizens, and especially by citizens well known for their virtues, is such an omnipresent element that even Rousseau proposes the adoption of an ancient Egyptian custom: after the death of a king, judgment should be passed on him by an assembly of chosen citizens, who evaluate his rule and decide if he deserves a royal tomb and other honors (Rousseau 2005, 234–5).

4 Autopoiesis of War Meets Autopoiesis of Nation (Clausewitz)

Rousseau showed good intuition in connecting the idea of the arming of the populace with that of the modern nation. However, what was much more problematic was his idea that this army could only be defensive. While it really did become a key source of the modern nation in the following century, it also transformed the nature of war to such an extent that it became hard to differentiate between offensive and defen-sive war.

We could continue with Herder and Fichte, if we wanted to reconstruct another "Marx and Weber" of nationalism. If we want a better understanding of the dynamics of nationalism, however, it is more helpful to turn our attention to one of Fichte's communication partners. When Fichte tried to introduce German readers to the ideas of Machiavelli in order to support their patriotic spirit, he found a sympathetic opponent in the shape of an anonymous Prussian officer who sent him a long letter.

Carl von Clausewitz, as the officer's name was, did not write this letter only to correct a philosopher's overly dogmatic lessons from reading Machiavelli (especially concerning artillery) and to express his opinion that Machiavelli's *Art of War* lacks the intellectual independence of Machiavelli's other books (of his *Discourses on Livy* above all). It is too dependent on his ancient sources. What Clausewitz was probably aiming to do was to present Fichte with an outline of the theory of war that might be more courageous than his own, more based on fresh experience, and at the same time more in keeping with Machiavelli's and Fichte's philosophy than was their own theory. "(U)nlike Machiavelli, we should not cling to methods that were successful in the past, reviving them in one form or another, but rather seek to restore the true spirit of war" (Clausewitz 1992, 282). And what is this "true spirit of war" according to Clausewitz? As opposed to a mechanical view of the army, he believes this spirit can be found in "mobilizing the energies of every soldier to the greatest possible extent and in infusing him with warlike feelings, so that the fire of war spreads to every component of the army" (Clausewitz 1992, 282). Clausewitz was at that time pressing for military reform which would include armed mobilization of the people, coinciding with Fichte's effort to mobilize Germans against Napoleon's invading armies.

Decades later, when Clausewitz wrote the draft of his never-finished classic *On War*, he made us see vividly how revolutionary this philosophy of war was. He tried to reconstruct war as something controlled by reason and its political purpose. However, at the same time he showed how the "paradoxical trinity" of war (blind hatred connected with the people, a play of chance attributed to the "commander and his army," and political purpose linked to the government) changes this original meaning of war (Clausewitz 2007, 31).

What Clausewitz had promoted in the 1800s he saw with ambivalence twenty years later. He showed how after the French Revolution war

> took on an entirely different character, or rather closely approached its true character, its absolute perfection. There seemed no end to the resources mobilized; all limits disappeared in the vigor and enthusiasm shown by governments and their subjects. [...] War, untrammeled by any conventional restraints, had broken loose in all its elemental fury. This was due to the peoples' new share in these great affairs of state. (Clausewitz 2007, 239)

Instead of the cabinet wars of princes, a new way of warfare had been invented in which the whole nation's existence was at stake, with all the brutality that implied (Schmitt 2004; Barša 2007, 209–13). Clausewitz was somehow terrified by the monster at whose birth he had assisted. He posed the key question:

> Will this always be the case in future? From now on will every war in Europe be waged with the full resources of the state, and therefore have to

be fought only over major issues that affect the people? Or shall we again see a gradual separation taking place between government and people? Such questions are difficult to answer, and we are the last to dare to do so. But the reader will agree with us when we say that once barriers – which in a sense consist only in man's ignorance of what is possible – are torn down, they are not so easily set up again. (Clausewitz 2007, 239)

The argument as to why it will not be easy (or maybe possible) to put genie back in Aladdin's bottle can be found in the first chapter of *On War*, where Clausewitz tried to reconstruct the nature and logic of war. Behind rhetoric depicting war as a "chameleon" and so on, he described above all the *logic of armed competition*, which causes a mutual relationship and dependence between opposite sides in a war. "So long as I have not overthrown my opponent I am bound to fear he may overthrow me. Thus I am not in control: he dictates to me as much as I dictate to him" (Clausewitz 2007, 16). This logic is the logic of the forced use of any trump card available – it is dictated by the fact that if I do not use it, my opponent (probably) will. Once we have lost "ignorance of what is possible", we will be forced to wage total wars where the fate and maybe physical survival of whole nations will be at stake.

5 Anxieties and Passions (Bibó and Benda)

Two authors from Central Europe have used the same definition for the "small nations" of which this part of Europe consists: István Bibó in 1946 and Milan Kundera in 1983. In both cases, a small nation is defined by the fact that it "is one whose very existence can be put in question in any moment; the small nation can disappear and it knows it" (Kundera 1984, 35). Both authors see the tragic moment of existence of small nations, but they differ very much in the consequences which they derive from this diagnosis. Kundera's description is affirmative: it is because of this situation that small nations have deeper insights into the Western condition. Their position on the borders of non-existence make their thinking more serious. Bibó, on the contrary, sees this very situation as the reason for shortcomings or defects in political culture. The "existential anxiety for the community" is exactly what is responsible for "the unbalanced Central-East European political mentality" (Bibó 2015, 149), characterized by mistrust of democracy and humanism. Openness and generosity can become dangerous; they might support the enemy and his annihilating agenda. At a moment when you are struggling for your existence, you cannot afford to be very generous...

This is exactly the reason, according to Bibó, why Central Europe (in his words Eastern Europe) became the promised region for "the greatest monstrosity of modern European political development: anti-democratic nationalism" (Bibó 2015, 151). It is fear that is the gravest enemy of democracy; "(t)o be a democrat is first and foremost not to be afraid" (Bibó 2015, 152).[1] Democracy, with its power to inhibit of bad decisions, may be perceived as "weak" and "too limiting" at moments when "everything is at stake". Understanding this not as moments but as an overall condition makes democracy an inadequate option.

However, this is not only about (liberal) democracy. The problem of limits and various forms of autonomy is present not only in politics. A total politics of existential anxiety can easily also overcome "apolitical" limits and subdue supposedly apolitical spheres. Of course, the culture then loses its autonomy; it becomes a servant of eternal national self-production. It is curious that Milan Kundera, often the guardian of the independence of the artist and his total freedom, writes with some nostalgia (and in a slightly Stalinist tone) about the social relevance of the writer (specifically in the context of the anti-Communist revolts of 1956 and 1968): "happy marriage of culture and life, of creative achievements and creative participation..." (Kundera 1984, 33). Bibó is much more bitter – and much more of a realist:

> All manifestations of national life were subjected to the most furious national teleology; all their genuine or imaginary achievements, from Nobel prizes to Olympic records, lost their spontaneous purpose in themselves and were put in the service of national self-documentation. (Bibó 2015, 155)

The problem of Bibó's precise analysis (revealing the generous political character and brilliant intellect of its author) is its western-centric parochialism. These problems in political culture are not specific to Central-Eastern Europe. We can find nations that have felt challenged in

---

[1] Today, we might ask ourselves if *anybody* could pass this definition of democrat, since democrats define themselves mostly by real or supposed fear of real or supposed anti-democrats. One could even ask if Bibó himself should not have been more afraid of Hungarian and Soviet communists at the moment of writing the essay in question. Not being afraid of them made him a better democrat, but it did not save Hungarian democracy.

their existence in an even more radical way – and it led them to even more drastic lessons. An interesting case is presented by Vladimir Tikhonov (2010) in his book on *fin-de-siècle* Korea under Japanese occupation. The Korean intellectuals' lesson was not to despise the values of their bloody imperialist occupiers but to imitate them and compete with them in their playground of violence: to be powerful enough to challenge their power. The holy grail they found was easily accessible to all nationalists, and was located in the modern achievements of Western science: Darwin and the social Darwinist imaginary.[2]

Above all, however, Bibó's vision of Eastern-Central anomaly in political culture needs some vision of "normality". Of course, this normality is found in the West – in Western and Northern Europe. Here (and only here), even Kundera is more precise than Bibó: he presents a fascinating description of a situation in which any nation may now, under the globalizing pressure of "civilization" and mass media, find itself in the position of a "small nation" that may disappear at any time – and the nation starts to realize this. As Trump, Johnson and others show us, this changed situation brings with it the implications darkly described by Bibó, not those celebrated by Kundera. Nevertheless, we could add that even these nations did not need to wait for this situation. As Julien Benda, *inter alia*, shows us, the colonization of culture in the name of the nation has been present here even without feelings of anxiety for the end of a "small" national community.

Modern nations, in Benda's view, are arenas producing political passions, "the chief of which are racial passions, class passions and national passions" (Benda 2006). The most important of them is "national passion", or "mystical adoration of the nation", partly because it works as some form of meta-passion, integrating many other important political passions. Benda names three as the most important: (i) the movement against the Jews; (ii) the movement of the possessing classes against the proletariat; (iii) the movement of the champions of authority against the democrats, but we could add also some parts of the workers' movement after their various compromises with nationalism.

---

2 Of course, we can agree with Hannah Arendt that various very different political ideas could find arguments or "arguments" for themselves in Darwin (Arendt 1973, 159–60); we may remember Kropotkin, who tried to reconstruct social Darwinism as argument for his vision of an anarchic-communist society based on solidarity. But at the same time the prevailing tendency in the political use of Darwin is simply the opposite: competition between individuals and struggle between nations.

For Benda, perfection of these passions became characteristic of his era, which he characterized as an "age of the intellectual organization of political hatreds". "Political passions" reached a level of "perfection never before known in history" (Benda 2006). There are more reasons than one for this. Julien Benda underlines the role of intellectuals: not only did the new political passions pretend to have scientific foundations, but they also attracted many intellectuals to develop them. The nation's educated classes for the most part sacrificed their intellectual independence and devotion to things of the spirit and exchanged them for a strange mixture of absolutized political passions and cynical realism, called by Benda *"divinized* realism" (Benda 2006). A strange combination of semi-religious belief in the power of one's own group means losing not only the transcendental horizon, but also human limitations. "The State, Country, Class, are now frankly God; we may even say that for many people (and some are proud of it) they alone are God" (Benda 2006).

The "betrayal of clerks", which became a catchphrase often borrowed from Benda (being mainly used simply to refer to intellectuals who think something different than the user of the phrase), is a description of a profound transformation in the mentality of men of spirit. They leave their unique position of "splendid isolation" from affairs of the day, their distance from the secular powers, and their care for the higher things of culture. They exchange their original role, characterized by this distance, for a new role: the feeding and manufacturing of political passions. While earlier the clerks intervened in politics very rarely, and only in order to defend some particular moral limit, now they intervene regularly, pretending to know the answers to all the important questions – both questions of the day and questions of history. Thus, "adhesion of the modern 'clerk' to patriotic fanaticism" (Benda 2006) is thus an introduction to the modern intellectual, a skillful partisan of *any* fanaticism. When an intellectual betrays his limits, he transforms not only himself but also patriotism; Benda favored limited patriotism, which makes it possible to "render unto Caesar the things that are Caesar's, and unto God the things that are God's" (Benda 2006). However, nationalism absolved from its limits and developed by intellectuals who forgot their original commitment to truth and care of the soul has become borderless and threatens to tear up the world, as "the logical end of the 'integral realism' professed by humanity to-day is the organized slaughter of nations or classes" (Benda 2006).

Even a reviewer as sympathetic and close to Benda's position as František X. Šalda felt compelled to say that Benda went too far. He criticized

Benda for his construction of mutually excluding contradictions and for placing the *clerk* outside the public sphere (Šalda 1928, 83–4). We can return here to Bibó's diagnosis that Central-Eastern European nations cannot have their own independent culture, that all culture is employed in the service of "national self-documentation". Maybe. However, the problem is deeper: how many active public intellectuals can be found even in countries that have not felt such a strong need to use culture in the "service of national self-documentation"? As eternal questions of ethics and values were posed in the brutal form of the question of the power of various groups, was it possible to escape complicity? Unlimited passions could not be separated from the production of limited *patrias* or ideas; they were a by-product of their reproduction. Was this by-product inevitable?

6 Imperialism: Negation or the Highest Stage of Nation? (Arendt)

Many consider imperialist ambitions to be an ultra- version of nationalism, its further step. Just as paleontologists look for a logically necessary "missing link" between apes and humans, the critical mission for the history of ideas is to find the "missing link" between nationalism and imperialism. Hannah Arendt (together with others such as the early theoretician of imperialism Hobson or the late theoretician of nationalism Anderson) promoted the opposite view: considering imperialism to be the opposite and the negation of the nation, she tried to develop an alternative explanation. It is provided in her fascinating genealogy of modern imperialism, and it is very convincing, but it is not clear if it really convinces for her argument about opposition between nationalism and imperialism.

Probably, in Arendt's story, the constitutive other for the nation is not another nation but the empire. A nation, as in Benda's case, is a limited set of institutions determined by borders. At the same time, imperialism means eternal expansion ("I would annex the planets if I could", she quotes from Cecil Rhodes; Arendt 1973, 121). Furthermore, Arendt shares Benda's diagnosis in other aspects: she also identifies in the basis of the imperialist mentality a ruthless version of aggressive "realism", "realism" of power which manifests itself in tautology: the winners are winners, the powerful have power etc. This "realism", of course, can often take on the form of superstition. We can identify many moments of this, such as when arguments using Darwinism are made in the pseu-do-science of Gobineau, Danilevsky or Spengler (Arendt 1973, 170–9, 223–4). However, these noisy forms can mislead us, causing us not to find the content under the cover.

In some ways it is hard to understand – how could Hannah Arendt become an iconic thinker for anti-totalitarian conservative post-dissidents, looking for the "original sin" of totalitarianism in Marxism? Did they not read her? Not only did she find a much more important source of totalitarianism in imperialism (and specifically in the "continental imperialisms" of Pan-Germanism and Pan-Slavism) but her book is one of the most serious charges against the bourgeoisie ever formulated (and the competition is stiff).

She believed it is precisely the calculating and competitive mentality of the bourgeoisie that is the root cause of this triumph of ruthless realism without limits. The "process of never-ending accumulation of power" was "necessary for the protection of a never-ending accumulation of capital" (Arendt 1973, 143). According to Arendt, the only political theorist who really elaborated the political implications of the rise of the bourgeoisie was Hobbes. It was his calculation of power and security that complemented the bourgeois world of unlimited calculations and competition of skills and wealth. It implies that the political complement of the bourgeois world is necessarily some form of tyranny (Arendt 1973, 144–7). As these tyrannies were replaced in the framework of nation-states, the space for this tyranny was found in territorial expansion.

> The bourgeoisie, so long excluded from government by the nation-state and by their own lack of interest in public affairs, was politically emancipated by imperialism. Imperialism must be considered the first stage in political rule of the bourgeoisie rather than the last stage of capitalism. (Arendt 1973, 138)

The export of "superfluous capital" and "superfluous working power" (Arendt 1973, 150) brought about an alternative version of this tyranny. In the context of colonial adventures and apparent racial differences, whiteness became the key to the redistribution of power. Even people who would be *lumpenproletarian* nobodies in their home societies in Europe automatically became a white *Somebodies* in colonies overseas. However, Hannah Arendt was led by her focus on the genealogy of Nazi and Stalinist totalitarianism to focus on the often-overlooked topic of the "continental imperialism" of Pan-Germanism and Pan-Slavism. She understood these movements in the context of imperialism. Their expansion differed in that it was predominantly terrestrial, not overseas (and had some bizarre peculiarities, given the relative backwardness of the German and Russian milieus, such as the non-developed economic discourse of these imperialisms).

Arendt identified the most critical aspects of pan-movements in "tribal nationalism" and "lawlessness". The reduction of nationalism to "tribal nationalism" (or "zoological nationalism", as she quotes from Masaryk's characteristic of Danilevsky; Arendt 1973, 224) is analogical to racism. The cultural creation of national specifics does not matter, neither culture-political vote in "everyday plebiscite". What is important is the almost biological identification of an individual as "German" or "Slavic". Meanings are not things that can be newly created in the framework of national culture. They become – in the form of the "chauvinist mystique" (Arendt 1973, 227) of ethnical greatness, mysterious origins, and great futures – simply attributes of an "objective" position which can be identified using natural science. Lawlessness was the result of the absolute stakes of this game. As both movements struggled for rule over the world, there was no possibility of limits or reservations. This aspiration can also explain the anti-Semitism broadly present in both these movements. According to Arendt, it is envy: as Jews are considered to be rulers of the world, they occupy the place which should be occupied by the victorious pan-movement.

Even Marx considered (limited) freedom to be the result of the rise of the bourgeoisie. Arendt is more critical, showing political despotism as a complement of prevalence bourgeois values. Here, maybe, we can find the "missing link" between limited nationalism and its supposed opposite, imperialist expansion. While "the nation" became a political weapon of the bourgeoisie against Estate-based society and a space for the cultivation of some elements of equality, bourgeois society also had to develop its need to find its complement in political despotism. Nationalism, with its internal solidarity and ambivalent positions towards the outside, makes it possible to externalize this tendency towards despotism and cultivate it in the form of chauvinism or imperialist expansion (or in form of "international solidarity", humanitarism – and imperialist expansion). Maybe this chauvinism and imperialism is the opposite of "real" nationalism, but at the same time it was at least partially produced and reproduced during its reproduction.

7 Instead of a Conclusion

If we turn to the title of our book, we might ask if we can understand the nation as an autopoietic system. There is a strong temptation to do so. Even the connotation of its name with birth might lead us to think about the nation as something that is constituting and eternally reproducing itself. In this study, however, I have touched on three problems with this. The first is the question of origins. The second is a problem with other (quasi-) autopoietic systems. The third is the logic of expansion.

Starting with the first problem, it is hard to identify the moment of the birth of a nation. Even the "fathers of the nation" who declare its independence or constitution are working with raw material already somehow present. However, the myth of self-constitution obscures more than it reveals. The nation never originates in itself, as we have seen in the debates of Rousseau and Clausewitz. It needs other nations to envy, imitate, feel danger from them, to constitute itself.

The second problem is intersections with other systems. As we have seen, especially in the debate between Clausewitz, Benda, and Arendt, the logic of nation does not work separately. It meets and interacts with other logics. The most important is the logic of war, the logic of construction of political passions, and the logic of bourgeois transformation of the world in a calculable object of competition. It is from these interactions that a nation receives its most essential characteristics. War makes the nation a community of common fate where everything is at stake. Political passions make this moment eternal. They produce a war-like mentality even in times of peace. Furthermore, bourgeois competition makes the world potentially inimical at any moment, and thus it creates two needs. The first is for a community that embraces individuals in this world and provides them with identity and solid ground. The second need is for the assertive self-promotion of this community in a supposedly or really inimical world.

As well as the nation, these three other logics also pretend, at least sometimes, to be autopoietic. Nevertheless, as we have seen, they make sense only in interaction. And it is precisely the nature of this interaction that brings us to our third problem.

Reproduction of the nation is connected with the idea of stability, the eternal return of the same. However, as we have seen, when the nation is reproduced it often accelerates. It is similar with bourgeois economy: it needs "growth" to be "stable". It is hard to sustain nation in a stable position; it needs to expand. We might thus say the nation is a *Uroboros* devouring its tail. However, this tail is much fatter at some times than it is at others.

References

Anderson, Benedict. 2006. *Imagined Communities: Reflections on the Origin and Spread of Nationalism*. London, New York: Verso.

Arendt, Hannah. 1973. *The Origins of Totalitarianism*. San Diego, CA: Harcourt Brace Jovanovich.

Barša, Pavel. 2007. *Síla a rozum. Spor realismu a idealismu v moderním politickém myšlení*, Praha: Filosofia.

Benda, Julien. 2006. *The Treason of the Intellectuals*. Translated by Richard Aldington. Piscataway, NJ: Transaction Publishers.

Bibó, István. 2015. *The Art of Peacemaking. Political Essays*. Translated by Péter Pásztor. New Haven, CT: Yale University Press.

Clausewitz, Carl von. 1992. *Historical and Political Writings*. Translated and edited by Peter Paret, and Daniel Moran. Princeton, NJ: Princeton University Press.

Clausewitz, Carl von. 2007. *On War*. Translated by Michael Howard, and Peter Paret. Oxford: Oxford University Press.

Kundera, Milan. 1984. "The Tragedy of Central Europe". *New York Review of Books* 26 April 1984: 33–8.

Mishra, Pankaj. 2017. *Age of Anger. A History of the Present*. New York: Farrar, Straus and Giroux.

Renan, Ernest. 2018. *What Is a Nation and Other Political Writings*. New York: Columbia University Press.

Rousseau, Jean-Jacques. 2005. *The Plan for Perpetual Peace, On the Government of Poland, and Other Writings on History and Politics*. Translated by Christopher Kelly, and Judith Bush. Lebanon, NH: University Press of New England.

Šalda, František X. 1928. "Poslání vzdělanců". *Šaldův zápisník* 1: 81–6.

Schmitt, Carl. 2004. *The Theory of the Partisan: A Commentary/Remark on the Concept of the Political*. Translated by A. C. Goodson. East Lansing: Michigan State University Press.

Tikhonov, Vladimir. 2010. *Social Darwinism and Nationalism in Korea: The Beginnings (1880s–1910s). "Survival" as an Ideology of Korean Modernity*. Leiden: Brill.

Wolff, Larry. 1994. *Inventing Eastern Europe. The Map of Civilization on the Mind of the Enlightenment*. Stanford, CA: Stanford University Press.

Abstract

Autopoiesis, or the ability of a *system* to create, re-create and maintain itself, is rather suspicious from both a scientific and commonsense point of view, suggesting a certain version of, or even improvement on, the *perpetuum mobile.* As such, though, it might be used as a defining feature of life and social issues in which the laws of thermodynamics simply do not hold. Arguably, there is no simpler fact than that we *are* the products of our own education.

With this belief modernity began, redefining creatively and self-consciously the traditional concepts of education (under the name of *Bildung*), citizenship, democracy, religi,nd innovation or are these just empty words? Is knowledge power or just a value to be nourished per se? Is culture different from technology, politics and industry or are these natural parts of it? Is religion just a relic from older times, a mere fairy-tale to be replaced by the positive sciences, or a vital part of society's reflective structure?

The purpose of this volume, being one of the milestones of the KREAS project (Operational Programme RDE, Excellent Research), is to put these questions concerning the autopoietic nature of our lives into a broad interdisciplinary perspective and answer them in a new and imaginative way. This consists, significantly, in the simultaneous account of the *dark side* of the autopoietic concept, its living from its own sources or devouring its own tail.